Mirror for Humanity

A Concise Introduction to Cultural Anthropology

Eleventh Edition

Conrad Phillip Kottak
University of Michigan

Mc
Graw
Hill
Education

MIRROR FOR HUMANITY: A CONCISE INTRODUCTION TO CULTURAL ANTHROPOLOGY, ELEVENTH EDITION

Published by McGraw-Hill Education, 2 Penn Plaza, New York, NY 10121. Copyright © 2018 by McGraw-Hill Education. All rights reserved. Printed in the United States of America. Previous editions © 2016, 2014, and 2012. No part of this publication may be reproduced or distributed in any form or by any means, or stored in a database or retrieval system, without the prior written consent of McGraw-Hill Education, including, but not limited to, in any network or other electronic storage or transmission, or broadcast for distance learning.

Some ancillaries, including electronic and print components, may not be available to customers outside the United States.

This book is printed on acid-free paper.

1 2 3 4 5 6 7 8 9 LCR 21 20 19 18 17

ISBN 978-1-259-81842-4
MHID 1-259-81842-X

Executive Brand Managing Director: *Claire Brantley*
Lead Product Developer: *Dawn Groundwater*
Senior Product Developer: *Briana Porco*
Marketing Manager: *Kaitlyn Lombardo*
Content Project Managers: *Rick Hecker/George Theofanopoulos*

Senior Buyer: *Laura M. Fuller*
Designer: *Egzon Shaqiri*
Content Licensing Specialist: *Lori Slattery*
Cover Image: © *1001nights/Getty Images*
Compositor: *Aptara®, Inc.*
Printer: *LSC Communications*

All credits appearing on this page or at the end of the book are considered to be an extension of the copyright page.

Library of Congress Cataloging-in-Publication Data

Names: Kottak, Conrad Phillip, author.
Title: Mirror for humanity : a concise introduction to cultural anthropology / Conrad Phillip Kottak.
Description: Eleventh edition. | New York, NY : McGraw-Hill Education, [2018]
Identifiers: LCCN 2017025310| ISBN 9781259818424 (alk. paper) | ISBN 125981842X (alk. paper)
Subjects: LCSH: Ethnology.
Classification: LCC GN316 .K66 2018 | DDC 305.8--dc23 LC record available at https://lccn.loc.gov/2017025310

The Internet addresses listed in the text were accurate at the time of publication. The inclusion of a website does not indicate an endorsement by the author or McGraw-Hill Education, and McGraw-Hill Education does not guarantee the accuracy of the information presented at these sites.

mheducation.com/highered

To my daughter,
Dr. Juliet Kottak Mavromatis

Also available from McGraw-Hill by Conrad Phillip Kottak:

Window on Humanity: A Concise Introduction to Anthropology, 8th ed. (2018)

Anthropology: Appreciating Human Diversity, 17th ed. (2017)

Cultural Anthropology: Appreciating Cultural Diversity, 17th ed. (2017)

CULTURE, 2nd ed. (2014) (Lisa Gezon and Conrad Phillip Kottak)

On Being Different: Diversity and Multiculturalism in the North American Mainstream, 4th ed. (2012) (with Kathryn A. Kozaitis)

Assault on Paradise: The Globalization of a Little Community in Brazil, 4th ed. (2006)

Brief Contents

Contents

Anthropology Today Boxes

Preface

Mirror for Humanity is intended to provide a concise, readable, introduction to cultural anthropology. The shorter length increases the instructor's options for assigning additional reading—case studies, readers, and other supplements—in a semester course. *Mirror* also works well in a quarter system, for which traditional texts may be too long.

Just as anthropology is a dynamic discipline that encourages new discoveries and explores the profound changes now affecting people and societies, *Mirror for Humanity* makes a concerted effort to keep pace with changes in the way students read and learn core content today. Our digital program, **Connect Anthropology,** includes assignable and assessable quizzes, exercises, and interactive activities, organized around course-specific learning objectives. Furthermore, **Connect** includes an adaptive testing program in **LearnSmart,** as well as **SmartBook,** the first and only truly adaptive reading experience. The tools and resources provided in **Connect Anthropology** are designed to engage students and enable them to improve their performance in the course. This 11th edition has benefited from feedback from over 2,000 students who worked with these tools and programs while using the 10th edition of *Mirror* or one of my other recent texts. We were able to respond to specific areas of difficulty that students encountered, chapter by chapter. I used this extensive feedback to revise, rethink, and clarify my writing in almost every chapter. In preparing this edition, I benefited tremendously from both students' and professors' reactions to my book.

As I work on each new edition, it becomes ever more apparent to me that while any competent and useful text must present core material, that text also must demonstrate the relevance of cultural anthropology to the 21st-century world we inhabit. Accordingly, each new edition contains substantial content changes as well as specific features relevant to our changing world. One of my primary goals is to help students make connections between what they read and their own lives. Accordingly, the "Anthropology Today" boxes placed near the end of each chapter examine recent developments in anthropology as well as contemporary topics and issues that are clearly related to anthropology's subject matter. I have written nine new "Anthropology Today" boxes highlighting important recent contributions as well as world events and issues in the news. Each chapter also contains a new feature that I call "Think Like an Anthropologist," which attempts to get students to do just that—to apply their critical thinking skills as an anthropologist might.

I realize that most students who read this book will not go on to become anthropologists, or even anthropology majors. For those who do, this book should provide a solid foundation to build on. For those who don't—that is, for most of my readers—my goal is to instill a sense of understanding and appreciation of human diversity and of cultural anthropology as a field. May this course and this text help students think differently about, and achieve greater understanding of, their own culture and its place within our globalizing world.

Updates and Revisions—Informed by Student Data

Revisions to this 11th edition of *Mirror for Humanity* were extensively informed by student data, collected anonymously by McGraw-Hill's LearnSmart adaptive learning system. Using this data, we were able to identify content areas with which students struggle. I relied on this data, which provided feedback at the paragraph and even sentence level (see the screen capture below), in making decisions about material to revise, update, and improve.

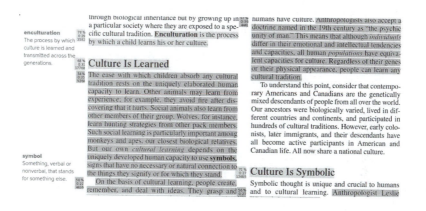

McGraw-Hill Connect Anthropology

Connect Anthropology is a premier digital teaching and learning tool that allows instructors to assign and assess course material. Connect Anthropology includes assignable and assessable quizzes, exercises, and interactive activities, organized around course-specific learning objectives. New to this edition, **NewsFlash** activities bring in articles on current events relevant to anthropology with accompanying assessment. In addition, Connect Anthropology includes LearnSmart, an adaptive testing program, and SmartBook, the first and only adaptive reading experience.

The system is praised by users—faculty and students alike—for helping to make both teaching and learning more efficient, saving time and keeping class time and independent study time focused on what is most important and only those things that still need reinforcing, and shifting the teaching/learning process away from memorization and cramming. The result is better grades, better concept retention, more students staying in class and passing, and less time spent preparing classes or studying for tests.

SMARTBOOK **SmartBook:** SmartBook makes study time as productive and efficient as possible. It identifies and closes knowledge gaps through a continually adapting reading experience that provides personalized learning resources at the precise moment of need. This ensures that every minute spent with SmartBook is returned to the student as the most value-added minute possible. The result? More confidence, better grades, and greater success.

Culture Is Learned

The ease with which children absorb any cultural tradition rests on the uniquely elaborated human capacity to learn. Other animals may learn from experience; for example, they avoid fire after discovering that it hurts. Social animals also learn from other members of their group. Wolves, for instance, learn hunting strategies from other pack members. Such social learning is particularly important among monkeys and apes, our closest biological relatives. But our own *cultural learning* depends on the uniquely developed human capacity to use symbols, signs that have no necessary or natural connection to the things they signify or for which they stand.

On the basis of cultural learning, people create, remember, and deal with ideas. They grasp and apply specific systems of symbolic meaning. Anthropologist Clifford Geertz defines culture as ideas based on cultural learning and symbols. Cultures have been characterized as sets of "control mechanisms—plans, recipes, rules, instructions, what computer engineers call programs for the governing of behavior" (Geertz 1973, p. 44). These programs are absorbed by people through enculturation in particular traditions. People gradually internalize a previously established system of meanings and symbols. They use this cultural system to define their world, express their feelings, and make their judgments. This system helps guide their behavior and perceptions throughout their lives.

Every person begins immediately, through a process of conscious and unconscious learning and interaction with others, to internalize, or incorporate, a cultural tradition through the process of enculturation. Sometimes culture is taught directly, as when parents tell their children to say "thank you" when someone gives them something or does them a favor.

Practice   «   ←   **22**   / 546   →   »   A

Children learn to avoid fire by being told that it is dangerous while animals learn to avoid fire by discovering that it burns them. The difference between the two is that human cultural learning depends on

Click the answer you think is right.

primate tendencies.

evolutionary psychology.

the capacity to use symbols.

cultural diffusion.

Do you know the answer?   Read about this

I know it   Think so   Unsure   No idea

ConnectINSIGHT   **Connect Insight:** Connect Insight is Connect's one-of-a-kind visual analytics dashboard—available for both instructors and students—that provides at-a-glance information regarding student performance, which is immediately actionable. By presenting assignment, assessment, and topical performance results together with a time metric that is easily visible for aggregate or individual results, Connect Insight gives the user the ability to take a just-in-time approach to teaching and learning.

Chapter-by-Chapter Changes

Updates were also informed by the many excellent reviews provided by faculty at 2- and 4-year schools across the country. In addition to the new "Think Like an Anthropologist" feature, as well as revisions and updates in nearly every section of the book, the following are this edition's major changes:

Chapter 1: What Is Anthropology?

- "The Subdivisions of Anthropology" features a thoroughly revised sub-section on "Biological Anthropology."

- The "Anthropology and Other Academic Fields" section has been fully revised and includes a new sub-section on "Cultural Anthropology and Sociology."
- A new "Anthropology Today" box, "School of Hope," has been added.

Chapter 2: Culture

- The opening section, "What Is Culture?," has been fully revised, with a new introduction differentiating more clearly between society and culture.
- The "Mechanisms of Cultural Change" section includes a new discussion of pidgin languages.
- A new "Anthropology Today" box, "Preserving Cultural Heritage," has been added.

Chapter 3: Doing Anthropology

- The "Ethnography: Anthropology's Distinctive Strategy" section (formerly "Ethnographic Techniques") features a new introduction with a clarified definition of ethnography, as well as a fully revised and expanded sub-section on "Problem-Oriented Ethnography.
- A new "Anthropology Today" box, "Online Ethnography," has been added.

Chapter 4: Language and Communication

- The "Nonverbal Communication" section includes a new sub-section, "Personal Space and Displays of Affection" (adapted from the previous edition's Chapter 2 "Anthropology Today" box).
- The "Sociolinguistics" section contains a new sub-section, "Linguistic Diversity in California" (adapted from the previous edition's Chapter 4 "Anthropology Today" box), as well as expanded discussion of regional speech patterns and examples of linguistic diversity within India.
- A new "Anthropology Today" box, "Words of the Year," has been added.

Chapter 5: Making a Living

- A new introduction to the "Adaptive Strategies" section better distinguishes the concept of food production.
- The "Foraging" section includes a clarified definition of foraging, as well as expanded discussion of the distribution of modern foragers, the Basarwa San, and social distinctions in egalitarian foraging societies.
- The "Adaptive Strategies Based on Food Production" section has been revised to clarify the discussions of horticulture, shifting cultivation, and slash-and-burn horticulture.
- The "Distribution, Exchange" section features revised discussions of redistribution, reciprocity, and potlatching.

Chapter 6: Political Systems

- The "What Is 'The Political'?" section features a revised introduction clarifying the difference between power and authority.
- The "Social Control" section has been thoroughly revised to clarify the concepts of public resistance, hidden transcripts, and shame and gossip.

- The "State Systems" section includes expanded discussion of the relative value of state systems.
- A new "Anthropology Today" box, "The Illegality Industry: A Failed System of Border Control," has been added.

Chapter 7: Families, Kinship, and Marriage

- The "Families" section has been extensively revised to include expanded discussion of the zadruga family system, industrialism and family organization, and changes in North American kinship, as well as new material on expanded family households and matrifocal households.
- The "Descent" section has been revised to foreground the concept of descent groups and clarify the discussion of demonstrated and stipulated descent.
- The "Same-Sex Marriage" has been thoroughly revised to include revised statistics regarding same-sex marriage worldwide and new material on the 2015 Supreme Court decision legalizing same-sex marriage in the United States.
- The "Divorce" section provides new discussion of divorce among foragers.
- The "Plural Marriages" section features a new introduction clarifying the difference between polygamy, polygyny, and polyandry, as well as expanded discussion of polygyny.
- A new "Anthropology Today" box, "What Anthropologists Could Teach the Supreme Court about the Definition of Marriage," has been added.

Chapter 8: Gender

- The "Sex and Gender" section features a new introduction foregrounding the concepts of nature and nurture.
- The "Recurrent Gender Patterns" section has been simplified for greater clarity.
- The "Gender Roles and Gender Stratification" section provides expanded discussion of patriarchy and violence (with new examples, including the Boko Haram kidnappings) as well as resistance to it (with the case of Pakistani Nobel Prize winner Malala Yousafzai's work).
- The "Gender in Industrialized Societies" section has been heavily revised, with a new introduction. Its sub-section "Changes in Gendered Work" contains new statistics and new material on the effects of automation and education on women's professional employment. A new sub-section "Work and Family: Reality and Stereotypes" examines the changing roles of women and men regarding work and family responsibilities, as well as persisting stereotypes. The sub-sections on "The Feminization of Poverty" and "Work and Happiness" have been thoroughly reworked.
- The "Beyond Male and Female" section has been revised to clarify the difference between intersex and transgender, and expanded to discuss the increased visibility of, and legal challenges faced by, transgender individuals in the United States.
- A new "Anthropology Today" box, "Gender, Ethnicity, and a Gold Medal for Fiji," has been added.

Chapter 9: Religion

- The "Social Control" section features a new discussion of accusations of witchcraft as a means of religiously-based social control.
- The "World Religions" section has been fully revised to incorporate the latest statistics.
- The "Religion and Cultural Globalization" section has been extensively revised and includes expanded discussion of the relationship between antimodernism and religious fundamentalism in Christianity and Islam, as well as a new sub-section "Religious Radicalism Today" focusing on Scott Atran's research into militant groups like al Qaeda and ISIS.
- A new "Anthropology Today" box, "Newtime Religion," has been added.

Chapter 10: Ethnicity and Race

- The "Ethnic Groups and Ethnicity" section has been substantially revised, including a new introduction and statistics, as well as an expanded "Status and Identity" section (previously "Shifting Status") clarifying the definition of status as well as the difference between ascribed and achieved status.
- The "Human Biological Diversity and the Race Concept" section features a clarified discussion of "Races Are Not Biologically Distinct."
- The "Race and Ethnicity" section provides clarification about the difficulty in defining both terms.
- "The Social Construction of Race" section includes clarified discussion of racial attitudes in Japan.
- The "Ethnic Groups, Nations, and Nationalities" section provides a revised discussion of nationalism.
- The "Ethnic Tolerance and Accommodation" section includes updated discussions of assimilation and multiculturalism.
- The "Changing Demographics" section provides updated demographic statistics as well as a new sub-section "The Backlash to Multiculturalism," which explores the growth of the Tea Party movement during the Obama presidency and ethno-nationalism during and since the Trump presidential campaign and presidency.
- The "Ethnic Conflict" section (previously "Roots of Ethnic Conflict") has new coverage of sectarian violence in Iraq and Syria and of the Black Lives Matter movement, as well as updated discussions of anti-ethnic discrimination and violence in Darfur, Syria, and Ukraine, and new material on the backlash against undocumented immigrants in the United States.

Chapter 11: Applying Anthropology

- "The Role of the Applied Anthropologist" section has been heavily revised, with an expanded sub-section on "Early Applications" and an updated section on "Applied Anthropology Today."
- The "Development Anthropology" section has been thoroughly revised, particularly the "Equity" and "Negative Equity Impact" sub-sections.

- The "Strategies for Innovation" section includes an expanded and revised discussion of overinnovation.
- The "Urban Anthropology" section has updated statistics.
- The "Medical Anthropology" section has been rewritten and reorganized and features three new sub-head sections to clarify the discussion: "Disease Theory Systems," "Scientific Medicine versus Western Medicine," and "Industrialization, Globalization, and Health."
- The "Anthropology and Business" section now includes expanded discussion and numerous examples of how anthropologists can contribute to market research and applied ethnography in business settings.

Chapter 12: The World System, Colonialism, and Inequality

- "The World System" section features a new introduction foregrounding the concept of the modern world system, as well as revised sub-sections on "World System Theory" and "The Emergence of the World System."
- "The Persistence of Inequality" section (previously "Socioeconomic Effects of Inequality") has been thoroughly revised to incorporate new statistics and extensive new discussion of the water crisis in Flint, Michigan.
- The "Colonialism and Imperialism" section (previously "Colonialism") has been heavily revised and includes clarified discussion of the difference between colonialism and imperialism, as well as a new sub-section "The First Phase of European Colonialism: Spain and Portugal."
- The "Communism, Socialism, and Postsocialism" section (previously "The Second World") provides expanded discussion of postsocial transitions.

Chapter 13: Anthropology's Role In a Globalizing World

- The "Globalization: Its Meanings and Its Nature" section has been clarified and simplified.
- The "Energy Consumption and Industrial Degradation" section has been heavily updated to incorporate new statistics and coverage of recent global developments, such as the Ebola and Zika virus crises, cyber attacks, and climate change.
- The "Global Climate Change" section has been fully revised to incorporate the latest statistics and an expanded discussion of the greenhouse effect.
- The "Environmental Anthropology" section includes an updated sub-section on "Emerging Diseases," especially zoonotic diseases.
- The "Interethnic Contact" section features a new introduction focused on shifting cultural patterns and a revised sub-section "A Global Culture of Consumption."
- The "Indigenous Peoples" section features updated statistics and new coverage of the United Nations' commitment to the rights of indigenous peoples.
- A new "Anthropology Today" box, "Diversity under Siege: Global Forces and Indigenous Peoples," has been added.

Content and Organization

No single or monolithic theoretical perspective orients this book. My e-mail, along with reviewers' comments, confirms that instructors with a very wide range of views and approaches have been pleased with *Mirror* as a teaching tool.

- In Chapter 1, anthropology is introduced as an integrated four-field discipline, with academic and applied dimensions, that examines human biological and cultural diversity in time and space. Anthropology is discussed as a comparative and holistic science, featuring biological, social, cultural, linguistic, humanistic, and historical approaches. Chapter 2 examines the central anthropological concept of culture, including its symbolic and adaptive features. Chapter 3 is about doing anthropology—the methods and ethics of ethnographic research and other approaches in cultural anthropology.

- Chapters 4-13 are organized to place related content close together—although they are sufficiently independent to be assigned in any order the instructor might select. Thus, "Political Systems" (Chapter 6) logically follows "Making a Living" (Chapter 5). Chapters 7 and 8 ("Families, Kinship, and Marriage" and "Gender," respectively) also form a coherent unit. The chapter on religion (9) covers not just traditional religious practices but also contemporary world religions and religious movements. It is followed by four chapters (10–13) that form a natural unit exploring sociocultural transformations and expressions in today's world.

- Those last four chapters address several important questions: How are race and ethnicity socially constructed and handled in different societies, and how do they generate prejudice, discrimination, and conflict? How and why did the modern world system emerge and expand? How has world capitalism affected patterns of stratification and inequality within and among nations? What were colonialism, imperialism, and Communism, and what are their legacies? How do people today actively interpret and confront the world system and the products of globalization? What factors threaten continued human diversity? How can anthropologists work to ensure the preservation of that diversity?

- Let me also single out two chapters present in *Mirror for Humanity* but not found consistently in other anthropology texts: "Ethnicity and Race" (Chapter 10) and "Gender" (Chapter 8). I believe that systematic consideration of race, ethnicity, and gender is vital in any introductory anthropology text. Anthropology's distinctive four-field approach can shed special light on these topics, as we see especially in Chapter 10 ("Ethnicity and Race"). Race and gender studies are fields in which anthropology always has taken the lead. I'm convinced that anthropology's special contributions to understanding the biological, social, cultural, and linguistic dimensions of race, ethnicity, and gender should be highlighted in any introductory text.

Teaching Resources

The following instructor resources can be accessed through the Library tab in **Connect Anthropology**:

- Instructor's manual
- PowerPoint lecture slides

- Computerized Test Bank
- Word version of the test bank

Create

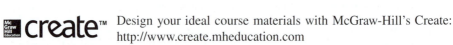 Design your ideal course materials with McGraw-Hill's Create: http://www.create.mheducation.com

Rearrange or omit chapters, combine materials from other sources, and/or upload any other content you have written to make the perfect resource for your students. You can even personalize your book's appearance by selecting the cover and adding your name, school, and course information. When you order a Create book, you receive a complimentary review copy. Get a printed copy in three to five business days or an electronic copy (eComp) via e-mail in about an hour. Register today at http://www.create.mheducation.com and craft your course resources to match the way you teach.

Acknowledgments

I'm grateful to many colleagues at McGraw-Hill. I offer particular thanks to Product Developer Emily Pecora, who synthesized and summarized the prepublication reviews, helped me plan and implement this revision, and worked with me to complete and submit the manuscript ahead of schedule. I have always appreciated Emily's keen editorial eye for style, language, and presentation, as well as content. She has helped guide me through several revisions. I also thank Bruce Cantley for his work as product developer as *Mirror for Humanity* moved toward publication. Thanks also to Gina Boedeker, McGraw-Hill's former Managing Director for anthropology, and to Rhona Robbin, former Lead Product Developer, for their help and support over many years and editions, including the start of this revision. I am privileged to be working now with Claire Brantley, Executive Portfolio Manager, and Dawn Groundwater, Lead Product Developer. Thanks as well to McGraw-Hill's entire team of sales reps and regional managers for the work they do in helping professors and students gain access to my books. I also acknowledge Michael Ryan, Vice President for Portfolio and Learning Content.

As usual Rick Hecker has done a great job as Content Project Manager, guiding the manuscript through production and keeping everything moving on schedule. Laura Fuller, Buyer, worked with the printer to make sure everything came out right. Thanks, too, to Charlotte Goldman, freelance photo researcher, and to Scott Lukas, Lake Tahoe Community College, who created the content for the Connect products for this book. I also thank Amy Marks for copyediting, Marlena Pechan for proofreading, and Egzon Shaqiri for executing the design.

Lori Slattery also deserves thanks as Content Licensing Specialist.

The names and schools of the reviewers contracted by McGraw-Hill to review the 10th edition of *Mirror for Humanity,* in preparation for the 11th edition, or the 7th edition of *Window on Humanity,* in preparation for the 8th edition, are as follows:

Jenna Andrews-Swann
Georgia Gwinnett College
Margaret Bruchez
Blinn College
Jessica H. Craig
Central New Mexico Community College
Anna R. Dixon
University of South Florida, St. Petersburg
Shasta Gaughen
California State University, San Marcos
Fred Heifner
Cumberland University
Joshua A. Irizarry
Bridgewater State University

Lily Malekfar
Triton College
Scotty Moore
Houston Community College
Elizabeth Scharf
University of North Dakota
Marjorie M. Snipes
University of West Georgia
Julie Vazquez
College of the Canyons
Jessica Worden-Jones
Schoolcraft College
Catherine Wright
Jacksonville State Community College

I'm grateful to all these reviewers and professors for their enthusiasm and their suggestions for changes, additions, and deletions (sometimes in very different directions!). Very, very special thanks as well to the more than 2,000 students whose responses in LearnSmart helped me pinpoint content and writing that needed clarification. Never have so many voices contributed to a revision as to this one. My readers also share their insights about *Mirror* via e-mail. Anyone—student or instructor—can reach me at the following e-mail address: **ckottak@bellsouth.net**.

As usual, my family provides me with understanding, support, and inspiration in my writing projects. Dr. Nicholas Kottak, my son and a fellow anthropologist, and Isabel Wagley Kottak, my wife and companion in field work throughout my career, regularly share their insights with me. Once again, I dedicate this book to my daughter. Dr. Juliet Kottak Mavromatis, who continues our family tradition of exploring and writing about human diversity and diagnosing and treating the human condition.

During my long academic career, I've benefited from the knowledge, help, and advice of so many friends, colleagues, teaching assistants (graduate student instructors—GSIs), and students that I can no longer fit their names into a short preface. I hope they know who they are and accept my thanks. I do especially thank my co-authors of other books: Lara Descartes (*Media and Middle Class Moms*), Lisa Gezon (*Culture*), and Kathryn Kozaitis (*On Being Different*). Kathryn (with whom I have worked on four editions), Lisa (two editions), and Lara are prized former students of mine. Today they all are accomplished anthropologists in their own right, and they continue to share their wisdom with me.

Feedback from students and from my fellow anthropologists keeps me up-to-date on the interests, needs, and views of the people for whom *Mirror* is written, as does my ongoing participation in workshops on the teaching of anthropology. I continue to believe that effective textbooks are based in the enjoyment of teaching and respect for students. I hope this product of my experience will continue to be helpful to others.

Conrad Phillip Kottak

Seabrook Island, South Carolina

ckottak@bellsouth.net

About the Author

© Juliet Kottak Mavromatis

Conrad Phillip Kottak,

who received his AB and PhD degrees from Columbia University, is the Julian H. Steward Collegiate Professor Emeritus of Anthropology at the University of Michigan, where he served as anthropology department chair from 1996 to 2006. He has been honored for his teaching by the university and the state of Michigan and by the American Anthropological Association. He is an elected member of the American Academy of Arts and Sciences and the National Academy of Sciences, where he chaired Section 51, Anthropology from 2010 to 2013.

Professor Kottak has done ethnographic fieldwork in Brazil, Madagascar, and the United States. His general interests are in the processes by which local cultures are incorporated—and resist incorporation—into larger systems. This interest links his earlier work on ecology and state formation in Africa and Madagascar to his more recent research on globalization, national and international culture, and media, including new media and social media.

Kottak's popular case study *Assault on Paradise: The Globalization of a Little Community in Brazil* (2006) describes his long-term and continuing fieldwork in Arembepe, Bahia, Brazil. His book *Prime-Time Society: An Anthropological Analysis of Television and Culture* (2009) is a comparative study of the nature and impact of television in Brazil and the United States.

Kottak's other books include *The Past in the Present: History, Ecology and Cultural Variation in Highland Madagascar* (1980), *Researching American Culture: A Guide for Student Anthropologists* (1982), *Madagascar: Society and History* (1986), and *Media and Middle Class Moms: Images and Realities of Work and Family* (with Lara Descartes, 2009). The most recent editions (17th) of his texts *Anthropology: Appreciating Human Diversity* and *Cultural Anthropology: Appreciating Cultural Diversity* were published by McGraw-Hill in 2017. He also is the author of *Window on Humanity: A Concise Introduction to Anthropology* (8th ed., McGraw-Hill, 2018), and of this book—*Mirror for Humanity: A Concise Introduction to Cultural Anthropology* (11th ed., McGraw-Hill, 2018).

Conrad Kottak's articles have appeared in academic journals, including *American Anthropologist, Journal of Anthropological Research, American Ethnologist, Ethnology, Human Organization,* and *Luso-Brazilian Review.* He also has written for more popular journals, including *Transaction/SOCIETY, Natural History, Psychology Today,* and *General Anthropology.*

In other research projects, Professor Kottak and his colleagues have investigated ecological awareness in Brazil, biodiversity conservation in Madagascar, and media use by modern American families. Professor Kottak currently is collaborating with Professor Richard Pace and several graduate students on research investigating "The Evolution of Media Impact: A Longitudinal and Multi-Site Study of Television and New Electronic/Digital Media in Brazil," a project supported by the National Science Foundation.

Conrad Kottak appreciates comments about his books from professors and students. He can be reached at the following e-mail address: **ckottak@bellsouth.net.**

Chapter 1

What Is Anthropology?

The Cross-Cultural Perspective

"That's just human nature." "People are pretty much the same all over the world." Such opinions, which we hear in conversations, in the mass media, and in a dozen scenes in daily life, promote the erroneous idea that people in other countries have the same desires, feelings, values, and aspirations that we do. Such statements proclaim that because people are essentially the same, they are eager to receive the ideas, beliefs, values, institutions, practices, and products of an expansive North American culture. Often this assumption turns out to be wrong.

Anthropology offers a broader view—a distinctive comparative, cross-cultural perspective. Most people think that anthropologists study nonindustrial societies, and they do. My research has taken me to remote villages in Brazil and Madagascar, a large island off the southeast coast of Africa. In Brazil I sailed with fishers in simple sailboats on Atlantic waters. Among Madagascar's Betsileo people, I worked in rice fields and took part in ceremonies in which I entered tombs to rewrap the corpses of decaying ancestors.

However, anthropology is much more than the study of nonindustrial peoples. It is a comparative science that examines all societies, ancient and modern, simple and complex. Most of the other social sciences tend to focus on a single society, usually an industrial nation such as the United States or Canada. Anthropology offers a unique cross-cultural perspective, constantly comparing the customs of one society with those of others.

Among scholarly disciplines, anthropology stands out as the field that provides the cross-cultural test. How much would we know about human behavior, thought, and feeling if we studied only our own kind? What if our entire understanding of human behavior were based on analysis of questionnaires filled out by college students in Oregon? That is a radical question, but one that should make you think about the basis for statements about what humans are like, individually or as a group. A primary reason anthropology can uncover so much about what it means to be human is that the discipline is based on the cross-cultural perspective. A single culture simply cannot tell us everything we need to know about what it means to be human. We need to compare and contrast.

To become a cultural anthropologist, one typically does *ethnography* (the firsthand, personal study of local settings). Ethnographic fieldwork usually entails spending a year or more in another society, living with the local people and learning about their way of life. No matter how much the ethnographer discovers about that society, he or she remains an alien there. That experience of alienation has a profound impact. Having learned to respect other customs and beliefs, anthropologists can never forget that there is a wider world. There are normal ways of thinking and acting other than our own.

Human Adaptability

Anthropologists study human beings wherever and whenever they find them—in a Turkish café, a Mesopotamian tomb, or a North American shopping mall. Anthropology is the exploration of human diversity in time and space. Anthropology studies the whole of the human condition: past, present, and future; biology, society, language, and culture. Of particular interest is the diversity that comes through human adaptability.

Humans are among the world's most adaptable animals. In the Andes of South America, people wake up in villages 16,000 feet above sea level and then trek 1,500 feet higher to work in tin mines. Tribes in the Australian desert worship animals and discuss philosophy. People survive malaria in the tropics. Men have walked on the moon. The model of the *Star Trek* starship *Enterprise* in Washington's Smithsonian Institution is a symbol of the *Star Trek* mission "to seek out new life and new civilizations, to boldly go where no one has gone before." Wishes to know the unknown, control the uncontrollable, and create order out of chaos find expression among all peoples. Creativity, adaptability, and flexibility are basic human attributes, and human diversity is the subject matter of anthropology.

Students often are surprised by the breadth of **anthropology,** which is the study of humans around the world and through time. Anthropology is a uniquely comparative and **holistic** science. *Holism* refers to the study of the whole of the human condition: past, present, and future; biology, society, language, and culture.

People share **society**—organized life in groups—with other animals, including baboons, wolves, mole rats, and even ants. Culture, however, is more distinctly human.

Cultures are traditions and customs, transmitted through learning, that form and guide the beliefs and behavior of the people exposed to them. Children learn such a tradition by growing up in a particular society, through a process called *enculturation.* Cultural traditions include customs and opinions, developed over the generations, about proper and improper behavior. These traditions answer such questions as: How should we do things? How do we make sense of the world? How do we tell right from wrong? A culture produces a degree of consistency in behavior and thought among the people who live in a particular society.

The most critical element of cultural traditions is their transmission through learning rather than through biological inheritance. Culture is not itself biological, but it rests on certain features of human biology. For more than a million years, humans have had at least some of the biological capacities on which culture depends. These abilities are to learn, to think symbolically, to use language, and to employ tools and other products in organizing their lives and adapting to their environments.

Anthropology confronts and ponders major questions of human existence as it explores human biological and cultural diversity in time and space. By examining ancient bones and tools, we unravel the mysteries of human origins. When did our ancestors separate from those remote great-aunts and great-uncles whose descendants are the apes? Where and when did *Homo sapiens* originate? How has our species changed? What are we now, and where are we going? How have changes in culture and society influenced biological change? Our genus, *Homo,* has been changing for more than 2 million years. Humans continue to adapt and change both biologically and culturally.

Adaptation, Variation, and Change

Adaptation refers to the processes by which organisms cope with environmental forces and stresses, such as those posed by climate and *topography* or terrains, also called landforms. How do organisms change to fit their environments, such as dry climates or high mountain altitudes? Like other animals, humans use biological means of adaptation. But humans are unique in also having cultural means of adaptation. Table 1.1 summarizes the cultural and biological means that humans use to adapt to high altitudes.

TABLE 1.1   **Forms of Cultural and Biological Adaptation (to High Altitude)**

Form of Adaptation	Type of Adaptation	Example
Technology	Cultural	Pressurized airplane cabin with oxygen masks
Genetic adaptation (occurs over generations)	Biological	Larger "barrel chests" of native highlanders
Long-term physiological adaptation (occurs during growth and development of the individual organism)	Biological	More efficient respiratory system, to extract oxygen from "thin air"
Short-term physiological adaptation (occurs spontaneously when the individual organism enters a new environment)	Biological	Increased heart rate, hyperventilation

Mountainous terrains pose particular challenges, those associated with high altitude and oxygen deprivation. Consider four ways (one cultural and three biological) in which humans may cope with low oxygen pressure at high altitudes. Illustrating cultural (technological) adaptation would be a pressurized airplane cabin equipped with oxygen masks. There are three ways of adapting biologically to high altitudes: genetic adaptation, long-term physiological adaptation, and short-term physiological adaptation. First, native populations of high-altitude areas, such as the Andes of Peru and the Himalayas of Tibet and Nepal, seem to have acquired certain genetic advantages for life at very high altitudes. The Andean tendency to develop a voluminous chest and lungs probably has a genetic basis. Second, regardless of their genes, people who grow up at a high altitude become physiologically more efficient there than genetically similar people who have grown up at sea level would be. This illustrates long-term physiological adaptation during the body's growth and development. Third, humans also have the capacity for short-term or immediate physiological adaptation. Thus, when lowlanders arrive in the highlands, they immediately increase their breathing and heart rates. Hyperventilation increases the oxygen in their lungs and arteries. As the pulse also increases, blood reaches their tissues more rapidly. All these varied adaptive responses—cultural and biological—achieve a single goal: maintaining an adequate supply of oxygen to the body.

As human history has unfolded, the social and cultural means of adaptation have become increasingly important. In this process, humans have devised diverse ways of coping with a wide range of environments. The rate of cultural adaptation and change has accelerated, particularly during the past 10,000 years. For millions of years, hunting and gathering of nature's bounty—*foraging*—was the sole basis of human subsistence. However, it took only a few thousand years for **food production** (the cultivation of plants and domestication of animals), which originated some 12,000–10,000 years ago, to replace foraging in most areas. Between 6000 and 5000 B.P. (before the present), the first civilizations arose. These were large, powerful, and complex societies, such as ancient Egypt, that conquered and governed large geographic areas.

Much more recently, the spread of industrial production and the forces of globalization have profoundly affected human life. Throughout human history, major innovations have spread at the expense of earlier ones. Each economic revolution has had social and cultural repercussions. Today's global economy and communications link all contemporary people, directly or indirectly, in the modern world system. People must cope with forces generated by progressively larger systems—region, nation, and world. The study of such contemporary adaptations generates new challenges for anthropology: "The cultures of world peoples need to be constantly rediscovered as these people reinvent them in changing historical circumstances" (Marcus and Fischer 1986, p. 24).

Cultural Forces Shape Human Biology

Anthropology's comparative, biocultural perspective recognizes that cultural forces constantly mold human biology. (**Biocultural** refers to using and combining both biological and cultural perspectives and approaches to analyze and understand a particular issue or problem.) Culture is a key environmental force in determining how human bodies grow and develop. Cultural traditions promote certain activities and abilities, discourage others, and set standards of physical well-being and attractiveness. Consider

Athletes primed for the start of the 10 kilometer women's marathon swim at the 2016 Summer Olympics in Rio de Janeiro. Years of swimming sculpt a distinctive physique—an enlarged upper torso and neck, and powerful shoulders and back. ©Tim de Waele/Corbis via Getty Images

how this works in sports. North American girls are encouraged to pursue, and therefore do well in, competition involving figure skating, gymnastics, track and field, swimming, diving, and many other sports. Brazilian girls, although excelling in the team sports of basketball and volleyball, haven't fared nearly as well in individual sports as have their American and Canadian counterparts.

Cultural standards of attractiveness and propriety influence participation and achievement in sports. Americans run or swim not just to compete but also to keep trim and fit. Brazil's beauty standards traditionally have accepted more fat, especially in female buttocks and hips. Brazilian men have had significant international success in swimming and running, but Brazil rarely sends female swimmers or runners to the Olympics. One reason why Brazilian women avoid competitive swimming in particular may be that sport's effects on the body. Years of swimming sculpt a distinctive physique: an enlarged upper torso, a massive neck, and powerful shoulders and back. Successful female swimmers tend to be big, strong, and bulky. The countries that have produced them most consistently are the United States, Canada, Australia, Germany, the Scandinavian nations, the Netherlands, and the former Soviet Union, where this body type isn't as stigmatized as it is in Latin countries. For women, Brazilian culture prefers ample hips and buttocks to a muscled upper body. Many young female swimmers in Brazil choose to abandon the sport rather than their culture's "feminine" body ideal.

When you grew up, which sport did you appreciate the most—soccer, swimming, football, baseball, tennis, golf, or some other sport (or perhaps none at all)? Is this because of "who you are" or because of the opportunities you had as a child to practice and participate in this particular activity? When you were young, your parents might have told you that drinking milk and eating vegetables would help you grow up "big and strong." They probably didn't as readily recognize the role that *culture* plays in shaping bodies, personalities, and personal health. If nutrition matters in growth, so, too, do cultural guidelines. What is proper behavior for boys and girls? What kinds of work should men and women do? Where should people live? What are proper uses of their leisure time? What role should religion play? How should people relate to their family, friends, and neighbors? Although our genetic attributes provide a foundation for growth and development, human biology is fairly plastic—that is, it is malleable. Culture is an environmental force that affects our development as much as do nutrition, heat, cold, and altitude. Culture also guides our emotional and cognitive growth and helps determine the kinds of personalities we have as adults.

General Anthropology

The academic discipline of anthropology, also known as **general anthropology** or "four-field" anthropology, includes four main subdisciplines, or subfields. They are sociocultural anthropology, anthropological archaeology, biological anthropology, and linguistic anthropology. (From here on, the shorter term *cultural anthropology* will be used as a synonym for *sociocultural anthropology*.) Of the subfields, cultural anthropology has the largest membership. Most departments of anthropology teach courses in all four subfields.

Early American anthropology was especially concerned with the history and cultures of Native North Americans. Ely S. Parker, or Ha-sa-no-an-da, was a Seneca Indian who made important contributions to early anthropology. Parker also served as commissioner of Indian affairs for the United States. Source: National Archives and Records Administration

There are historical reasons for the inclusion of four subfields in a single discipline. The origin of anthropology as a scientific field, and of American anthropology in particular, can be traced to the 19th century. Early American anthropologists were concerned especially with the history and cultures of the native peoples of North America. Interest in the origins and diversity of Native Americans brought together studies of customs, social life, language, and physical traits. Anthropologists still are pondering such questions as these: Where did Native Americans come from? How many waves of migration brought them to the New World? What are the linguistic, cultural, and biological links among Native Americans and between them and Asia? (Note that a unified four-field anthropology did not develop in Europe, where the subfields tend to exist separately.)

There also are logical reasons for the unity of American anthropology. Each subfield considers variation in time and space (that is, in different geographic areas). Cultural anthropologists and anthropological archaeologists study changes in social life and customs (among many other topics). Archaeologists use studies of living societies to imagine what life might have been like in the past. Biological anthropologists examine evolutionary changes in human biology. Linguistic anthropologists may reconstruct the basics of ancient languages by studying modern ones.

The subfields influence each other as anthropologists talk to each other, read books and journals, and meet in professional organizations. General anthropology explores the basics of human biology, society, and culture and considers their interrelations. Anthropologists share certain key assumptions. Perhaps the most fundamental is the idea that sound conclusions about "human nature" cannot be derived from studying a single population, nation, society, or cultural tradition. A comparative, cross-cultural approach is essential.

The Subdisciplines of Anthropology

Cultural Anthropology

Cultural anthropology is the study of human society and culture. This subfield describes, analyzes, interprets, and explains social and cultural similarities and differences. To study and interpret cultural diversity, cultural anthropologists engage in two kinds of activity: ethnography (based on fieldwork) and ethnology (based on cross-cultural comparison). **Ethnography** provides an account of a particular culture, society, or community. During ethnographic fieldwork, the ethnographer gathers data that he or she organizes, analyzes, and interprets to develop that account, which may be in the form of a book, an article, or a film. Traditionally, ethnographers have lived in small communities and studied local behavior, beliefs, customs, social life, economic activities, politics, and religion (see Okely 2012; Wolcott 2008).

An anthropological perspective derived from ethnographic fieldwork often differs radically from that of economics or political science. Those fields focus on national and official organizations and policies and often on elites. However, the groups that anthropologists traditionally have studied usually have been relatively poor and powerless. Ethnographers often observe discriminatory practices directed toward such people, who experience food shortages, dietary deficiencies, and other aspects of poverty. Political scientists tend to study programs that national planners develop, whereas anthropologists discover how these programs work on the local level.

Communities and cultures are less isolated today than ever before. As noted by Franz Boas (1940/1966) many years ago, contact between neighboring tribes always has existed and has extended over enormous areas. "Human populations construct their cultures in interaction with one another, and not in isolation" (Wolf 1982, p. ix). Villagers increasingly participate in regional, national, and world events. Exposure to external forces comes through education, the mass media, migration, and modern transportation. (The "Anthropology Today" box at the end of this chapter examines the role of a residential school in eastern India in bridging barriers between cultures.) City and nation increasingly invade local communities with the arrival of teachers, tourists, development agents, government and religious officials, and political candidates. Such linkages are prominent components of regional, national, and international systems of politics, economics, and information. These larger systems increasingly affect the people and places anthropology traditionally has studied. The study of such linkages and systems is part of the subject matter of modern anthropology.

Ethnology examines, compares, analyzes, and interprets the results of ethnography—the data gathered in different societies. Ethnologists use such data to compare, contrast, and generalize about society and culture. Looking beyond the particular to the more general, they attempt to identify and explain cultural differences and similarities, to test hypotheses, and to build theory to enhance our understanding of how social and cultural systems work. Ethnology gets its data for comparison not only from ethnography but also from the other subfields, particularly from anthropological archaeology, which reconstructs social systems of the past. (Table 1.2 summarizes the main contrasts between ethnography and ethnology.)

Anthropological Archaeology

Anthropological archaeology (more simply, "archaeology") reconstructs, describes, and interprets human behavior and cultural patterns through material remains. At sites where people live or have lived, archaeologists find artifacts—material items that humans have made, used, or modified—such as tools, weapons, campsites, buildings, and garbage. Plant and animal remains and ancient garbage tell stories about consumption and activities. Wild and domesticated grains have different characteristics, which allow archaeologists to distinguish between gathering and cultivation. Examination of animal bones reveals the ages of slaughtered animals and provides other information useful in determining whether species were wild or domesticated.

Analyzing such data, archaeologists answer several questions about ancient economies: Did the group get its meat from hunting, or did it domesticate and breed animals, killing only those of a certain age and sex? Did plant food come from wild plants or from sowing, tending, and harvesting crops? Did the residents make, trade for, or buy particular items? Were raw materials available locally? If not, where did they come from? From such information, archaeologists reconstruct patterns of production, trade, and consumption.

Archaeologists have spent considerable time studying potsherds, fragments of earthenware. Potsherds are more durable than many other artifacts, such as textiles and wood. The quantity of pottery fragments allows estimates of population size and density. The discovery that potters used materials that were not available locally suggests systems of trade. Similarities in manufacture and decoration at different sites may be proof of cultural connections. Groups with similar pots may share a common history. They might

TABLE 1.2 **Ethnography and Ethnology—Two Dimensions of Cultural Anthropology**

Ethnography	Ethnology
Requires fieldwork to collect data	Uses data collected by a series of researchers
Is often descriptive	Is usually synthetic
Is specific to a group or community	Is comparative and cross-cultural

have common cultural ancestors. Perhaps they traded with each other or belonged to the same political system.

Many archaeologists examine paleoecology. *Ecology* is the study of interrelations among living things in an environment. The organisms and environment together constitute an *ecosystem,* a patterned arrangement of energy flows and exchanges. Human ecology studies ecosystems that include people, focusing on the ways in which human use "of nature influences and is influenced by social organization and cultural values" (Bennett 1969, pp. 10–11). *Paleoecology* looks at the ecosystems of the past.

In addition to reconstructing ecological patterns, archaeologists may infer cultural transformations, for example, by observing changes in the size and type of sites and the distance between them. A city develops in a region where only towns, villages, and hamlets existed a few centuries earlier. The number of settlement levels (city, town, village, hamlet) in a society is a measure of social complexity. Buildings offer clues about political and religious features. Temples and pyramids suggest that an ancient society had an authority structure capable of marshaling the labor needed to build such monuments. The presence or absence of certain structures, like the pyramids of ancient Egypt and Mexico, reveals differences in function between settlements. For example, some towns were places where people went to attend ceremonies. Others were burial sites; still others were farming communities.

Archaeologists also reconstruct behavior patterns and lifestyles of the past by excavating. This involves digging through a succession of levels at a particular site. In a

Anthropological archaeologists from the University of Pennsylvania work to stabilize the original plaster at an Anasazi (Native American) site in Colorado's Mesa Verde National Park. ©George H.H. Huey/Alamy Stock Photo

given area, through time, settlements may change in form and purpose, as may the connections between settlements. Excavation can document changes in economic, social, and political activities.

Although archaeologists are best known for studying prehistory, that is, the period before the invention of writing, they also study the cultures of historical and even living peoples (see Sabloff 2008). Studying sunken ships off the Florida coast, underwater archaeologists have been able to verify the living conditions on the vessels that brought ancestral African Americans to the New World as enslaved people. In a well-known research project in Tucson, Arizona, archaeologist William Rathje learned a great deal about contemporary life by studying modern garbage (Zimring 2012). The value of "garbology," as Rathje called it, is that it provides "evidence of what people did, not what they think they did, what they think they should have done, or what the interviewer thinks they should have done" (Harrison, Rathje, and Hughes 1994, p. 108). What people report may contrast strongly with their real behavior as revealed by garbology. For example, the three Tucson neighborhoods that reported the lowest beer consumption actually had the highest number of discarded beer cans per household (Rathje and Murphy 2001; Zimring 2012)!

Biological Anthropology

Biological anthropology is the study of human biological diversity through time and as it exists in the world today. There are five specialties within biological anthropology:

1. Human biological evolution as revealed by the fossil record (paleoanthropology).
2. Human genetics.
3. Human growth and development.
4. Human biological plasticity (the living body's ability to change as it copes with environmental conditions, such as heat, cold, and altitude).
5. Primatology (the study of monkeys, apes, and other nonhuman primates).

A common thread that runs across all five specialties is an interest in biological variation among humans, including their ancestors and their closest animal relatives (monkeys and apes).

These varied interests link biological anthropology to other fields: biology, zoology, geology, anatomy, physiology, medicine, and public health. Knowledge of osteology—the study of bones—is essential for anthropologists who examine and interpret skulls, teeth, and bones, whether of living humans or of our fossilized ancestors. *Paleontologists* are scientists who study fossils. *Paleoanthropologists* study the fossil record of human evolution. Paleoanthropologists often collaborate with archaeologists, who study artifacts, in reconstructing biological and cultural aspects of human evolution. Fossils and tools often are found together. Different types of tools provide information about the habits, customs, and lifestyles of the ancestral humans who used them.

More than a century ago, Charles Darwin noticed that the variety that exists within any population permits some individuals (those with the favored characteristics) to do better than others at surviving and reproducing. Genetics, which developed after Darwin, enlightens us about the causes and transmission of the variety on which evolution depends. However, it isn't just genes that cause variety. During any individual's lifetime, the environment works along with heredity to determine biological features. For example, people with a genetic tendency to be tall will be shorter if they have poor nutrition during childhood. Thus, biological anthropology also investigates the influence of environment on the body as it grows and matures. Among the environmental factors that influence the body as it develops are nutrition, altitude, temperature, and disease, as well as cultural factors, such as the standards of attractiveness that were discussed previously.

Biological anthropology (along with zoology) also includes primatology. The primates include our closest relatives—apes and monkeys. Primatologists study their biology, evolution, behavior, and social life, often in their natural environments. Primatology assists paleoanthropology, because primate behavior and social organization may shed light on early human behavior and human nature.

Linguistic Anthropology

We don't know (and probably never will) when our ancestors acquired the ability to speak, although biological anthropologists have looked to the anatomy of the face and the skull to speculate about the origin of language. Primatologists have described the communication systems of monkeys and apes. We do know that grammatically complex languages have existed for thousands of years. Linguistic anthropology offers further illustration of anthropology's interest in comparison, variation, and change. **Linguistic anthropology** studies language in its social and cultural context, throughout the world and over time. Some linguistic anthropologists make inferences about universal features of language, linked perhaps to uniformities in the human brain. Others reconstruct ancient languages by comparing their contemporary descendants. Still others study linguistic differences to discover varied perceptions and patterns of thought in different cultures (see Bonvillain 2012, 2016).

Historical linguistics considers variation in time, such as the changes in sounds, grammar, and vocabulary between Middle English (spoken from approximately C.E. [formerly A.D.] 1050 to 1550) and modern English. **Sociolinguistics** investigates relationships between social and linguistic variation. How do different speakers use a given language? How do linguistic features correlate with social factors, including class and gender differences (Eckert and McConnell-Ginet 2013)? One reason for variation is geography, as in regional dialects and accents. Linguistic variation also is expressed in the bilingualism of ethnic groups. Linguistic and cultural anthropologists collaborate in studying links between language and many other aspects of culture, such as how people reckon kinship and how they perceive and classify colors.

Applied Anthropology

What sort of man or woman do you envision when you hear the word *anthropologist*? Although anthropologists have been portrayed as quirky and eccentric, bearded and bespectacled, anthropology is not a science of the exotic carried on by quaint scholars in ivory towers. Rather, anthropology has a lot to tell the public. Anthropology's foremost professional organization, the American Anthropological Association (AAA), has formally acknowledged a public service role by recognizing that anthropology has two dimensions: (1) academic anthropology and (2) practicing, or **applied, anthropology**. The latter refers to the application of anthropological data, perspectives, theory, and methods to identify, assess, and solve contemporary social problems. As American anthropologist Erve Chambers (1987) has stated, applied anthropology is "concerned with the relationships between anthropological knowledge and the uses of that knowledge in the world beyond anthropology" (p. 309). More and more anthropologists from the four subfields now work in "applied" areas such as public health, family planning, business, market research, economic development, and cultural resource management.

Because of anthropology's breadth, applied anthropology has many applications. For example, applied medical anthropologists consider both the sociocultural and the biological contexts and implications of disease and illness. Perceptions of good and bad health, along with actual health threats and problems, differ among societies. Various ethnic groups recognize different illnesses, symptoms, and causes and have developed different health care systems and treatment strategies.

Applied archaeology, usually called *public archaeology,* includes such activities as cultural resource management, public educational programs, and historic preservation. Legislation requiring evaluation of sites threatened by dams, highways, and other construction activities has created an important role for public archaeology. To decide what

Applied anthropology in action. Professor Robin Nagle of New York University is also an anthropologist-in-residence at New York City's Department of Sanitation. Nagle studies curbside garbage as a mirror into the lives of New Yorkers. Here she accompanies sanitation worker Joe Damiano during his morning rounds in August 2015. ©Richard Drew/AP Images

TABLE 1.3   The Four Subfields and Two Dimensions of Anthropology

Anthropology's Subfields (General Anthropology)	Examples of Application (Applied Anthropology)
Cultural anthropology	Development anthropology
Anthropological archaeology	Cultural resource management (CRM)
Biological anthropology	Forensic anthropology
Linguistic anthropology	Study of linguistic diversity in classrooms

needs saving, and to preserve significant information about the past when sites cannot be saved, is the work of **cultural resource management** (CRM). CRM involves not only preserving sites but also allowing their destruction if they are not significant. The *management* part of the term refers to the evaluation and decision-making process. Cultural resource managers work for federal, state, and county agencies and other clients. Applied cultural anthropologists sometimes work with public archaeologists, assessing the human problems generated by the proposed change and determining how they can be reduced. Table 1.3 relates anthropology's four subfields to its two dimensions.

Anthropology and Other Academic Fields

As mentioned previously, one of the main differences between anthropology and the other fields that study people is holism, anthropology's unique blend of biological, social, cultural, linguistic, historical, and contemporary perspectives. Paradoxically, while distinguishing anthropology, this breadth is what also links it to many other disciplines. Techniques used to date fossils and artifacts have come to anthropology from physics, chemistry, and geology. Because plant and animal remains often are found with human bones and artifacts, anthropologists collaborate with botanists, zoologists, and paleontologists.

A Humanistic Science

As a discipline that is both scientific and humanistic, anthropology has links with many other academic fields. Anthropology is a **science**—a "systematic field of study or body of knowledge that aims, through experiment, observation, and deduction, to produce reliable explanations of phenomena, with references to the material and physical world" (*Webster's New World Encyclopedia* 1993, p. 937). The chapters that follow present anthropology as a humanistic science devoted to discovering, describing, understanding, and explaining similarities and differences in time and space among humans and our ancestors. Clyde Kluckhohn (1944) described anthropology as "the science of human similarities and differences" (p. 9). His statement of the need for such a field still stands: "Anthropology provides a scientific basis for dealing with the crucial dilemma of the world today: how can peoples of different appearance, mutually unintelligible languages, and dissimilar ways of life get along peaceably together?" (p. 9). Anthropology has compiled an impressive body of knowledge, which this textbook attempts to encapsulate.

Besides its links to the natural sciences (e.g., geology, zoology) and social sciences (e.g., sociology, psychology), anthropology also has strong links to the humanities. The humanities include English, comparative literature, classics, folklore, philosophy, and the arts. These fields study languages, texts, philosophies, arts, music, performances, and other forms of creative expression. Ethnomusicology, which studies forms of musical expression on a worldwide basis, is especially closely related to anthropology. Also linked is folklore, the systematic study of tales, myths, and legends from a variety of cultures. One might well argue that anthropology is among the most humanistic of all academic fields because of its fundamental respect for human diversity. Anthropologists listen to, record, and represent voices from a multitude of nations and cultures. Anthropology values local knowledge, diverse worldviews, and alternative philosophies. Cultural anthropology and linguistic anthropology in particular bring a comparative and nonelitist perspective to forms of creative expression, including language, art, narratives, music, and dance, viewed in their social and cultural context.

Cultural Anthropology and Sociology

Students often ask about how anthropology differs from sociology, which is probably the discipline that is closest to anthropology, specifically to sociocultural anthropology. Like anthropologists, particularly cultural anthropologists, sociologists study society—consisting of human social behavior, social relations, and social organization. Key differences between sociology and anthropology reflect the kinds of societies traditionally studied by each discipline. Sociologists typically have studied contemporary Western, industrial societies. Anthropologists, by contrast, have focused on nonindustrial and non-Western societies. Sociologists and anthropologists developed different methods to study these different kinds of society. To study contemporary Western societies, which tend to be large-scale, complex nations, sociologists have relied on surveys and other means of gathering quantifiable data. Sociologists must use sampling and statistical techniques to collect and analyze such data, and statistical training has been fundamental in sociology. Working in much smaller societies, such as a village, anthropologists can get to know almost everyone and have less need for sampling and statistics. However, because anthropologists today are working increasingly in modern nations, use of sampling and statistics is becoming more common.

Traditionally, ethnographers studied small and nonliterate (without writing) populations and developed methods appropriate to that context. An ethnographer participates directly in the daily life of another culture and must be an attentive, detailed observer of what people do and say. The focus is on a real, living population, not just a sample of a population. During ethnographic fieldwork, the anthropologist takes part in the events she or he is *observing*, describing, and analyzing. Anthropology, we might say, is more personal and less formal than sociology.

In today's interconnected world, however, the interests and methods of anthropology and sociology are converging—coming together—because they are studying some of the same topics and areas. For example, many sociologists now work in non-Western countries, smaller communities, and other settings that used to be mainly within the anthropological orbit. As industrialization and urbanization have spread across the globe, anthropologists now work increasingly in industrial nations and cities, rather

Anthropology Today *School of Hope*

A school is one kind of community in which culture is transmitted—a process known as enculturation. A boarding school where students reside for several years is fully comparable as a enculturative setting to a village or other local community. You've all heard of Hogwarts. Although fictional, is it not a setting in which enculturation takes place?

Often, schools serve as intermediaries between one cultural tradition and another. As students are exposed to outsiders, they inevitably change. In today's world, opportunities to become bilingual and bicultural—that is, to learn more than one language and to participate in more than one cultural tradition—are greater than ever before.

The Kalinga Institute of Social Sciences (KISS) is a boarding school in Bhubaneswar, India, whose mission is to instill in indigenous students a "capacity to aspire" to a better life (Finnan 2016). KISS is the world's largest residential school for tribal children. Located in Odisha, one of India's poorest states, KISS supports 25,000 students from first grade through graduate training. Its students represent 62 of India's tribal groups. Children as young as age 6 travel to KISS by bus or train, sometimes from hundreds of miles away. They leave their families for up to 10 months at a time, returning to their villages only during the summer.

During six months of research at KISS in 2014–2015, anthropologist Christine Finnan gathered stories and personal accounts about the school and its effects. Working with three Indian research partners, she interviewed 160 people: students, former students, parents, staff, teachers, administrators, and visitors. Her team observed classes, meals, celebrations, and athletic competitions. They also visited several tribal villages to find out why parents send their children so far

KISS students at an assembly for visiting foreign dignitaries. KISS officials use such events not only to showcase the school to visitors, but also to help build solidarity among students. Courtesy of Christine Finnan

continued

Anthropology Today *continued*

away to school. Finnan wanted to determine what children gained and lost from growing up at KISS. (For a fuller account of the research described here, see Finnan 2016 at www.sapiens.org).

Acceptance to KISS is based on need, so that the poorest of the poor are chosen to attend. The school offers cost-free room and board, classes, medical care, and vocational and athletic training to all its students. The value system at KISS encourages responsibility, orderliness, and respect. Children learn those behaviors not only from KISS employees, but also from each other—especially from older students. Students are repeatedly reminded that they are special, that they can rise out of poverty and become change agents for their communities. Many students hope to return to their villages as teachers, doctors, or nurses.

KISS receives no government support. Most of its funding comes from its profitable sister institution, the Kalinga Institute of Industrial Technology (KIIT), a respected private university. By targeting indigenous children, KISS meets an educational need that is unmet by the government. In India's tribal villages, the presence of teachers is unreliable, even when there are village schools. At KISS, in sharp contrast, teachers don't just instruct; they also serve in loco parentis, living in the dormitories or in nearby housing, and viewing many of their students as family members.

During her fieldwork, Finnan found attitudes about KISS among all parties to be overwhelmingly positive. Students contrasted their KISS education with the poor quality of their village schools. Teachers mentioned their shared commitment to poverty reduction. Parents were eager for their children to be admitted. Although KISS encourages students to take pride in their native language and culture, both students and parents understand that change is inevitable. Students will adopt new beliefs, values, and behaviors, and they will learn Odia, the state language used at KISS. They will become bilingual and bicultural.

When Finnan began her research, she was aware of the now-notorious boarding schools for indigenous students that were established during the 19th and 20th centuries in the United States and Australia. Native American and Aboriginal children were forcibly removed from their families, required to speak English and accept Christianity, and taught that their native cultures were inferior. The educational style was authoritarian, and its goal was forced assimilation. Finnan found KISS's positive educational philosophy and respect for indigenous cultures to be very different from those archaic institutions.

To fully evaluate KISS's success in meeting its goals, we would need reliable data—currently unavailable—on job placements, academic achievement levels, and dropout rates. Finnan (2016) does note that pass rates for KISS students on state-mandated tests are higher than the state average and considerably higher than averages for tribal children. KISS also can point to a series of successful scholars, ambassadors, and athletes among its graduates. Each year, 5 percent of its graduating class is admitted tuition-free to KIIT. At that highly selective university, students can study engineering, medicine, and law, among other subjects.

This chapter examined the difference between applied and academic anthropology. Think about whether Finnan's research was academic or applied, and whether there is a sharp distinction between these two dimensions of anthropology. Even if Finnan did not intend her work to be applied anthropology, her findings certainly suggest educational lessons that can be applied beyond this case. What are some of those lessons?

than villages. Among the many topics studied by contemporary cultural anthropologists are rural-urban and transnational (from one country to another) migration, urban adaptation, inner-city life, ethnic diversity and conflict, crime, and warfare. Anthropologists today may be as likely as sociologists are to study issues of globalization and inequality.

Summary

1. Anthropology is the holistic, biocultural, and comparative study of humanity. It is the systematic exploration of human biological and cultural diversity across time and space. Examining the origins of, and changes in, human biology and culture, anthropology provides explanations for similarities and differences among humans and their societies.

2. The four subfields of general anthropology are (socio)cultural anthropology, anthropological archaeology, biological anthropology, and linguistic anthropology. All consider variation in time and space. Each also examines adaptation—the process by which organisms cope with environmental stresses. Anthropology's biocultural perspective is a particularly effective way of approaching interrelations between biology and culture. Cultural forces mold human biology, including our body types and images.

3. Cultural anthropology explores the cultural diversity of the present and the recent past. Archaeology reconstructs cultural patterns, often of prehistoric populations. Biological anthropology documents diversity involving fossils, genetics, growth and development, bodily responses, and nonhuman primates. Linguistic anthropology considers diversity among languages. It also studies how speech changes in social situations and over time. Anthropology has two dimensions: academic and applied. Applied anthropology is the use of anthropological data, perspectives, theory, and methods to identify, assess, and solve contemporary social problems.

4. Concerns with biology, society, culture, and language link anthropology to many other fields—sciences and humanities. Sociologists traditionally study Western, industrial societies, whereas anthropologists have focused on rural, nonindustrial peoples.

Think Like an Anthropologist

1. If, as Franz Boas illustrated early on in American anthropology, cultures are not isolated, how can ethnography provide an account of a particular community, society, or culture? Note: There is no easy answer to this question! Anthropologists continue to deal with it as they define their research questions and projects.

2. The American Anthropological Association has formally acknowledged a public service role by recognizing that anthropology has two dimensions: (1) academic anthropology and (2) practicing, or applied, anthropology. What is applied

anthropology? Based on your reading of this chapter, identify examples from current events where an anthropologist could help identify, assess, and solve contemporary social problems.

Key Terms

adaptation, *3*
anthropological archaeology, *8*
anthropology, *2*
applied anthropology, *12*
biocultural, *4*
biological anthropology, *10*

cultural anthropology, *7*
cultural resource management (CRM), *13*
culture, *3*
ethnography, *7*
ethnology, *8*
food production, *4*

general anthropology, *6*
holistic, *2*
linguistic anthropology, *11*
science, *13*
society, *2*
sociolinguistics, *11*

Chapter

2

Culture

What Is Culture?

In Chapter 1 we saw that humans share *society,* organized life in groups, with social animals, such as apes, monkeys, wolves, and ants. Although other animals, especially apes, have rudimentary cultural abilities, only humans have fully elaborated cultures—distinctive traditions and customs transmitted over the generations through learning and through language.

The concept of culture has long been basic to anthropology. Well over a century ago, in his book *Primitive Culture,* the British anthropologist Edward Tylor proposed that cultures, systems of human behavior and thought, obey natural laws and therefore can be studied scientifically. Tylor's definition of culture still offers an overview of the subject matter of anthropology, and it is widely quoted.

"Culture . . . is that complex whole which includes knowledge, belief, arts, morals, law, custom, and any other capabilities and habits acquired by man as a member of society" (Tylor 1871/1958, p. 1). The crucial phrase here is "acquired . . . as a member of society." Tylor's definition focuses on attributes that people acquire not through biological inheritance but by growing up in a particular society in which they are exposed to a specific cultural tradition. **Enculturation** is the process by which a child *learns* his or her culture.

Culture Is Learned

The ease with which children absorb any cultural tradition rests on the uniquely elaborated human capacity to learn. Other animals may learn from experience, so that, for example, they avoid fire after discovering that it hurts. Social animals also learn from other members of their group. Wolves, for example, learn hunting strategies from other pack members. Such social learning is particularly important among monkeys and apes, our closest biological relatives. But our own *cultural learning* depends on the uniquely developed human capacity to use **symbols,** signs that have no necessary or natural connection to the things they stand for, or signify.

Through cultural learning, people create, remember, and deal with ideas. They understand and apply specific systems of symbolic meaning. Anthropologist Clifford Geertz (1973) described cultures as sets of "control mechanisms—plans, recipes, rules, instructions" and likens them to computer programs that govern human behavior (p. 44). During enculturation, people gradually absorb and internalize their particular culture—a previously established system of meanings and symbols that helps guide their behavior and perceptions throughout their lives.

Every person begins immediately, through a process of conscious and unconscious learning and interaction with others, to internalize, or incorporate, a cultural tradition through the process of enculturation. Sometimes culture is taught directly, as when parents tell their children to say "thank you" when someone gives them something or does them a favor.

We also acquire culture through observation. Children pay attention to the things that go on around them. They modify their behavior not just because other people tell them to do so, but also because of their own observations and growing awareness of what their culture considers right and wrong. Many aspects of culture are absorbed unconsciously. North Americans acquire their culture's notions about how far apart people should stand when they talk, not by being told directly to maintain a certain distance but through a gradual process of observation, experience, and conscious and unconscious behavior modification. No one tells Brazilians or Italians to stand closer together than North Americans do; they learn to do so as part of their cultural tradition.

Culture Is Symbolic

Symbolic thought is unique and crucial to humans and to cultural learning. A symbol is something verbal or nonverbal, within a particular language or culture, that comes to stand for something else. There need be no obvious, natural, or necessary connection between a symbol and the thing that it symbolizes. The familiar pet that barks is no more naturally a *dog* than it is a *chien, Hund,* or *mbwa,* the words for "dog" in French, German, and Swahili, respectively. Language is one of the distinctive possessions of *Homo sapiens.* No other animal has developed anything approaching the complexity of language, with its multitude of symbols.

There also is a rich array of nonverbal symbols. Flags, for example, stand for various countries, as arches do for a hamburger chain. Holy water is a potent symbol in Roman Catholicism. As is true of all symbols, the association between water and what it stands for (holiness) is arbitrary and conventional. Water probably is not intrinsically holier than milk, blood, or other natural liquids. Nor is holy water chemically different from ordinary water. Holy water is a symbol within Roman Catholicism, which is part of an international cultural system. A natural thing has been associated arbitrarily with a particular meaning for Catholics, who share beliefs and experiences that are based on learning and transmitted across the generations. Our cultures immerse us in a world of symbols that are both linguistic and nonverbal. Particular items and brands of clothing, such as jeans, shirts, or shoes, can acquire symbolic meanings, as can our gestures, posture, and body decoration and ornamentation.

All humans possess the abilities on which culture rests—the abilities to learn, to think symbolically, to manipulate language, and to use tools and other cultural products in organizing their lives and coping with their environments. Every contemporary human population has the ability to use symbols and thus to create and maintain culture. Our nearest relatives—chimpanzees and gorillas—have rudimentary cultural abilities. However, no other animal has elaborated cultural abilities to the extent that *Homo* has.

Culture Is Shared

Culture is an attribute not of individuals per se but of individuals as members of *groups*. Culture is transmitted in society. We learn our culture by observing, listening, talking, and interacting with many other people. Shared beliefs, values, memories, and expectations link people who grow up in the same culture. Enculturation unifies people by providing us with common experiences. Today's parents were yesterday's children. If they grew up in North America, they absorbed certain values and beliefs transmitted over the generations. People become agents in the enculturation of their children, just as their parents were for them. Although a culture constantly changes, certain fundamental beliefs, values, worldviews, and child-rearing practices endure. One example of enduring shared enculturation is the American emphasis on self-reliance and independent achievement.

Despite characteristic American notions that people should "make up their own minds" and "have a right to their opinion," little of what we think is original or unique. We share our opinions and beliefs with many other people—nowadays not just in person but also via new media. Think about how often (and with whom) you share information or an opinion via texting, Facebook, Instagram, and Twitter. Illustrating the power of shared cultural background, we are most likely to agree with and feel comfortable with people who are socially, economically, and culturally similar to ourselves. This is one reason Americans abroad tend to socialize with each other, just as French and British colonials did in their overseas empires. Birds of a feather flock together, but for people, the familiar plumage is culture.

Culture and Nature

Culture takes the natural biological urges we share with other animals and teaches us how to express them in particular ways. People have to eat, but culture teaches us what, when, and how. In many cultures, people have their main meal at noon, but most North Americans prefer a large dinner. English people eat fish (e.g., kippers—kippered herring) for breakfast, but North Americans prefer hot cakes and cold cereals. Brazilians put hot milk into strong coffee, whereas many North Americans pour cold milk into a weaker brew. Midwesterners dine at 5 or 6, Spaniards at 10.

Cultural habits, perceptions, and inventions mold "human nature" into many forms. People have to eliminate wastes from their bodies. But some cultures teach people to defecate standing, while others tell them to do it sitting down. Peasant women in the Andean highlands squat in the streets and urinate, getting all the privacy they need from their massive skirts. All these habits are parts of cultural traditions that have converted natural acts into cultural customs.

Culture influences how we perceive nature, human nature, and "the natural," and cultural advances have overcome many "natural" limitations. We can prevent and cure diseases, such as polio and smallpox, that felled our ancestors. We can use pills to enhance or restore sexual potency. Through cloning, scientists have challenged the way we think about biological identity and the meaning of life itself. Culture, of course, does not always protect us. Hurricanes, earthquakes, tsunamis, floods, and other natural forces regularly thwart our efforts to modify the environment through building, development, and expansion.

Culture Is All-Encompassing and Integrated

For anthropologists, culture includes much more than refinement, good taste, sophistication, education, and appreciation of the fine arts. Not only college graduates but all people are "cultured." The most interesting and significant cultural forces are those that affect people every day of their lives, particularly those that influence children during enculturation.

Culture, as defined anthropologically, encompasses features that sometimes are considered trivial or unworthy of serious study, such as those of "popular" culture. To understand contemporary North American culture, we must consider holidays, mass media, the Internet, fast-food restaurants, sports, and games. As a cultural manifestation, a rock star may be as interesting as a symphony conductor (or vice versa); a comic book may be as significant as a book-award winner.

The term **popular culture** encompasses aspects of culture that have meaning for many or most people within the same national culture. American examples include July 4th, Halloween, Thanksgiving, football, homecoming dances, dinner-and-a-movie dates, and retirement parties. Although popular culture is available to us all, we use it selectively, and its meaning varies from one person to the next. For example, the World Cup, the Super Bowl, Taylor Swift, *Star Wars,* and *The Simpsons* mean something different to each of their fans. All of us creatively consume and interpret print media, music, television, films, theme parks, celebrities, politicians, and other popular culture products.

Cultures are not haphazard collections of customs and beliefs. Cultures are integrated, patterned systems. If one part of the system (e.g., the economy) changes, other parts also change. For example, during the 1950s, most American women planned domestic careers as homemakers and mothers. Since then, an increasing number of American women, including wives and mothers, have entered the workforce. Only 32 percent of married American women worked outside the home in 1960, compared to about 60 percent today.

What are some of the social repercussions of this particular economic change? Attitudes and behavior regarding marriage, family, and children have changed. Late marriage, "living together," and divorce have become more common. Work competes with marriage and family responsibilities and reduces the time available to invest in child care.

Cultures are integrated not simply by their dominant economic activities and related social patterns but also by sets of values, ideas, symbols, and judgments. Cultures train their individual members to share certain personality traits. A set of characteristic **core values** (key, basic, central values) integrates each culture and helps distinguish it from others. For instance, the work ethic and individualism are core values that have integrated American culture for generations. Different sets of dominant values influence the patterns of other cultures.

Culture Is Instrumental, Adaptive, and Maladaptive

Culture is the main reason for human adaptability and success. Other animals rely on biological means of adaptation (such as fur or blubber, which are adaptations to cold). Humans also adapt biologically—for example, by shivering when we get cold or sweating when we get hot. But in addition to biological responses, people also have cultural ways of adapting. To cope with environmental stresses, we habitually use technology, or tools. We hunt cold-adapted animals and use their fur coats as our own. We turn the thermostat up in the winter and down in the summer. In summer, we have a cold drink, jump in a pool, or travel to someplace cooler. In winter we have hot chocolate, seek out a sauna, or vacation in warmer climates. People use culture *instrumentally*, that is, to fulfill their basic biological needs for food, drink, shelter, comfort, and reproduction.

People also use culture to fulfill psychological and emotional needs, such as friendship, companionship, approval, and sexual desirability. People seek *informal support—* help from people who care about them—as well as *formal support* from associations and institutions. To these ends, individuals cultivate ties with others on the basis of common experiences, political interests, aesthetic sensibilities, or personal attraction.

On one level, cultural traits (e.g., air conditioning) may be called *adaptive* if they help individuals cope with environmental stresses. But on a different level, such traits can also be *maladaptive*. That is, they may threaten a group's continued existence. Thus, chlorofluorocarbons (e.g., as found in old air conditioners) have been banned in the United States because they deplete the ozone layer and, by doing so, can harm humans and other life. Many modern cultural patterns may be maladaptive in the long run. Some examples of maladaptive aspects of culture are policies that encourage overpopulation, poor food-distribution systems, overconsumption, and environmental degradation.

Cultures are integrated systems. When one behavior pattern changes, others also change. During the 1950s, most American women expected to have careers as wives, mothers, and domestic managers. As more and more women have entered the workforce, attitudes toward work and family have changed. In the earlier photo, a 1950s mom and kids do the dishes. In the recent photo, a doctor and two nurses examine a patient's record. Will their work day end when they get home? (top): ©William Gottlieb/Corbis; (bottom): ©Tom Tracy Photography/Alamy Stock Photo

Culture's Evolutionary Basis

The human capacity for culture has an evolutionary basis that extends back perhaps 3 million years, the date of the earliest evidence of tool manufacture in the archaeological record. Tool making by our distant ancestors may extend even farther back, based on observations of tool manufacture by chimpanzees in their natural habitats (Mercader, Panger, and Boesch 2002).

Similarities between humans and apes, our closest relatives, are evident in anatomy, brain structure, genetics, and biochemistry. Most closely related to us are the African great apes: chimpanzees and gorillas. *Hominidae* is the zoological family that includes fossil and living humans, as well as chimps and gorillas. We refer to members of this family as **hominids.** The term **hominins** is used for the group that leads to humans but not to chimps and gorillas and that encompasses all the human species that ever have existed.

Many human traits are part of an ancestral arboreal heritage that we share with monkeys and apes. These traits developed as our ancestors adapted to life in the trees millions of years ago. They include (1) grasping ability and manual dexterity (especially opposable thumbs), (2) depth and color vision, (3) learning ability based on a large, visually oriented, brain, and (4) substantial parental investment in a limited number of offspring. All these traits continue to be key features of human adaptation. Manual dexterity, for example, is essential to a major human adaptive capacity: tool making.

What We Share with Other Primates

There is a substantial gap between primate *society* (organized life in groups) and fully developed human *culture,* which is based on symbolic thought. Nevertheless, studies of nonhuman primates reveal many similarities with humans, such as the ability to learn from experience and change behavior as a result. Monkeys, and especially apes, learn throughout their lives (see Choi 2011). In one group of Japanese macaques (land-dwelling monkeys), for example, a 3-year-old female started washing sweet potatoes before she ate them. First her mother, then her age peers, and finally the entire troop began washing sweet potatoes as well. The ability to benefit from experience confers a tremendous adaptive advantage, permitting the avoidance of fatal mistakes. Faced with environmental change, humans and other primates don't have to wait for a genetic or physiological response. They can modify learned behavior and social patterns instead.

Although humans employ tools much more than any other animal does, tool use also turns up among several nonhuman species, including birds, beavers, sea otters, and especially apes (see Campbell 2011). Humans are not the only animals that make tools with a specific purpose in mind. Chimpanzees living in the Taï forest of Ivory Coast make and use stone tools to break open hard, golf-ball-sized nuts (Mercader et al. 2002; Wilford 2007b). Nut cracking is a learned skill, with mothers showing their young how to do it. In 1960, Jane Goodall began observing wild chimps—including their tool use and hunting behavior—at Gombe Stream National Park in Tanzania, East Africa (see Goodall 2010). The most studied form of ape tool making involves "termiting," in which chimps make tools to probe termite hills. They choose twigs, which they modify by removing leaves and peeling off bark to expose the sticky surface beneath. They carry the twigs to termite hills, dig holes with their fingers, and insert the twigs. Finally, they pull out the twigs and dine on termites that were attracted to the sticky surface. Given what is known about ape tool use and manufacture, it is almost certain that early hominins shared this ability, although the first evidence for hominin stone tool making dates back only 2.6 million years. In addition, bipedalism (moving around upright on two legs) would have permitted the carrying and use of tools and weapons against predators and competitors in an open grassland habitat.

The apes have other abilities essential to culture. Wild chimpanzees and orangutans aim and throw objects. Gorillas build nests, and they throw branches, grass, vines, and other objects. Hominins have elaborated the capacity to aim and throw, without which we never would have developed projectile technology and weaponry—or baseball.

As with tool making, anthropologists used to regard hunting as a distinctive human activity not shared with the apes. Again, however, primate research shows that other primates, especially chimpanzees, are habitual hunters. For example, in Uganda's Kibale National Park, chimps form large hunting parties, including an average of 26 individuals (almost always adult and adolescent males). Most hunts (78 percent) result in at least one prey item being caught—a much higher success rate than that among lions (26 percent),

Different forms of tool use by chimps. Top photo shows a Liberian chimp using a hammer stone to crack palm nuts. The bottom photo shows using prepared twigs to "fish" for termites from an ant hill. (top): ©Clive Bromhall/Oxford Scientific/Getty Images; (bottom): ©Stan Osolinski/Oxford Scientific/Getty Images

hyenas (34 percent), or cheetahs (30 percent). Chimps' favored prey there is the red colobus monkey (Mitani and Watts 1999).

It is likely that human ancestors were doing some hunting by at least 3 million years ago, based on the existence of early stone tools designed to cut meat. Given our current understanding of chimp tool making and hunting, we can infer that hominids may have been hunting much earlier than the first archaeological evidence attests. Because chimps typically devour the monkeys they kill, leaving few remains, we may never find archaeological evidence for the first hominin hunt, especially if it proceeded without stone tools.

How We Differ from Other Primates

Although chimps often share meat from a hunt, apes and monkeys (except for nursing infants) tend to feed themselves individually. Cooperation and sharing are much more characteristic of humans. Until fairly recently (12,000 to 10,000 years ago), all humans were hunter-gatherers who lived in small social groups called bands. In some world areas, the hunter-gatherer way of life persisted into recent times, permitting study by ethnographers. In such societies, men and women take resources back to the camp and share them. Everyone shares the meat from a large animal. Nourished and protected by younger band members, elders live past reproductive age and are respected for their knowledge and experience. Humans are among the most cooperative of the primates— in the food quest and other social activities. As well, the amount of information stored in a human band is far greater than that in any other primate group.

Another difference between humans and other primates involves mating. Among baboons and chimps, most mating occurs when females enter **estrus,** during which they ovulate. In estrus, the vaginal area swells and reddens, and receptive females form temporary bonds with, and mate with, males. Human females, by contrast, lack a visible estrus cycle, and their ovulation is concealed. Not knowing when ovulation is occurring, humans maximize their reproductive success by mating throughout the year. Human pair bonds for mating are more exclusive and more durable than are those of chimps. Related to our more constant sexuality, all human societies have some form of marriage. Marriage gives mating a reliable basis and grants to each spouse special, though not always exclusive, sexual rights in the other.

Marriage creates another major contrast between humans and other primates: exogamy and kinship systems. Most cultures have rules of exogamy requiring marriage outside one's kin or local group. Exogamy confers adaptive advantages because it creates ties between the spouses' different kin groups. Their children have relatives, and therefore allies, in two kin groups rather than just one. Such ties of affection and mutual support between members of different local groups tend to be absent among primates other than *Homo.* Other primates tend to disperse at adolescence. Among chimps and gorillas, females tend to migrate, seeking mates in other groups. Humans also choose mates from outside the natal group, and usually at least one spouse moves. However, *humans maintain lifelong ties with sons and daughters.* The systems of kinship and marriage that preserve these links provide a major contrast between humans and other primates (see Chapais 2008; Hill et al. 2011). Table 2.1 lists differences in the cultural abilities of humans and chimpanzees, our nearest relatives.

TABLE 2.1 **Cultural Features of Chimpanzees (Rudimentary) and Humans (Fully Developed)**

	Chimpanzees	Humans
Cultural learning	Rudimentary	Fully developed
Tool use	Occasional	Habitual
Tool manufacture	Occasional: hammer stones, termiting	Habitual and sophisticated
Aimed throwing	Occasional objects, not tools	Projectile technology
Hunting	Significant, but no tools	Basic hominin subsistence strategy, with tools
Food sharing	Meat sharing after hunt	Basic to human life
Cooperation	Occasional in hunting	Basic to human life
Mating and marriage	Female estrus cycle, limited pair bonds	Year-round mating, marriage, and exogamy
Kin ties	Limited by dispersal at adolescence	Maintained through sons and daughters

Universality, Generality, and Particularity

Anthropologists agree that cultural learning is uniquely elaborated among humans and that all humans have culture. Anthropologists also agree that although *individuals* differ in their emotional and intellectual tendencies and capacities, all human *populations* have equivalent capacities for culture. Regardless of their genes or their physical appearance, people can learn *any* cultural tradition. To understand this point, consider that contemporary North Americans are the genetically mixed descendants of people from all over the world. Our ancestors were biologically varied, lived in different countries and continents, and participated in hundreds of cultural traditions. However, successive waves of immigrants and their descendants now share a national culture.

In studying human diversity in time and space, anthropologists distinguish among the universal, the generalized, and the particular. Certain biological, psychological, social, and cultural features are **universal,** found in every culture. Others are merely **generalities,** common to several but not all human groups. Still other traits are **particularities,** unique to certain cultural traditions.

Universals and Generalities

Biologically based universals include a long period of infant dependency; year-round (rather than seasonal) sexuality; and a complex brain that enables us to use symbols, languages, and tools. Among the social universals is life in groups and in some kind of family. Generalities occur in certain times and places but not in all cultures. They may be widespread, but they are not universal. One cultural generality that is present in many but not all societies is the nuclear family, a kinship group consisting of parents and children. Many middle-class Americans still view the "traditional" nuclear family, consisting of a married man and woman and their children, as a proper and "natural" group.

This view persists despite the fact that nuclear families now comprise only 20 percent of contemporary American households. Cross-culturally, too, this kind of "traditional" family is far from universal. Consider the Nayars, who live on the Malabar Coast of India. Traditionally, the Nayars lived in female-headed households, and husbands and wives did not live together. In many other societies, the nuclear family is submerged in larger kin groups, such as extended families, lineages, and clans (see Chapter 7).

Societies can share beliefs and customs because of borrowing or (cultural) inheritance from a common cultural ancestor. Speaking English is a generality shared by North Americans and Australians because both countries had English settlers. Another reason for generalities is domination, as in colonial rule, when a more powerful nation imposes its customs and procedures on another group. In many countries, use of the English language reflects colonial history. More recently, English has spread through **diffusion** (cultural borrowing, either directly or through intermediaries) to many other countries, as it has become the world's foremost language for business and travel.

Particularity: Patterns of Culture

A cultural particularity is a trait or feature of culture that is not generalized or widespread; rather, it is confined to a single place, culture, or society. Yet because of cultural borrowing, which has accelerated through modern transportation and communication systems, traits that once were limited in their distribution have become more widespread. Traits that are useful, that have the capacity to please large audiences, and that don't clash with the cultural values of potential adopters are more likely to be borrowed than are others. Nevertheless, certain cultural particularities persist—for example, foods such as the pork barbecue with a mustard-based sauce available only in South Carolina and the "pasty," beef stew baked in pie dough, characteristic of Michigan's Upper Peninsula. Besides diffusion (which, for example, has spread McDonald's food outlets, once confined to San Bernadino, California, across the globe), there are other reasons that cultural particularities are increasingly rare. Many cultural traits are shared as cultural universals and as a result of independent invention. Facing similar problems, people in different places have come up with similar solutions. Again and again, similar cultural causes have produced similar cultural results.

At the level of the individual cultural trait or element (e.g., bow and arrow, hot dog, Netflix), particularities may be getting rarer. But at a higher level, particularity is more obvious. Different cultures emphasize different things. *Cultures are integrated and patterned differently and display tremendous variation and diversity.* When cultural traits are borrowed, they are modified to fit the culture that adopts them. They are *reintegrated*—patterned anew—to fit their new setting. Patterned beliefs, customs, and practices lend distinctiveness to particular cultural traditions.

Consider the universal life-cycle events, such as birth, puberty, marriage, parenthood, and death, that many cultures observe and celebrate. The occasions (e.g., marriage, death) may be the same and universal, but the patterns of ceremonial observance may be dramatically different. Cultures vary in just which events merit special celebration. Americans, for example, regard expensive weddings as more socially appropriate than lavish funerals. The Betsileo of Madagascar take the opposite view. The marriage ceremony is a minor event that brings together just the couple and a few close relatives.

However, a funeral is a measure of the deceased person's social position and lifetime achievement, and it may attract a thousand people. Why use money on a house, the Betsileo say, when one can use it on the tomb where one will spend eternity in the company of dead relatives? Cremation, an increasingly common option in the United States, would horrify the Betsileo, for whom ancestral bones and relics are important ritual objects (see Sack 2011).

Cultures vary tremendously in their beliefs, practices, integration, and patterning. By focusing on and trying to explain alternative customs, anthropology forces us to reappraise our familiar ways of thinking. In a world full of cultural diversity, contemporary American culture is just one cultural variant, more powerful perhaps but no more natural than the others.

Culture and the Individual

Generations of anthropologists have theorized about the relationship between the "system" on one hand and the "person" or "individual" on the other. *System* can refer to various concepts, including culture, society, social relations, or social structure. Individual human beings always make up, or constitute, the system. Within that system, however, humans also are constrained (to some extent, at least) by its rules and by the actions of other individuals. Cultural rules provide guidance about what to do and how to do it, but people don't always do what the rules say should be done. People use their culture actively and creatively, rather than blindly following its dictates (see Handwerker 2009). Cultures are dynamic and constantly changing. People learn, interpret, and manipulate the same rule in different ways—or they emphasize different rules that better suit their interests. Culture is *contested:* Different groups in society struggle with one another over whose ideas, values, goals, and beliefs will prevail. Even common symbols may have radically different *meanings* to different individuals and groups in the same culture. Golden arches may cause one person to salivate, while someone else plots a vegetarian protest. Different people may wave the same flag to support or oppose a particular war or political candidate.

Even when they agree about what should be done, people don't always do as their culture directs or as other people expect. Many rules are violated, some very often (e.g., automobile speed limits). Some anthropologists find it useful to distinguish between ideal and real culture. The *ideal culture* consists of what people say they should do and what they *say* they do. *Real culture* refers to their actual behavior as observed by the anthropologist.

Culture is both public and individual, both in the world and in people's heads. Anthropologists are interested not only in public and collective behavior but also in how *individuals* think, feel, and act. The individual and culture are linked because human social life is a process in which individuals internalize the meanings of *public* (i.e., cultural) messages. Then, alone and in groups, people influence culture by converting their private (and often divergent) understandings into public expressions (D'Andrade 1984).

Conventionally, culture has been seen as social glue transmitted across the generations, binding people through their common past, rather than as something being continually created and reworked in the present. The tendency to view culture as an entity rather than as a process is changing. Contemporary anthropologists now emphasize how day-to-day action, practice, or resistance can make and remake culture (Gupta and Ferguson 1997b). *Agency* refers to the actions that individuals take, both alone and in groups, in forming and transforming cultural identities.

The approach to culture known as *practice theory* (Ortner 1984) recognizes that individuals within a society or culture have diverse motives and intentions and different degrees of power and influence. Such contrasts may be associated with gender, age, ethnicity, class, and other social variables. Practice theory focuses on how such varied individuals—through their ordinary and extraordinary actions and practices—manage to influence, create, and transform the world they live in. Practice theory appropriately recognizes a reciprocal relation between culture (the system) and the individual. The system shapes how individuals experience and respond to external events, but individuals also play an active role in how society functions and changes. Practice theory recognizes both constraints on individuals and the flexibility and changeability of cultures and social systems.

Levels of Culture

Anthropologists also recognize cultural systems—levels of culture—that are larger and smaller than nation-states. **National culture** encompasses those beliefs, learned behavior patterns, values, and institutions that are shared by citizens of the same nation. **International culture** extends beyond and across national boundaries. Because culture is transmitted through learning rather than genetics, cultural traits can spread through borrowing, or diffusion, from one group to another.

Because of diffusion, migration, colonialism, and globalization, many cultural traits and patterns have acquired international scope. The contemporary United States, Canada, Great Britain, and Australia share cultural traits they have inherited from their common linguistic and cultural ancestors in Great Britain. Roman Catholics in many countries share beliefs, symbols, experiences, and values transmitted by their church. The World Cup has become an international cultural event, as people in many countries know the rules of, play, and follow soccer.

Cultures also can be smaller than nations. Although people who live in the same country share a national cultural tradition, all cultures also contain diversity. Individuals, families, communities, regions, classes, and other groups within a culture have different learning experiences, as well as shared ones. **Subcultures** are different symbol-based patterns and traditions associated with particular groups in the same complex society. In large or diverse nations such as the United States or Canada, a variety of subcultures originate in region, ethnicity, language, class, and religion. The religious backgrounds of Jews, Baptists, and Roman Catholics create subcultural differences among them. While sharing a national culture, U.S. northerners and southerners also differ in their beliefs, values, and customary behavior as a result of national and regional history. Italian Americans have ethnic traditions different from those of Irish, Polish, Hispanic, or African Americans.

Nowadays, many anthropologists are reluctant to use the term *subculture*. They feel that the prefix *sub-* is offensive because it means "below." Subcultures thus may be perceived as "less than" or somehow inferior to a dominant, elite, or national culture. In this discussion of levels of culture, I intend no such implication. My point is simply that nations may contain many different culturally defined groups. As mentioned earlier, culture is contested. Various groups may strive to promote the correctness and value of their own practices, values, and beliefs in comparison with those of other groups or the nation as a whole.

Ethnocentrism, Cultural Relativism, and Human Rights

Ethnocentrism is the tendency to view one's own culture as superior and to apply one's own cultural values in judging the behavior and beliefs of people raised in other cultures. We hear ethnocentric statements all the time. Ethnocentrism contributes to social solidarity, a sense of value and community, among people who share a cultural tradition. People everywhere think that the familiar explanations, opinions, and customs are true, right, proper, and moral. They regard different behavior as strange, immoral, or savage. Often other societies are not considered fully human. Their members may be castigated as cannibals, thieves, or people who do not bury their dead.

Opposing ethnocentrism is **cultural relativism,** the viewpoint that behavior in one culture should not be judged by the standards of another culture. This position also can present problems. At its most extreme, cultural relativism argues that there is no superior, international, or universal morality, that the moral and ethical rules of all cultures deserve equal respect. In the extreme relativist view, Nazi Germany would be evaluated as nonjudgmentally as Athenian Greece.

In today's world, human rights advocates challenge many of the tenets of cultural relativism. For example, several societies in Africa and the Middle East have traditions of female genital modification (FGM). *Clitoridectomy* is the removal of a girl's clitoris. *Infibulation* involves sewing the lips (labia) of the vagina, to constrict the vaginal opening. Both procedures reduce female sexual pleasure and, it is believed in some cultures, the likelihood of adultery. Such practices have been opposed by human rights advocates, especially women's rights groups. The idea is that the tradition infringes on a basic human right—disposition over one's body and one's sexuality. Some African countries have banned or otherwise discouraged the procedures, as have Western nations that receive immigration from such cultures. Similar issues arise with circumcision and other male genital operations. Is it proper to require adolescent boys to undergo collective circumcision to fulfill cultural tradition, as has been done in parts of Africa and Australia? Is it right to circumcise a baby boy without his permission, as has been done routinely in the United States and as is customary among Jews and Muslims?

Some would argue that the problems with relativism can be solved by distinguishing between methodological and moral relativism (see Kellenberger 2008). In anthropology, cultural relativism is not a moral position but a methodological one. It states: To understand another culture fully, you must try to determine how the people in that culture see things. What motivates them—what are they thinking—when they do the things they do? Such an approach does not preclude making moral judgments or taking action. When faced with Nazi atrocities, a methodological relativist would have a moral obligation to stop doing anthropology and take action to intervene. In the FGM example, we can best understand the motivations for the practice by considering the perspective of those who engage in it. Having done this, one then faces the moral question of whether to intervene to stop it. We should recognize as well that different people and groups living in the same society—for example, women and men, old and young, the more and less powerful—can have widely different views about what is proper, necessary, and moral (see Hunt 2007).

The idea of **human rights** invokes a realm of justice and morality beyond and superior to the laws and customs of particular countries, cultures, and religions (see Donnelly 2013). Human rights include the rights to speak freely; to hold religious beliefs without persecution; and not to be murdered, injured, or enslaved or imprisoned without charge. Such rights are seen as *inalienable* (nations cannot abridge or terminate them) and international (larger than and superior to individual nations and cultures). Four United

Top: A Maori haka. Maori men dressed as warriors perform their traditional haka during a festival celebrating Maori heritage in January, 2016 in Auckland, New Zealand. Bottom: Illustrating cultural appropriation, members of New Zealand's Kiwis rugby team enact their version of the haka prior to an October 2016 match against England. The notion of indigenous property rights states that any society has a fundamental right to preserve and manage its cultural base. Does the rugby team have the right to perform the haka?
(top): ©Hannah Peters/Getty Images News/Getty Images; (bottom): ©Jan Kruger/Getty Images Sport/Getty Images

Nations documents describe nearly all the human rights that have been recognized internationally. Those documents are the U.N. Charter; the Universal Declaration of Human Rights; the International Covenant on Economic, Social and Cultural Rights; and the International Covenant on Civil and Political Rights.

Alongside the human rights movement has arisen an awareness of the need to preserve cultural rights. Unlike human rights, **cultural rights** are vested not in individuals but in *groups,* such as religious and ethnic minorities and indigenous societies. Cultural rights include a group's ability to preserve its culture, to raise its children in the ways of its forebears, to continue its language, and not to be deprived of its economic base by the nation in which it is located. The related notion of indigenous **intellectual property rights (IPR)** has arisen in an attempt to conserve each society's cultural base—its core beliefs, knowledge, and practices. Much traditional cultural knowledge has commercial value. Examples include ethnomedicine (traditional medical knowledge and techniques), cosmetics, cultivated plants, foods, folklore, arts, crafts, songs, dances, costumes, and rituals. According to the IPR concept, a particular group may determine how indigenous knowledge and its products may be used and distributed and the level of compensation required. (This chapter's "Anthropology Today" discusses the related concept of "cultural heritage.")

The notion of cultural rights is related to the idea of cultural relativism, and the problem discussed previously arises again. What does one do about cultural rights that interfere with human rights? I believe that anthropology's main job is to present accurate accounts and explanations of cultural phenomena. The anthropologist doesn't have to approve infanticide, cannibalism, or torture to record their existence and determine their causes and the motivations behind them. However, each anthropologist has a choice about where he or she will do fieldwork. Some anthropologists choose not to study a particular culture because they discover in advance or early in fieldwork that behavior they consider morally repugnant is practiced there. Anthropologists respect human diversity. Most ethnographers try to be objective, accurate, and sensitive in their accounts of other cultures. However, objectivity, sensitivity, and a cross-cultural perspective don't mean that anthropologists have to ignore international standards of justice and morality. What do you think?

Mechanisms of Cultural Change

Why and how do cultures change? One way is through diffusion, or borrowing, of traits between cultures. Such exchange of information and products has gone on throughout human history because cultures never have been truly isolated. Contact between neighboring groups has always existed and has extended over vast areas (Boas 1940/1966). Diffusion is *direct* when two cultures trade with, intermarry among, or wage war on one another. Diffusion is *forced* when one culture subjugates another and imposes its customs on the dominated group. Diffusion is *indirect* when items or traits move from group A to group C via group B without any firsthand contact between A and C. In this case, group B might consist of traders or merchants who take products from a variety of places to new markets. Or group B might be geographically situated between A and C, so that what it gets from A eventually winds up in C, and vice versa. In today's world, much international diffusion is indirect—culture spread by the mass media and advanced information technology.

Acculturation, a second mechanism of cultural change, is the ongoing exchange of cultural features that results when groups have continuous firsthand contact. This contact may change the cultures of either or both groups, but each group remains distinct. In situations of acculturation, cultures have exchanged and blended foods, recipes, music, dances, clothing, tools, languages, and technologies.

One example of acculturation is a *pidgin,* a mixed language that develops to ease communication between members of different societies in contact. This usually happens in situations of trade or colonialism. Pidgin English, for example, is a simplified form of English that blends English grammar with the grammar of a native language. Pidgin English first developed to facilitate commerce in Chinese ports. Similar pidgins developed later in Papua New Guinea and West Africa.

Independent invention—the process by which humans innovate, creatively finding solutions to problems—is a third mechanism of cultural change. Faced with comparable problems and challenges, people in different societies have innovated and changed in similar ways, which is one reason cultural generalities exist. One example is the independent invention of agriculture in the Middle East and Mexico. Often a major invention, such as agriculture, triggers a series of subsequent, interrelated changes. Thus, in both Mexico and the Middle East, agriculture led to many social, political, and legal changes, including notions of property and distinctions in wealth, class, and power.

Globalization

The term **globalization** encompasses a series of processes that work transnationally to promote change in a world in which nations and people are increasingly interlinked and mutually dependent. The forces of globalization include international commerce and finance, travel and tourism, transnational migration, and the media—including the Internet and other high-tech information flows (see Friedman and Friedman 2008; Haugerud, Stone, and Little 2011; Kjaerulff 2010). New economic unions (which have met considerable resistance in their member nations) have been created through the World Trade Organization (WTO), the International Monetary Fund (IMF), and the European Union (EU).

The media, including the Internet, play a key role in globalization. Long-distance communication is faster and easier than ever and now covers most of the globe. I can now e-mail, call, Skype, or Facetime families in Arembepe, Brazil, which lacked phones and even postal service when I first began to study the community. Information about Arembepe is now available to anyone, including potential tourists, on hundreds of websites. Anything can be Googled. The media help propel a transnational culture of consumption, as they spread information about products, services, rights, institutions, lifestyles, and the perceived costs and benefits of globalization. Emigrants transmit information and resources transnationally, as they maintain their ties with home (phoning, Skyping, Facetiming, texting, e-mailing, visiting, sending money). In a sense, such

Anthropology Today   *Preserving Cultural Heritage*

Heritage refers to something that has been passed on from previous generations. *Cultural heritage*—the culture, values, and traditions of a particular group—includes not only such material things as artifacts, artwork, and buildings but also intangibles such as language, music, dances, and stories. Every human group has a shared heritage. Members of that group are its proper guardians. Heritage becomes a matter of international concern when one group seizes it from another, or destroys it for political or religious purposes.

As the world system has expanded, heritage items often have been collected, purchased, and stolen from indigenous people for museums and private collections. Many times they were sold by people (e.g., explorers or colonial officials) who had no right to sell them. Among the world's most famous items of cultural heritage are the Parthenon Sculptures, also known as the Elgin Marbles, on display at—and one of the most prized possessions of—London's famed British Museum. Lord Elgin, the British ambassador to the Ottoman empire, acquired these sculptures in the early 19th century in Athens, Greece. Their ownership remains a point of contention between Greece and the United Kingdom.

Some items are recognized as important to the shared heritage of humanity as a whole. This is what UNESCO (the United Nations Educational, Scientific and Cultural Organization) has in mind when it designates sites as having "*World* Heritage" value. Their significance extends beyond their particular geographic location. The disappearance or destruction of such sites would deprive future generations of key aspects of our shared history. Surveying the globe, UNESCO has designated (as of this writing) 1,052 World Heritage sites (see http://whc.unesco.org/en/list/). Of those, 203 were chosen because of their natural resources, such as waterfalls, glaciers, rivers, flora, and fauna. However, the overwhelming majority (814 sites) are cultural heritage sites, so chosen because of their archaeological or historical value. The final 35 sites are mixed cultural and natural, such as the Tikal National Park in Guatemala, which is an archaeological site in a rainforest. Fifty-five of the World Heritage sites are currently considered endangered. Many of those are in areas of war and instability, including six sites in Syria, five in Libya, and three each in Iraq and Mali (see http://whc.unesco.org/en/list/?&danger=1).

In 2012, Islamic extremists occupied and wreaked havoc on Timbuktu, Mali, one of those endangered sites, where they destroyed mausoleums and other heritage items, which they considered to be objects of idolatry. One of the perpetrators, Ahmad al-Faqi al-Mahdi, was successfully prosecuted in 2016 by the International Criminal Court, where he pleaded guilty and was sentenced to nine years in prison.

In 2015, members of the Islamic State (known variously as ISIS, IS, ISIL, and Daesh) destroyed architectural ruins—and murdered a prominent Syrian archaeologist—at Palmyra, Syria, a major cultural center of the ancient world and another endangered UNESCO World Heritage site. The structures destroyed included Palmyra's almost 2,000-year-old Arch of Triumph and Temple of Baalshamin. In both these cases, items of cultural heritage were intentionally destroyed, in violation of The Hague's 1954 Convention for the Protection of Cultural Property in the Event of Armed Conflict.

Responding to ongoing threats to cultural preservation, local activists, cultural historians, anthropologists, and others have taken various steps to ensure that indigenous groups maintain or recover items of cultural heritage. The United Nations has enacted a number of measures, including those mentioned previously, as well as the 1972 Convention Concerning the Protection of the World Cultural and Natural Heritage and its 2007 Declaration on the Rights of Indigenous Peoples. Both affirm that indigenous peoples have the right to keep, control, protect, and develop their particular cultural heritage, traditional knowledge, and cultural expressions. An American example is the Native American Graves Protection and Repatriation Act (NAGPRA), which affirms that Native American remains belong to Native Americans. NAGPRA requires American museums to return remains and artifacts to any tribe that requests them and can prove a "cultural affiliation" between itself and the remains or artifact.

We see that different groups may value cultural heritage sites, artifacts, and remains for different reasons. Anthropologists value the skeleton known as "Kennewick Man" for its scientific importance—what this early fossil from Oregon can tell us about the peopling of North America.

Native American tribes in Oregon, by contrast, value Kennewick Man as "the Ancient One," an ancestor whose remains need to be buried in a culturally appropriate manner. For Lord Elgin, the Parthenon friezes were a valuable commodity that he could (and did) sell to the British government. For the British Museum, the Elgin Marbles are prized works of art proudly displayed in a chamber far from their point of origin. Athenians value the Marbles as a creation of their classic civilization that should be returned to Greece, where descendants of their makers can determine their use. Khaled al-Asaad, an 81-year-old Syrian archaeologist known for his work in preservation, died in Palmyra at the hands of ISIS, who view ancient buildings as objects of idolatry, but who also view ancient artifacts as commodities that can be traded for money. Cultural heritage items, then, can be viewed in multiple ways—as a source of identity, as a commodity, or as a threat to be destroyed.

On March 31, 2016, in Palmyra, Syria, a photographer holds up his photo of the Temple of Bel taken two years earlier. Members of ISIS destroyed this historic temple in September 2015. ©Joseph Eid/AFP/ Getty Images

people live multilocally—in different places and cultures at once. They learn to play various social roles and to change behavior and identity depending on the situation.

Local people must cope increasingly with forces generated by progressively larger systems—region, nation, and world. An army of outsiders and potential change agents now intrudes on people everywhere. Tourism has become the world's number one industry. Economic development agents and the media promote the idea that work should be for cash rather than mainly for subsistence. The effects of globalization aren't always welcome. Indigenous peoples and traditional societies have devised various strategies to deal with threats to their autonomy, identity, and livelihood (Maybury-Lewis, Macdonald, and Maybury-Lewis 2009). New forms of cultural expression and political mobilization, including the rights movements discussed previously, are emerging from the interplay of local, regional, national, and international cultural forces (see Ong and Collier 2005).

Illustrating political mobilization against globalization are regular protests at meetings of the principal agencies concerned with international trade. Protesters continue to show their disapproval of policies of the WTO, the IMF, and the World Bank. Anti-globalization activists fault those organizations for policies that, they say, promote corporate wealth at the expense of farmers, workers, and others at or near the bottom of the economy. Protesters also include environmentalists seeking tougher environmental regulations and trade unionists advocating global labor standards. Related to these protests was the 2011 Occupy movement, which spread quickly from Wall Street to other American (and Canadian) cities. That movement protested growing North American inequality—between the top 1 percent and everyone else. Similar sentiments motivated Vermont senator Bernie Sanders's 2016 presidential campaign.

Summary

1. *Culture,* which is distinctive to humanity, refers to customary behavior and beliefs that are passed on through enculturation. Culture rests on the human capacity for cultural learning. Culture encompasses rules for conduct internalized in human beings, which lead them to think and act in characteristic ways.

2. Although other animals learn, only humans have cultural learning, dependent on symbols. Humans think symbolically—arbitrarily bestowing meaning on things and events. By convention, a symbol stands for something with which it has no necessary or natural relation. Symbols have special meaning for people who share memories, values, and beliefs because of common enculturation.

3. Cultural traditions mold biologically based desires and needs in particular directions. Everyone is cultured, not just people with elite educations. Cultures may be integrated and patterned through economic and social forces, key symbols, and core values. Cultural rules don't rigidly dictate our behavior. There is room for creativity, flexibility, diversity, and disagreement within societies. Cultural means of adaptation have been crucial in human evolution. Aspects of culture also can be maladaptive.

4. The human capacity for culture has an evolutionary basis that extends back at least 2.6 million years—to early toolmakers whose products survive in the archaeological

record (and most probably even further back—based on observation of tool use and manufacture by apes). Humans share with monkeys and apes such traits as manual dexterity (especially opposable thumbs), depth and color vision, learning ability based on a large brain, substantial parental investment in a limited number of off-spring, and tendencies toward sociality and cooperation.

5. Many hominin traits are foreshadowed in other primates, particularly in the African apes, which, like us, belong to the hominid family. The ability to learn, basic to culture, is an adaptive advantage available to monkeys and apes. Chimpanzees make tools for several purposes. They also hunt and share meat. Sharing and coop-eration are more developed among humans than among the apes, and only humans have systems of kinship and marriage that permit us to maintain lifelong ties with relatives in different local groups.

6. Using a comparative perspective, anthropology examines biological, psychological, social, and cultural universals and generalities. There also are unique and distinctive aspects of the human condition (cultural particularities). North American cultural tradi-tions are no more natural than any others. Levels of culture can be larger or smaller than a nation. Cultural traits may be shared across national boundaries. Nations also include cultural differences associated with ethnicity, region, and social class.

7. Ethnocentrism describes judging other cultures by using one's own cultural stan-dards. Cultural relativism, which anthropologists may use as a methodological position rather than a moral stance, is the idea of avoiding the use of outside stan-dards to judge behavior in a given society. Human rights are those based on justice and morality beyond and superior to particular countries, cultures, and religions. Cultural rights are vested in religious and ethnic minorities and indigenous societies, and intellectual property rights, or IPR, apply to an indigenous group's collective knowledge and its applications.

8. Diffusion, migration, and colonialism have carried cultural traits and patterns to different world areas. Mechanisms of cultural change include diffusion, accultura-tion, and independent invention. Globalization comprises a series of processes that promote change in a world in which nations and people are interlinked and mutu-ally dependent.

Think Like an Anthropologist

1. Our culture—and cultural changes—affect how we perceive nature, human nature, and "the natural." This theme continues to fascinate science fiction writers. Recall a recent science fiction book, movie, or TV program that creatively explores the boundaries between nature and culture. How does the story develop the tension between nature and culture to craft a plot?

2. What are some issues about which you find it hard to be culturally relativistic? If you were an anthropologist with the task of investigating these issues in real life, can you think of a series of steps that you would take to design a project that would, to the best of your ability, practice methodological cultural relativism?

Key Terms

acculturation, *35*
core values, *23*
cultural
    relativism, *32*
cultural rights, *34*
diffusion, *29*
enculturation, *20*
estrus, *27*
ethnocentrism, *32*

generality, *28*
globalization, *35*
hominids, *25*
hominins, *25*
human rights, *33*
independent
    invention, *35*
intellectual property
    rights (IPR), *34*

international
    culture, *31*
national culture, *31*
particularity, *28*
popular culture, *22*
subcultures, *31*
symbol, *20*
universal, *28*

Chapter 3

Doing Anthropology

What Do Anthropologists Do?

"Been on any digs lately?" Ask your professor how many times she or he has been asked this question. Then ask how often he or she actually has been on a dig. Remember that anthropology has four subfields, only two of which (archaeology and biological anthropology) require much digging—in the ground, at least. To be sure, cultural anthropologists "dig out" information about varied lifestyles, as linguistic anthropologists do about the features of language. Traditionally, cultural anthropologists have done a variant on the *Star Trek* theme of seeking out, if not new, at least different "life" and "civilizations," sometimes boldly going where no scientist has gone before.

Despite globalization, the cultural diversity under anthropological scrutiny right now may be as great as ever before, because the anthropological universe has expanded to modern nations. Today's cultural anthropologists are as likely to be studying artists in Miami or bankers in Beirut as Polynesians in outrigger canoes. Still, we can't forget that anthropology did originate in non-Western, nonindustrial societies. Its research techniques, especially those subsumed under the label "ethnography," were developed to

World famous anthropologist Margaret Mead in the field in Bali, Indonesia, in 1957. ©AP Images

deal with small populations. Even when working in modern nations, anthropologists still consider ethnography with small groups to be an excellent way of learning about how people live their lives and make decisions.

Before this course, did you know the names of any anthropologists? If so, which ones—real or fictional? For the general public, biological anthropologists and archaeologists tend to be better known than cultural anthropologists because of what they study and discover—making them attractive subjects for the Discovery Channel. You're more likely to have watched the TV series *Bones,* seen film of Jane Goodall with chimps, or seen a paleoanthropologist holding a skull than to have seen a linguistic or cultural anthropologist at work. One cultural anthropologist was an important public and media figure for much of the 20th century. Margaret Mead, famed for her work on teen sexuality in Samoa and gender roles in New Guinea, may well be the most famous anthropologist who ever lived. Mead, one of my own professors at Columbia University, appeared regularly on NBC's *Tonight Show*. In all her venues, including teaching, museum work, television, anthropological films, popular books, and magazines, Mead helped Americans appreciate the relevance of anthropology to understanding their daily lives. That's a worthy goal that more contemporary anthropologists should emulate.

This chapter is about what cultural anthropologists do. Linguistic methods are discussed in Chapter 4; applied anthropology, in Chapter 11.

Research Methods in Cultural Anthropology

Early students of society, such as the French scholar Émile Durkheim, were among the founders of both sociology and anthropology. Durkheim studied the religions of Native Australians (Durkheim 1912/2001), as well as mass phenomena, such as suicide rates, in modern nations (Durkheim 1897/1951). Key differences between anthropology and sociology eventually emerged from the kinds of societies each studied. Sociologists focused on the industrial West; anthropologists, on nonindustrial societies. Different methods of data collection and analysis were developed to deal with those different kinds of societies. To study large-scale, complex nations, sociologists came to rely on questionnaires and other means of gathering masses of quantifiable data. For many years, sampling and statistical techniques have been basic to sociology, whereas statistical training has been less common in anthropology (although this is changing somewhat as anthropologists increasingly work in modern nations).

Traditional ethnographers studied small, nonliterate (without writing) populations and relied on ethnographic methods appropriate to that context. According to Marcus and Fischer (1986), "[e]thnography is a research process in which the anthropologist closely observes, records, and engages in the daily life of another culture—an experience labeled as the fieldwork method—and then writes accounts of this culture, emphasizing descriptive detail" (p. 18).

Ethnography: Anthropology's Distinctive Strategy

Traditionally, the process of becoming a cultural anthropologist has required an ethnographic field experience in another society. Early ethnographers studied small-scale, relatively isolated societies with simple technologies and economies. Ethnography thus emerged as a research strategy in societies with less social differentiation than is found in large, modern nations (see Konopinski 2014; Moore 2012). Traditionally, ethnographers have tried to understand the whole of a particular culture (or, more realistically, as much as they can, given limitations of time and perception). To pursue this goal, ethnographers adopt a free-ranging strategy for gathering information. The ethnographer moves from setting to setting, person to person, and place to place to discover the totality and interconnectedness of social life. Ethnographers draw on varied techniques to piece together a picture of otherwise alien lifestyles (see Bernard 2011; Bernard and Gravlee 2014; Wolcott 2010). We turn now to a consideration of those techniques.

Observation and Participant Observation

Ethnographers must pay attention to hundreds of details of daily life, seasonal events, and unusual happenings. They should record what they see as they see it. Things never will seem quite as strange as they do during the first few weeks in the field. The ethnographer eventually gets used to, and accepts as normal, cultural patterns that initially were alien. Staying a bit more than a year in the field allows the ethnographer to repeat the season of his or her arrival, when certain events and processes may have been missed because of initial unfamiliarity and culture shock.

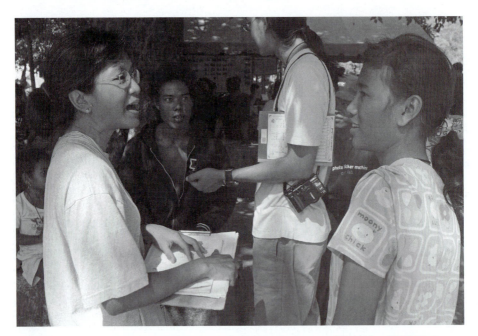

A month after the devastating Indian Ocean earthquake and tsunami of December 2004, Thai anthropologist Narumon Hinshiranan (left) helped guide the relief effort among the Moken, a maritime people who live on the Surin Islands along Thailand's Andaman coast. Dr. Hinshiranan had done prior fieldwork among the Moken people and speaks their language. ©Aroon Thaewchatturat/ Alamy Stock Photo

Many ethnographers record their impressions in a personal diary, or notebook, which is kept separate from more formal field notes. Later, this record of early impressions will help point out some of the most basic aspects of cultural difference. Such aspects include distinctive smells, noises people make, how they cover their mouths when they eat, and how they gaze at others. These patterns, which are so basic as to seem almost trivial, are part of what Bronislaw Malinowski (1922/1961) called "the *imponderabilia* of native life and of typical behavior" (p. 20). These features of culture are so fundamental that natives take them for granted. They are too basic even to talk about, but the unaccustomed eye of the fledgling ethnographer picks them up. Thereafter, becoming familiar, they fade to the edge of consciousness. Initial impressions are valuable and should be recorded. First and foremost, ethnographers should try to be accurate observers, recorders, and reporters of what they see in the field.

Ethnographers strive to establish *rapport,* a good, friendly working relationship based on personal contact, with their hosts. One of ethnography's most characteristic procedures is **participant observation**—taking part in the events one is observing, describing, and analyzing. As human beings living among others, we cannot be totally impartial and detached observers. We take part in many events and processes we are observing and trying to comprehend. By participating, we may learn why people find such events meaningful, as we see how they are organized and conducted.

In Arembepe, Brazil, I learned about fishing by sailing on the Atlantic with local fishers. I gave Jeep rides to malnourished babies and their parents, to pregnant mothers, and once to a teenage girl possessed by a spirit. All those people needed to consult specialists outside the village. I danced on Arembepe's festive occasions, drank libations commemorating new births, and became a godfather to a village girl. Most anthropologists have similar field experiences. The common humanity of the student and the studied, the ethnographer and the research community, makes participant observation inevitable.

Conversation, Interviewing, and Interview Schedules

Participating in local life means that ethnographers continually talk to people and ask questions. As their knowledge of the local language and culture increases, they understand more. There are several stages in learning a field language. First is the naming phase—asking name after name of the objects around us. Later we are able to pose more complex questions and understand the replies. We begin to understand simple conversations between two villagers. If our language expertise proceeds far enough, we eventually become able to comprehend rapid-fire public discussions and group conversations.

One data-gathering technique I have used in both Arembepe and Madagascar involves an ethnographic survey that includes an interview schedule. Soon after I began research in Arembepe, my fellow field workers and I attempted to complete an interview schedule in each of Arembepe's (then) 160 households. We entered almost every household (fewer than 5 percent refused to participate) to ask a set of questions on a printed form. Our results provided us with a census and basic information about the village. We wrote down the name, age, and gender of each household member. We gathered data on family type, religion, present and previous jobs, income, expenditures, diet, possessions, and many other items on our eight-page form.

Although we were doing a survey, our approach differed from the survey research design routinely used by sociologists and other social scientists working in large, industrial nations. That survey research, discussed later in the chapter, involves sampling (choosing a **sample**—a small, manageable study group from a larger population). We did not select a partial sample from the total population. Instead, we tried to interview in all households in the community (that is, to have a total sample). We used an interview schedule rather than a questionnaire. With the **interview schedule,** the ethnographer talks face to face with people, asks the questions, and writes down the answers. Questionnaire procedures tend to be more impersonal; often the respondent fills in the form.

Our goal of getting a total sample allowed us to meet almost everyone in the village and helped us establish rapport. Decades later, Arembepeiros still talk warmly about how we were interested enough in them to visit their homes and ask them questions. We stood in sharp contrast to the other outsiders the villagers had known, who considered them too poor and backward to be taken seriously.

Like other survey research, however, our interview schedule did gather comparable quantifiable information. It gave us a basis for assessing patterns and exceptions in village life. Our schedules included a core set of questions posed to everyone. However, some interesting side issues often came up during the interview, which we would pursue then or later.

We followed such leads into many dimensions of village life. One woman, for instance, a midwife, became the key cultural consultant we sought out later when we wanted detailed information about local childbirth. Another woman had done an internship in an Afro-Brazilian cult (*candomblé*) in the city. She still went there regularly to study, dance, and get possessed. She became our candomblé expert.

Thus, our interview schedule provided a structure that directed but did not confine us as researchers. It enabled our ethnography to be both quantitative and qualitative. The quantitative part consisted of the basic information we gathered and later analyzed statistically. The qualitative dimension came from our follow-up questions, open-ended discussions, pauses for gossip, and work with key consultants.

The Genealogical Method

Many of us learn about our own ancestry and relatives by tracing our genealogies. Websites like ancestry.com allow us to trace our "family trees" and degrees of relationship. The **genealogical method** is a well-established ethnographic technique. Early ethnographers developed notation and symbols to deal with kinship, descent, and marriage. Genealogy is a prominent building block in the social organization of nonindustrial societies, where people live and work each day with their close kin. Anthropologists need to collect genealogical data to understand current social relations and to reconstruct history. Indeed, another term for such cultures is *kin-based societies,* because everyone is related and spends most of his or her time with relatives. Rules of behavior attached to particular kin relations are basic to everyday life. Marriage also is crucial in organizing nonindustrial societies because strategic marriages between villages, tribes, and clans create political alliances.

Key Cultural Consultants

Every community has people who by accident, experience, talent, or training can provide the most complete or useful information about particular aspects of life. These people are **key cultural consultants,** also called *key informants*. In Ivato, the Betsileo village in Madagascar where I spent most of my time, a man named Rakoto was particularly knowledgeable about village history. However, when I asked him to work with me on a genealogy of the 50 to 60 people buried in the village tomb, he called in his cousin Tuesdaysfather, who knew more about that subject. Tuesdaysfather had survived an epidemic of influenza that ravaged Madagascar, along with much of the world, around 1919. Immune to the disease himself, Tuesdaysfather had the grim job of burying his kin as they died. He kept track of everyone buried in the tomb. Tuesdaysfather helped me with the tomb genealogy. Rakoto joined him in telling me personal details about the deceased villagers.

Life Histories

In nonindustrial societies—as in our own—individual personalities, interests, and abilities vary. Some villagers prove to be more interested in the ethnographer's work and are more helpful, interesting, and pleasant than others are. Anthropologists develop likes and dislikes in the field, as we do at home. Often, when we find someone unusually interesting, we collect his or her **life history.** This recollection of a lifetime of experiences provides a more intimate and personal cultural portrait than would be possible otherwise. Life histories, which may be audio- or video-recorded for later review and analysis, reveal how specific people perceive, react to, and contribute to changes that affect their lives. Many ethnographers include the collection of life histories as an important part of their research strategy.

Local Beliefs and Perceptions, and the Ethnographer's

One goal of ethnography is to discover local (native) views, beliefs, and perceptions, which may be compared with the ethnographer's own observations and conclusions. In the field, ethnographers typically combine two research strategies, the emic (local-oriented) and the etic (scientist-oriented). These terms, derived from linguistics, have been applied to ethnography by various anthropologists. Marvin Harris (1968/2001) popularized the following meanings of the terms: An **emic** approach investigates how local people think. How do they perceive and categorize the world? What are their rules for behavior? What has meaning for them? How do they imagine and explain things? Operating emically, the ethnographer relies on local people to explain things and to say whether something is significant or not. The term **cultural consultant,** or informant, refers to individuals the ethnographer gets to know in the field, the people who teach him or her about their culture, who provide the emic perspective.

The **etic** (scientist-oriented) approach shifts the focus from local observations, categories, explanations, and interpretations to those of the anthropologist. The etic approach realizes that members of a culture often are too involved in what they are doing to interpret their cultures impartially. Operating etically, the ethnographer emphasizes what he or she (the observer) notices and considers important. As a trained scientist, the ethnographer should try to bring an objective and comprehensive viewpoint to the study of other cultures. Of course, the ethnographer, like any other scientist, is also a human being with cultural blinders that prevent complete objectivity. As in other sciences, proper training can reduce, but not totally eliminate, the observer's bias. But anthropologists do have special training to compare behavior between different societies.

What are some examples of emic versus etic perspectives? Consider our holidays. For North Americans, Thanksgiving Day has special significance. In our view (emically), it is a unique cultural celebration that commemorates particular historical themes. But a wider, etic, perspective sees Thanksgiving as just one more example of the post-harvest festivals held in many societies. Another example: Local people give folk explanations for illnesses caused by germs and other pathogens. Emic agents that cause illness include angry or envious spirits, ancestors, witches, and sorcerers. *Illness* refers to a culture's (emic) perception and explanation of bad health, whereas *disease* refers to the scientific (etic) explanation of poor health, involving known pathogens.

Ethnographers typically combine emic and etic strategies in their fieldwork. The statements, perceptions, categories, and opinions of local people help ethnographers understand how cultures work. Local beliefs are also interesting and valuable in themselves. However, people often fail to admit, or even recognize, certain causes and consequences of their behavior. This is as true of North Americans as it is of people in other societies.

The Evolution of Ethnography

Bronislaw Malinowski (1884–1942), a prolific Polish anthropologist who spent most of his professional life in England, is generally considered the founder of ethnography. Like most anthropologists of his time, Malinowski did *salvage ethnography*, in the belief that the ethnographer's job is to study and record cultural diversity threatened by Westernization. Early ethnographic accounts (*ethnographies*), such as Malinowski's classic *Argonauts of the Western Pacific* (1922/1961), were similar to earlier traveler and explorer accounts in describing the writer's discovery of unknown people and places. However, the *scientific* aims of ethnographies set them apart from books by explorers and amateurs.

The style that dominated "classic" ethnographies was *ethnographic realism*. The writer's goal was to present an accurate, objective, scientific account of a different way of life, written by someone who knew it firsthand. This knowledge came from immersion in an alien language and culture. Ethnographers derived their authority—both as scientists and as voices of "the native" or "the other"—from this personal research experience.

Malinowski (1922/1961) argued that a primary task of the ethnographer is "to grasp the native's point of view, *his* relation to life, to realize his vision of *his* world" (p. 25—Malinowski's italics and pronouns). This is a good statement of the need for the emic perspective, as was discussed in the previous section. Since the 1970s, *interpretive anthropology* has focused on describing and interpreting aspects of culture that are meaningful to natives (see Geertz 1973).

Bronislaw Malinowski (1884–1942), who was born in Poland but spent most of his professional life in England, did fieldwork in the Trobriand Islands from 1914 to 1918. Malinowski is generally considered to be the founder of ethnography. Does this photo suggest anything about his relationship with Trobriand villagers? ©Mary Evans Picture Library/The Image Works

Linked to salvage ethnography was the idea of the *ethnographic present*—the period before Westernization, when the "true" native culture flourished. Attempts to portray an ethnographic present often give classic ethnographies an unrealistic timeless quality. Providing the only jarring note in such an idealized picture are occasional comments by the author about traders or missionaries, suggesting that the natives already were part of the world system. Anthropologists now recognize that the ethnographic present is a rather unrealistic construct. Cultures have been in contact—and have been changing—throughout history. Most native cultures had at least one major foreign encounter before any anthropologist ever came their way. Most of them already had been incorporated in some fashion into nation-states or colonial systems.

Contemporary ethnographers by and large have abandoned the goals of salvage ethnography and ethnographic realism for more dynamic approaches that recognize connectedness and change. George Marcus and Michael Fischer (1986) have encouraged innovation and experimentation in ethnographic writing, because all peoples and cultures have already been "discovered" and must now be "*re*discovered…in changing historical circumstances" (p. 24). Contemporary ethnographies usually recognize that cultures change constantly and that an ethnographic account applies to a particular moment.

Problem-Oriented Ethnography

Although anthropologists remain interested in the totality of people's lives in a particular community or society, it is impossible to study everything. As a result, contemporary ethnographic fieldwork generally is aimed at investigating one or more specific topics or problems (see Murchison 2010; Sunstein and Chiseri-Strater 2012). Topics that an ethnographer might choose to investigate include marriage practices, gender roles, religion, or economic change. Examples of problem-oriented research include various impact studies done by anthropologists, such as the impact on a particular community or society of television, the Internet, education, drought, a hurricane, or a change in government.

In researching a specific problem, today's anthropologists often need to look beyond local people for relevant data. Government agencies or international organizations may have gathered information on such matters as climate and weather conditions, population density, and settlement patterns. Often, however, depending on the problem they are investigating, anthropologists have to do their own measurements of such variables as field size, yields, dietary quantities, or time allocation. Information of interest to ethnographers extends well beyond what local people can and do tell us. In an increasingly interconnected and complicated world, local people lack knowledge about many factors that may affect their lives—for example, international terrorism, warfare, or the exercise of power from regional, national, and international centers (see Sanjek 2014).

Longitudinal Studies, Team Research, and Multisited Ethnography

Geography limits anthropologists much less now than in the past, when it could take months to reach a field site and return visits were rare. Modern transportation systems allow anthropologists to return to the field repeatedly. Ethnographic reports now routinely include data from two or more field stays. We can even follow the people we study as they move from village to city, cross the border, or travel internationally. **Longitudinal research** is the long-term study of an area or a population, usually based on repeated visits.

One example is the study of Gwembe District, Zambia. This study, planned in 1956 as a longitudinal project by Elizabeth Colson and Thayer Scudder, has continued with Colson, Scudder, and their associates and successors of various nationalities. As is often the case with longitudinal research, the Gwembe study also illustrates *team research—* coordinated research by multiple ethnographers (Scudder and Colson 1980). Researchers have studied four villages in different areas for 60 years. Periodic censuses provide basic data on population, economy, kinship, and religious behavior. Censused people who have moved are traced and interviewed to see how their lives compare with those of people who have stayed behind. The initial focus of study was the impact of a large hydroelectric dam, which subjected the Gwembe people to forced resettlement. Thereafter, Scudder and Colson (1980) examined how education provided access to new opportunities, even as it also widened a social gap between people with different educational levels. The anthropologists next focused on a change in brewing and drinking patterns, including a rise in alcoholism (Colson and Scudder 1988). When Colson, who died in 2016 at the age of 99, retired from the University of California at Berkeley, she moved to Gwembe district, where she spent her last days and is buried.

As mentioned, longitudinal research often is team research. My own field site of Arembepe, Brazil, first entered the world of anthropology as a field-team village in 1962. It was one of four sites for the now defunct Columbia-Cornell-Harvard-Illinois Summer Field Studies Program in Anthropology. For at least three years, that program sent a total of about 20 undergraduates annually, the author included, to do summer research abroad. The teams were stationed in rural communities in four countries: Brazil, Ecuador, Mexico, and Peru. Since my wife, Isabel Wagley Kottak, and I began studying it in 1962, Arembepe has become a longitudinal field site. Generations of researchers have monitored various aspects of change and development. The community has changed from a village into a town and illustrates the process of globalization at the local level. Its economy, religion, and social life have been transformed (see Kottak 2006).

Brazilian and American researchers worked with us on team research projects during the 1980s (on the impact of television) and the 1990s (on ecological awareness and environmental risk perception). Students from various universities have drawn on our baseline information from the 1960s in their more recent studies in Arembepe. Their topics have included standards of physical attractiveness, family planning, conversion to Protestantism, changing food habits, and the influence of the Internet and social media. Arembepe is thus a site where various field workers have worked as members of a longitudinal, multigenerational team. The more recent researchers have built on prior contacts and findings to increase knowledge about how local people meet and manage new circumstances. As of this writing (2017), researchers have recently completed fieldwork in Arembepe and other Brazilian communities, updating our study of media impact, which began during the 1980s.

Traditional ethnographic research focused on a single community or "culture," treated as more or less isolated and unique in time and space. In recent years, ethnography has shifted toward studies of change and of contemporary flows of people, technology, images, and information. Reflecting today's world, fieldwork must be more flexible and on

Janet Dunn, one of many anthropologists who have worked in Arembepe. Where is Arembepe, and what kinds of research have been done there? ©Christopher M. O'Leary

a larger scale. Ethnography increasingly is *multitimed* and *multisited*. That is, it studies people through time and at multiple research sites. Malinowski could focus on Trobriand culture and spend most of his field time in a particular community. Nowadays we cannot afford to ignore, as Malinowski did, the outside forces that increasingly impinge on the places we study. Integral to our analyses are the external entities (e.g., governments, corporations, nongovernmental organizations, new social movements) laying claim to land, people, and resources throughout the world. Also important in contemporary ethnography is increased recognition of power differentials and how they affect cultures, and of the importance of diversity within cultures and societies.

Anthropologists increasingly study people in motion. Examples include people living on or near national borders, nomads, seasonal migrants, homeless and displaced people, immigrants, and refugees (see Andersson 2014; Lugo 1997). As fieldwork changes, with less and less of a spatially set field, what can we take from traditional ethnography? Gupta and Ferguson (1997a) correctly cite the "characteristically anthropological emphasis on daily routine and lived experience" (p. 5). The treatment of communities as discrete entities may be a thing of the past. However, "anthropology's traditional attention to the close observation of particular lives in particular places" has an enduring importance (Gupta and Ferguson 1997b, p. 25). The method of close observation helps distinguish cultural anthropology from sociology and survey research, to which we now turn.

Survey Research

Working increasingly in large-scale societies, anthropologists have developed innovative ways of blending ethnography and survey research (Fricke 1994; Kottak 2009; Pace and Hinote 2013). Before examining such mixed field methods, let's consider the main differences between survey research and ethnography. Sociologists have developed and refined the **survey research** design, which involves sampling, impersonal data collection, and statistical analysis. Survey research draws a sample (a manageable study group) from a much larger population. A properly selected and representative sample permits accurate inferences about the larger population.

In small communities, ethnographers can get to know almost everyone. Given the greater size and complexity of nations, survey research can't help being more impersonal. Survey researchers call the people they study *respondents*—those who respond to questions during a survey. Sometimes survey researchers interview their sample of respondents personally or by phone. Sometimes they ask them to fill out a questionnaire, often online.

Probably the most familiar example of survey research and sampling is the polling done to predict political races. An ever-increasing number of organizations now gather information designed to estimate outcomes and to determine what kinds of people voted for which candidates. During sampling, researchers gather information about age, gender, religion, occupation, income, and political party preference. These characteristics (**variables**—attributes that vary among members of a sample or population) are known to influence political decisions.

Many more variables affect social identities, experiences, and activities in a modern nation than in the small communities where ethnography grew up. In contemporary North America, hundreds of factors influence our behavior and attitudes. These *social predictors* include age; religion; level of education; the region of the country we grew up in; whether we come from a town, suburb, or city; and our parents' professions,

In China's Shandong Province, census takers gathered personal information from a family during the Sixth National Population Census. From November 1 to November 10, more than six million census takers visited over 400 million households across the country. ©Imaginechina via AP Images

ethnic origins, and income levels. In any large nation, many predictor variables (social indicators) influence behavior and opinions. Because we must be able to detect, measure, and compare the influence of social indicators, many contemporary anthropological studies have a statistical foundation. Even in rural fieldwork, more anthropologists now draw samples, gather quantitative data, and use statistics to interpret them (see Bernard 2011, 2013; Bernard and Gravlee 2014). Quantifiable information may permit a more precise assessment of similarities and differences among communities. Statistical analysis can support and round out an ethnographic account of local social life.

In the best studies, however, the hallmark of ethnography remains: Anthropologists enter the community and get to know the people. They participate in local activities, networks, and associations. They observe and experience social conditions and problems. They watch the effects of national policies and globalization on local life. The ethnographic method and the emphasis on personal relationships in social research are valuable gifts that cultural anthropology brings to the study of any society.

Doing Anthropology Right and Wrong: Ethical Issues

Science exists in society and in the context of law and ethics. Anthropologists can't study things simply because they happen to be interesting or of value to science. Ethical issues also must be considered. Anthropologists typically have worked abroad, outside their own society. In the context of international contacts and cultural diversity, different ethical codes and value systems will meet, and sometimes challenge, one another.

Anthropologists must be sensitive to cultural differences and aware of procedures and standards in the host country (where the research takes place). The researcher must inform officials and colleagues in the host country about the purpose, funding, and likely results, products, and impacts of their research. **Informed consent** (agreement to take part in the research—after having been informed about its nature, procedures, and possible impacts) should be obtained from anyone who provides information or who might be affected by the research.

It is appropriate for North American anthropologists working in another country to (1) include host country colleagues in their research planning and requests for funding; (2) establish truly collaborative relationships with those colleagues and their institutions before, during, and after fieldwork; (3) include host country colleagues in dissemination, including publication, of the research results; and (4) ensure that something is "given back" to host country colleagues. For example, research equipment and technology are allowed to remain in the host country. Or funding is provided for host country colleagues to do research, attend international meetings, or visit foreign institutions—especially those where their international collaborators work.

The Code of Ethics

To guide its members in making decisions involving ethics and values, the American Anthropological Association (AAA) offers a Code of Ethics (http://www.americananthro.org/ParticipateAndAdvocate/Content.aspx?ItemNumber=1656.) The most recent code, approved in 2012, points out that anthropologists have obligations to their scholarly field, to the wider society and culture, and to the human species, other species, and the environment. Like physicians who take the Hippocratic oath, the anthropologist's first concern should be to *do no harm* to the people, animals, or artifacts being studied. The stated aim of the AAA code is to offer guidelines and to promote discussion and education, rather than to investigate possible misconduct. The code addresses several contexts in which anthropologists work. Some of its main points are highlighted in the next paragraph.

Anthropologists should be open and honest about their research projects with all parties affected by the research. Those parties should be informed about the nature, procedures, purpose(s), potential impacts, and source(s) of support for the research. Researchers should pay attention to proper relations between themselves as guests and the host nations and communities where they work. The AAA does not advise anthropologists to avoid taking stands on issues. Indeed, seeking to shape actions and policies may be as ethically justifiable as inaction.

Anthropologists and the Military

The AAA has deemed it of "paramount importance" that anthropologists study the causes of terrorism and violence. How should such studies be conducted? What ethical issues might arise?

Consider a Pentagon program, Project Minerva, initiated late in the George W. Bush administration, designed to draw on social science expertise to combat national security threats. Project Minerva sought scholars to translate documents captured in Iraq, study China's shifting political scene, and explain ongoing violence in Afghanistan (Cohen 2008). Project Minerva and related programs raised concerns that governments might use anthropological research in ethically problematic ways. Government policies and military operations have the potential to harm the people anthropologists study.

More recently, anthropologists have been especially critical of the Pentagon's Human Terrain System (HTS) program. Launched in February 2007, HTS has embedded anthropologists and other social scientists in military teams in Iraq and Afghanistan. On October 31, 2007, the AAA Executive Board issued a statement of disapproval of HTS—outlining how HTS violates the AAA Code of Ethics (see http://www.aaanet.org/about/Policies/statements/Human-Terrain-System-Statement.cfm). The Board noted that HTS places anthropologists, as contractors with the U.S. military, in war zones, where they are charged with collecting cultural and social data for use by the military. The ethical concerns raised by these activities include the following:

1. In a war zone, it may be impossible for anthropologists to identify themselves as anthropologists, as distinct from military personnel. This constrains their ethical responsibility as anthropologists to disclose who they are and what they are doing.
2. HTS anthropologists are asked to negotiate relations among several groups, including local populations and the military units in which they are embedded. Their responsibilities to their units may conflict with their obligations to the local people they consult. This may interfere with the obligation, stipulated in the AAA Code of Ethics, to do no harm.

Anthropology Today *Online Ethnography*

The relatively recent creation of virtual worlds has attracted contemporary ethnographers to venture into online communities. Tom Boellstorff, Bonnie Nardi, Celia Pearce, and T. L. Taylor offer a handbook for fieldwork in virtual worlds (2012). All four have researched gaming-oriented online environments, including *Second Life, World of Warcraft, Dreamscape, There. com,* and *Myst Online: Uru Live.* Ethnographers have used various techniques to study those virtual worlds. Most important has been participant observation: The ethnographic researchers became skilled players as they observed the online environment and the interactions within it.

Each virtual world has developed its own culture, which includes rules and governance, customary practices and events, social roles and modes of interaction, and power differentials. When *Uru Live* was discontinued in 2008, Uru refugees moved on to other virtual worlds, where they have created and retain a strong ethnic Uru identity. Although virtual environments are created by software designers, those who enter and thrive in these worlds can innovate within the constraints set by "the system"—either the software program or other participants. Within these worlds, the online ethnographers have observed and described various forms of play, performance, creativity, and ritual.

Virtual worlds have been heavily influenced by works of science fiction and fantasy. Early games owed a debt to the imaginary world of Middle Earth created by J. R. R. Tolkien, of *The Hobbit* and *The Lord of the Rings* fame. Online worlds are sophisticated places of imagination with their own species, artifacts, characters,

and customs. The avatar is the representation of self in a virtual world. People in cyberspace can have multiple identities, which often contrast—in gender, for example—with their real-world identities. A person's multiple avatars are known as alts—alternative identities or personalities.

The online ethnographer sometimes moves offline to visit players in their real-world setting (e.g., a home or an Internet café). In some cases, ethnographers have traveled abroad to see how a given game is played in different countries and how real-world culture influences participation in the virtual world. There are virtual world fan conventions, which the ethnographer may attend. Interviews can be conducted online and/or offline in a participant's virtual or real-world home. Informal conversations online reveal what players are thinking about as they play. To understand the social organization of their virtual field site, ethnographers may draw diagrams of social relations, similar to genealogies drawn during real-world fieldwork. Timelines are useful for understanding the succession of virtual events such as dances, festivals, or auctions. Brief site drop-ins can be used to respond to instant messages, keep up with announcements, and find out when players typically log in. Virtual research offers various means of record keeping, note taking, and recording typical of the online environment. These include chat logs and screenshots, as well as audio- and video-recording.

This box has summarized some features of online research as discussed by Boellstorff and his coauthors (2012). Readers interested in doing virtual world fieldwork should consult that handbook.

3. In an active war zone, it is difficult for local people to give "informed consent" without feeling coerced to provide information. As a result, "voluntary informed consent" (as stipulated by the AAA Code of Ethics) is compromised.

4. Information supplied by HTS anthropologists to military field commanders could help target specific groups for military action. Such use of fieldwork-derived information would violate the AAA Code of Ethics stipulation that those studied not be harmed.

5. The identification of anthropology and anthropologists with the U.S. military may indirectly (through "guilt by association") endanger the research, and even the personal safety, of other anthropologists and their consultants throughout the world.

How should anthropologists study terrorism? What do you think about anthropologists' role in war?

Summary

1. Ethnographic methods include firsthand and participant observation, rapport building, interviews, genealogies, work with key consultants or informants, collection of life histories, discovery of local beliefs and perceptions, problem-oriented and longitudinal research, and team research. Ethnographers work in communities and form personal relationships with local people as they study their lives.

2. An interview schedule is a form an ethnographer completes as he or she visits a series of households. Key consultants, or informants, teach us about particular areas of local life. Life histories document personal experiences with culture and culture change. Genealogical information is particularly useful in societies in which principles of kinship and marriage organize social and political life. Emic approaches focus on native perceptions and explanations. Etic approaches give priority to the ethnographer's own observations and conclusions. Longitudinal research is the systematic study of an area or a population over time. Longitudinal, team, and multisited ethnographic research are increasingly common.

3. Traditionally, anthropologists worked in small-scale societies; sociologists, in modern nations. Different techniques developed to study these different kinds of societies. Anthropologists do their fieldwork in communities and study the totality of social life. Sociologists use surveys and study samples to make inferences about a larger population. Anthropologists may employ ethnographic procedures to study cities, towns, or rural areas.

4. Because science exists in society, and in the context of law and ethics, anthropologists can't study things simply because they happen to be interesting or of scientific value. Anthropologists have obligations to their scholarly field, to the wider society and culture (including that of the host country), and to the human species, other species, and the environment. The AAA Code of Ethics offers ethical guidelines for anthropologists. Ethical problems often arise when anthropologists work for governments, especially the military.

Think Like an Anthropologist

1. What do you see as the strengths and weaknesses of ethnography compared with survey research? Which provides more accurate data? Might one be better for finding questions, while the other is better for finding answers? Or does it depend on the context of research?

2. Many of the ethical issues that affect the work of anthropologists have some legal dimension, whether in their own country, in another country, or even among several nations. Have you thought about law as a possible future career? (If not, think of a friend who has!) Write a convincing argument about why anthropology could be a valuable tool for a lawyer.

Key Terms

cultural
  consultant, 47
emic, 47
etic, 47
genealogical
  method, 46
informed
  consent, 53

interview
  schedule, 45
key cultural
  consultants, 46
life history, 46
longitudinal
  research, 50

participant
  observation, 44
sample, 45
survey research, 52
variables, 52

Chapter 4

Language and Communication

Language

Linguistic anthropology illustrates anthropology's characteristic interests in diversity, comparison, and change—but here the focus is on language (see Ahearn 2012; Bonvillain 2016; Duranti 2009; Ottenheimer 2013). Language, whether spoken (*speech*) or written (*writing*—which has existed for less than 6,000 years), is our primary means of communication. Like culture in general, of which language is a part, language is transmitted through learning. Language is based on arbitrary, learned associations between words and the things they stand for. Unlike the communication systems of other animals, language allows us to discuss the past and future, share our experiences with others, and benefit from their experiences.

Anthropologists study language in its social and cultural context (see Bonvillain 2012; Salzmann, Stanlaw, and Adachi 2015). Some linguistic anthropologists reconstruct ancient languages by comparing their contemporary descendants. Others study languages to discover the varied worldviews and patterns of thought in different cultures. Sociolinguists examine dialects and styles in a single language to show how speech reflects social differences. Linguistic anthropologists also explore the role of language in colonization and globalization (Blommaert 2010; Trudgill 2010).

Nonhuman Primate Communication

Call Systems

No other animal has anything approaching the complexity of language. The communication systems of other primates (monkeys and apes) are **call systems.** These vocal systems consist of a limited number of sounds—*calls*—that are produced only when particular environmental stimuli are encountered. Such calls may be varied in intensity and duration, but they are much less flexible than language because they are automatic and can't be combined. At some point in human evolution, however, our ancestors began to combine calls and to understand the combinations. The number of calls also expanded, eventually becoming too great to be transmitted, from generation to generation, even partly through the genes. Communication came to rely almost totally on learning.

Although wild primates use call systems, the vocal tract of apes is not suitable for speech. Until the 1960s, attempts to teach spoken language to apes suggested that they lack linguistic abilities. In the 1950s, a couple raised a chimpanzee, Viki, as a member of their family and systematically tried to teach her to speak. However, Viki learned only four words ("mama," "papa," "up," and "cup").

Sign Language

More recent experiments have shown that apes can learn to use, if not speak, true language (Fouts 1997). Several apes have learned to converse with people through means other than speech. One such communication system is American Sign Language, or ASL, which is widely used by deaf Americans. ASL employs a limited number of basic gesture units that are analogous to sounds in spoken language. These units combine to form words and larger units of meaning.

The first chimpanzee to learn ASL was Washoe, a female, who died in 2007 at the age of 42. Captured in West Africa, Washoe was acquired by R. Allen Gardner and Beatrice Gardner, scientists at the University of Nevada in Reno, in 1966, when she was a year old. Four years later, she moved to Norman, Oklahoma, to a converted farm that had become the Institute for Primate Studies. Washoe revolutionized the discussion of the language-learning abilities of apes (Carey 2007). At first she lived in a trailer and heard no spoken language. The researchers always used ASL to communicate with each other in her presence. The chimp gradually acquired a vocabulary of more than 100 signs representing English words (Gardner, Gardner, and Van Cantfort, 1989). At the age of 2, Washoe began to combine as many as five signs into rudimentary sentences such as "you, me, go out, hurry."

The second chimp to learn ASL was Lucy, Washoe's junior by one year. Lucy died, or was murdered by poachers, in 1986, after having been introduced to "the wild" in

Apes, such as these Congo chimpanzees, use call systems to communicate in the wild. Their vocal systems consist of a limited number of sounds—calls—that are produced only when particular environmental stimuli are encountered. ©Michael Nichols/National Geographic Creative

Africa in 1979 (Carter 1988). From her second day of life until her move to Africa, Lucy lived with a family in Norman, Oklahoma. Roger Fouts, a researcher from the nearby Institute for Primate Studies, came twice a week to test and improve Lucy's knowledge of ASL. During the rest of the week, Lucy used ASL to converse with her foster parents. After acquiring language, Washoe and Lucy exhibited several human traits: swearing, joking, telling lies, and trying to teach language to others (Fouts 1997).

When irritated, Washoe called her monkey neighbors at the institute "dirty monkeys." Lucy insulted her "dirty cat." On arrival at Lucy's place, Fouts once found a pile of excrement on the floor. When he asked the chimp what it was, she replied, "dirty, dirty," her expression for feces. Asked whose "dirty, dirty" it was, Lucy named Fouts's coworker, Sue. When Fouts refused to believe her about Sue, the chimp blamed the excrement on Fouts himself.

Fundamental to any language is its **cultural transmission** through learning. People talk to you and around you, and you learn. Washoe, Lucy, and other chimps have tried to teach ASL to other animals, including their own offspring. Washoe taught gestures to other institute chimps, including her son Sequoia, who died in infancy (Fouts, Fouts, and Van Cantfort 1989).

Because of their size and strength as adults, gorillas are less likely subjects than chimps for such experiments. Psychologist Francine "Penny" Patterson's work with gorillas at Stanford University therefore seems more daring than the chimp experiments. Patterson raised the now full-grown female gorilla Koko, born in 1971, in a trailer next to a Stanford museum. Koko's vocabulary surpasses that of any chimp. She has learned more than 1,000 signs, of which she regularly uses over 800. She also recognizes at least 2,000 spoken words in English when she hears them (see http://www.koko.org/sign-language).

Koko and the chimps also show that apes share still another linguistic ability with humans: **productivity.** Speakers use the rules of their language to produce entirely new expressions that are comprehensible to other native speakers. I can, for example, create "baboonlet" to refer to a baboon infant. I do this by analogy with English words in which the suffix *-let* designates the young of a species. Anyone who speaks English immediately understands the meaning of my new word. Apes can also use language productively. Lucy used gestures she already knew to create "drinkfruit" for "watermelon." Washoe, seeing a swan for the first time, coined "waterbird." Koko, who knew the gestures for "finger" and "bracelet," formed "finger bracelet" when she was given a ring.

Although apes have never invented their own meaningful gesture system in the wild, when given such a system, they show many humanlike abilities in learning it. They can employ it productively and creatively, although not with the sophistication of human ASL users.

Apes also have demonstrated linguistic **displacement.** Absent in call systems, displacement is our ability to talk about things that are not present. We don't have to see the objects before we say the words. We can discuss the past and future, share our experiences with others, and benefit from theirs. Patterson has described several examples of Koko's capacity for displacement. The gorilla once expressed sorrow about having bitten Patterson three days earlier. Koko has used the sign "later" to postpone doing things she doesn't want to do. Table 4.1 summarizes the contrasts between language, whether sign or spoken, and call systems.

No one denies the huge difference between human language and gorilla signs. There is surely a major gap between the ability to write a book or say a prayer and an ape's use of signs. Apes may not be people, but they aren't just animals, either. Let Koko express

TABLE 4.1 **Language Contrasted with Call Systems**

Human Language	Primate Call Systems
Has the capacity to speak of things and events that are not present (displacement)	Are stimuli dependent (e.g., the food call will be made only in the presence of food); it cannot be faked
Has the capacity to generate new expressions by combining other expressions (productivity)	Consist of a limited number of calls that cannot be combined to produce new calls
Is group specific in that all humans have the capacity for language, but each linguistic community has its own language, which is culturally transmitted	Tend to be species specific, with little variation among communities of the same species for each call

it: When asked by a reporter whether she was a person or an animal, Koko signed "fine animal gorilla" (Patterson 1978). For the latest on Koko, see http://www.koko.org.

The Origin of Language

Although the capacity to remember and combine linguistic symbols may be latent in the apes, human evolution was needed for this seed to sprout into language. A mutated gene known as *FOXP2* helps explain why humans speak and chimps don't (Paulson 2005). The key role of *FOXP2* in speech came to light in a study of a British family, identified only as KE, half of whose members had an inherited, severe speech deficit (Trivedi 2001). The same variant form of *FOXP2* that is found in chimpanzees causes this disorder. Those with the nonspeech version of the gene can't make the tongue and lip movements necessary for clear speech, and their speech is unintelligible—even to other family members (Trivedi 2001). Chimps have the same (genetic) sequence as the KE family members with the speech deficit. Based on genomics, it appears that the speech-friendly form of *FOXP2* took hold in humans around 150,000 years ago (Paulson 2005). We know now that other genes and a series of anatomical changes were necessary for fully evolved human speech. It would be an oversimplification to call *FOXP2* "the language gene," as was done initially in the popular press, because other genes also determine language development.

Nonverbal Communication

Language is our principal means of communicating, but it isn't the only one we use. We *communicate* when we transmit information about ourselves to others and receive such information from them. Our expressions, stances, gestures, and movements, even if unconscious, convey information and are part of our communication styles. Deborah Tannen (1990) discusses differences in the communication styles of American men and women, and her comments go beyond language. She notes that American girls and women tend to look directly at each other when they talk, whereas boys and men do not. Males are more likely to look straight ahead rather than turn and make eye contact with someone, especially another man, seated beside them. Also, in conversational groups, American men tend to relax and sprawl out. Consider the phenomenon known as "manspreading"—the tendency for men using public transportation to open their legs and thus take up more than one place. American women may relax their posture in all-female groups, but when they are with men, they tend to draw in their limbs and assume a tighter stance.

Kinesics

The study of communication through body movements, stances, gestures, and expressions is known as **kinesics.** Linguists pay attention not only to what is said but also to how it is said. A speaker's enthusiasm is conveyed not only through words but also through facial expressions, gestures, and other signs of animation. We use gestures, such as a jab of the hand, for emphasis. We vary our intonation and the pitch or loudness of our voices. We communicate through strategic pauses, and even by being silent. An effective communication strategy may include altering pitch, voice level, and grammatical forms such as declaratives ("I am . . ."), imperatives ("Go forth . . ."), and questions ("Are you . . . ?"). Culture teaches us that certain manners and styles should accompany certain kinds of speech.

Much of what we communicate is nonverbal and reflects our emotional states and intentions. This can create problems when we use rapid means of communication such as texting and online messaging. People can use emoticons (☺, ☹, :~/ [confused], :~0 ["hah!" no way!]) and abbreviations (lol—laugh out loud; lmao—laugh my a** off; wtf—what the f***; omg—oh my god) to fill in what would otherwise be communicated by tone of voice, laughter, and facial expression (see Baron 2009; Tannen and Trester 2012). This chapter's "Anthropology Today" considers the growing role of emojis in digital communication. An *emoji* is a digital image or pictograph, widely available on smartphones and tablets, used to express an idea or emotion, such as happiness or sadness.

Culture always plays a role in shaping the "natural." Cross-culturally, nodding does not always mean affirmative, nor does head shaking from side to side always mean negative. Americans say "uh huh" to affirm, whereas in Madagascar a similar sound is made to deny. Americans point with their fingers; the people of Madagascar point with their lips.

Body movements communicate social differences. In Japan, bowing is a regular part of social interaction, but different bows are used depending on the social status of the people who are interacting. In Madagascar and Polynesia, people of lower status should not hold their heads above those of people of higher status. When one approaches someone older or of higher status, one bends one's knees and lowers one's head as a sign of respect. In Madagascar, one always does this, for politeness, when passing between two people. Although our gestures, facial expressions, and body stances have roots in our primate heritage, and can be seen in the monkeys and the apes, they have not escaped cultural shaping (see Salzmann et al. 2015).

Personal Space and Displays of Affection

The world's nations and cultures have strikingly different notions about personal space and displays of affection. Cocktail parties in international meeting places such as the United Nations can resemble an elaborate insect mating ritual as diplomats from different countries advance, withdraw, and sidestep. When Americans talk, walk, and dance, they maintain a certain distance from others. Italians and Brazilians, who need less personal space, may interpret such "standoffishness" as a sign of coldness. In conversational pairs, the Italian or Brazilian typically moves in, while the American "instinctively" retreats from a "close talker." Such bodily movements illustrate culture—behavior programmed by years of exposure to a particular cultural tradition.

Consider, too, some striking contrasts between a national culture (American) that tends to be reserved about displays of physical affection and a national culture (Brazilian) in which the opposite is true. Brazilians approach, touch, and kiss one another much more frequently than North Americans do. Middle-class Brazilians teach their kids to kiss (on the cheek, two or three times, coming and going) all their adult relatives. Given the size of Brazilian extended families, this can mean hundreds of people. Women continue kissing those people throughout their lives. Until they are adolescents, boys kiss adult relatives. Thereafter, with extended family men and close male friends, they may adopt the characteristic Brazilian hug (abraço). Men typically continue to kiss female relatives and friends, as well as their fathers and uncles, throughout their lives.

Do you kiss your father? Your uncle? Your grandfather? How about your mother, aunt, or grandmother? The answers to these questions may differ between men and women, and for male and female relatives. In the United States, a cultural homophobia (fear of homosexuality) may deter American men from displays of affection with other men. American girls are typically encouraged to show affection; this is less true for boys.

However, culture is not static. Sarah Kershaw (2009) describes a surge of teenage hugging behavior in American schools. Concerned about potential sexual harassment issues, parents and school officials are suspicious of such public displays of affection, even if the younger generation is more tolerant. Even American boys appear to be more likely nowadays to share nonromantic hugs, as such expressions as "bromance" and "man crush" have entered our vocabulary. What's your position on displays of affection?

The Structure of Language

The scientific study of a spoken language (**descriptive linguistics**) involves several interrelated areas of analysis: phonology, morphology, lexicon, and syntax (see McGregor 2015). **Phonology,** the study of speech sounds, considers which sounds are present and meaningful in a given language. **Morphology** studies how sounds combine to form *morphemes*—words and their meaningful parts. Thus, the word *cats* would be analyzed as containing two morphemes—*cat,* the name for a kind of animal, and *-s,* a morpheme indicating plurality. A language's **lexicon** is a dictionary containing all its morphemes and their meanings. **Syntax** refers to the arrangement and order of words in phrases and sentences. For example, do nouns usually come before or after verbs? Do adjectives normally precede or follow the nouns they modify?

Syntax refers to the arrangement and order of words in phrases and sentences. A photo of Yoda from *Star Wars* (*Revenge of the Sith*) this is. What's odd about Yoda's syntax? ©Lucas Film/Topham/The Image Works

From the media, and from meeting foreigners, we know something about foreign accents and mispronunciations. We know that someone with a marked French accent doesn't pronounce *r* as an American does. But at least someone from France can distinguish between "craw" and "claw," which someone from Japan may not be able to do. The difference between *r* and *l* makes a difference in English and in French, but it doesn't in Japanese. In linguistics we say that the difference between *r* and *l* is *phonemic* in English and French but not in Japanese. In English and French *r* and *l* are phonemes but not in Japanese. A **phoneme** is a sound contrast that makes a difference, that differentiates meaning.

We find the phonemes in a given language by comparing *minimal pairs,* words that resemble each other in all but one sound. The words have different meanings, but they differ in just one sound. The contrasting sounds therefore are phonemes in that language. An example in English is the minimal pair *pit/bit*. These two words are distinguished by a single sound contrast between /p/ and /b/ (we enclose phonemes in slashes). Thus, /p/ and /b/ are phonemes in English. Another example is the different vowel sound of *bit* and *beat* (see Figure 4.1). This contrast distinguishes these two words and the two vowel phonemes written /I/ and /i/ in English.

FIGURE 4.1   **Vowel Phonemes in Standard American English**

The phonemes are shown according to height of the tongue and tongue position at the front, center, or back of the mouth. Phonetic symbols are identified by English words that include them; note that most are minimal pairs.

Source: Bolinger, Dwight *Aspects of Language,* 3rd ed., Independence, KY: Cengage Learning, Inc., 1981, fig. 2.1. Copyright © 1981 Cengage Learning, Inc.

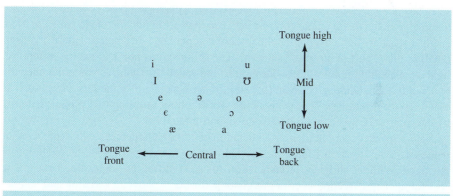

high front (spread)	[i]	as in *beat*
lower high front (spread)	[I]	as in *bit*
mid front (spread)	[e]	as in *bait*
lower mid front (spread)	[ɛ]	as in *bet*
low front	[æ]	as in *bat*
central	[ə]	as in *butt*
low back	[a]	as in *pot*
lower mid back (rounded)	[ɔ]	as in *bought*
mid back (rounded)	[o]	as in *boat*
lower high back (rounded)	[ʊ]	as in *put*
high back (rounded)	[u]	as in *boot*

Standard (American) English (SE), the "region-free" dialect of TV network newscasters, has about 35 phonemes—at least 11 vowels and 24 consonants. The number of phonemes varies from language to language—from 15 to 60, averaging between 30 and 40. The number of phonemes also varies between dialects of a given language. In North American English, for example, vowel phonemes vary noticeably from dialect to dialect. Readers should pronounce the words in Figure 4.1, paying attention to (or asking someone else) whether they distinguish each of the vowel sounds. Most North Americans don't pronounce them all.

My grandson Lucas thinks it's funny that I make a phonemic distinction he doesn't make. I pronounce words beginning with *wh* as though they began with *hw*. My personal set of phonemes includes both /hw/ and /w/. This enables me to distinguish between *white* and *Wight* (as in the Isle of Wight) and between *where* and *wear*. Lucas pronounces all four of those words as though they begin with [w], so that he does not distinguish between *white* and *Wight* or between *where* and *wear*. How about you?

Phonetics is the study of speech sounds in general, what people actually say in various languages or dialects (see the "Sociolinguistics" section of this chapter). **Phonemics** studies only the *significant* sound contrasts (phonemes) of a given language. In English, like /r/ and /l/ (remember *craw* and *claw*), /b/ and /v/ also are phonemes, occurring in minimal pairs like *bat* and *vat*. In Spanish, however, the contrast between [b] and [v] doesn't distinguish meaning, and they therefore are not phonemes (we enclose sounds that are not phonemic in brackets). Spanish speakers normally use the [b] sound to pronounce words spelled with either *b* or *v*.

In any language, a given phoneme extends over a phonetic range. In English the phoneme /p/ ignores the phonetic contrast between the $[p^h]$ in *pin* and the [p] in *spin*. Most English speakers don't even notice that there is a phonetic difference. The $[p^h]$ is aspirated, so that a puff of air follows the [p]. The [p] in *spin* is not. (To see the difference, light a match, hold it in front of your mouth, and watch the flame as you pronounce the two words.) The contrast between $[p^h]$ and [p] *is* phonemic in some languages, such as Hindi (spoken in India). That is, there are words whose meaning is distinguished only by the contrast between an aspirated and an unaspirated [p].

Native speakers vary in their pronunciation of certain phonemes, such as the /e/ phoneme in the midwestern United States. This variation is important in the evolution of language. Without shifts in pronunciation, there could be no linguistic change. The "Sociolinguistics" section later in this chapter considers phonetic variation and its relationship to social divisions and the evolution of language.

Language, Thought, and Culture

The well-known linguist Noam Chomsky (1957, 2014) has argued that the human brain contains a limited set of rules for organizing language, so that all languages have a common structural basis. (Chomsky calls this set of rules *universal grammar*.) That people can learn foreign languages and that words and ideas translate from one language to another support Chomsky's position that all humans have similar linguistic abilities and thought processes. Another line of support comes from creole languages. Such languages develop from *pidgins,* which form during acculturation, when different societies come into contact and must devise a system of communication (see Gu 2012; Lim and Ansaldo 2016). After generations of being spoken, pidgins may develop into *creole* languages, which have fully developed grammatical rules and native speakers (people who learn the language as their primary one during enculturation).

Creoles are spoken in several Caribbean societies. Gullah, which is spoken by African Americans on coastal islands in South Carolina and Georgia, is a creole language. Supporting the idea that creoles are based on universal grammar is the fact that such languages all share certain features. Syntactically, all use particles (e.g., *will, was*) to form future and past tenses and multiple negation to deny or negate (e.g., "he don't got none"). Also, all form questions by changing inflection rather than by changing word order—for example, "You're going home for the holidays?" (with a rising tone at the end) rather than "Are you going home for the holidays?"

The Sapir-Whorf Hypothesis

Other linguists and anthropologists take a different approach to the relation between language and thought. Rather than seeking universal linguistic structures and processes, they believe that different languages produce different ways of thinking. This position sometimes is known as the **Sapir-Whorf hypothesis** after Edward Sapir (1931) and his student Benjamin Lee Whorf (1956), its prominent early advocates. Sapir and Whorf argued that the grammatical categories of different languages lead their speakers to think about things in particular ways. For example, English divides time (tenses) into past, present, and future. Hopi, a language of the Pueblo region of the Native American Southwest, does not. Rather, Hopi distinguishes between events that exist or have existed (what we use present and past to discuss) and those that don't or don't yet (our future events, along with imaginary and hypothetical events). Whorf argued that this difference leads Hopi speakers to think about time and reality in different ways than English speakers do.

A similar example comes from Portuguese, which employs a future subjunctive verb form, introducing a degree of uncertainty into discussions of the future. In English we routinely use the future tense to talk about something we think will happen. We don't hesitate to proclaim "I'll see you next year," even when we can't be absolutely sure we will. The Portuguese future subjunctive qualifies the future event, recognizing that the future can't be certain. Our way of expressing the future as certain is so ingrained that we don't even think about it, just as the Hopi don't see the need to distinguish between present and past, both of which are real, while the future remains hypothetical. However, language restricts thought and perception only partially, because cultural changes can produce changes in thought and in language, as we'll see in the next section.

Focal Vocabulary

A lexicon (vocabulary) is a language's dictionary, its set of names for things, events, and ideas. Lexicon influences perception. Thus, Eskimos (Inuit) have several distinct words for different types of snow that in English are all called *snow*. Eskimos recognize and think about differences in snow that English speakers don't see because our language gives us just one word.

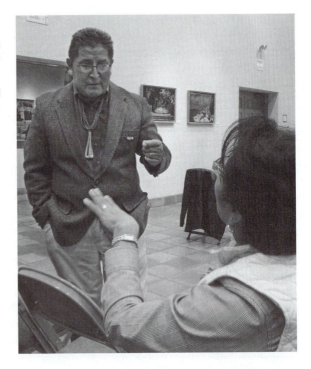

Clark Tenakhongva, who was (or is) a candidate to be Hopi tribal chairman, spoke (or speaks) to an audience member during a forum in Flagstaff, Arizona. The Hopi language would not distinguish between *was* and *is* or *spoke* and *speaks* in the previous sentence. For the Hopi, present and past are real and are expressed grammatically in the same way, while the future remains hypothetical and has a different grammatical expression. ©Felicia Fonseca/AP Images

Similarly, the Nuer of South Sudan have an elaborate vocabulary to describe cattle. Eskimos have several words for snow and Nuer have dozens for cattle because of their particular histories, economies, and environments (Robson 2013). When the need arises, English speakers can also elaborate their snow and cattle vocabularies. For example, skiers name varieties of snow with words that are missing from the lexicons of Florida retirees. Similarly, the cattle vocabulary of a Texas rancher is much more ample than that of a salesperson in a New York City department store. Such specialized sets of terms and distinctions that are particularly important to certain groups (those with particular *foci* of experience or activity) are known as **focal vocabulary.**

Vocabulary is the area of language that changes most readily. New words and distinctions, when needed, appear and spread. For example, who would have "texted" or "emailed" anything a generation ago? Names for items get simpler as they become common and important. A television has become a *TV,* an automobile a *car,* and an application for a smartphone an *app* (see this chapter's Anthropology Today for a discussion of recent changes in word use in English).

Language, culture, and thought are certainly interrelated. In opposition to Sapir-Whorf, however, it is probably more accurate to say that changes in *culture* produce changes in language and thought than to say the reverse. Consider differences in the color terms used by American men and women (Lakoff 2004). Distinctions implied by such terms as *salmon, rust, peach, beige, teal, mauve, cranberry,* and *dusky orange* aren't in the vocabularies of most American men. However, many of them weren't even in American women's lexicons 60–70 years ago. Color terms and distinctions have increased with the growth of the fashion and cosmetic industries. Thus, cultural contrasts and changes affect lexical distinctions (for instance, *peach* versus *salmon*) within semantic domains (for instance, color terminology). **Semantics** refers to a language's meaning system.

The ways in which people divide the world—the lexical contrasts they perceive as meaningful or significant—reflect their experiences. Anthropologists have discovered that certain sets of vocabulary items evolve in a determined order. For example, after studying more than 100 languages, Berlin and Kay (1969/1992) discovered 10 basic color terms: *white, black, red, yellow, blue, green, brown, pink, orange,* and *purple* (they evolved in more or less that order). The number of terms varied with cultural complexity. Representing one extreme were Papua New Guinea cultivators and Australian hunters and gatherers, who used only two basic terms, which translate as *black* and *white* or *dark* and *light*. At the other end of the continuum were European and Asian languages with all the color terms. Color terminology was most developed in areas with a history of using dyes and artificial coloring.

Sociolinguistics

Social and Linguistic Variation

Is there anything distinctive or unusual about the way you talk? If you're from Canada, Virginia, or Savannah, you may say "oot" instead of "out." A southerner might request a "soft drink" rather than a New Yorker's "soda" or someone else's "pop." Can you imitate how a "Valley Girl" or "surfer dude" might talk? Usually when we pay attention to how we talk, it's because someone comments on our speech. It may be only when students move from one state or region to another that they realize how much of a regional accent they have. I moved as a teenager from Atlanta to New York City. Previously I hadn't realized I had a southern accent, but some guardians of linguistic correctness in my new high school did. They put me in a speech class, pointing out linguistic flaws I never knew I had. One was my "dull *s*," particularly in terminal consonant clusters, as in the words *tusks* and *breakfasts*. Apparently I didn't pronounce all three consonants at the ends of those words. Later it occurred to me that these weren't words I used very often. As far as I know, I've never had a conversation about tusks or proclaimed, "I ate seven breakfasts last week."

We all have stereotypes about how people in other regions talk. Some stereotypes, spread by the media, are more generalized than others are. Most Americans think they can imitate a "Southern accent." We also stereotype speech in Boston ("I pahked the kah in Hahvahd Yahd") and Canada ("oot" for "out"). Although many people assume, erroneously, that midwesterners don't have accents, people from that region do exhibit significant linguistic variation (see Eckert 1989, 2000). One of the best examples is pronunciation of the *e* vowel sound (called the /e/ phoneme), in such words as *ten, rent, section, lecture, effect, best,* and *test*. In southeastern Michigan, there are four different ways of pronouncing this *e* sound. African Americans and immigrants from Appalachia often pronounce *ten* as "tin," just as Southerners habitually do. Some Michiganders say "ten," the correct pronunciation in Standard English. However, two other pronunciations also are common. Instead of "ten," many Michiganders say "tan" or "tun" (as though they were using the word *ton,* a unit of weight).

I remember, for example, how one of my Michigan-raised teaching assistants appeared deliriously happy one afternoon. When I asked why, she replied, "I've just had the best suction." "What?" I asked, and she replied more precisely. "I've just had the best saction." She considered this a clearer pronunciation of the word *section.* Another TA complimented me, "You luctured to great effuct today." After an exam, a student lamented that she had not done her "bust on the tust" (i.e., "best on the test"). The truth is, regional patterns affect the way we speak.

Unlike grammarians, linguists and anthropologists are interested in what people do say, rather than what they should say. Speech differences are associated with, and tell us a lot about, social variation, such as region, education, ethnic background, and gender. Men and women talk differently. I'm sure you can think of examples based on your own experience, although you probably never realized that women tend to peripheralize their vowels (think of the sounds in *weasel* and *whee*), whereas men tend to centralize them (think of *rough* and *ugh*). Men are more likely to speak "ungrammatically" than women are. As mentioned previously, men and women differ in their use of color terms. In another lexical domain, sports vocabulary, men typically know more terms, make more distinctions among them (e.g., *runs* versus *points*), and try to use the terms more precisely than women do. Correspondingly, women use more color terms and attempt to use them more specifically than men do. To make this point when I lecture, I bring an off-purple shirt to class. Holding it up, I first ask women to say aloud what color the shirt is. The women rarely answer with a uniform voice, as they try to distinguish the actual shade (mauve, lilac, lavender, wisteria, or some other purplish hue). I then ask the men, who consistently answer as one, "PURPLE."

No language is a uniform system in which everyone talks just like everyone else. The field of **sociolinguistics** investigates relationships between social and linguistic variation (Edwards 2013; Spencer 2010; Wardhaugh and Fuller 2015). How do linguistic features correlate with social diversity and stratification, including class, ethnic, and gender differences (Eckert and McConnell-Ginet 2013; McConnell-Ginet 2010; Tannen 1990, 1993)? How is language used to express, reinforce, or resist power (Fairclough 2015; Mesthrie 2011; Mooney 2011; Trudgill 2010)? To study variation, sociolinguists must observe, define, and measure variable use of language and speakers in real-world situations.

The Language of Food

In his book *The Language of Food*, linguist Dan Jurafsky (2014) describes a recent study based on measurement of sociolinguistic variation. Jurafsky and his colleagues analyzed the menus of 6,500 contemporary American restaurants. One of their goals was to see how the food vocabularies of upscale restaurants differed from those of cheaper establishments. One key difference they found was that upscale menus paid much more attention to the sources of the foods they served. They named specific farms, gardens, ranches, pastures, woodlands, and farmers' markets. They were careful to mention, if the season was right, that their tomatoes or peas were heirloom varieties. Very expensive restaurants mentioned the origin of food more than 15 times as often as inexpensive restaurants.

Word length was another differentiator. Upscale menu words averaged half a letter longer than in the cheaper restaurants. Cheaper eateries, for instance, were more likely to use *decaf,* rather than *decaffeinated,* and *sides* rather than *accompaniments.* Diners had to pay higher prices for those longer words: Every increase of one letter in the average length of words describing a dish meant an average increase of $.18 in the price of that dish.

Cheaper restaurants were more apt to use linguistic fillers. These included positive but vague words like *delicious, tasty, mouthwatering,* and *flavorful,* or other positive, but impossible to measure, adjectives such as *terrific, wonderful, delightful,* and *sublime.* Each positive vague word for a dish in a modest restaurant reduced its average price by 9 percent. Downscale restaurants also were more likely to assure their diners that their offerings were "fresh." Expensive restaurants expected their patrons to assume that their offerings were fresh, without having to say it.

Study these menus from two restaurants, one more upscale than the other. Note the use of names of farms (food origin) in one menu and the use of adjectives such as *delicious, fresh,* and *premium* in the other. Which menu is from the more upscale restaurant? ©McGraw-Hill Education. Mark Dierker, photographer

Jurafsky and his associates also analyzed vocabulary used in 1 million online Yelp restaurant reviews, representing seven American cities—Boston, Chicago, Los Angeles, New York, Philadelphia, San Francisco, and Washington. The researchers found that good and bad reviews differed linguistically. Reviewers used a greater variety of words, with more differentiated meanings, to express negative rather than positive opinions. This tendency, known as negative differentiation, extends to other linguistic domains in English, and even to other languages. People seem to need more varied and elaborate ways of being negative. Negative reviewers wanted to comment on the restaurant's failings as fully as possible and to present it as a shared experience. Bad reviews were much more likely than good ones to use the inclusive pronouns *we* and *us.* Psychologists know that traumatized people seek comfort in groups by emphasizing their belonging, using the words *we* and *us* with high frequency when reporting about negative experiences. Next time you eat out and/or are tempted to write a review, pay attention to these findings about "the language of food."

Linguistic Diversity within Nations

As an illustration of the linguistic variation encountered in all nations, consider the contemporary United States. Ethnic diversity is revealed by the fact that millions of Americans learn first languages other than English. Spanish is the most common. Many of

In Renton, Washington, this King County Department of Elections sign shows the word "vote" in English, Chinese, Korean, Vietnamese, and Spanish. Washington, Oregon and Colorado are three states that conduct all elections by mail, with no traditional polling places. The U.S. Voting Rights Act mandates that certain counties provide bilingual or multilingual ballots and voting instructions.
©Jason Remond/AFP/ Getty Images

those people eventually become bilingual, adding English as a second language. In many multilingual (including colonized) nations, people use two or more languages on different occasions—one in the home, for example, and the other on the job or in public. In India, where some 22 languages are spoken, a person may need to use three different languages when talking, respectively, with a boss, a spouse, and a parent. Only about one-tenth of India's population speaks English, the colonial language. As they interact today with one of the key instruments of globalization—the Internet—even those English speakers appreciate being able to read, and to find Internet content in, their own regional languages.

Whether bilingual or not, we all vary our speech in different contexts; we engage in **style shifts.** In 2013, I traveled to India with a friend, an India-born American who speaks perfectly good Standard (American) English (SE). During the time we spent in India, it was fascinating to watch as he shifted back and forth between Hindi, English with a strong Indian accent (when speaking to Indians in English), and SE (when speaking to his American fellow travelers).

In certain parts of Europe, people regularly switch dialects. This phenomenon, known as **diglossia,** applies to "high" and "low" variants of the same language, for example, in German and Dutch. People employ the high variant at universities and in writing, professions, and the mass media. They use the low variant for ordinary conversation with family members and friends.

Just as social situations influence our speech, so do geographic, cultural, and socioeconomic differences. Many dialects coexist in the United States with SE, which itself is a dialect that differs from, say, "BBC English," the preferred dialect in Great Britain. Different dialects are equally effective as systems of communication, which is the main job of language. Our tendency to think of particular dialects as cruder or more sophisticated than others is a social rather than a linguistic judgment. We rank certain speech patterns as better or worse because we recognize that they are used by groups that we also rank. People who say *dese, dem,* and *dere* instead of *these, them,* and *there* communicate perfectly well with anyone who recognizes that the *d* sound systematically replaces the *th* sound in their speech. However, this form of speech has become an indicator of low social rank. We call it, like the use of *ain't,* "uneducated speech." The use of *dese, dem,* and *dere* is one of many phonological differences that Americans recognize and look down on (see Labov 2012).

Linguistic Diversity in California

Popular stereotypes of how Californians talk reflect media images of White, blonde, Valley girls and White, blond surfers, who say things like "dude," "gnarly," and "Like, totally!" These stereotypes have some accuracy. Among coastal California Whites, a distinctive "Valley girl accent" has been developing since the 1940s. That accent is most evident in vowels. For example, the vowels in *hock* and *hawk,* or *cot* and *caught,* are pronounced the same, so that *awesome* rhymes with *possum.* Second, the vowel sound in *boot* and *dude* has shifted and now is pronounced as in *cute* or *pure* (thus, *boot* becomes "beaut," and *dude* becomes "dewed," rather than "dood") (see Eckert and Mendoza-Denton 2002).

California is even more notable, however, for its linguistic diversity. To document this variation, Penelope Eckert, a sociolinguist at Stanford University, leads an ongoing research project called Voices of California. Recently, her team has focused on inland California. The researchers always test certain words that elicit specific pronunciations associated with social differentiation. Those words include *wash,* sometimes pronounced "warsh," *greasy* ("greezy"), and *pin* and *pen,* which some people pronounce the same. Depression-era migrants from Oklahoma's Dust Bowl have left their mark on inland California speech, as in their alternate pronunciations of *wash, greasy,* and *pen* (see King 2012).

Another factor contributing to diversity is how people feel about their home community versus the outside world. In California's Central Valley, which is economically depressed, young people must choose whether to stay put or move elsewhere. When people want to stay involved in their home community, they tend to talk like locals. A desire *not* to be perceived as being from a particular place can motivate people to change their speech (King 2012).

Ethnicity also influences speech patterns. So strong is California's Spanish heritage that Spanish-like vowels influence the way English is spoken even by Hispanics who learn English as their first, or native, language. For example, among Mexican-American English speakers in northern California, the vowel in the second syllable of *nothing* has come to resemble the Spanish "ee" sound (see Eckert and Mendoza-Denton 2002).

Gender Speech Contrasts

According to Robin Lakoff (2004), the use of certain types of words and expressions has been associated with women's traditional lesser power in American society. For example, *Oh dear, Oh fudge,* and *Goodness!* are less forceful than *Hell* and *Damn.* Watch the lips of a disgruntled athlete in a televised competition, such as a football game. What's the likelihood he's saying "Phooey on you"? Women are more likely to use such adjectives as *adorable, charming, sweet, cute, lovely,* and *divine* than men are.

Differences in the linguistic strategies and behavior of men and women are examined in several books by the well-known sociolinguist Deborah Tannen (1990, 1993). Tannen uses the terms *rapport* and *report* to contrast women's and men's overall linguistic styles. Women, says Tannen, typically use language and the body movements that accompany it to build rapport, social connections with others. Men, on the other hand, tend to make reports, reciting information to establish a place for themselves in a hierarchy, as they also attempt to determine the relative ranks of their conversation mates.

Stratification and Symbolic Domination

We use and evaluate speech in the context of *extralinguistic* forces—social, political, and economic. Mainstream Americans evaluate the speech of low-status groups negatively, calling it "uneducated." This is not because these ways of speaking are bad in themselves but because they have come to symbolize low status. Consider variation in the pronunciation of *r*. In some parts of the United States, *r* is regularly pronounced, and in other (*r*less) areas it is not. Originally, American *r*less speech was modeled on the fashionable speech of England. Because of its prestige, *r*lessness was adopted in many areas and continues as the norm around Boston and in the South.

New Yorkers sought prestige by dropping their *r*'s in the 19th century, after having pronounced them in the 18th. However, contemporary New Yorkers are going back to the 18th-century pattern of pronouncing *r*'s. What matters, and what governs linguistic change, is not the reverberation of a strong midwestern *r* but *social* evaluation, whether *r*'s happen to be "in" or "out."

Studies of *r* pronunciation in New York City have clarified the mechanisms of phonological change. William Labov (1972b) focused on whether *r* was pronounced after vowels in such words as *car, floor, card,* and *fourth*. To get data on how this linguistic variation correlated with social class, he used a series of rapid encounters with employees in three New York City department stores, each of which had prices and locations that attracted a different socioeconomic group. Saks Fifth Avenue (68 encounters) catered to the upper middle class, Macy's (125) attracted middle-class shoppers, and S. Klein's (71) had predominantly lower-middle-class and working-class customers. The class origins of store personnel reflected those of their customers.

Having already determined that a certain department was on the fourth floor, Labov approached ground-floor salespeople and asked where that department was. After the salesperson had answered, "Fourth floor," Labov repeated his "Where?" in order to get a second response. The second reply was more considered and emphatic, the salesperson presumably thinking that Labov hadn't heard or understood the first answer. For each salesperson, therefore, Labov had two samples of *r* pronunciation in two words.

Labov calculated the percentages of workers who pronounced *r* at least once during the interview. These were 62 percent at Saks, 51 percent at Macy's, but only 20 percent at S. Klein's. He also found that personnel on upper floors, where he asked, "What floor is this?" (and where more expensive items were sold), pronounced *r* more often than ground-floor salespeople did (see also Labov 2006).

In Labov's study, *r* pronunciation was clearly associated with prestige. Certainly the job interviewers who had hired the salespeople never counted *r*'s before offering employment. However, they did use speech evaluations to make judgments about how effective certain people would be in selling particular kinds of merchandise. In other words, they practiced sociolinguistic discrimination, using linguistic features in deciding who got certain jobs.

Our speech habits help determine our access to employment and other material resources. Because of this, "proper language" itself becomes a strategic resource—and a path to wealth, prestige, and power. Illustrating this, many ethnographers have described the importance of verbal skill and oratory in politics (Lakoff 2008; Lakoff and Wehling 2012). Ronald Reagan, known as a "great communicator," dominated American society in the 1980s as a two-term president. Another twice-elected president, Bill Clinton, despite his Arkansas accent, was known for his verbal skills in certain contexts (e.g., televised debates and town-hall meetings). Communications flaws may have helped doom the presidencies of Gerald Ford, Jimmy Carter, and George Bush the elder. Does the current U.S. president's use of language affect your perception of that officeholder?

The French anthropologist Pierre Bourdieu views linguistic practices as *symbolic capital* that properly trained people may convert into economic and social capital. The value of a dialect—its standing in a "linguistic market"—depends on the extent to which it provides access to desired positions in the labor market. In turn, this reflects its legitimation by formal institutions—educational institutions, state, church, and prestige media. Even people who don't use the prestige dialect accept its authority and correctness, its "symbolic domination" (Bourdieu 1982, 1984; Labov 2012). Thus, linguistic forms, which lack power in themselves, take on the power of the groups they symbolize (see Mooney and Evans 2015). The education system, however (defending its own worth), denies linguistic relativity. It misrepresents prestige speech as being inherently better. The linguistic insecurity often felt by lower-class and minority speakers is a result of this symbolic domination.

Certain dialects are stigmatized, not because of actual linguistic deficiencies, but because of a symbolic association between a certain way of talking and low social status. In this scene from the movie *My Fair Lady,* Professor Henry Higgins (Rex Harrison) teaches Eliza Doolittle (Audrey Hepburn), formerly a Cockney flower girl, how to speak "proper English." ©Warner Brothers/Album/Newscom

African American Vernacular English (AAVE)

The sociolinguist William Labov and several associates, both White and Black, have conducted detailed studies of what they call **African American Vernacular English (AAVE)**. (*Vernacular* means ordinary, casual speech.) AAVE is the "relatively uniform dialect spoken by the majority of Black youth in most parts of the United States today, especially in the inner city areas of New York, Boston, Detroit, Philadelphia, Washington, Cleveland, . . . and other urban centers. It is also spoken in most rural areas and used in the casual, intimate speech of many adults" (Labov 1972a, p. xiii). This does not imply that all, or even most, African Americans speak AAVE.

AAVE is a complex linguistic system with its own rules, which linguists have described. Consider some of the phonological and grammatical differences between AAVE and SE. One phonological difference is that AAVE speakers are less likely to pronounce *r* than SE speakers are. Actually, many SE speakers don't pronounce *r*'s that come right before a consonant (ca*r*d) or at the end of a word (ca*r*). But SE speakers usually do pronounce an *r* that comes right before a vowel, either at the end of a word (fou*r* o'clock) or within a word (Ca*r*ol). AAVE speakers, by contrast, are much more likely to omit such intervocalic (between vowels) *r*'s. The result is that speakers of the two dialects have different *homonyms* (words that sound the same but have different meanings). AAVE speakers who don't pronounce intervocalic *r*'s have the following homonyms: *Carol/Cal*; *Paris/pass*.

Observing different phonological rules, AAVE speakers pronounce certain words differently than SE speakers do. Particularly in the elementary school context, the homonyms of AAVE-speaking students typically differ from those of their SE-speaking teachers. To evaluate reading accuracy, teachers should determine whether students are recognizing the different meanings of such AAVE homonyms as *passed, past,* and *pass*. Teachers need to make sure students understand what they are reading, which is probably more important than whether they are pronouncing words correctly according to the SE norm.

Phonological rules may lead AAVE speakers to omit *-ed* as a past-tense marker and *-s* as a marker of plurality. However, other speech contexts demonstrate that AAVE speakers do understand the difference between past- and present-tense verbs, and between singular and plural nouns. Confirming this are irregular verbs (e.g., *tell, told*) and irregular plurals (e.g., *child, children*), in which AAVE works the same as SE.

SE is not superior to AAVE as a linguistic system, but it does happen to be the prestige dialect—the one used in the mass media, in writing, and in most public and professional contexts. SE is the dialect that has the most "symbolic capital." In areas of Germany where there is diglossia, speakers of Plattdeusch (Low German) learn the High German dialect (originally spoken in the highlands of southern Germany) to communicate appropriately in the national context. High German is the standard literary and spoken form of German. Similarly, upwardly mobile AAVE-speaking students learn SE.

Historical Linguistics

Sociolinguists study contemporary variation in speech, which is language change in progress. **Historical linguistics** deals with longer-term change. Historical linguists can reconstruct many features of past languages by studying contemporary

FIGURE 4.2   **PIE Family Tree**

Main languages and subgroups of the Indo-European language stock, showing approximate time to their divergence.

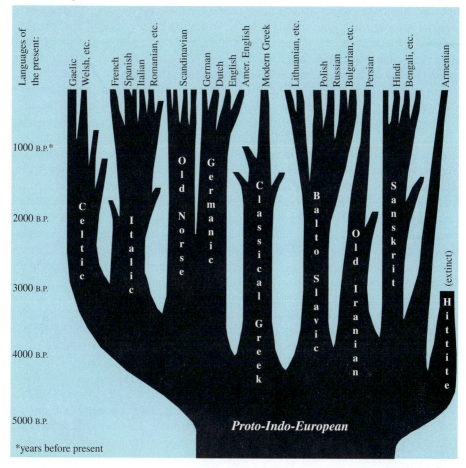

daughter languages. These are languages that descend from the same parent language and that have been changing separately for hundreds or even thousands of years. We call the original language from which they diverge the **protolanguage.** Romance languages such as French and Spanish, for example, are daughter languages of Latin, their common protolanguage. German, English, Dutch, and the Scandinavian languages are daughter languages of proto-Germanic. The Romance languages and the Germanic languages all belong to the Indo-European (IE) language family. Proto-Indo-European (PIE), spoken in the more distant past, was the common protolanguage of Latin, proto-Germanic, and many other ancient languages (see Figure 4.2).

When did PIE originate, and how did it spread? Decades ago, archaeologist Colin Renfrew (1987) traced the origin of PIE to a farming population living in Anatolia, in what is now Turkey, about 9,000 years ago. Recent studies by the evolutionary biologist Quentin

Atkinson and his colleagues in New Zealand support this Anatolian origin of PIE (see Bouckaert et al. 2012). Atkinson's team focused on a set of vocabulary items known to be resistant to linguistic change. These include pronouns, parts of the body, and family relations. For 103 IE languages, the researchers compared those words with the PIE ancestral word (as reconstructed by historical linguists). Words that clearly descend from the same ancestral word are known as *cognates*. For example, *mother* (English) is a cognate with all these words for the same relative: *mutter* (German), *mat* (Russian), *madar* (Persian), *matka* (Polish), and *mater* (Latin). All are descendants of the PIE word *mehter*.

For each language, when the word was a cognate, the researchers scored it 1; when it was not (having been replaced by an unrelated word), it was scored 0. With each language represented by a string of 1s and 0s, the researchers could establish a family tree showing the relationships among the 103 languages. Based on those relationships and the geographic areas where the daughter languages are spoken, the computer determined the likeliest routes of movement from an origin. The calculation pointed to Anatolia, southern Turkey. This is precisely the region originally proposed by Renfrew, because it was the area from which farming spread to Europe. Atkinson also ran a computer simulation on a grammar-based IE tree—once again finding Anatolia to be the most likely origin point for PIE (Wade 2012). Several lines of biological and archaeological evidence now indicate that the Neolithic economy spread more through the actual migration of farmers than through the diffusion of crops and ideas. This would seem to offer support to the Renfrew-Atkinson model of PIE origin and dispersal of Neolithic farmers.

Historically oriented linguists suspect that a very remote protolanguage, spoken perhaps 50,000 years ago in Africa, gave rise to all contemporary languages. Murray Gell-Mann and Merritt Ruhlen (2011), who co-direct the Evolution of Human Languages project at the Sante Fe Institute, have reconstructed the syntax (word ordering) of this ancient protolanguage. Their study focused on how subject (S), objects (O), and verbs (V) are arranged in phrases and sentences in some 2,000 contemporary languages. There are six possible word orders: SOV, SVO, OSV, OVS, VSO, and VOS. Most common is SOV ("I you like," e.g., Latin), present in more than half of all languages. Next comes SVO ("I like you," e.g., English). Much rarer are OSV, OVS, VSO, and VOS. Gell-Mann and Ruhlen constructed a family tree of relationships among 2,000 contemporary languages. The directions of change involving the six word orders were clear. All the languages that were SVO, OVS, and OSV derived from SOV languages—never the other way around. Furthermore, any language with VSO or VOS word order always came from an SVO language (see Figure 4.3). The fact that SVO always comes from SOV confirms SOV as the original, ancestral word order.

Language changes over time. It evolves—varies, spreads, and divides into **subgroups** (languages within a taxonomy of related languages that are most closely related). Dialects of

FIGURE 4.3 **Evolution of Word Order from Original SOV (Subject, Object, Verb) in Ancient Ancestral Protolanguage**

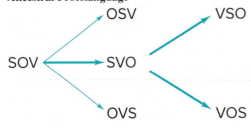

a single parent language become distinct daughter languages, especially if they are isolated from one another. Some of them split, and new "granddaughter" languages develop. If people remain in the ancestral homeland, their speech patterns also change. The evolving speech in the ancestral homeland should be considered a daughter language like the others.

Language, Culture, and History

A close relationship between languages doesn't necessarily mean that their speakers are closely related biologically or culturally, because people can adopt new languages. In the equatorial forests of Africa, "pygmy" hunters have discarded their ancestral languages and now speak those of the cultivators who have migrated to the area. Immigrants to the United States spoke many different languages on arrival, but their descendants now speak fluent English.

Cultural features may (or may not) correlate with the distribution of language families. Groups that speak related languages may (or may not) be more culturally similar to each other than they are to groups whose speech derives from different linguistic ancestors. Of course, cultural similarities aren't limited to speakers of related languages. Even groups whose members speak unrelated languages have contact through trade, intermarriage, and warfare. Many items of vocabulary in contemporary English, particularly food items such as "beef" and "pork," come from French. Even without written documentation of France's influence after the Norman Conquest of England in 1066, linguistic evidence in contemporary English would reveal a long period of important firsthand contact with France. Similarly, linguistic evidence may confirm cultural contact and borrowing when written history is lacking. By considering which words have been borrowed, we also can make inferences about the nature of the contact.

Language Loss

One aspect of linguistic history is language loss. According to linguist K. David Harrison, "When we lose a language, we lose centuries of thinking about time, . . . seasons, mathematics, landscapes, myths, music, the unknown and the everyday" (quoted in Maugh 2007). Harrison's book *When Languages Die* (2007) notes that an indigenous language goes extinct every two weeks. The world's linguistic diversity has been cut in half (measured by number of distinct languages) in the past 500 years, and half of the remaining languages are predicted to disappear during this century. Colonial languages (e.g., English, Spanish, Portuguese, French, Dutch, Russian) have expanded at the expense of indigenous ones. Of approximately 7,000 remaining languages, about 20 percent are endangered, compared with 18 percent of mammals, 8 percent of plants, and 5 percent of birds (Harrison 2010; Maugh 2007).

National Geographic's Enduring Voices Project strives to preserve endangered languages by identifying the geographic areas with unique, poorly understood, or threatened languages and by documenting those languages and cultures. The website shows various language hot spots where the endangerment rate ranges from low to severe. The rate is high in an area encompassing Oklahoma, Texas, and New Mexico, where 40 Native American languages are at risk. The top hot spot is northern Australia, where 153 Aboriginal

Anthropology Today *Words of the Year*

Annual lists of "words of the year" provide an excellent illustration of how vocabulary shifts in response to cultural changes. Organizations in various countries routinely publish such lists, which usually choose one increasingly common word as the winner—the "word of the year." According to various lists, the 2015 winners in English included single words, words in combination (such as "binge watch"), and even, in one case, a pictograph, known as the "Face with Tears of Joy" emoji. Among the 2015 words of the year listed by the American Dialect Society were *they* (as a *singular* pronoun), *binge watch, sharing economy, identity, austerity, content marketing, microaggression, refugee, feardom,* and *ammosexual.* These words are viewed as reflecting the ethos, mood, and preoccupations of 2015 (Northover 2016). Let's consider two of the more interesting choices, the singular *they* and the "Face with Tears of Joy" emoji.

The Face with Tears of Joy emoji—a recent "word" of the year. Have you ever used this, or a similar, emoji? ©Maksym Chechel/ Shutterstock.com RF

Several organizations chose singular *they* as their word of the year (Baron 2015). *They* is a third-person pronoun that is gender neutral; it includes males and females. For centuries it also has been used informally in speech and writing as a singular pronoun. Someone can use *they* when they want to avoid having to use "he or she" in a sentence—as I just did. Historical documents show that *they* has been used as a singular pronoun for over 600 years (Baron 2015). The popularity of the singular *they* has been growing recently because it fills an important linguistic niche—the need for a gender-neutral third-person singular pronoun.

The word *they* itself was introduced into the English language by Danish immigrants in the ninth century. It gradually replaced the then-existing English third-person plural pronoun. For centuries thereafter, English writers and speakers commonly used both the singular and the plural *they.* Its use as a singular pronoun began to meet resistance around 1800. Grammarians discouraged the use of the singular *they* because of lack of agreement between an apparently plural pronoun and a singular verb (e.g., "They eats dinner."). Those grammatical purists who continue to resist the singular *they* might be reminded that the singular pronoun *you* in English began as a plural pronoun, which eventually replaced *thou* and *thee* as a singular pronoun. According to various "word of the year" lists, the time has come for a similar shift to using *they* instead of the more unwieldy "he or she." If someone wants to do that, they won't get any flak from me.

Another illustration of lexical change in progress today is Oxford Dictionaries' first-ever choice of an emoji as 2015's word of the year (Oxford University Press 2015). An *emoji* is a digital image used to express an idea or emotion in electronic communication. Despite its similarity to the English word *emoticon* (coined from *emotion* and *icon*), the word *emoji* actually comes from Japanese. Emojis have been around since the late 1990s, but their use, along with the use of the term *emoji* itself, have increased substantially. No doubt this reflects the growing availability of these pictographs on smartphones, tablets, computers, and other devices we use to communicate on a daily basis. Between 2014 and 2015, use of the word *emoji* tripled in the United States and the United Kingdom (Northover 2016). According to a study done by Oxford University Press and the mobile technology company SwiftKey, the most popular emoji—the "Face with Tears of Joy"—represented 20 percent of all emojis used in the United Kingdom, and 17 percent of those used in the United States, in 2015 (Northover 2016). The growing role of digital transmission in our everyday lives, including reliance on emojis, illustrates once again how language and communication continue to evolve in our globalizing world. Google some of the sources mentioned here to see the most recent words of the year.

About 30 Native American groups are using a device known as the "phraselator" as an aid in preserving their endangered indigenous language. Shown here, Dakota tribal elder Curtis Campbell (left) and Dakota language teacher Wayne Wells work with the device at the Prairie Island Reservation in Minnesota. ©Elizabeth Flores/ZUMA Press/Newscom

languages are endangered (Maugh 2007). Other hot spots are in central South America, the Pacific Northwest of North America, and eastern Siberia. In all these areas, indigenous tongues have yielded, either voluntarily or through coercion, to a colonial language (see Harrison 2010).

Summary

1. Wild primates use call systems to communicate. Contrasts between language and call systems include displacement, productivity, and cultural transmission. Over time, our ancestral call systems grew too complex for genetic transmission, and hominin communication began to rely on learning. Humans still use nonverbal communication, such as facial expressions, gestures, and body stances and movements. But language is the main system humans use to communicate. Chimps and gorillas can understand and manipulate nonverbal symbols based on language.

2. No language uses all the sounds the human vocal tract can make. Phonology—the study of speech sounds—focuses on sound contrasts (phonemes) that distinguish meaning. The grammars and lexicons of particular languages can lead their speakers to perceive and think in certain ways.

3. Linguistic anthropologists share anthropology's general interest in diversity in time and space. Sociolinguistics investigates relationships between social and linguistic variation by focusing on the actual use of language. Only when features of speech acquire social meaning are they imitated. If they are valued, they will spread. People vary their speech, shifting styles, dialects, and languages.

4. As linguistic systems, all languages and dialects are equally complex, rule-governed, and effective for communication. However, speech is used, is evaluated, and changes in the context of political, economic, and social forces. Often the linguistic traits of a low-status group are negatively evaluated. This devaluation is not because of linguistic features per se. Rather, it reflects the association of such features with low social status. One dialect, supported by the dominant institutions of the state, exercises symbolic domination over the others.

5. Historical linguistics is useful for anthropologists interested in historical relationships among populations. Cultural similarities and differences often correlate with linguistic ones. Linguistic clues can suggest past contacts between cultures. Related languages—members of the same language family—descend from an original protolanguage. Relationships between languages don't necessarily mean there are biological ties between their speakers, because people can learn new languages.

6. One aspect of linguistic history is language loss. The world's linguistic diversity has been cut in half in the past 500 years, and half of the remaining 7,000 languages are predicted to disappear during this century.

Think Like an Anthropologist

1. What dialects and languages do you speak? Do you tend to use different dialects, languages, or speech styles in different contexts? Why or why not?

2. Consider how changing technologies have affected how you communicate with family, friends, and even strangers. Suppose your best friend decides to study sociolinguistics in graduate school. What ideas about the relationship among changing technologies, language, and social relations could you suggest to him or her as worth studying?

Key Terms

Chapter 5

Making a Living

Adaptive Strategies

In today's globalizing world, communities and societies are being incorporated, at an accelerating rate, into larger systems (Caldararo 2014). The first major acceleration in the growth of human social systems can be traced back to around 12,000–10,000 years ago, when humans started intervening in the reproductive cycles of plants and animals. **Food production** refers to human control over the reproduction of plants and animals, and it contrasts with the foraging economies that preceded it and that still persist in some parts of the world. To make their living, foragers hunt, gather, and collect what nature has to offer. Foragers may harvest, but they don't plant. They may hunt animals, but (except for the dog) they don't domesticate them. Only food producers systematically select and breed for desirable traits in plants and animals. With the advent of food production, which includes plant cultivation and animal domestication, people, rather than nature, become selective agents. Human selection replaces natural selection as food collectors become food producers.

The origin and spread of food production accelerated human population growth and led to the formation of larger and more powerful social and political systems. The pace of cultural transformation increased enormously. This chapter provides a framework for understanding a variety of human adaptive strategies and economic systems.

The anthropologist Yehudi Cohen (1974) used the term *adaptive strategy* to describe a society's main system of economic production. Cohen argued that the most important reason for similarities between two (or more) unrelated societies is their possession of a similar adaptive strategy. In other words, similar economic causes have similar sociocultural effects. For example, there are clear similarities among societies that have a foraging (hunting and gathering) strategy. Cohen developed a typology of societies based on correlations between their economies and their social features. His typology includes these five adaptive strategies: foraging, horticulture, agriculture, pastoralism, and industrialism. Industrialism is the focus of the last two chapters of this book. The present chapter focuses on the first four adaptive strategies, which are characteristic of nonindustrial societies.

Foraging

Foraging—an economy and way of life based on hunting and gathering—was humans' only way of making a living until about 12,000 years ago, when people began experimenting with food production. To be sure, environmental differences created substantial contrasts among foragers living in different parts of the world. Some, like the people who lived in Europe during the ice ages, were big-game hunters. Today, hunters in the Arctic still focus on large animals. Those far northern foragers have much less vegetation and variety in their diets than do tropical foragers. Moving from colder to hotter areas, the number of species increases. The tropics contain tremendous biodiversity, and tropical foragers typically hunt and gather a wide range of plant and animal species. Some temperate areas also offer abundant and varied species. For example, on the North Pacific Coast of North America, foragers could draw on varied sea, river, and land species, such as salmon and other fish, sea mammals, mountain goats, and berries. Despite differences caused by such environmental variation, all foraging economies have shared one essential feature: People rely on nature to make their living. They don't grow crops or breed and tend animals.

Animal domestication (initially of sheep and goats) and plant cultivation (of wheat and barley) began 12,000 to 10,000 years ago in the Middle East. Cultivation based on different crops, such as corn (maize), manioc (cassava), and potatoes, arose independently in the Americas. In both hemispheres most societies eventually turned from foraging to food production. Today most foragers have at least some dependence on food production or on food producers (Kent 2002).

Foraging economies survived into modern times in certain forests, deserts, islands, and very cold areas—places where cultivation was not practicable with simple technology (see Lee and Daly 1999). Figure 5.1 presents a partial distribution of recent

FIGURE 5.1 **Locations of Some Recent Hunter-Gatherers**

Source: Kelly, Robert, L., *The Foraging Spectrum: Diversity in Hunter-Gatherer Lifeways,* fig. 1.1. Copyright © 2007 by Eliot Werner Publications, Inc. All rights reserved. Used with permission.

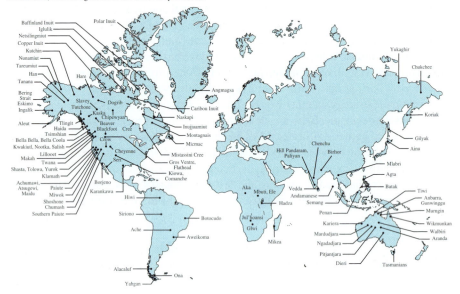

foragers. Their habitats tend to have one thing in common—their marginality. Posing major obstacles to food production, these environments did not attract farmers or herders. The difficulties of cultivating at the North Pole are obvious. In southern Africa, the Dobe Ju/'hoansi San area studied by Richard Lee and others is surrounded by a huge waterless belt (Solway and Lee 1990). Farming could not exist in much of California without irrigation, which is why its native populations were foragers.

We should not assume that foragers will inevitably turn to food production once they learn of its existence. In fact, foragers in many areas have been—and still are—in contact with farmers or herders, but they have chosen to maintain their hunter-gatherer lifestyle. Their traditional economy supports them well enough, lacks the labor requirements associated with farming and herding, and provides an adequate and nutritious diet. In some places, people have tried food production, only to abandon it eventually and return to foraging.

All surviving foragers now live in nation-states. Typically they are in contact with food-producing neighbors as well as with missionaries and other outsiders. We should not view contemporary foragers as isolated or pristine survivors of the Stone Age. Modern foragers are influenced by national and international policies and political and economic events in the world system.

Geographic Distribution of Foragers

It will be helpful to refer to Figure 5.1 throughout this section. Africa contains two broad belts of contemporary or recent foraging. One is the Kalahari Desert of southern Africa.

This is the home of the San ("Bushmen"), who include the Ju/'hoansi (Lee 2003, 2012). The other main African foraging area is the equatorial forest of central and eastern Africa, home of the Mbuti, Efe, and other "pygmies."

People still do, or until recently did, subsistence foraging in certain remote forests in Madagascar, in South and Southeast Asia, in Malaysia, in the Philippines, and on certain islands off the Indian coast. In addition, some of the best-known recent foragers are the Aborigines of Australia. Those Native Australians lived on their island continent for perhaps 50,000 years without developing food production.

The Western Hemisphere also had recent foragers. The Eskimos, or Inuit, of Alaska and Canada are well-known hunters. These (and other) northern foragers now use modern technology, including rifles and snowmobiles, in their subsistence activities. The native populations of the North Pacific Coast of North America (northern California, Oregon, Washington, British Columbia, and southern Alaska) all were foragers, as were those of inland subarctic Canada and the Great Lakes. For many Native Americans, fishing, hunting, and gathering remain important subsistence (and sometimes commercial) activities. Considering South America, there were coastal foragers along that continent's southern tip, in Patagonia. Additional foragers inhabited the grassy plains of Argentina, southern Brazil, Uruguay, and Paraguay.

Jana Fortier (2009) summarizes key attributes of foragers in South Asia, which today is home to more full- and part-time hunter-gatherers than any other world area. In India, Nepal, and Sri Lanka, about 40 societies and an estimated 150,000 people continue to derive their subsistence from full- or part-time foraging. The Hill Kharia and the Yanadi are the largest contemporary South Asian foraging populations, with about 20,000 members each. Several other ethnic groups are highly endangered, with fewer than 350 members still engaging in subsistence foraging.

Surviving South Asian foraging societies are those whose members, despite having lost many of their natural resources to deforestation and spreading farming populations, have been unwilling to adopt food cultivation and its cultural correlates. These hunter-gatherers share features with other foragers worldwide: small social groups, mobile settlement patterns, sharing of resources, immediate food consumption, egalitarianism, and decision making by mutual consent (Fortier 2009).

As is true elsewhere, specific foraging techniques reflect variations in environment and resource distribution. Hill and mountain South Asian foragers favor focused hunting of medium-sized prey (langur monkey, macaque, porcupine). Other groups pursue several small species or practice broad-spectrum foraging of bats, porcupines, and deer. Larger groups use communal hunting techniques, such as spreading nets over large fig trees to entangle sleeping bats. Some South Indian foragers focus on such wild plant resources as yams, palms, and taro, in addition to more than 100 locally available plants. Harvesting honey and beeswax has been prominent in many South Asian foraging societies (Fortier 2009).

Members of these societies cherish their identities as people who forage for a living in biologically rich and diverse environments. They stress their need for continued access to rich forest resources to continue their lifestyles, yet many have been evicted from their traditional habitats. Their best chances for cultural survival depend on national governments that maintain healthy forests, allow foragers access to their traditional resources, and foster cultural survival rather than assimilation (Fortier 2009).

Some governments have done quite the opposite. For example, between 1997 and 2002, the government of Botswana (in southern Africa) carried out a relocation scheme affecting about 3,000 Basarwa San Bushmen (Motseta 2006). The government forced these people to leave their ancestral territory, which became a wildlife reserve. After some of them sued, Botswana's High Court eventually ruled that the Basarwa had been wrongly evicted, and issued a court order allowing them to return, but under very restrictive conditions. Although 3,000 people had been relocated, only the 189 people who actually filed the lawsuit were granted an automatic right of return with their children. The many other Basarwa San who wanted to return to their ancestral territory would need to apply for special permits. Even the 189 favored people would be allowed to build only temporary structures and to use only enough water for subsistence needs. Water would be a major obstacle, because the government had shut down the main well. Furthermore, anyone wishing to hunt would have to apply for a permit. This case illustrates how contemporary governments can limit the independence of indigenous peoples and restrict their traditional lifestyle.

Correlates of Foraging

Typologies, such as Cohen's adaptive strategies, are useful because they suggest **correlations**—that is, associations or covariations between two or more variables. (Correlated variables are factors that are linked and interrelated, such as food intake and body weight. When one increases or decreases, the other changes as well.) Ethnographic studies in hundreds of societies have revealed many correlations between the economy and social life. Associated (correlated) with each adaptive strategy is a bundle of particular sociocultural features. Correlations, however, rarely are perfect. Some foragers lack cultural features usually associated with foraging, and some of those features are found in groups with other adaptive strategies.

What, then, are some correlates of foraging? People who subsisted by hunting and gathering often, but not always, lived in band-organized societies. Their basic social unit, the **band,** was a small group of fewer than a hundred people, all related by kinship or marriage. Among some foragers, band size stayed about the same year-round. In others, the band split up for part of the year. Families left to gather resources that were better exploited by just a few people. Later, they regrouped for cooperative work and ceremonies.

Typical characteristics of the foraging life are flexibility and mobility. In many San groups, as among the Mbuti of Congo, people shifted band membership several times in a lifetime. One could be born, for example, in a band in which one's mother had kin. Later, one's family could move to a band in which the father had relatives. Because bands were exogamous (people married outside their own bands), one's parents came from two different bands, and one's grandparents could have come from four. People could join any band to which they had kin or marital links. A couple could live in, or shift between, the husband's and the wife's bands.

Foraging societies tend to be *egalitarian*. That is, they make few status distinctions, and the ones they make are based mainly on age, gender, and personal qualities or achievements. For example, old people—elders—may receive respect as guardians of myths, legends, stories, and traditions. Younger people may value the elders' special knowledge of ritual and practical matters. A good hunter, an especially productive gatherer, or a skilled midwife or shaman may be recognized as such. But foragers are known for sharing rather than bragging. Their status distinctions are not associated with differences in wealth and power, nor are they inherited. When considering issues of "human nature," we should remember that the egalitarian society associated with foraging was a basic form of human social life for most of our history. Food production has existed less than 1 percent of the time *Homo* has spent on Earth. However, it has produced huge social differences. We now consider the main economic features of food-producing strategies.

Adaptive Strategies Based on Food Production

In Cohen's typology, the three adaptive strategies based on food production in nonindustrial societies are horticulture, agriculture, and pastoralism. With horticulture and agriculture, plant cultivation is the mainstay of the economy, whereas with pastoralism, herding is key. All three strategies originated in nonindustrial societies, although they may persist as ways of making a living even after some degree of industrialization reaches the nation-states that include them. In fully industrial societies, such as the United States and Canada, most cultivation has become large-scale, commercial, mechanized, agrochemical-dependent farming. Rather than simple pastoralism, industrial societies use technologically sophisticated systems of ranch and livestock management. These industrial societies, and their global context, are the focus of the last two chapters of this book. This chapter's focus is on nonindustrial strategies of adaptation.

Food producers typically carry out a variety of economic activities. In Cohen's typology, each adaptive strategy refers to the main economic activity. Pastoralists (herders), for example, consume milk, blood, and meat from their animals as mainstays of their diet. However, they also add grain to their diet by doing some cultivating or by trading with neighbors.

Horticulture

The two types of plant cultivation found in nonindustrial societies are **horticulture** (nonintensive, shifting cultivation) and **agriculture** (intensive, continuous cultivation). Both differ from the commercially oriented farming systems of industrial nations, which use large land areas and rely on machinery and agrochemicals.

When food production arose, both in the Middle East and in Mexico, the earliest cultivators were rainfall-dependent horticulturalists. More recently, horticulture has been—and in many cases still is—the primary form of cultivation in parts of Africa, Southeast Asia, the Pacific islands, Mexico, Central America, and the South American tropical forest.

Horticulturalists use simple tools such as hoes and digging sticks to grow their crops. Horticulturalists typically rely on *slash-and-burn* techniques. Farmers clear land by cutting down (slashing) trees, saplings, and brush. Then they burn that vegetation. They also may set fire directly to grasses and weeds on their farm plots before planting. Slashing and burning not only gets rid of unwanted vegetation, but it also kills pests and provides ashes that help fertilize the soil. The farmers then sow, tend, and harvest their crops on the cleared plot. They do not use that plot continuously; often they farm it for only a year or two.

In slash-and-burn horticulture, the land is cleared by cutting down (slashing) and burning trees and brush, using simple technology, as is done here among mountain rice farmers in the hills of Thailand.
©Universal Images Group via Getty Images

Horticulture also is known as *shifting cultivation*, because farmers shift back and forth between plots, rather than using any one of those plots continuously. With shifting cultivation, horticulturalists farm a plot for a year or two, then abandon it, clear another plot, cultivate it for a year or two, then abandon it, and so on. After the original plot lies fallow for several years (the duration varies in different societies), it can be farmed again.

Shifting cultivation doesn't mean that whole villages must move when plots are abandoned. Horticulture can support large, permanent villages. Among the Kuikuru of the South American tropical forest, for example, one village of 150 people remained in the same place for 90 years (Carneiro 1956). Kuikuru houses are large and well made. Because the work involved in building them is great, the Kuikuru preferred to walk farther to their fields, rather than construct a new village. They chose to shift their plots rather than their villages. By contrast, other horticulturalists in the montaña (Andean foothills) of Peru maintained small villages of about 30 people (Carneiro 1961/1968). Their houses were small, simple, and easy to rebuild. They would stay a few years in one place, then move on to a different site near their fields where they would build new homes. They preferred rebuilding to walking even a half-mile to their fields.

Agriculture

The greater labor demands associated with agriculture, as compared with horticulture, reflect the former's use of domesticated animals, irrigation, or terracing.

Domesticated Animals

Many agriculturists use animals as means of production—for transport, as cultivating machines, and for their manure. Asian farmers typically incorporate cattle and/or water buffalo into their agricultural economies. Those rice farmers may use cattle to trample pre-tilled flooded fields, thus mixing soil and water, before transplanting. Many agriculturists attach animals to plows and harrows for field preparation before planting or transplanting. Also, agriculturists typically collect manure from their animals, using it to fertilize their plots, thus increasing yields. Animals are attached to carts for transport and to implements of cultivation.

Irrigation

Whereas horticulturalists must await the rainy season, agriculturists can schedule their planting in advance because they control water. Like other irrigation experts in the Philippines, the Ifugao water their fields with canals from rivers, streams, springs, and ponds. Irrigation makes it possible to cultivate a plot year after year. Irrigation enriches the soil because the irrigated field is a unique ecosystem with several species of plants and animals, many of them minute organisms, whose wastes fertilize the land.

An irrigated field is a capital investment that usually increases in value. It takes time for a field to start yielding; it reaches full productivity only after several years of cultivation. The Ifugao, like other irrigators, have farmed the same fields for generations. In some agricultural areas, including the Middle East, however, salts carried in the irrigation water can make fields unusable after 50 or 60 years.

Terracing

Terracing is another agricultural technique the Ifugao have mastered. Their homeland has small valleys separated by steep hillsides. Because the population is dense, people need to farm the hills. However, if they simply planted on the steep hillsides, fertile soil and crops would be washed away during the rainy season. To prevent this, the Ifugao cut into the hillside and build stage after stage of terraced fields rising above the valley floor. Springs located above the terraces supply their irrigation water. The labor

Agriculture requires longer work hours than horticulture does and uses land intensively and continuously. Labor demands associated with agriculture reflect its use of domesticated animals, irrigation, and terracing. Shown here, rice terraces surround a farming village in Longsheng, Guangxi province, China. ©KingWu/iStockphoto.com RF

necessary to build and maintain a system of terraces is great. Terrace walls crumble each year and must be partially rebuilt. The canals that bring water down through the terraces also demand attention.

Costs and Benefits of Agriculture

Agriculture requires human labor to build and maintain irrigation systems, terraces, and other works. People must feed, water, and care for their animals. But agricultural land can yield one or two crops annually for years, or even generations. An agricultural field does not necessarily produce a higher single-year yield than does a horticultural plot. The first crop grown by horticulturalists on long-idle land may be larger than that from an agricultural plot of the same size. Furthermore, because agriculturists have to work more hours than horticulturalists do, agriculture's yield relative to the labor time invested also is lower. Agriculture's main advantage is that the long-term yield per area is far greater and more dependable. Because a single field sustains its owners year after year, there is no need to maintain a reserve of uncultivated land as horticulturalists do. This is why agricultural societies tend to be more densely populated than horticultural ones.

The Cultivation Continuum

Because some nonindustrial economies have features of both horticulture and agriculture, it is useful to discuss cultivators as being arranged along a **cultivation continuum.** Horticultural systems stand at one end—the "low-labor, shifting-plot" end. Agriculturalists are at the other—the "labor-intensive, permanent-plot" end.

We speak of a continuum because there are intermediate economies, which combine horticultural and agricultural features. In such economies, cultivation is more intensive than with annually shifting horticulture, but less so than with permanent agriculture. The South American Kuikuru, for example, grow two or three crops of manioc, or cassava—an edible tuber—before abandoning their plots. Cultivation is even more intensive in certain densely populated areas of Papua New Guinea, where plots are planted for two or three years, allowed to rest for three to five, and then recultivated. After several of these cycles, the plots are abandoned for a longer fallow period. These intermediate economies, which support denser populations than does simple horticulture, also are found in parts of West Africa and in the highlands of Mexico, Peru, and Bolivia.

The one key difference between horticulture and agriculture is that *horticulture always has a fallow period,* whereas agriculture does not.

Agricultural Intensification: People and the Environment

The range of environments available for cultivation has widened as people have increased their control over nature. Agriculturists have been able to colonize many areas that are too arid for nonirrigators or too hilly for nonterracers. Agriculture's increased labor intensity and permanent land use have major demographic, social, political, and environmental consequences.

How, specifically, does agriculture affect society and the environment? Because of their permanent fields, agriculturists tend to be sedentary. People live in larger and more permanent communities located closer to other settlements. Growth in population size and density increases contact between individuals and groups. There is more need to regulate interpersonal relations, including conflicts of interest. Economies that support more people usually require more coordination in the use of land, labor, and other resources (see Chapter 6).

Intensive agriculture has significant environmental effects. Irrigation ditches and paddies (fields with irrigated rice) become repositories for organic wastes, chemicals (such as salts), and disease microorganisms. Intensive agriculture typically spreads at the expense of trees and forests, which are cut down to be replaced by fields. Accompanying such deforestation is loss of environmental diversity (see Dove and Carpenter 2008). Compared with horticulture, agricultural economies are specialized. They focus on one or a few caloric staples, such as rice, and on the animals that aid the agricultural economy. Because tropical horticulturalists typically cultivate dozens of plant species simultaneously, a horticultural plot mirrors the botanical diversity found in a tropical forest. Agricultural plots, by contrast, reduce ecological diversity by cutting down trees and concentrating on just a few staple foods. Such crop specialization is true of agriculturists both in the tropics (e.g., Indonesian paddy farmers) and outside the tropics (e.g., Middle Eastern irrigation farmers).

Agriculturists attempt to reduce risk in production by favoring stability in the form of a reliable annual harvest and long-term production. Tropical foragers and horticulturalists, by contrast, attempt to reduce risk by relying on multiple species and benefiting from ecological diversity. The agricultural strategy is to put all one's eggs in one big and very dependable basket. The strategy of tropical foragers and horticulturalists is to have several smaller baskets, a few of which may fail without endangering subsistence. The agricultural strategy makes sense when there are lots of children to raise and adults to be fed. Foraging and horticulture, of course, are associated with smaller, sparser, and more mobile populations.

Agricultural economies also pose a series of regulatory problems. How is water to be managed? How are disputes about access to and distribution of water to be resolved? With more people living closer together on more valuable land, agriculturists have more opportunities for interpersonal contact and conflict than foragers and horticulturalists do. The social and political implications of food production and intensification are examined more fully in Chapter 6, on political systems.

Anthropologists know that many indigenous groups—especially foragers and nonintensive cultivators—have done a reasonable job of managing their resources and preserving their ecosystems (see Menzies 2006). Such societies had traditional ways of categorizing resources and regulating their use. Increasingly, however, these traditional management systems have been challenged by national and international incentives to exploit and degrade the environment (see Dove, Sajise, and Doolittle 2011). These challenges are the focus of the last two chapters of this book.

Pastoralism

Herders, or **pastoralists,** are people whose activities focus on such domesticated animals as cattle, sheep, goats, camels, yak, and reindeer. They live in North and sub-Saharan Africa, the Middle East, Europe, and Asia. East African pastoralists, like many others, live in symbiosis with their herds. (*Symbiosis* is an obligatory interaction between groups—here, humans and animals—that is beneficial to each.) Herders attempt to protect their animals and to ensure their reproduction in return for food (dairy products and meat) and other products, such as leather.

People use livestock in various ways. Natives of North America's Great Plains, for example, didn't eat, but only rode, their horses. (They got those horses after Europeans reintroduced them to the Western Hemisphere; the native American horse had gone extinct thousands of years earlier.) For Plains Indians, horses served as "tools of the trade," means of production used to *hunt* buffalo, the main target of their economies. So the Plains Indians were not true pastoralists but hunters who used horses—as many agriculturists use animals—as means of production.

Pastoralists, by contrast, typically use their herds for food. They consume their meat, blood, and milk, from which they make yogurt, butter, and cheese. Although some pastoralists rely on their herds more completely than others do, it is impossible to base subsistence solely on animals. Most pastoralists therefore supplement their diet by hunting, gathering, fishing, cultivating, or trading.

The Samis (also known as Lapps or Laplanders) of Norway, Sweden, and Finland domesticated the reindeer, which their ancestors had once hunted, in the 16th century. Like other herders, they follow their animals as they make an annual trek, in this case from coast to interior. Today's Samis use modern technology, such as snowmobiles and four-wheel-drive vehicles, to accompany their herds on their annual nomadic trek. Some of them probably use reindeer management software on their laptops, tablets, or smartphones. Although their environment is harsher, the Samis, like other herders, live in nation-states and must deal with outsiders, including government officials, as they follow their herds and make their living through animal husbandry, trade, and sales (Hoge 2001; Paine 2009).

Unlike foraging and cultivation, which existed throughout the world before the Industrial Revolution, pastoralism was confined almost totally to the Old World. Before European conquest, the only herders in the Americas lived in the Andean region of South America. They used their llamas and alpacas for food and wool and in agriculture and transport. Much more recently, the Navajo of the southwestern United States developed a pastoral economy based on sheep, which were brought to North America by Europeans. The populous Navajo became the major pastoral population in the Western Hemisphere.

Two patterns of movement occur with pastoralism: *nomadism* and *transhumance*. Both are based on the fact that herds must move to use pasture available in particular places in different seasons. In **pastoral nomadism,** the entire group—women, men, and children—moves with the animals throughout the year. The Middle East and North Africa provide numerous examples of pastoral nomads (see Salzman 2008). In Iran, for example, the Basseri and the Qashqai ethnic groups traditionally followed a nomadic route more than 300 miles (480 kilometers) long (see Salzman 2004).

With **transhumance,** part of the group moves with the herds but most people stay in the home village. There are examples from Europe and Africa. In Europe's Alps it is just the shepherds and goatherds—not the whole hamlet, village, or town—who accompany the flocks to highland meadows in summer. Among the Turkana of Uganda, men and boys take the herds to distant pastures, while much of the village stays put and does some horticultural farming. During their annual trek, pastoral nomads trade for crops and other products with more sedentary people. Transhumants don't have to trade for

Pastoralists may be nomadic or transhumant, but they don't typically live off their herds alone. They either trade or cultivate. Shown here, a transhumant shepherd with his herd in Eifel Rheinland Pfalz, Germany. ©tbkmedia.de/Alamy Stock Photo RF

crops. Because only part of the population accompanies the herds, transhumants can maintain year-round villages and grow their own crops.

Economic Systems

An **economy** is a system of production, distribution, and consumption of resources; *economics* is the study of such systems. Economists tend to focus on modern nations and capitalist systems. Anthropologists have broadened understanding of economic principles by gathering data on nonindustrial economies. Economic anthropology brings a comparative perspective to the study of economics (see Carrier 2012; Chibnik 2011; Gudeman 2016; Hann and Hart 2011; Sahlins 2011).

A **mode of production** is a way of organizing production—"a set of social relations through which labor is deployed to wrest energy from nature by means of tools, skills, organization, and knowledge" (Wolf 1982, p. 75). In the capitalist mode of production, money buys labor power, and a social gap exists between the people (bosses and workers) involved in the production process. By contrast, in nonindustrial societies, labor usually is not bought but is given as a social obligation. In such a *kin-based* mode of production, mutual aid in production is one among many expressions of a larger web of social relations (see Marshall 2011). A kin-based mode of production typifies foragers, horticulturalists, pastoralists, and many agriculturalists, especially those lacking state organization.

Societies with the same strategy of adaptation (e.g., foraging) and the same mode of production (e.g., kin-based), can organize the specifics of production differently. For example, foraging can be done by individual hunters or teams, depending on whether the game is solitary, or a herd or flocking animal. Gathering usually is more individualistic than is hunting, although collecting teams may assemble when abundant resources ripen and must be harvested quickly. Fishing may be done alone (as in ice or spear fishing) or in crews (as with open-sea fishing and hunting of sea mammals).

Organization of Production in Nonindustrial Societies

Although some kind of division of economic labor related to age and gender is a cultural universal, the specific tasks assigned to each sex and to people of different ages vary (see Chapter 8). Many horticultural societies assign a major productive role to women, but some make men's work primary. Similarly, among pastoralists, men generally tend large animals, but in some societies women do the milking. Jobs accomplished through teamwork in some cultivating societies are done in other societies by smaller groups or by individuals working over a longer period.

The Betsileo of Madagascar have two stages of teamwork in rice cultivation: transplanting and harvesting. Both activities feature a traditional division of labor by age and gender that is well known to all Betsileo and is repeated across the generations. The first job in the transplanting process is the trampling of a previously tilled and flooded field by young men driving cattle, in order to mix earth and water. The young men yell at and beat the cattle, striving to drive them into a frenzy, so that they will trample the fields properly. Trampling breaks up clumps of earth and mixes irrigation water with soil to form a smooth mud, into which women will soon transplant seedlings. Once the tramplers leave the field, older men arrive. With their spades, they break up the clumps that the cattle missed. Meanwhile, the owner and other adults uproot rice seedlings and take them to the field, where women will transplant them.

At harvest time, four or five months later, young men cut the rice off the stalks. Young women carry it to the clearing above the field. Older women arrange and stack it. The oldest men and women then stand on the stack, stomping and compacting it. Three days later, young men thresh the rice, beating the stalks against a rock to remove the grain. Older men then beat the stalks with sticks to make sure all the grains have fallen off.

Means of Production

In nonindustrial societies the relationship between the worker and the means of production is more intimate than it is in industrial nations. **Means, or factors, of production** include land (territory), technology, and the available labor supply.

Land as a Means of Production

Among foragers, ties between people and land are less permanent than they are among food producers. The borders between foraging territories are neither precisely demarcated nor enforced. A hunter's stake in pursuit of an animal is more important than where that animal finally dies. One acquires the right to use a band's territory by being born in that band or by joining it through a tie of kinship or marriage. On changing bands, one immediately acquires rights to hunt or gather in its territory.

Among food producers, rights to the means of production also come through kinship and marriage. Descent groups (groups whose members claim common ancestry) are common among nonindustrial food producers. Those who descend from the founder share the group's territory and resources. If the adaptive strategy is horticulture, the estate includes gardens and fallow land for shifting cultivation. With pastoralism, descent group members have access to animals to start their own herds, to grazing land, to garden land, and to other means of production.

Labor, Tools, and Specialization

Like land, the labor supply is a means of production. In nonindustrial societies, access to both land and labor comes through social links such as kinship, marriage, and descent. Mutual aid in production is merely one aspect of ongoing social relations that are expressed on many other occasions.

Nonindustrial societies contrast with industrial nations regarding another means of production—technology. Manufacturing often is linked to age and gender. Women may weave and men may make pottery, or vice versa. Most people of a particular age and gender share the technical knowledge associated with that age and gender. If married women customarily make baskets, most married women know how to make baskets. Neither technology nor technical knowledge is very specialized.

Some tribal societies, however, do promote specialization. Among the Yanomami of Venezuela and Brazil, for instance, certain villages manufacture clay pots and others make hammocks. They don't specialize, as one might suppose, because certain raw materials happen to be available near particular villages. Clay suitable for pots is widely available. Everyone knows how to make pots, but not everybody does so. Craft specialization reflects the social and political environment rather than the natural environment. Such specialization promotes trade, which is the first step in creating an alliance with enemy villages (Chagnon 2013).

Alienation in Industrial Economies

There are significant contrasts between nonindustrial economies and industrial ones. In the former, economic relations are just one part of a larger, multidimensional social matrix. People don't just work for and with others; they live with those same people; they pray with, feast with, and care about them. One works for and with people with whom one has long-term personal and social bonds (e.g., kin and in-laws).

In industrial societies, by contrast, workers sell their labor to bosses who can fire them. Work and the workplace are separated—*alienated*—from one's social essence. Rather than expressing an ongoing, mutual social relationship, labor becomes a thing (commodity) to be paid for, bought, and sold—and from which the boss can generate an individual profit. Furthermore, industrial workers usually don't work with their relatives and neighbors. If coworkers are friends, the personal relationship often develops out of their common employment rather than a previous social tie.

In nonindustrial societies, an individual who makes something can use or dispose of it as he or she sees fit. The maker may feel pride in such a personal product and, if it is given away, a renewed commitment to the social relationship that is reinforced by the gift. On the other hand, when factory workers produce for their employer's profit, their

In a garment factory in Hlaing Tharyar, Myanmar, Burmese women stitch sports clothing for a Taiwanese company. Their average wage is less than one American dollar per day. Throughout Southeast Asia, hundreds of thousands of young women from peasant families now work in factories. Chances are good that you own one of their products. ©Paula Bronstein/Getty Images News/Getty Images

products as well as their labor are alienated. Their bosses have use or disposal rights. Human labor and its products belong to someone other than the individual producer. Unlike assembly-line workers, producers in nonindustrial societies typically see their work through from start to finish and feel a sense of accomplishment.

Thus, industrial workers have impersonal relations with their employers, coworkers, and products. People sell their labor for cash in a market economy, and work stands apart from family life. In nonindustrial societies, by contrast, the relations of production, distribution, and consumption are social relations with economic aspects. Economy is not a separate entity but is *embedded* in the society.

A Case of Industrial Alienation

For decades, the government of Malaysia has promoted export-oriented industry, allowing transnational companies to install manufacturing operations in rural Malaysia. In search of cheaper labor, corporations headquartered in Japan, Western Europe, and the United States have moved labor-intensive factories to developing countries. Malaysia has hundreds of Japanese and American subsidiaries, which produce garments, foodstuffs, and electronics components. Thousands of young Malaysian women from rural families now assemble microchips and microcomponents for transistors and capacitors. Aihwa Ong (1987; Ong and Collier 2010) did a study of electronics assembly workers in an area where 85 percent of the workers were young, unmarried females from nearby villages.

Ong found that, unlike village women, female factory workers had to cope with a rigid work routine and constant supervision by men. The discipline that factories enforce was being taught in local schools, where uniforms helped prepare girls for the factory dress code. Village women wore loose, flowing tunics, sarongs, and sandals, but factory workers had to don tight overalls and heavy rubber gloves, in which they felt constrained. Assembling electronics components requires precise, concentrated labor. Labor in these factories illustrates the separation of intellectual and manual activity— the alienation that Karl Marx considered the defining feature of industrial work. One woman said about her bosses, "They exhaust us very much, as if they do not think that we too are human beings" (Ong 1987, p. 202). Nor does factory work bring women a substantial financial reward, given low wages, job uncertainty, and family claims on wages. Although young women typically work just a few years, production quotas, three daily shifts, overtime, and surveillance take their toll in mental and physical exhaustion.

One response to factory relations of production has been spirit possession (factory women are possessed by spirits). Ong interprets this phenomenon as the women's unconscious protest against labor discipline and male control of the industrial setting. Sometimes possession takes the form of mass hysteria. Spirits have simultaneously invaded as many as 120 factory workers. Weretigers (the Malay equivalent of the werewolf) arrive to avenge the construction of a factory on local burial grounds. Disturbed earth and grave spirits swarm on the shop floor. First the women see the spirits; then their bodies are invaded. The weretigers send the women into sobbing, laughing, and shrieking fits. To deal with possession, factories employ local medicine men, who sacrifice chickens and goats to fend off the spirits. This solution works only some of the time; possession still goes on. Ong argues that spirit possession expresses anguish at, and resistance to, the capitalist mode of production. By engaging in this form of rebellion, however, factory women avoid a direct confrontation with the source of their distress. Ong concludes that spirit possession, while expressing repressed resentment, doesn't do much to modify factory conditions. (Other tactics, such as unionization, would do more.) Spirit possession may even help maintain the current system by operating as a safety valve for accumulated tensions.

Economizing and Maximization

Economic anthropologists have been concerned with two main questions:

1. How are production, distribution, and consumption organized in different societies? This question focuses on *systems* of human behavior and their organization.
2. What motivates people in different societies to produce, distribute or exchange, and consume? Here the focus is not on systems of behavior but on the *individuals* who participate in those systems.

Anthropologists view economic systems and motivations in a cross-cultural perspective. Motivation is a concern of psychologists, but it also has been a concern of economists and anthropologists. American economists assume that people make decisions rationally, guided by the *profit motive*. Although anthropologists know that the profit motive is not universal, the assumption that individuals try to maximize profits is basic to capitalism and to Western economic theory. In fact, the subject matter of economics often is defined as economizing, or the rational allocation of scarce means (or resources) to alternative ends (or uses) (see Chibnik 2011).

What does that mean? Classical economic theory assumes that our wants are infinite, while our means are limited. People must make choices about how to use their scarce resources—their time, labor, money, and capital. (This chapter's "Anthropology Today" disputes the idea that people always make economic choices based on scarcity.) Western economists assume that when confronted with choices and decisions, people tend to make the one that maximizes profit. This is assumed to be the most rational choice.

The idea that individuals choose to maximize profits was a basic assumption of the classical economists of the 19th century and one held by many contemporary economists. However, certain economists now recognize that individuals may be motivated by many other goals. Depending on the society and the situation, people may try to maximize profit, wealth, prestige, pleasure, comfort, social harmony, or spiritual goals. Individuals may want to realize their personal, family, or community ambitions, or those of some other group to which they belong (see Chibnik 2011; Sahlins 2011).

Alternative Ends

To what uses do people put their scarce resources? Throughout the world, people devote some of their time and energy to building up a *subsistence fund* (Wolf 1966). In other words, they have to work to eat, to replace the calories they use in daily activity. People also must invest in a *replacement fund*. They must maintain their technology and other items essential to production. If a hoe or plow breaks, they must repair or replace it. They also must obtain and replace items that are essential not to production but to everyday life, such as clothing and shelter.

People everywhere also have to invest in a *social fund*. They must help their friends, relatives, in-laws, and neighbors. It is useful to distinguish between a social fund and a *ceremonial fund*. The latter term refers to expenditures on ceremonies or rituals. To prepare a festival honoring one's ancestors, for example, requires time and the outlay of wealth.

Citizens of nation-states also must allocate scarce resources to a *rent fund*. We think of rent as payment for the use of property. Rent fund, however, has a wider meaning. It refers to resources that people must render to an individual or agency that is superior politically or economically. Tenant farmers and sharecroppers, for example, either pay rent or give some of their produce to their landlords, as peasants did under feudalism. The rent fund also includes taxes, which people typically pay in state-organized societies.

Peasants are small-scale farmers who live in state-organized societies and have rent fund obligations. They produce to feed themselves, to sell their produce, and to pay rent. All peasants have two things in common:

1. They live in state-organized societies.
2. They produce food without the elaborate technology—chemical fertilizers, tractors, airplanes to spray crops, and so on—of modern farming or agribusiness.

Besides paying rent to landlords, peasants must satisfy government obligations, paying taxes in the form of money, produce, or labor. The rent fund is not simply an *additional* obligation for peasants. Often it becomes their foremost and unavoidable duty. Sometimes their own diets suffer as a result. The demands of social superiors may divert resources from subsistence, replacement, social, and ceremonial funds.

Motivations vary from society to society, and people often lack freedom of choice in allocating their resources. Because of obligations to pay rent, peasants may allocate their scarce means toward ends that are not their own but those of government officials. Thus, even in societies in which there is a profit motive, people often are prevented from rationally maximizing self-interest by factors beyond their control.

Distribution, Exchange

The economist Karl Polanyi (1968) was a key early contributor to the comparative study of exchanges (e.g., gift giving, trade between individuals and/or groups), and several anthropologists followed his lead. Polanyi defined three principles that guide exchanges: the market principle, redistribution, and reciprocity. These principles all can be present in the same society, but in that case they govern different kinds of transactions. In any society, one of them usually dominates. The principle that dominates in a given society is the one that determines how the means of production are exchanged (see Chibnik 2011; Hann and Hart 2011).

The Market Principle

In today's world capitalist economy, the **market principle** dominates. It governs the distribution of the means of production—land, labor, natural resources, technology, knowledge, and capital. With market exchange, items are bought and sold, using money, with an eye to maximizing profit, and value is determined by the *law of supply and demand* (things cost more the scarcer they are and the more people want them). Bargaining is characteristic of market-principle exchanges. The buyer and seller strive to maximize something—to get what they feel is their "money's worth." Bargaining doesn't require that the buyer and seller meet. Consumers bargain whenever they shop around or use advertisements or the Internet in their decision making (see Hann and Hart 2009; Madra 2004).

Redistribution

Redistribution occurs when products, such as a portion of the annual harvest, move from the local level to a center, from which they eventually flow back out. That center may be a capital, a regional collection point, or a storehouse near a chief's residence. Redistribution typically occurs in societies that have chiefs. To reach the center, where they will be stored, products often move through a hierarchy of officials. Along the way, those officials and their dependents may consume some, but never all, of the products. After reaching the center, the flow of goods eventually will reverse direction—out from the center, down through the hierarchy, and back to the common people. Redistribution is a way of moving a variety of goods from different areas to a central point, where they are stored and eventually supplied to the public. The custom of tithing encouraged by many religions is a form of redistribution, in that what the church receives can be used (redistributed) to benefit the needy.

One example of redistribution comes from the Cherokee, Native Americans who were the original inhabitants of the Tennessee Valley. The Cherokee were productive cultivators of maize, beans, and squash, which they supplemented by hunting and fishing. They also had chiefs. Each of their main villages had a central plaza, where meetings of the chief's council took place and where redistributive feasts were held. According to Cherokee custom, each family farm had an area where the family could set aside part of its annual harvest for the chief. This supply of corn was used to feed the needy, as well as travelers and warriors journeying through Cherokee territory. This store of food was available to all who needed it, with the understanding that it "belonged" to the chief and was available through his generosity. The chief also hosted the redistributive feasts held in the main settlements. On those occasions, ordinary people were able to consume some of the produce they had previously given in the chief's name (Harris 1978).

Reciprocity

Reciprocity is the act of reciprocating—giving back, returning a favor, repaying a debt. More specifically, economic anthropologists use the term **reciprocity** to refer to exchanges between social equals, people who are related by some kind of personal tie, such as kinship or marriage. Because it occurs between social equals, reciprocity is the dominant exchange principle in the more egalitarian societies—among foragers, cultivators, and pastoralists.

There are three forms of reciprocity: generalized, balanced, and negative (Sahlins 1968, 2011; Service 1966). These may be imagined as areas along a continuum defined by these questions:

1. How closely related are the parties to the exchange?
2. How quickly and unselfishly are gifts reciprocated?

The exchanges that occur between the most closely related people illustrate *generalized reciprocity*. There is no expectation of immediate return of a gift or favor. With *balanced reciprocity,* social distance increases, as does the need to reciprocate. In *negative reciprocity,* social distance is greatest and reciprocation is most calculated. This range, from generalized through balanced to negative, is called the **reciprocity continuum.**

With **generalized reciprocity,** someone gives to another person and expects nothing immediately in return. Such exchanges are not primarily economic transactions but expressions of personal relationships. Most parents don't keep accounts of all the time, money, and energy they expend on behalf of their children. They merely hope their children will respect their culture's customs involving obligations to parents.

Among foragers, generalized reciprocity—unselfish giving with no immediate expectation of return—tends to govern exchanges. People routinely share with other band members. So strong is the ethic of sharing that most foragers lack an expression for "thank you." To offer thanks would be impolite because it would imply that a particular act of sharing, which is the keystone of egalitarian society, was unusual. Among the Semai, foragers of central Malaysia (Dentan 2008), to express gratitude would suggest surprise at a hunter's success (see also Zhang 2016).

Balanced reciprocity characterizes exchanges between people who are more distantly related than are members of the same band or household. In a horticultural society, for example, a man presents a gift to a distant cousin, a trading partner, or a brother-in-law. The giver expects something in return. This may not come immediately, but the social relationship will be strained if there is no reciprocation.

Exchanges in nonindustrial societies also may illustrate **negative reciprocity,** mainly in dealing with people beyond their social systems. To people who live in a world of close personal relations, exchanges with outsiders are full of ambiguity and distrust. Exchange is one way of establishing friendly relations, but when trade begins, the relationship is still tentative. Initially, people seek to get something back immediately. Just as in market economies, but without using money, they try to get the best possible immediate return for their investment (see Clark 2010; Hann and Hart 2009).

Generalized reciprocity and balanced reciprocity are based on trust and a social tie. With negative reciprocity, the goal is to get something for as little as possible, even if it means being cagey or deceitful or cheating. Among the most extreme and "negative" examples was 19th-century horse thievery by North American Plains Indians. Men would sneak into camps of neighboring tribes to steal horses. Such thefts were likely to be reciprocated. A similar pattern of livestock (cattle) raiding continues today in East Africa, among tribes such as the Kuria (Fleisher 2000). In these cases, the party that starts the raiding can expect reciprocity—a raid on their own village—or worse. The Kuria hunt down cattle thieves and kill them. It's still reciprocity, governed by "Do unto others as they have done unto you."

One way of reducing the tension in situations of potential negative reciprocity is to engage in "silent trade." One example was the silent trade of the Mbuti pygmy foragers of the African equatorial forest and their neighboring horticultural villagers. There was no personal contact during their exchanges. A Mbuti hunter left game, honey, or another forest product at a customary site. Villagers collected it and left crops in exchange. Often the parties bargained silently. If one felt the return was insufficient, he or she simply left it at the trading site. If the other party wanted to continue trade, it was increased.

Coexistence of Exchange Principles

In contemporary North America, the market principle governs most exchanges, from the sale of the means of production to the sale of consumer goods. We also have redistribution. Some of our tax money goes to support the government, but some of it also comes back to us in the form of social services, education, health care, and infrastructure. We also have reciprocal exchanges. Generalized reciprocity characterizes the relationship between parents and children. However, even here the dominant market mentality surfaces in comments about the high cost of raising children and in the stereotypical statement of the disappointed parent: "We gave you everything money could buy."

Exchanges of gifts, cards, and invitations exemplify reciprocity, usually balanced. Everyone has heard remarks like "They invited us to their daughter's wedding, so when ours gets married, we'll have to invite them" and "They've been here for dinner three times and haven't invited us yet. I don't think we should ask them back until they do." Such precise balancing of reciprocity would be out of place in a foraging band, where resources are communal (common to all) and daily sharing based on generalized reciprocity is an essential ingredient of social life and survival.

Generalized reciprocity would appear to be the most widespread form of exchange, because it exists in every kind of society, from foraging bands to industrial nations. Societies with productive economies based on food production have expanded social and economic networks, which allow for wider and more distant exchanges characterized by balanced and even negative reciprocity. Societies with chiefs have redistribution. The market principle tends to dominate exchanges in state-organized societies, to be examined further in Chapter 6.

Potlatching

The **potlatch** is a festive event within a regional exchange system among tribes of the North Pacific Coast of North America, including the Salish and Kwakiutl of Washington and British Columbia, and the Tsimshian of Alaska. At each potlatch, the sponsoring community gave away food and wealth items, such as blankets and pieces of copper,

The fantastic Potlatch Dancers, Indian Village of Klinkwan, Alaska.
Copyright 1904 by Underwood & Underwood.

This historic (1904) photo shows potlatch participants at the Haida village of Klinkwan, Alaska.

Source: Stereograph Cards collection, Prints & Photographs Division, Library of Congress, LC-USZ62-50908

to visitors from other villages in its network. In return for its giveaway of food and wealth, the sponsoring community received prestige. Prestige increased with the lavishness of the potlatch, the value of the goods distributed. Some North Pacific tribes still practice the potlatch, sometimes as a memorial to the dead (Kan 1986, 1989).

The potlatching tribes were foragers, but not typical ones. Rather than living in nomadic bands, they were sedentary and had chiefs. They enjoyed access to a wide variety of land and sea resources. Among their most important foods were salmon, herring, candlefish, berries, mountain goats, seals, and porpoises (Piddocke 1969).

The economist and social commentator Thorstein Veblen cited potlatching as a prime example of conspicuous consumption in his influential book *The Theory of the Leisure Class* (1934), claiming that potlatching was based on an economically irrational drive for prestige. His analysis emphasized the lavishness and supposed wastefulness, especially of the Kwakiutl displays, to support his contention that in some societies people strive to maximize prestige at the expense of their material well-being. This interpretation has been challenged.

Ecological anthropology, also known as *cultural ecology,* is a theoretical school that attempts to interpret cultural practices, such as the potlatch, in terms of their long-term role in helping humans adapt to their environments (see Haenn, Wilk, and Harnish 2016). Wayne Suttles (1960) and Andrew Vayda (1961/1968) saw potlatching not in terms of its immediate wastefulness but in terms of its long-term role as a cultural adaptive mechanism. This view also helps us understand similar patterns of lavish feasting throughout the world. Here is the ecological interpretation: *Customs such as the potlatch are cultural adaptations to alternating periods of local abundance and shortage.*

How did this work? Although the natural environment of the North Pacific Coast is favorable, resources do fluctuate from year to year and place to place. Salmon and herring aren't equally abundant every year in a given locality. One village can have a good year while another is experiencing a bad one. Later, their fortunes reverse. In this context, the potlatch cycle had adaptive value; the potlatch was not a competitive display that brought no material benefit.

A village enjoying an especially good year had a surplus of subsistence items, which it could trade for more durable wealth items, such as blankets, canoes, or pieces of copper. Such wealth, in turn, could be given away and thereby converted into prestige. Members of several villages were invited to any potlatch and got to take home the resources that were distributed. In this way, potlatching linked villages together in a regional economy—an exchange system that distributed food and wealth from wealthy to needy communities. In return, the potlatch sponsors and their villages got prestige. The decision to potlatch was determined by the health of the local economy. If there had been subsistence surpluses, and thus a buildup of wealth over several good years, a village could afford a potlatch to convert its surplus food and wealth into prestige.

The long-term adaptive value of potlatching becomes clear when a formerly prosperous village had a run of bad luck. Its people started accepting invitations to potlatches in villages that were doing better. The tables were turned as the temporarily rich became temporarily poor and vice versa. The newly needy accepted food and wealth items. They were willing to receive rather than bestow gifts and thus to relinquish some of their stored-up prestige. They hoped their luck would eventually improve, so that resources could be recouped and prestige regained.

Anthropology Today   *Scarcity and the Betsileo*

In the realm of cultural diversity, perceptions and motivations can change substantially over time. Consider some changes I've observed among the Betsileo of Madagascar during the decades I've been studying them. Initially, compared with modern consumers, the Betsileo had little perception of scarcity. Now, with population increase and the spread of a cash-oriented economy, their perceived wants and needs have increased relative to their means. Their motivations have changed, too, as people increasingly seek profits, even if it means stealing from their neighbors or destroying ancestral farms.

In the late 1960s my wife and I first lived among the Betsileo, studying their economy and social life (Kottak 1980). Soon after our arrival we met two well-educated schoolteachers (first cousins) who were interested in our research. The woman's father was a congressional representative who became a cabinet minister during our stay. Their family came from a historically important and typical Betsileo village called Ivato, which they invited us to visit with them.

We had visited many other Betsileo villages, where often, as we drove up, children would run away screaming. Women would hurry inside, and men would retreat to doorways. This behavior expressed their fear of the *mpakafo*. Believed to cut out and devour his victim's heart and liver, the mpakafo is the Malagasy vampire. These cannibals are said to have fair skin and to be very tall. Because I have light skin and stand over 6 feet tall, I was a natural suspect. The fact that such creatures were not known to travel with their wives helped convince the Betsileo that I wasn't really a mpakafo.

When we visited Ivato, however, its people were friendly and hospitable. Our very first day there we did a brief census and found out who lived in which households. We learned people's names and their relationships to our schoolteacher friends and to each other. We met an excellent informant who knew all about the local history. In a few afternoons I learned much more than I had in the other villages in several sessions.

Ivatans were so willing to talk because we had powerful sponsors, villagers who had made it in the outside world, people the Ivatans knew would protect them. The schoolteachers vouched for us, but even more significant was the cabinet minister, who was like a grandfather and benefactor to everyone in town. The Ivatans had no reason to fear us because their more influential native son had asked them to answer our questions.

Once we moved to Ivato, the elders established a pattern of visiting us every evening. They came to talk, attracted by the inquisitive foreigners but also by the wine, tobacco, and food we offered. I asked question after question about their customs and beliefs.

As our stay neared its end, our Ivatan friends lamented, saying, "We'll miss you. When you leave, there won't be any more cigarettes, any more wine, or any more questions." They wondered what it would be like for us back in the United States. They knew we had an automobile and that we regularly purchased things, including the items we shared with them. We could afford to buy products they never would have. They commented, "When you go back to your country, you'll need a lot of money for things like cars, clothes, and food. We don't need to buy those things. We make almost everything we use. We don't need as much money as you, because we produce for ourselves."

The Betsileo weren't unusual for nonindustrial people. Strange as it may seem to an American consumer, those rice farmers actually believed *they had all they needed.* The lesson from the Betsileo of the 1960s is that scarcity, which economists view as universal, is variable. Although shortages do arise in nonindustrial societies, the concept of scarcity (insufficient means) is much less developed in stable, subsistence-oriented economies than in industrial societies that rely on a host of consumer goods.

But with globalization over the past few decades, significant changes have affected the Betsileo—and most nonindustrial peoples. On my most recent visit to Ivato, the effects of cash and of population increase were evident there—and throughout Madagascar—where the population growth rate has been about 3 percent annually. Madagascar's population has quadrupled since 1966, to about 24 million. One result of population pressure has been agricultural intensification. In Ivato, farmers who formerly grew only rice in their fields now use the same land for commercial crops, such as carrots, after the annual rice harvest. More tragically, Ivato has witnessed a breakdown of social and political order, fueled by increasing demand for cash.

Cattle rustling has become a growing threat. Cattle thieves (sometimes from neighboring villages) have terrorized peasants who previously felt secure in their villages. Some of the rustled cattle are driven to the coasts for commercial export. Prominent among the rustlers are relatively well-educated young men who have studied long enough to be comfortable negotiating with outsiders, but who have been unable to find formal work, and who are unwilling to work the rice fields as their peasant ancestors did. The formal education system has familiarized them with external institutions and norms, including the need for cash. The concepts of

Women hull rice in a Betsileo village. In the village of Ivato, farmers who traditionally grew only rice in their fields now use the same land for commercial crops, such as carrots, after the annual rice harvest. ©Carl D. Walsh/Aurora Photos

continued

Anthropology Today *continued*

scarcity, commerce, and negative reciprocity now thrive among the Betsileo.

I've witnessed other striking evidence of the new addiction to cash during my most recent visits to Betsileo country. Near Ivato's county seat, people now sell precious stones—tourmalines, which were found by chance in local rice fields. We saw an amazing sight: dozens of villagers destroying an ancestral resource, digging up a large rice field, seeking tourmalines—clear evidence of the encroachment of cash on the local subsistence economy.

Throughout the Betsileo homeland, population growth and density are propelling emigration. Locally, land, jobs, and money are all scarce. One woman with ancestors from Ivato, herself now a resident of the national capital (Antananarivo), remarked that half the children of Ivato now lived in that city. Although she was exaggerating, a census of all the descendants of Ivato reveals a substantial emigrant and urban population.

Ivato's recent history is one of increasing participation in a cash economy. That history, combined with the pressure of a growing population on local resources, has made scarcity not just a concept but a reality for Ivatans and their neighbors.

The potlatch linked local groups along the North Pacific Coast into a regional alliance and exchange network. Potlatching and intervillage exchange had adaptive functions, regardless of the motivations of the individual participants. The anthropologists who stressed rivalry for prestige were not wrong. They were merely emphasizing *motivations* at the expense of an analysis of economic and ecological *systems*.

The use of feasts to enhance individual and community reputations and to redistribute wealth is not unique to populations of the North Pacific Coast. Competitive feasting is widely characteristic of nonindustrial food producers. But among most foragers, who live, remember, in marginal areas, resources are too meager to support feasting on such a level. Among foragers living in marginal areas, sharing rather than competition prevails.

The potlatch does not, and did not, exist apart from larger world events. For example, within the spreading world capitalist economy of the 19th century, the potlatching tribes, particularly the Kwakiutl, began to trade with Europeans (fur for blankets, for example). Their wealth increased as a result. Simultaneously, a huge proportion of the Kwakiutl population died from diseases brought by the Europeans. The increased wealth from trade flowed into a drastically reduced population. With many of the traditional potlatch organizers dead (such as chiefs and their families), the Kwakiutl extended the right to give a potlatch to everyone. This resulted in intense competition for prestige, to such an extent that Kwakiutl potlatches began to incorporate the ostentatious destruction of wealth, including blankets, pieces of copper, and even their wooden houses. Blankets and homes were burned, and pieces of copper were buried at sea. Being rich enough to destroy wealth conveyed prestige. European trade and local depopulation caused Kwakiutl potlatching to change its nature. It became much more destructive than it had been previously.

Note, however, that this destructive potlatching also worked to prevent the formation of sharply divided social classes. Wealth relinquished or destroyed was converted into a nonmaterial item: prestige. Under capitalism, we reinvest our profits (rather than burning our cash), with the hope of making an additional profit. The potlatchers, by contrast, were content to relinquish their surpluses rather than use them to widen the social distance between themselves and their fellow tribe members.

Summary

1. Cohen's adaptive strategies include foraging (hunting and gathering), horticulture, agriculture, pastoralism, and industrialism. Foraging was the only human adaptive strategy until the transition to food production (farming and herding), which began about 12,000 years ago. Food production eventually replaced foraging in most places. Almost all modern foragers have some dependence on food production or food producers.

2. Horticulture doesn't use land or labor intensively. Horticulturalists cultivate a plot for one or two years (sometimes longer) and then abandon it. There is always a fallow period. Agriculturists farm the same plot of land continuously and use labor intensively. They use one or more of the following: irrigation, terracing, domesticated animals as a means of production, and manure for fertilizer.

3. The pastoral strategy is mixed. Nomadic pastoralists trade with cultivators. Part of a transhumant pastoral population cultivates while another part takes the herds to pasture. Except for some Peruvians and the Navajo, who are recent herders, the New World lacks native pastoralists.

4. Economic anthropology is the cross-cultural study of systems of production, distribution, and consumption. In nonindustrial societies, a kin-based mode of production prevails. One acquires rights to resources and labor through membership in social groups, not impersonally through purchase and sale. Work is just one aspect of social relations expressed in varied contexts.

5. Economics has been defined as the science of allocating scarce means to alternative ends. Western economists assume the notion of scarcity is universal—which it isn't—and that in making choices, people strive to maximize personal profit. In nonindustrial societies, indeed as in our own, people often maximize values other than individual profit.

6. In nonindustrial societies, people invest in subsistence, replacement, social, and ceremonial funds. States add a rent fund: People must share their output with their social superiors. In states, the obligation to pay rent often becomes primary.

7. Besides studying production, economic anthropologists study and compare exchange systems. The three principles of exchange are the market principle, redistribution, and reciprocity, which may coexist in a given society. The primary exchange mode is the one that allocates the means of production.

8. Patterns of feasting and exchanges of wealth among villages are common among nonindustrial food producers, as among the potlatching societies of North America's North Pacific Coast. Such systems help even out the availability of resources over time.

Think Like an Anthropologist

1. When considering issues of "human nature," why should we remember that the egalitarian band was a basic form of human social life for most of our history?

2. Give examples from your own exchanges of different degrees of reciprocity. Why are anthropologists interested in studying exchange across cultures?

Key Terms

agriculture, *89*
balanced
    reciprocity, *103*
band, *88*
correlation, *88*
cultivation
    continuum, *92*
economy, *95*
food production, *84*
foraging, *85*

generalized
    reciprocity, *102*
horticulture, *89*
market principle, *101*
means (factors) of
    production, *96*
mode of
    production, *95*
negative
    reciprocity, *103*

pastoral
    nomadism, *94*
pastoralists, *93*
peasants, *100*
potlatch, *104*
reciprocity, *102*
reciprocity
    continuum, *102*
redistribution, *101*
transhumance, *94*

Chapter  6

Political Systems

What Is "The Political"?

Anthropologists share with political scientists an interest in political systems, power, and politics. Here again, however, the anthropological approach is global and comparative and includes nonstates, whereas political scientists tend to focus on contemporary nations. Anthropological studies have revealed substantial variation in power, authority, and legal systems in different societies (see Pirie 2013; Walton and Suarez 2016). (**Power** is the ability to exercise one's will over others; **authority** is the formal, socially approved use of power—e.g., by government officials.)

Morton Fried (1967) offered the following definition of political organization:

> Political organization comprises those portions of social organization that specifically relate to the individuals or groups that manage the affairs of public policy or seek to control the appointment or activities of those individuals or groups. (pp. 20–21)

This definition certainly fits contemporary North America and other nation-states. Under "individuals or groups that manage the affairs of public policy" come various

Seeking to influence public policy, hundreds of demonstrators march in midtown Manhattan, New York, in solidarity with protests in North Dakota against construction of the Dakota Access Pipeline. Opposed particularly by Native Americans and environmentalists, the pipeline passes near the Standing Rock Sioux reservation. ©Erik McGregor/Pacific Press/LightRocket via Getty Images

agencies and levels of government. Those who seek to influence public policy include political parties, unions, corporations, consumers, lobbyists, activists, political action committees (including super PACs), religious groups, and nongovernmental organizations (NGOs).

In nonstates, by contrast, it's often difficult to detect any "public policy." For this reason, I prefer to speak of *socio*political organization in discussing the exercise of power and the regulation of relations among groups and their representatives. *Political regulation* includes such processes as decision making, dispute management, and conflict resolution. The study of political regulation draws our attention to those who make decisions and resolve conflicts, for example, by raising the question of whether there are formal leaders (see Rhodes and Hart 2014; Schwartz et al. 2011; Stryker and Gonzalez 2014).

Types and Trends

Ethnographic and archaeological studies in hundreds of places have revealed many correlations between the economy and social and political organization. Decades ago, the anthropologist Elman Service (1962) listed four types, or levels, of political organization: band, tribe, chiefdom, and state. Today, none of the first three types can be studied as a self-contained form of political organization, because all now exist within the context of nation-states and are subject to state control. There is archaeological evidence for early bands, tribes, and chiefdoms that existed before the first states appeared. However, because anthropology came into being long after the origin of the state, anthropologists never have been able to observe "in the flesh" a band, tribe, or chiefdom outside the influence of some state. There still may be local political leaders (e.g., village heads) and regional figures (e.g., chiefs) of the sort discussed in this chapter, but all now exist and function within the context of state organization.

A band is a small, kin-based group (all its members are related by kinship or marriage) found among foragers. **Tribes** typically have economies based on horticulture and pastoralism. Living in villages and organized into kin groups based on common descent, tribes have no formal government and no reliable means of enforcing political decisions. **Chiefdom** refers to a form of sociopolitical organization intermediate between the tribe and the state. In chiefdoms, social relations are based mainly on kinship, marriage, descent, age, generation, and gender—just as in bands and tribes. However, although chiefdoms are kin based, they feature **differential access** to resources (some people have more wealth, prestige, and power than others do) and a permanent political structure. The **state** is a form of sociopolitical organization based on a formal government structure and socioeconomic stratification.

The four labels in Service's typology are much too simple to account for the full range of political diversity and complexity known to anthropologists. We'll see, for instance, that tribes have varied widely in their political systems and institutions. Nevertheless, Service's typology does highlight significant contrasts in political organization, especially those between states and nonstates. For example, in bands and tribes—unlike states, which have clearly visible governments—political organization does not stand out as separate and distinct. In bands and tribes, it is difficult to characterize an act or event as political rather than merely social.

Service's labels "band," "tribe," "chiefdom," and "state" are categories or types within a **sociopolitical typology.** These types are correlated with the adaptive strategies (an *economic typology*) discussed in Chapter 5. Thus, foragers (an economic type) tend to have band organization (a sociopolitical type). Similarly, many horticulturalists and pastoralists live in tribes. Although most chiefdoms have farming economies, herding is important in some Middle Eastern chiefdoms. Nonindustrial states usually have an agricultural base.

Food production led to larger, denser populations and more complex economies than was the case among foragers. Many sociopolitical trends reflect the increased regulatory demands associated with cultivation and herding. Archaeologists have studied these trends through time, and cultural anthropologists have observed them across a range of more contemporary societies (see Shore, Wright, and Peró 2011).

Bands and Tribes

This chapter discusses a series of societies, as case studies, with different political systems. A common set of questions will be addressed for each one. What kinds of social groups does the society have? How do those groups represent themselves to each other? How are their internal and external relations regulated? To answer these questions, we begin with bands and tribes and then consider chiefdoms and states.

Foraging Bands

The strong ties that contemporary and recent foragers maintain with sociopolitical groups beyond the band make them markedly different from Stone Age hunter-gatherers. Modern foragers live in nation-states and an interlinked world. All foragers now trade with food producers. The pygmies of Congo, for example, for generations have shared a social world and economic exchanges with their neighbors who are cultivators. Furthermore, most contemporary hunter-gatherers rely on governments and on missionaries for at least part of what they consume.

The San

Anthropologists once viewed contemporary and recent foragers (inaccurately) as primitive, isolated survivors of the Stone Age. A more recent and accurate view of contemporary and recent foragers sees them as groups forced into marginal environments by states, colonialism, and world events (Kent 2002).

In Chapter 5, we saw how the Basarwa San of Botswana have been affected by government policies that relocated them after converting their ancestral lands into a wildlife reserve (Motseta 2006). More generally, San speakers ("Bushmen") of southern Africa have been influenced by Bantu speakers (farmers and herders) for 2,000 years and by Europeans for centuries. Edwin Wilmsen (1989) argues that many San descend from herders who were pushed into the desert by poverty or oppression. He sees the San today as a rural underclass in a larger political and economic system dominated by Europeans and Bantu food producers. Within this system, many San now tend cattle for wealthier Bantu rather than foraging independently. San also have their own domesticated animals, further illustrating their movement away from a foraging lifestyle.

An Aboriginal elder stands next to his home in the Anangu Pitjantjara lands, South Australia. Like this man, most recent and contemporary foragers and their descendants participate in the modern world system. ©Susie Bennett/ Alamy Stock Photo

The nature of San life has changed considerably since the 1950s and 1960s, when a series of anthropologists from Harvard University, including Richard B. Lee, embarked on a systematic study of their lives. Studying the San over time, Lee and others have documented many changes (see Lee 2003, 2012). Such longitudinal research monitors variation in time, while fieldwork in many San areas has revealed variation in space. One of the most important contrasts is between settled (sedentary) and nomadic groups (Kent and Vierich 1989). Although sedentism has increased substantially in recent years, some San groups (along rivers) have been sedentary for generations. Others, including the Dobe Ju/'hoansi San studied by Lee (1984, 2003, 2012) and the Kutse San whom Susan Kent studied, have retained more of the hunter-gatherer lifestyle.

To the extent that foraging continues to be their subsistence base, groups like the San can illustrate links between a foraging economy and other aspects of life in bands. For example, San groups that still are mobile, or that were so until recently, emphasize social, political, and gender equality, which are traditional band characteristics. A social system based on kinship, reciprocity, and sharing is appropriate for an economy with few people and limited resources. People have to share meat when they get it; otherwise, it rots. The nomadic pursuit of wild plants and animals tends to discourage permanent settlement, wealth accumulation, and social distinctions.

Marriage and kinship create ties between members of different bands. Trade and visiting also link them. Band leaders are leaders in name only. Bands are *egalitarian* societies. That is, they make only a few social distinctions, based mainly on age, gender, and individual talents or achievements. In these egalitarian societies, the "leaders" are merely first among equals. If they give advice or make decisions, they have no sure way to enforce those decisions.

The Inuit

The Aboriginal Inuit (Hoebel 1954, 2006), another group of foragers, provide a classic example of methods of settling disputes—**conflict resolution**—in stateless societies. All societies have ways of settling disputes (of variable effectiveness) along with cultural rules or norms about proper and improper behavior. **Norms** are cultural standards or guidelines that enable individuals to distinguish between appropriate and inappropriate behavior in a given society (N. Kottak 2002). Although rules and norms are cultural universals, only state societies, those with established governments, have formal *laws* that are formulated, proclaimed, and enforced (see Donovan 2007; Dresch and Skoda 2012; Pirie 2013).

Foragers lacked formal **law** in the sense of a legal code with trial and enforcement, but they did have methods of social control and dispute settlement. The absence of law did not mean total anarchy. As described by E. A. Hoebel (1954, 2006) in a classic ethnographic study of conflict resolution, a sparse population of some 20,000 Inuit spanned 6,000 miles (9,500 kilometers) of the Arctic region. The most significant social groups were the nuclear family and the band. Some bands had headmen. There also were shamans (part-time religious specialists). However, these positions conferred little power on those who occupied them. Each Inuit had access to the resources he or she needed to sustain life. Every man could hunt, fish, and make the tools necessary for subsistence. Every woman could obtain the materials needed to make clothing, prepare food, and do domestic work. Inuit men could even hunt and fish in the territories of other local groups. There was no notion of private ownership of territory or animals.

Hunting and fishing by men were the primary subsistence activities. The diverse and abundant plant foods available in warmer areas, where female labor in gathering is important, were absent in the Arctic. Traveling on land and sea in a bitter environment, Inuit men faced more dangers than women did. The traditional male role took its toll in lives, so that adult women outnumbered men. This permitted some men to have two or three wives. The ability to support more than one wife conferred a certain amount of prestige, but it also encouraged envy. (*Prestige* is social esteem, respect, or approval.) If a man seemed to be taking additional wives just to enhance his reputation, a rival was likely to steal one of them. Most Inuit disputes were between men and originated over women, caused by wife stealing or adultery.

A jilted husband had several options. He could try to kill the wife thief. However, if he succeeded, one of his rival's kinsmen surely would try to kill him in retaliation. One dispute might escalate into several deaths as relatives avenged a succession of murders. No government existed to intervene and stop such a *blood feud* (a murderous feud between families). However, one also could challenge a rival to a song battle. In a public setting, contestants made up insulting songs about each other. At the end of the match, the audience proclaimed the winner. However, if the winner was the man whose wife had been stolen, there was no guarantee she would return. Often she stayed with her abductor.

Tribal Cultivators

As is true of foraging bands, there are no totally autonomous tribes in today's world. Still, there are societies, for example, in Papua New Guinea and in South America's tropical forests, in which tribal principles continue to operate. Tribes typically have a horticultural or pastoral economy and are organized into villages and/or *descent groups* (kin groups whose members trace descent from a common ancestor). Tribes lack socioeconomic stratification (i.e., a class structure) and a formal government of their own. A few tribes still conduct small-scale warfare, in the form of intervillage raiding. Tribes have more effective regulatory mechanisms than foragers do, but tribal societies have no sure means of enforcing political decisions (see Gluckman 2012). The main regulatory officials are village heads, "big men," descent-group leaders, village councils, and leaders of pantribal associations (described later in this section). All these figures and groups have limited authority.

Like foragers, horticulturalists tend to be egalitarian, although some have marked *gender stratification:* an unequal distribution of resources, power, prestige, and personal freedom between men and women (see Chapter 8). Horticultural villages usually are small, with low population density and open access to strategic resources. Age, gender, and personal traits determine how much respect people receive and how much support they get from others. Egalitarianism diminishes, however, as village size and population density increase. Horticultural villages usually have headmen—rarely, if ever, headwomen.

The Village Head

The Yanomami (Chagnon 1997, 2013; Ferguson 1995; Ramos 1995) live in southern Venezuela and the adjacent part of Brazil. When anthropologists first studied them, they numbered about 26,000 people living in 200 to 250 widely scattered villages, each with a population between 40 and 250. The Yanomami are horticulturalists who also hunt and gather. Their staple crops are bananas and plantains (a banana-like crop). The Yanomami have more social groups than exist in a foraging society. They have families, villages, and descent groups. Their descent groups, which span more than one village, are *patrilineal* (ancestry is traced back through males only) and *exogamous* (people must marry outside their own descent group). However, branches of two different descent groups may live in the same village and intermarry.

Traditionally the only leadership position has been that of **village head** (always a man). A village head is chosen based on his personal characteristics (e.g., bravery, persuasiveness) and the support he can muster from fellow villagers. The position is not inherited, and the authority of the village head, like that of the leader of a foraging band, is severely limited. The headman lacks the right to issue orders. He can only persuade, harangue, and try to influence public opinion. For example, if he wants people to clean up the central plaza in preparation for a feast, he must start sweeping it himself, hoping his covillagers will take the hint and relieve him.

When conflict erupts within the village, the headman may be called on as a mediator who listens to both sides. He will give an opinion and advice. If a disputant is unsatisfied, the headman has no power to back his decisions and no way to impose punishments. Like the band leader, he is first among equals.

A Yanomami village headman also must lead in generosity. Expected to be more generous than any other villager, he cultivates more land. His garden provides much of the food consumed when his village hosts a feast for another village. The headman represents the village in its dealings with outsiders, including Venezuelan and Brazilian government agents.

Napoleon Chagnon (1983/1992, 2013) describes how one village headman, Kaobawa, guaranteed safety to a delegation from a village with which a covillager of his wanted to start a war. Kaobawa was a particularly effective headman. He had demonstrated his mettle in battle, but he also knew how to use diplomacy to avoid offending other villagers. No one in his village had a better personality for the headmanship. Nor (because Kaobawa had many brothers) did anyone have more supporters. Among the Yanomami, when a village is dissatisfied with its headman, its members can leave and found a new village. This happens from time to time and is called *village fissioning*.

With its many villages and descent groups, Yanomami sociopolitical organization is more complicated than that of a band-organized society. The Yanomami face more problems in regulating relations between groups and individuals. Although a headman sometimes can prevent a specific violent act, intervillage raiding has been common in some areas of Yanomami territory, particularly those studied by Chagnon (1997, 2013).

It's important to recognize as well that the Yanomami are not isolated from outside events. They live in two nation-states, Venezuela and Brazil, and attacks by outsiders, especially Brazilian ranchers and miners, have plagued them (Chagnon 2013; *Cultural Survival Quarterly* 1989; Ferguson 1995). During a Brazilian gold rush between 1987 and 1991, one Yanomami died each day, on average, from such attacks. By 1991, there were some 40,000 miners in the Brazilian Yanomami homeland. Some Yanomami were killed outright. The miners introduced new diseases, and the swollen population ensured that old diseases became epidemic. Brazilian Yanomami were dying at a rate of

10 percent annually, and their fertility rate had dropped to zero. Since then, one Brazilian president declared a huge Yanomami territory off-limits to outsiders. Unfortunately, local politicians, miners, and ranchers have managed to evade the ban. The future of the Yanomami remains uncertain (see Romero 2008).

The "Big Man"

Many societies of the South Pacific, particularly on the Melanesian Islands and in Papua New Guinea, had a kind of political leader that we call the big man. The **big man** (almost always a male) was an elaborate version of the village head, but with one significant difference. Unlike the village head, whose leadership is limited to one village, the big man had supporters in several villages. The big man thus was a regulator of *regional* political organization.

Consider the Kapauku Papuans, inhabitants of Irian Jaya, Indonesia (located on the island of New Guinea). Anthropologist Leopold Pospisil (1963) studied the Kapauku (then 45,000 people), who grew crops (with the sweet potato as their staple) and raised pigs. Their cultivation system was too labor intensive to be described as simple horticulture. It required mutual aid in turning the soil before planting. The digging of long drainage ditches, which a big man often helped organize, was even more complex. Kapauku cultivation supported a larger and denser population than does the simpler horticulture of the Yanomami. The Kapauku economy required collective cultivation and political regulation of the more complex tasks. The key political figure was the big man.

Attributes that distinguished the big man from his fellows included wealth, generosity, eloquence, physical fitness, bravery, supernatural powers, and the ability to gain the support and loyalty of others. Men became big men because they had certain personalities; they did not inherit their position but created it through hard work and good judgment. Wealth resulted from successful pig breeding and trading. As a man's pig herd and prestige grew, he attracted supporters. He sponsored pig feasts in which pork (provided by the big man and his supporters) was distributed to guests, bringing him more prestige and widening his network of support (see also O'Connor 2015).

The big man's supporters, acknowledging his past favors and anticipating future rewards, recognized him as a leader and accepted his decisions as binding. The Kapauku big man, known as the *tonowi*, was an important regulator of regional events. He helped

The big man persuades people to organize feasts, which distribute pork and wealth. Shown here is a big man from the Huli (or Haroli) tribe of the southern highlands of Papua New Guinea. Does your own society have equivalents of big men? ©Edward Reeves/Alamy Stock Photo

determine the dates for feasts and markets. He initiated economic projects requiring the cooperation of a regional community.

The Kapauku big man again exemplifies a generalization about leadership in tribal societies: If someone achieves wealth and widespread respect and support, he or she must be generous. The big man worked hard not to hoard wealth but to be able to give away the fruits of his labor, to convert wealth into prestige and gratitude. A stingy big man would lose his support. Selfish and greedy big men sometimes were killed by their fellows (Zimmer-Tamakoshi 1997).

How similar are contemporary politicians to the big man? Big men get their loyalists to produce and deliver pigs, just as modern politicians persuade their supporters to make campaign contributions. And like big men, successful American politicians try to be generous with their supporters. Payback may take the form of a night in the Lincoln bedroom, a strategic dinner invitation, an ambassadorship, or largesse to a place that was particularly supportive. Big men amass wealth, then distribute pigs and their meat. Successful American politicians also give away "pork." As with the big man, eloquence and communication skills contribute to political success (e.g., Ronald Reagan, Bill Clinton, Barack Obama), although lack of such skills isn't necessarily fatal (e.g., either President Bush). What about physical fitness? Hair, height, and health are still political advantages. Bravery, in the form of military service, also helps political careers (e.g., John Kerry and John McCain), but it certainly isn't required, nor does it guarantee success. Supernatural powers? Candidates who proclaim themselves atheists are even rarer than self-identified witches (or not witches). Almost all political candidates claim to belong to a mainstream religion. Some even present their candidacies as promoting God's will. (How does the current leader of your country fare in terms of the attributes discussed in this paragraph?)

On the other hand, contemporary politics isn't just about personality, as it is in big man systems. We live in a state-organized, stratified society with inherited wealth, power, and privilege, all of which have political implications. As is typical of states, inheritance and kin connections play a role in political success. Just think of the Kennedys, Bushes, Clintons, and Gandhis.

Pantribal Sodalities

Big men could forge regional political organization, albeit temporarily, by mobilizing supporters from several villages. Other principles in tribal societies—such as a belief in common ancestry, kinship, or descent—could be used to link local groups within a region. The same descent group, for example, might span several villages, and its dispersed members might recognize the same leader.

Principles other than kinship also can link local groups, especially in modern societies. People who live in different parts of the same nation may belong to the same labor union, sorority or fraternity, political party, or religious denomination. In tribes, nonkin groups called *associations* or *sodalities* may serve a similar linking function. Often, sodalities are based on common age or gender, with all-male sodalities more common than all-female ones.

Pantribal sodalities are groups that extend across the whole tribe, spanning several villages. Such sodalities were especially likely to develop in situations of warfare with a neighboring tribe. Mobilizing their members from multiple villages within the same tribe, pantribal sodalities could assemble a force to attack, defend, or retaliate against another tribe.

The best examples of pantribal sodalities come from the Central Plains of North America and from tropical Africa. During the 18th and 19th centuries, Native American populations of the Great Plains of the United States and Canada experienced a rapid growth of pantribal sodalities. This development reflected an economic change that followed the spread of horses, which had been reintroduced to the Americas by the Spanish, to the area between the Rocky Mountains and the Mississippi River. Many Plains societies changed their adaptive strategies because of the horse. At first they had been foragers who hunted bison (buffalo) on foot. Later they adopted a mixed economy based on hunting, gathering, and horticulture. Finally they changed to a much more specialized economy based on horseback hunting of bison (eventually with rifles).

As the Plains tribes were undergoing these changes, other groups also adopted horseback hunting and moved into the Plains. Attempting to occupy the same area, groups came into conflict. A pattern of warfare developed in which the members of one tribe raided another, usually for horses. The economy demanded that people follow the movement of the bison herds. During the winter, when the bison dispersed, a tribe fragmented into small bands and families. In the summer, when huge herds assembled on the Plains, the tribe reunited. They camped together for social, political, and religious activities, but mainly for communal bison hunting.

Two activities demanded strong leadership: organizing and carrying out raids on enemy camps (to capture horses) and managing the summer bison hunt. All the Plains societies developed pantribal sodalities, and leadership roles within them, to police the summer hunt. Leaders coordinated hunting efforts, making sure that people did not cause a stampede with an early shot or an ill-advised action. Leaders imposed severe penalties, including seizure of a culprit's wealth, for disobedience.

Many tribes that adopted this Plains strategy of adaptation had once been foragers for whom hunting and gathering had been individual or small-group affairs. They never had come together previously as a single social unit. Age and gender were available as social principles that could quickly and efficiently forge unrelated people into pantribal sodalities.

Raiding of one tribe by another, this time for cattle rather than horses, was common in eastern and southeastern Africa, where pantribal sodalities also developed. Among the pastoral Masai of Kenya, men born during the same four-year period were circumcised together and belonged to the same named group, an age set, throughout their lives. The sets moved through *age grades,* the most important of which was the warrior grade. Members of a set felt a strong allegiance to one another. Masai women lacked comparable set organization, but they also passed through culturally recognized age grades: the initiate, the married woman, and the female elder.

In certain parts of western and central Africa, pantribal sodalities are secret societies, made up exclusively of men or women. Like our college fraternities and sororities, these associations have secret initiation ceremonies. Among the Mende of Sierra Leone, men's and women's secret societies were very influential. The men's group, the Poro, trained boys in social conduct, ethics, and religion and supervised political and economic activities. Leadership roles in the Poro often overshadowed village headship and played an important part in social control, dispute management, and tribal political regulation. Age, gender, and ritual can link members of different local groups into a single social collectivity in a tribe and thus create a sense of ethnic identity, of belonging to the same cultural tradition.

Nomadic Politics

The political systems associated with pastoralism varied considerably, ranging from tribal societies to chiefdoms. The Masai (just discussed) live in a tribal society. The sociopolitical organization of such tribal herders is based on descent groups and pantribal sodalities. Other pastoralists, however, have chiefs and live in nation-states. The scope of political authority among pastoralists expands considerably as regulatory problems increase in densely populated regions (see Salzman 2008). Consider two Iranian pastoral nomadic tribes—the Basseri and the Qashqai (Salzman 1974). Starting each year from a plateau near the coast, these groups took their animals to grazing land 17,000 feet (5,400 meters) above sea level. The Basseri and the Qashqai shared this route with one another and with several other ethnic groups.

Use of the same pasture land at different times of year was carefully scheduled. Ethnic-group movements were tightly coordinated. Expressing this schedule is *il-rah,* a concept common to all Iranian nomads. A group's il-rah is its customary path in time and space. It is the schedule, different for each group, of when specific areas can be used in the annual trek.

Each tribe had its own leader, known as the *khan* or *il-khan.* The Basseri khan, because he dealt with a smaller population, faced fewer problems in coordinating its movements than did the leaders of the Qashqai. Correspondingly, his rights, privileges, duties, and authority were weaker. Nevertheless, his authority exceeded that of any political figure discussed so far. The khan's authority still came from his personal traits rather than from his office. That is, the Basseri followed a particular khan not because of a political position he happened to fill but because of their personal allegiance and loyalty to him as a man. The khan relied on the support of the heads of the descent groups into which Basseri society was divided.

Among the Qashqai, however, allegiance shifted from the person to the office. The Qashqai had multiple levels of authority and more powerful chiefs or khans. Managing 400,000 people required a complex hierarchy. Heading it was the il-khan, helped by a deputy, under whom were the heads of constituent tribes, under each of whom were descent-group heads.

A case illustrates just how developed the Qashqai authority structure was. A hailstorm prevented some nomads from joining the annual migration at the appointed time. Although all the nomads recognized that they were not responsible for their delay, the il-khan assigned them less favorable grazing land, for that year only, in place of their usual pasture. The tardy herders and other Qashqai considered the judgment fair and didn't question it. Thus, Qashqai authorities regulated the annual migration. They also adjudicated disputes between people, tribes, and descent groups (see Salzman 2008).

These Iranian cases illustrate the fact that pastoralism often is just one among many specialized economic activities within a nation-state. As part of a larger whole, pastoral tribes are continually pitted against other ethnic groups. Within the context of the modern nation-state, that government becomes a final authority, a higher-level regulator that attempts to limit conflict between ethnic groups. State organization arose not just to manage agricultural economies but also to regulate the activities of ethnic groups within expanding social and economic systems (see Das and Poole, 2004; Saleh 2013).

Chiefdoms

The first states emerged in the Old World around 5,500 years ago. The first chiefdoms developed perhaps a thousand years earlier, but few survive today. In many parts of the world, the chiefdom was a transitional form of organization that emerged during the evolution of tribes into states. State formation began in Mesopotamia (currently Iran and Iraq). It next occurred in Egypt, the Indus Valley of Pakistan and India, and northern China. A few thousand years later, states arose in two parts of the Western Hemisphere—Mesoamerica (Mexico, Guatemala, Belize) and the central Andes (Peru and Bolivia). Early states are known as *archaic,* or *nonindustrial,* states, in contrast to modern industrial nation-states. Robert Carneiro (1970) defines the state as "an autonomous political unit encompassing many communities within its territory, having a centralized government with the power to collect taxes, draft men for work or war, and decree and enforce laws" (p. 733).

The chiefdom and the state, like many categories used by social scientists, are *ideal types.* That is, they are labels that make social contrasts seem sharper than they really are. In reality there is a continuum from tribe to chiefdom to state. Some societies had many attributes of chiefdoms but retained tribal features. Some advanced chiefdoms had many attributes of archaic states and thus are difficult to assign to either category. Recognizing this "continuous change" (Johnson and Earle 2000), some anthropologists speak of "complex chiefdoms" (Earle 1997), which are almost states.

Political and Economic Systems

Geographic areas where chiefdoms existed included the circum-Caribbean (e.g., Caribbean islands, Panama, Colombia), lowland Amazonia, what is now the southeastern

Chiefdoms as widespread as Mexico's Olmecs, England's Stonehenge, and Polynesia's Easter Island (Rapa Nui) are famed for their major works in stone. The statues shown here are Easter Island's major tourist attraction.
©David Madison/The Image Bank/Getty Images

United States, and Polynesia. Chiefdoms created the megalithic cultures of Europe, including the one that built Stonehenge. Bear in mind that chiefdoms and states can fall (disintegrate) as well as rise. Before Rome's expansion, much of Europe was organized at the chiefdom level, to which it reverted for centuries after the fall of Rome in the 5th century C.E.

Much of our ethnographic knowledge about chiefdoms comes from Polynesia, where they were common at the time of European exploration. In chiefdoms, social relations are based mainly on kinship, marriage, descent, age, generation, and gender—just as in bands and tribes. This is a fundamental difference between chiefdoms and states. States bring nonrelatives together and oblige them to pledge allegiance to a government.

Unlike bands and tribes, however, chiefdoms administer a clear-cut and permanent regional political system. Chiefdoms may include thousands of people living in many villages or hamlets. Regulation is carried out by the chief and his or her assistants, who occupy political offices. An **office** is a permanent position, which must be refilled when it is vacated by death or retirement. Such vacancies are filled systematically, so that the political system that is the chiefdom endures across the generations, thus ensuring permanent political regulation.

Polynesian chiefs were full-time specialists whose duties included managing the economy. They regulated production by commanding or prohibiting (using religious taboos) the cultivation of certain lands and crops. Chiefs also regulated distribution and consumption. At certain seasons—often on a ritual occasion such as a first-fruit ceremony—people would offer part of their harvest to the chief through his or her representatives. Products moved up the hierarchy, eventually reaching the chief. Conversely, illustrating obligatory sharing with kin, chiefs sponsored feasts at which they gave back some of what they had received (see O'Connor 2015). Unlike big men, chiefs were exempt from ordinary work and had rights and privileges unavailable to the masses. Like big men, however, they still returned a portion of the wealth they took in.

Such a flow of resources to and then from a central place is known as *chiefly redistribution,* which offers economic advantages. If different parts of the chiefdom specialized in particular products, chiefly redistribution made those products available to the entire society. Chiefly redistribution also helped stimulate production beyond the basic subsistence level and provided a central storehouse for goods that might become scarce in times of famine (Earle 1997).

Status Systems

Social status (one's position in society) in chiefdoms was based on seniority of descent. Polynesian chiefs kept extremely long genealogies. Some chiefs (without writing) managed to trace their ancestry back 50 generations. All the people in the chiefdom were thought to be related to each other. Presumably, all were descended from a group of founding ancestors.

The chief would be the oldest child (usually son) of the oldest child of the oldest child, and so on. Degrees of seniority were calculated so intricately on some islands that there were as many ranks as people. For example, the third son would rank below the second, who in turn would rank below the first. The children of an eldest brother, however, would rank above the children of the next brother, whose children in turn would outrank those of younger brothers. However, even the lowest-ranking man or woman in a chiefdom was still the chief's relative, and everyone, including the chief, had to share with their relatives. It was difficult to draw a line between elites and common people.

Nevertheless, in chiefdoms as in states, some men, women, and even children had more prestige, wealth, and power than others did. These elites controlled strategic resources such as land and water. Earle (1987) characterizes chiefs as "an incipient aristocracy with advantages in wealth and lifestyle" (p. 290).

Compared with chiefdoms, archaic states drew a much firmer line between elites and masses, distinguishing at least between nobles and commoners. Kinship ties did not extend from the nobles to the commoners because of *stratum endogamy*—marriage within one's own group. Commoners married commoners; elites married elites.

The Emergence of Stratification

We see that a key difference between chiefdom and state was the chiefdom's kinship basis. However, chiefs and their closest relatives, backed by their differential wealth and power, sometimes launched attacks on the kinship basis of their chiefdom. In Madagascar they would do this by demoting their more distant relatives to commoner status and banning marriage between nobles and commoners (Kottak 1980). Such moves, if accepted by the society, created separate *social strata*—unrelated groups that differ in their access to wealth, prestige, and power. (A *stratum* is one of two or more groups that contrast in social status and access to strategic resources. Each stratum includes people of both sexes and all ages.) The creation of separate social strata is called *stratification,* and its emergence signified the transition from chiefdom to state. The presence of stratification is one of the key distinguishing features of a state.

The influential sociologist Max Weber (1922/1968) defined three related dimensions of social stratification: (1) Economic status, or **wealth,** encompasses a person's material assets, including income, land, and other types of property. (2) Power, the ability to exercise one's will over others—to get what one wants—is the basis of political status. (3) **Prestige**—the basis of social status—refers to esteem, respect, or approval for acts, deeds, or qualities considered exemplary. Prestige, or "cultural capital" (Bourdieu 1984), gives people a sense of worth and respect, which they may often convert into economic advantage (see Table 6.1).

In archaic states—for the first time in human history—there were contrasts in wealth, power, and prestige between entire groups (social strata) of men and women. The **superordinate** (the higher, or elite) stratum had privileged access to valued resources. Access to those resources by members of the **subordinate** (lower, or underprivileged) stratum was limited by the privileged group.

TABLE 6.1 Max Weber's Three Dimensions of Stratification		
wealth	economic status
power	political status
prestige	social status

State Systems

Table 6.2 summarizes the information presented so far on bands, tribes, chiefdoms, and states. States, remember, are autonomous political units with social strata and a formal government. States tend to be large and populous, and certain systems and subsystems with specialized functions are found in all states (see Sharma and Gupta 2006). They include the following:

- Population control: fixing of boundaries, border control, establishment of citizenship categories, and censusing.
- Judiciary: laws, legal procedure, and judges.
- Enforcement: permanent military and police forces.
- Fiscal support: taxation.

In archaic states, these subsystems were integrated by a ruling system or government composed of civil, military, and religious officials. Let's look at the four subsystems one by one.

TABLE 6.2 **Economic Basis of and Political Regulation in Bands, Tribes, Chiefdoms, and States**

Sociopolitical Type	Economic Type	Examples	Type of Regulation
Band	Foraging	Inuit, San	Local
Tribe	Horticulture, pastoralism	Yanomami, Masai, Kapauku	Local, temporary, regional
Chiefdom	Intensive horticulture, pastoral nomadism, agriculture	Qashqai, Polynesia, Cherokee	Permanent, regional
State	Agriculture, industrialism	Ancient Mesopotamia, contemporary U.S., Canada	Permanent, regional

Population Control

To keep track of whom they govern, states conduct censuses. States demarcate boundaries—borders—that separate that state from other societies. (See this chapter's "Anthropology Today" for a discussion of border control issues in today's world.) Customs agents, immigration officers, navies, and coast guards patrol frontiers. States also regulate population through administrative subdivision: provinces, districts, "states," counties, and parishes. Lower-level officials manage the populations and territories of the subdivisions.

States often promote geographic mobility and resettlement, severing long-standing ties among people, land, and kin. Population displacements have increased with globalization and as war, famine, and job seeking churn up migratory currents. Within states, people claim new identities based on their region, ethnicity, occupation, political party, religion, and team or club affiliation—rather than only as members of a descent group or an extended family.

States also manage their populations by granting different rights and obligations to citizens and noncitizens. Social distinctions among citizens also are common. Archaic states granted different rights to nobles, commoners, and slaves. In American history before the Emancipation Proclamation, there were different laws for enslaved and free people. In European colonies, separate courts judged cases involving only natives and cases involving Europeans. In contemporary America, a military judiciary coexists alongside the civil system.

Judiciary

All states have laws based on precedent and legislative proclamations. Without writing, laws may be preserved in oral tradition. *Crimes* are violations of the legal code ("breaking the law"), with specified types of punishment. To handle crimes and disputes, all states have courts and judges (see Donovan 2007; Pirie 2013).

A striking contrast between states and nonstates is intervention in internal and domestic disputes, such as violence within and between families. Governments step in to halt blood feuds and regulate previously private disputes. However, states aren't always successful in their attempts to curb *internal* conflict. About 85 percent of the world's armed conflicts since the end of World War II have begun within states—in efforts to overthrow a ruling regime or as disputes over ethnic, religious, or human rights issues (see Chatterjee 2004; Nordstrom 2004; Stavenhagen 2013; Tishkov 2004).

Enforcement

How do states enforce laws and judicial decisions? All states have enforcement agents—some kind of police force. The duties of these enforcement officers may include apprehending and imprisoning criminals (those who have broken the law). Confinement requires prisons and jailers. If there is a death penalty, executioners are needed. Government officials have the power to collect fines and confiscate property. The government uses its enforcement agents to maintain internal order, suppress disorder, and guard against external threats (with the military and border officials—see Maguire, Frois, and Zurawski 2014).

Armies help states subdue and conquer neighboring nonstates, but conquest isn't the only reason state organization has spread. Although states impose hardships, they also offer advantages. States have formal mechanisms (e.g., an army and a police force) designed to protect against external threats and to preserve internal order. When they are successful in promoting internal peace, states enhance production. Their economies can support massive, dense populations, which supply armies and colonists to promote expansion.

Fiscal Support

All states have fiscal systems. States could not maintain the government apparatus and agents just discussed without a secure means of financial support. Governments rely on financial, or **fiscal,** mechanisms (e.g., taxation) to support their officials and numerous other specialists. As in the chiefdom, the state intervenes in production, distribution, and consumption. The state may require a certain area to produce specific things or ban certain activities in particular places. Although, like chiefdoms, states have redistribution ("spreading the wealth around"), less of what comes in from the people goes directly back to the people.

In nonstates, people customarily share with their relatives, but people who live in states also have to turn over a significant portion of what they produce to the state. Markets and trade usually are under at least some state oversight, with officials overseeing distribution and exchange, standardizing weights and measures, and collecting taxes on goods passing into or through the state. Of the revenues the state collects, it reallocates part for the general good and keeps another part (often larger) for itself—its agents and agencies. State organization doesn't bring more freedom or leisure to the common people, who may be conscripted to build monumental public works. Some projects, such as dams and irrigation systems, may be economically necessary, but residents of archaic states also had to build temples, palaces, and tombs for the elites. Those elites reveled in the consumption of sumptuary goods— jewelry, exotic food and drink, and stylish clothing reserved for, or affordable only by, the rich. Peasants' diets suffered as they struggled to meet government demands for produce, currency, or labor. Commoners perished in territorial wars that had little relevance to their own needs. To what extent are these observations true of contemporary states?

Although it offers advantages, we should not think of the state as "better" than other forms of sociopolitical organization. Stratification and the state are antithetical to the egalitarian and free-ranging way of life practiced by our foraging ancestors. We have just considered some of the demands that states place on ordinary people. It should not be surprising, then, that populations in various parts of the world have resisted, and tried to avoid or escape, state organization. We saw in Chapter 5 that foragers do not necessarily adopt food production just because they know of its existence. Similarly, certain societies have managed to resist or escape state organization by adopting nomadic lifestyles that are difficult for states to supervise. For example, James C. Scott (2009) discusses how a belt of highland societies with economies based on shifting cultivation in Southeast Asia have survived for generations outside the control of states based in the lowlands of the same countries.

Social Control

In studying political systems, anthropologists pay attention not only to formal, governmental institutions but to other forms of social control as well. The concept of social control is broader than "the political." **Social control** refers to "those fields of the social system (beliefs, practices, and institutions) that are most actively involved in the maintenance of any norms and the regulation of any conflict" (N. Kottak 2002, p. 290). *Norms,* as defined earlier in this chapter, are cultural standards or guidelines that enable individuals to distinguish between appropriate and inappropriate behavior.

Previous sections of this chapter have focused more on formal political organization than on sociopolitical process. We've seen how the scale and strength of political systems have expanded in relation to economic changes. We've examined means of conflict resolution, or their absence, in various types of society. We've looked at political decision making, including leaders and their limits. We've also recognized that all contemporary humans have been affected by states, colonialism, and the spread of the world system (Kaplan 2014; Shore et al. 2011).

Sociopolitical was introduced as a key concept at the beginning of this chapter. So far, we've focused mainly on the *political* part of sociopolitical; now we focus on the *social* part. In this section we'll see that political systems have their informal, social, and subtle aspects along with their formal, governmental, and public dimensions.

Hegemony and Resistance

In addition to the formal mechanisms discussed in the section "State Systems," what mechanisms do states employ to maintain social order? Antonio Gramsci (1971) developed the concept of **hegemony** for a stratified social order in which subordinates comply with domination by internalizing their rulers' values and accepting the "naturalness" of domination (this is, the way things were meant to be). According to Pierre Bourdieu (1977, p. 164), every social order tries to make its own arbitrariness (including its mechanisms of control and domination) seem natural and in everyone's interest—even when that is not the case. Both Bourdieu (1977) and Michel Foucault (1979) argue that it is easier and more effective to dominate people in their minds than to try to control their bodies. Nonphysical forms of social control include various techniques of persuading and managing people and of monitoring and recording their beliefs, activities, and contacts.

Hegemony, the internalization of a dominant ideology, is one way in which elites curb resistance to their power and domination. Another way to discourage resistance is to make subordinates believe they eventually will gain power—as young people usually foresee when they let their elders dominate them. Yet another way to curb resistance is to separate or isolate people while supervising them closely, as is done in prisons (Foucault 1979).

Some contexts enable or encourage public resistance, particularly when people are allowed to assemble. The setting of a crowd offers anonymity, while also reinforcing and encouraging the common sentiments that have brought those people together. The elites, sensing the threat of surging crowds and public rebellion, often discourage such gatherings.

They try to limit and control holidays, funerals, dances, festivals, and other occasions that might unite the oppressed. For example, in the American South before the Civil War, gatherings of five or more slaves were prohibited unless a White person was present.

Also working to discourage resistance are factors that interfere with community formation—such as geographic, linguistic, and ethnic separation. Elites want to isolate the oppressed rather than bringing them together in a group. Consequently, southern U.S. plantation owners sought slaves with diverse cultural and linguistic backgrounds, and limited their rights to assemble. Despite the measures used to divide them, the slaves resisted, developing their own popular culture, linguistic codes, and religious vision. The masters stressed portions of the Bible that emphasized compliance (e.g., the book of Job). The slaves, however, preferred the story of Moses and deliverance. The cornerstone of slave religion became the idea of a reversal in the conditions of Whites and Blacks. Slaves also resisted directly, through sabotage and flight. In many New World areas, slaves managed to establish free communities in the hills and other isolated areas (Price 1973).

Weapons of the Weak

The study of sociopolitical systems also should consider the sentiments and activity that may be hiding beneath the surface of evident, public behavior. In public, the oppressed may seem to accept their own domination, even when they are questioning it in private. Scott (1990) uses the term "public transcript" to describe the open, public interactions between oppressed people and their oppressors. Scott uses "hidden transcript" to describe the critique of the power structure that goes on out of sight of those who hold power. In public, the elites and the oppressed may observe the etiquette of power relations. The dominants act like masters while their subordinates show humility and defer. But resistance often is seething beneath the surface.

Sometimes, the hidden transcript may include active resistance, but it is individual and disguised rather than collective and defiant. Scott (1985) uses Malay peasants, among whom he did fieldwork, to illustrate small-scale acts of resistance—which he calls "weapons of the weak." The Malay peasants used an indirect strategy to resist an Islamic tithe (religious tax). Peasants were expected to pay the tithe, usually in the form of rice, which was sent to the provincial capital. In theory, the tithe would come back as charity, but it never did. Peasants didn't resist the tithe by rioting, demonstrating, or protesting. Instead they used a "nibbling" strategy, based on small acts of resistance. For example, they failed to declare their land or lied about the amount they farmed. They underpaid, or they delivered rice contaminated with water, rocks, or mud, to add weight. Because of this resistance, only 15 percent of what was due actually was paid (Scott 1990, p. 89).

Hidden transcripts tend to be expressed publicly at certain times (festivals and carnavals) and in certain places (such as markets). Because of its costumed anonymity, Carnaval (Mardi Gras in New Orleans) is an excellent arena for expressing feelings that are typically suppressed. Carnavals celebrate freedom through immodesty, dancing, gluttony, and sexuality (DaMatta 1991). Carnaval may begin as a playful outlet for frustrations built up during the year. Over time, it may evolve into a powerful annual critique of stratification and domination and thus a threat to the established order (Gilmore 1987).

"Schwellkoepp," or "Swollen Heads," caricature local characters during a Carnaval parade in Mainz, Germany. Because of its costumed anonymity, Carnaval is an excellent arena for expressing feelings that are typically suppressed. Is there anything like Carnaval in your society? ©Daniel Roland/AP Images

Shame and Gossip

Many anthropologists have noted the importance of "informal" processes of social control, such as fear, stigma, shame, and gossip, especially in small-scale societies (see Freilich, Raybeck, and Savishinsky 1991). Gossip and shame, for example, can function as effective processes of social control when a direct or formal sanction is risky or impossible (Herskovits 1937). Gossip can be used to shame someone who has violated a social norm. Margaret Mead (1937) and Ruth Benedict (1946) distinguished between shame as an external sanction (i.e., forces set in motion by others, for example, through gossip) and guilt as an internal sanction, psychologically generated by the individual. They regarded shame as a more prominent form of social control in non-Western societies and guilt as a more dominant emotional sanction in Western societies. Of course, to be effective as a sanction, the prospect of being shamed or of shaming oneself must be internalized by the individual. In small-scale societies, in a social environment where everyone knows everyone else, most people try to avoid behavior that might shame them or otherwise spoil their reputations and alienate them from their social network.

Bronislaw Malinowski (1927, 2013) described how Trobriand Islanders might climb to the top of a palm tree and dive to their deaths because they couldn't tolerate the shame associated with public knowledge of some stigmatizing action. Nicholas Kottak (2002) heard Makua villagers in northern Mozambique tell the story of a man rumored to have fathered a child with his stepdaughter. The political authorities imposed no formal sanctions (e.g., a fine or jail time) on this man, but gossip about the affair circulated widely. The gossip crystallized in the lyrics of a song that groups of young women would perform. After the man heard his name and behavior mentioned in that song, he hanged himself by the neck from a tree. (Previously we saw the role of song in the social control system of the Inuit. We'll see it again in the case of the Igbo women's war, discussed in the next section.)

Although it isn't part of any formal or official authority structure, shame can be a powerful social sanction. People aren't just citizens of governments; they are members of society, and social sanctions exist alongside governmental ones. Such sanctions exemplify other "weapons of the weak," because they often are wielded most effectively by people, such as women or young people, who have limited access to the formal authority structure.

The Igbo Women's War

Shame and ridicule—used by women against men—played a key role in a decisive protest movement that took place in southeastern Nigeria in late 1929. This is remembered as the "Aba Women's Riots of 1929" in British colonial history and as the "Women's War" in Igbo history (see Dorward, 1983; Martin 1988; Mba 1982; Oriji 2000; Van Allen 1971). During this two-month "war," at least 25,000 Igbo women joined protests against British officials, their agents, and their colonial policies. This massive revolt touched off the most serious challenge to British rule in the history of what was then the British colony of Nigeria.

In 1914, the British had implemented a policy of indirect rule by appointing local Nigerian men as their agents—known as "warrant chiefs." These chiefs became increasingly oppressive, seizing property, imposing arbitrary regulations, and imprisoning people who criticized them. Colonial administrators further stoked local outrage when they announced plans to impose taxes on Igbo market women. These women were key suppliers of food for Nigeria's growing urban population; they feared being forced out of business by the new tax.

After hearing about the tax in November 1929, thousands of Igbo women assembled in various towns to protest both the warrant chiefs and the taxes on market women. They used a traditional practice of censoring and shaming men through all-night song and dance ridicule (often called "sitting on a man"). This process entailed constant singing and dancing around the houses and offices of the warrant chiefs. The women also followed the chiefs' every move, forcing the men to pay attention by invading their space (see also Walton and Suarez 2016). Disturbed by the whole process, wives of the warrant chiefs also pressured their husbands to listen to the protesters' demands.

The protests were remarkably effective. The tax was abandoned, and many of the warrant chiefs resigned, some to be replaced by women. Other women were appointed to the Native courts as judges. The position of women improved in Nigeria, where market women especially remain a powerful political force to this day. Many subsequent Nigerian political events were inspired by the Women's War, including additional tax protests. This Women's War inspired many other protests in regions all over Africa. The Igbo uprising is seen as the first major challenge to British authority in Nigeria and West Africa during the colonial period.

Anthropology Today   *The Illegality Industry: A Failed System of Border Control*

"Secure the border!" has become a familiar refrain in political discussion about undocumented immigrants to the United States. But what exactly does this mean? How can a border be truly secure in today's world, in which tens of millions of people are routinely on the move, and what can anthropologists contribute to the discussion?

Ruben Andersson is a Swedish anthropologist and postdoctoral fellow at the London School of Economics. His 2014 book *Illegality, Inc.* is based on his ethnographic study of actual and would-be migrants to Europe, along with the people and agencies—some supportive, the majority just the opposite—they encounter along the way. The book's title reflects Andersson's contention that the European Union's migration policies have created an "illegality industry," which is fueling, rather than curbing, illegal activity.

In less than half a year—between January 1 and June 19, 2016—214,691 migrants and refugees had arrived in Europe by sea, and another 7,457 by land, according to the International Organization for Migration (IOM). During that period, the IOM also reported 2,859 would-be migrants dead or missing, most through drowning, as their boats capsized in the Mediterranean (O'Donnell 2016). Most of these migrants are from West Africa, the Middle East, and Afghanistan. Lack of job opportunities at home is the main driver sending young West Africans toward Europe. Political instability and war have been pushing refugees from the Middle East (especially Syria and Iraq) and Afghanistan toward Europe.

Andersson did his fieldwork for the book between 2005 and 2014 and initially focused on would-be migrants from West Africa (mainly Senegal and Mali).

Although his study took place before the current refugee crisis in the Middle East, the lessons he derived can easily be applied to today's refugees.

Andersson began his research by focusing on a small sample of people, with whom he established close personal relationships. He wanted to understand how border controls affect individual migrants. He was particularly struck by his informants' accounts of the various people and organizations they encountered (or tried to avoid) as they moved, and he extended his study to those intermediaries. He discovered an entire "illegality industry" deployed around, and benefiting financially from, migrants and their misfortunes. This industry supports border guards and police; defense, monitoring, and construction companies; nongovernmental aid organizations; journalists; and even academics building their careers on the study of migrants. Benefiting especially are human smugglers and traffickers, who increase their prices whenever and wherever border control is tightest.

One of Andersson's main conclusions is that the current system of deterrence is complex and expensive, and is not working as intended. The EU's costly, militarized, high-tech border-control system includes razor-wire fences, naval blockades, drones, and command centers. In the nations through which migrants typically move (e.g., Turkey, Ukraine, Mauritania, Morocco, Libya), the EU subsidizes police officers to seek out and stop would-be migrants. Despite these numerous barriers, migrants and refugees keep coming.

In 2015, just over 1 million migrants entered Europe by sea, according to the IOM. Note, however, that this figure represents considerably less than 1 percent of

Europe's total population of about 740 million. Andersson contends that Europe is wealthy enough to easily absorb this number of arrivals. He also notes that, despite right-wing outrage in Europe and the United States, most refugees today wind up in poorer, rather than wealthier, nations (O'Donnell 2016).

A more effective policy than creating barriers to immigration, Andersson argues, would be to normalize migration and provide people with legal, safe, and efficient ways of moving across national and continental borders. For our 21st-century world, he continues, we need a "political strategy that takes into consideration the globalized nature of human movement." "Ultimately, we need to unfence migration" (both quotes from O'Donnell 2016).

Can you apply lessons from Andersson's study to border control issues in contemporary North America? Is building walls likely to be an effective way to secure the border?

In less than half a year—between January 1 and June 19, 2016—more than 200,000 migrants and refugees reached Europe by sea. Shown here in September, 2016, a rubber boat carrying 120 people is in distress a few miles northeast of Tripoli, Libya. Its passengers will soon be rescued by the rescue vessel Aquarius, operated by the NGOs SOS Méditerranée and Médicins Sans Frontières (MSF). ©Marco Panzetti/NurPhoto via Getty Images

At the beginning of this chapter, *power* was defined as the ability to exercise one's will over others. It was contrasted with *authority*—the formal, socially approved use of power by government officials and others. The case of the Igbo Women's War shows how women effectively used their social power (through song, dance, noise, and "in-your-face" behavior) to subvert the formal authority structure and, in so doing, gained greater influence within that structure. Can you think of other, perhaps recent examples? We see how gossip, ridicule, and shaming can be effective processes of social control, which can even result in governmental change. The Igbo case also shows the importance of community organizing and political mobilization in effective resistance.

Summary

1. Although no ethnographer has been able to observe a polity uninfluenced by some state, many anthropologists use a sociopolitical typology that classifies societies as bands, tribes, chiefdoms, or states. Foragers tended to live in egalitarian, band-organized societies. Personal networks linked individuals, families, and bands. Band leaders were first among equals, with no sure way to enforce decisions. Disputes rarely arose over strategic resources, which were open to all.

2. Political authority increased with growth in population size and density and in the scale of regulatory problems. More people mean more relations among individuals and groups to regulate. Increasingly complex economies pose further regulatory problems.

3. Heads of horticultural villages are local leaders with limited authority. They lead by example and persuasion. Big men have support and authority beyond a single village. They are regional regulators, but temporary ones. In organizing a feast, they mobilize labor from several villages. Sponsoring such events leaves them with little wealth but with prestige and a reputation for generosity.

4. Age and gender also can be used for regional political integration. Among North America's Plains tribes, men's associations (pantribal sodalities) organized raiding and buffalo hunting. Such sodalities provide offense and defense when there is intertribal raiding for animals. Among pastoralists, the degree of authority and political organization reflects population size and density, interethnic relations, and pressure on resources.

5. The state is an autonomous political unit that encompasses many communities. Its government collects taxes, drafts people for work and war, and decrees and enforces laws. The state is a form of sociopolitical organization based on central government and social stratification. Early states are known as archaic, or non-industrial, states, in contrast to modern industrial nation-states.

6. Unlike tribes, but like states, chiefdoms had permanent regional regulation and differential access to resources. But chiefdoms lacked stratification. Unlike states, but like bands and tribes, chiefdoms were organized by kinship, descent, and marriage. Chiefdoms emerged in several areas, including the circum-Caribbean, lowland Amazonia, the southeastern United States, and Polynesia.

7. Weber's three dimensions of stratification are wealth, power, and prestige. In early states—for the first time in human history—contrasts in wealth, power, and prestige between entire groups of men and women came into being. A socioeconomic stratum includes people of both sexes and all ages. The superordinate—higher, or elite—stratum enjoys privileged access to resources.

8. Certain systems are found in all states: population control, judiciary, enforcement, and fiscal support. These systems are integrated by a ruling system or government composed of civil, military, and religious officials. States conduct censuses and demarcate boundaries. Laws are based on precedent and legislative proclamations. Courts and judges handle disputes and crimes. A police force maintains internal order, as a military defends against external threats. A financial, or fiscal, system supports rulers, officials, judges, and other specialists and government agencies.

9. *Hegemony* describes a stratified social order in which subordinates comply with domination by internalizing its values and accepting its "naturalness." Situations that appear hegemonic may have resistance that is individual and disguised rather than collective and defiant. "Public transcript" refers to the open, public interactions between the dominators and the oppressed. "Hidden transcript" describes the critique of power that goes on where the power holders can't see it. Discontent also may be expressed in public rituals such as Carnaval.

10. Broader than the political is the concept of social control—those fields of the social system most actively involved in the maintenance of norms and the regulation of conflict. Sanctions are social as well as governmental. Shame and gossip can be effective social sanctions. In the Igbo Women's War, women effectively used their social power (through song, dance, noise, and "in-your-face" behavior) to subvert the formal authority structure and, in so doing, gained greater influence within that structure.

Think Like an Anthropologist

1. This chapter notes that the labels "band," "tribe," "chiefdom," and "state" are too simple to account for the full range of political diversity and complexity known to archaeologists and ethnographers. Why not get rid of this typology altogether if it does not accurately describe reality? What is the value, if any, of retaining the use of such ideal types to study society?

2. This chapter describes population control as one of the specialized functions found in all states. What are examples of population control? Have you had direct experiences with these controls? (Think of the last time you traveled abroad, registered to vote, paid taxes, or applied for a driver's license.) Do you think these controls are good or bad for society?

Key Terms

authority, *111*
big man, *118*
chiefdom, *113*
conflict
   resolution, *115*
differential
   access, *113*
fiscal, *127*
hegemony, *128*

law, *115*
norms, *115*
office, *123*
pantribal
   sodality, *119*
power, *111*
prestige, *124*
social
   control, *128*

sociopolitical
   typology, *113*
state, *113*
subordinate, *124*
superordinate, *124*
tribe, *113*
village head, *117*
wealth, *124*

Chapter 7

Families, Kinship, and Marriage

How Anthropologists View Families and Kinship

Although it still is something of an ideal in our culture, the nuclear family (parents and their children) now accounts for less than one-fifth of all American households. What kind of family raised you? Perhaps it was a nuclear family. Or maybe you were raised by a single parent, with or without the help of extended kin. Perhaps your extended kin acted as your parents. Or maybe you had a stepparent and/or step or half siblings in a blended family. Maybe you had two moms or two dads. Given the diversity of families in contemporary North America, your family may not have fit any of these descriptions, or perhaps it varied over time.

Although contemporary American family types are diverse, other cultures offer family alternatives that Americans might have trouble understanding. Imagine a society in which someone doesn't know for sure, and doesn't care much about, who his actual mother was. Consider Joseph Rabe, a Betsileo man who was my field assistant in Madagascar. Illustrating an adoptive pattern common among the Betsileo, Rabe was given as a toddler to his childless aunt, his father's sister. He knew that his birth mother lived far away but did not know which of two sisters in his birth mother's family was his biological mother. His mother and her sister both died in his childhood (as did his father), so he didn't really know them. But he was very close to his father's sister, for whom he used the term for mother. Indeed, he had to call her that, because the Betsileo have only one word, *reny,* for mother, mother's sister, and father's sister. (They also use a single term, *ray,* for father and all uncles.) The difference between "real" (biologically based) and socially constructed kinship didn't matter to Rabe.

Contrast this Betsileo case with the common American view that kinship is, and should be, biological. It's increasingly common for adopted children to seek out their birth mothers or sperm donors (which used to be discouraged as disruptive), even after a perfectly satisfactory upbringing in an adoptive family. The American emphasis on biology for kinship is seen also in the recent proliferation of DNA testing. Viewing our beliefs through the lens of cross-cultural comparison helps us appreciate that kinship and biology don't always converge, nor do they need to.

The societies anthropologists traditionally have studied have stimulated a strong interest in families, along with larger systems of kinship and marriage. The wide web of kinship—as vital in daily life in nonindustrial societies as work outside the home is in our own—has become an essential part of anthropology because of its importance to the people we study. We are ready to take a closer look at the systems of kinship and marriage that have organized human life for much of our history.

Families

One kind of kin group that is widespread is the nuclear family, consisting of parents and children, who typically live together in the same household. Other families are extended, including three or more generations. Members of an extended family get together from time to time, but they don't necessarily live together.

The term *family* is basic, familiar (so much so that it even shares its root with *familiar*), and difficult to define in a way that applies to all cultures. A **family** is a group of people (e.g., parents, children, siblings, grandparents, grandchildren, uncles, aunts, nephews, nieces, cousins, spouses, siblings-in-law, parents-in-law, children-in-law) who are considered to be related in some way, for example, by "blood" (common ancestry or descent) or marriage. Some families, such as the nuclear family, are residentially based; its members live together. Others are not; they live apart but come together for family reunions of various sorts from time to time.

Nuclear and Extended Families

Most people belong to at least two nuclear families at different times in their lives. They are born into a family consisting of their parents and siblings. Reaching adulthood, they may establish a nuclear family that includes their spouse (or domestic partner) and eventually their children. Some people establish more than one family through successive marriages or domestic partnerships.

Anthropologists distinguish between the **family of orientation** (the family in which one is born and grows up) and the **family of procreation** (formed when one marries and has children). From the individual's point of view, the critical relationships are with parents and siblings in the family of orientation and with spouse and children in the family of procreation.

In most societies, relations with nuclear family members (parents, siblings, and children) take precedence over relations with other kin. Nuclear family organization is widespread but not universal, and its significance varies from one place to another. In a few societies, such as the classic Nayar case described later in this section, nuclear families are rare or nonexistent. In others, the nuclear family plays no special role in social life. Other social units, such as extended families and descent groups, can assume many of the functions otherwise associated with the nuclear family.

The following example from Bosnia illustrates how an extended family—known as the *zadruga*—can be the most important kinship unit, overshadowing the nuclear family. Among the Muslims of western Bosnia (Lockwood 1975), nuclear families did not exist as independent units. People customarily resided in a household called a zadruga. Living in this household was an extended family headed by a senior man and his wife, the senior woman. Also living in the zadruga were their married sons and their wives and children, as well as unmarried sons and daughters. Each married couple had a sleeping room, decorated and partly furnished from the bride's trousseau. However, possessions— even clothing items—were shared freely by zadruga members. Even trousseau items could be used by other zadruga members.

Within the zadruga, social interaction was more usual among its women, its men, or its children than between spouses, or between parents and children. When the zadruga was particularly large, its members ate at three successive sittings: for men, women, and children, respectively. Traditionally, all children over 12 slept together in boys' or girls' rooms. When a woman wanted to visit another village, she asked permission not from her husband, but from the male zadruga head. Although men may have felt closer to their own children than to those of their brothers, they were obliged to treat all of the zadruga's children equally. Any adult in the household could discipline a child. When a marriage broke up, children under 7 went with the mother. Older children could choose between their parents. Children were considered part of the household where they were born even if their mother left. One widow who remarried had to leave her five children, all over 7, in their father's zadruga, headed by his brother.

Another example of an alternative to the nuclear family is provided by the Nayars (or Nair), a large and powerful caste on the Malabar Coast of southern India (Gough 1959; Shivaram 1996). Their traditional kinship system was matrilineal (descent traced only through females). Nayar lived in matrilineal extended family compounds called *tarawads*. Headed by a senior woman, assisted by her brother, the tarawad housed her siblings, sisters' children, and other matrikin—matrilineal relatives.

Traditional Nayar marriage was barely more than a formality: a kind of coming-of-age ritual. A young woman would go through a marriage ceremony with a man, after

A matrilineal extended family of the Khasi ethnic group in India's northeastern city of Shillong. The Khasis trace descent through women, taking their maternal ancestors' surnames. Women choose their husbands, family incomes are pooled, and extended family households are managed by older women. ©DINODIA/ Dinodia Photo/age fotostock

which they might spend a few days together at her tarawad. Then the man would return to his own tarawad, where he lived with his mother, aunts, uncles, siblings, and other matrikin. Nayar men belonged to a warrior class, who left home regularly for military expeditions, returning permanently to their tarawad on retirement. Nayar women could have multiple sexual partners. Children became members of the mother's tarawad; they were not considered to be relatives of their biological father. Indeed, many Nayar children didn't even know who their biological father was.

Industrialism and Family Organization

The geographic mobility associated with industrialism works to fragment kinship groups larger than the nuclear family. As people move, often for economic reasons, they are separated from their parents and other kin. Eventually, most North Americans will enter a marriage or domestic partnership and establish a family of procreation. With only about 2 percent of the U.S. population now working in farming, relatively few Americans are tied to the land—to a family farm or estate. A nonfarming nation can be a mobile nation. Americans can move to places where jobs are available, even if they have to leave home to do so. Individuals and married couples often live hundreds of miles from their parents. This pattern of postmarital residence, in which married couples establish a new place of residence away from their parents, is called **neolocality.** The prefix *neo* means new; the couple establishes a new residence, a "home of their own." For middle-class North Americans, neolocality is both a cultural preference and a statistical norm. That is, they both want to, and eventually do, establish homes and nuclear families of their own.

It should be noted, however, that there are significant differences involving kinship between middle-class and poorer North Americans. One example is the association between poverty and single-parent households. Another example is the higher incidence of *expanded family households* among Americans who are less well off. An **expanded family household** is one that includes a group of relatives other than, or in addition to, a married couple and their children. Expanded family households take various forms. When the expanded household includes three or more generations, it is an **extended family household,** like the Bosnian zadruga. Another type of expanded family household is the *collateral household,* which includes siblings and their spouses and children. Yet another form is a *matrifocal household,* which is headed by a woman and includes other adult relatives and children. The higher proportion of expanded family households among poorer Americans has been explained as an adaptation to poverty (Stack 1975). Unable to survive economically as independent nuclear family units, relatives band together and pool their resources (see Hansen 2005).

Changes in North American Kinship

Although the nuclear family remains a cultural ideal for many Americans, we see in Table 7.1 that nuclear families now account for less than 20 percent of American households. Other domestic arrangements outnumber the "traditional" American household more than five to one. There are several reasons for this changing household composition. Women increasingly have joined men in the cash workforce. This allows them to leave their family of orientation while making it economically feasible to delay (or even forgo) marriage. Often, job demands compete with romantic attachments. More than a third (35 percent) of American men and 30 percent of American women had never married as of 2015. The median age at first marriage for American women in 2015 was

TABLE 7.1 **Changes in Family and Household Organization in the United States, 1970 versus 2016**

Source: Vespa, Jonathan, Jamie M. Lewis, and Rose M. Kreider, 2013, "America's Families and Living Arrangements: 2012," *Current Population Reports, P20-570.* Washington, DC: U.S. Census Bureau, 2013; United States Census Bureau, America's Families and Living Arrangements, 2016, https://www.census.gov/data/tables/2016/demo/families/cps-2016.html.

	1970	2016
Numbers:		
Total number of households	63 million	126 million
Number of people per household	3.1	2.5
Percentages:		
Married couples living with children	40%	19%
Married couples living without children	30%	29%
Family households	81%	65%
Households with five or more people	21%	10%
People living alone	17%	28%
Percentage of single-mother families	5%	12%
Percentage of single-father families	0%	5%
Households with own children under 18	45%	27%

One among many kinds of American family. This single mother, seen here baking with her daughter, used donor insemination to become pregnant. What do you see as the main differences between nuclear families and single-parent families?
©Steve Russell/Toronto Star via Getty Images

27 years, compared with 21 years in 1970. For men the comparable ages were 29 and 23. Fewer than half (47 percent) of American women lived with a husband in 2015, compared with 65 percent in 1950.

Another important trend is the increasing number of single-parent families, which has tripled from fewer than 4 million in 1970 to over 12 million in 2015. (The overall American population in 2015 was about 1.6 times its size in 1970.) Most of those single-parent families (83 percent) are single-mother families, leaving 17 percent as single-father families.

Household size in both the United States and Canada has declined from 2.9 in 1980 to 2.5 today. The typical American family now has 3.1 members versus 3.3 in 1980. The trend toward smaller families and living units also is detectable in Western Europe and other industrial nations. To be sure, contemporary Americans maintain social lives through school, work, friendship, sports, clubs, religion, and organized social activities. However, the growing isolation from kin that these figures suggest may well be unprecedented in human history.

What does "family" mean in different cultures? Consider a striking contrast between the United States and Brazil, the two most populous nations of the Western Hemisphere, in the meaning of "family." Contemporary North American adults usually define their families as consisting of their spouse (or domestic partner) and their children. However, when Brazilians talk about their families, they mean their parents, siblings, aunts, uncles, grandparents, and cousins. Later they add their children, but rarely the spouse, who has his or her own family. The children are shared by the two families. Because middle-class Americans lack an extended family support system, marriage assumes more importance. The spousal relationship is supposed to take precedence over either spouse's relationship with his or her own parents. This places a significant strain on American marriages.

Living in a less mobile society, Brazilians stay in closer contact with their relatives, including members of the extended family, than North Americans do. Residents of Rio de Janeiro and São Paulo, two of South America's largest cities, are reluctant to leave those urban centers to live away from family and friends. Brazilians find it hard to imagine, and unpleasant to live in, social worlds without relatives. Contrast this with a characteristic American theme: learning to live with strangers.

The Family among Foragers

Foraging societies are far removed from industrial nations in terms of population size and social complexity, but they do feature geographic mobility, which is associated with nomadic or seminomadic hunting and gathering. Here again, a mobile lifestyle favors the nuclear family as the most significant kin group, although in no foraging society is the nuclear family the only group based on kinship. The two basic social units of traditional foraging societies are the nuclear family and the band. Both are based on kinship ties.

Unlike middle-class couples in industrial nations, foragers don't usually reside neolocally. Instead, they join a band in which either the husband or the wife has relatives. However, couples and families may move from one band to another several times. Although nuclear families are ultimately as impermanent among foragers as they are in any other society, they usually are more stable than bands are.

Many foraging societies lacked year-round band organization. The Native American Shoshone of Utah and Nevada provide an example. The resources available to the Shoshone were so meager that for most of the year families traveled alone through the countryside, hunting and gathering. In certain seasons, families assembled to hunt cooperatively as a band, but after just a few months together they dispersed.

In neither industrial nor foraging economies are people permanently tied to the land. The mobility and the emphasis on small, economically self-sufficient family units promote the nuclear family as a basic kin group in both types of societies.

Descent

We've seen that the nuclear family is important in industrial nations and among foragers. The descent group, by contrast, is the key kinship group among nonindustrial farmers and herders. A **descent group** includes people who share common ancestry—they *descend* from the same ancestor(s). Descent groups typically are spread out among several villages, so that all their members do not reside together; only some of them do—those who live in a given village.

Unlike nuclear families, descent groups are permanent. They last for generations. The group endures even as its membership changes. Individual members are born and die, move in and move out. Descent groups may take their names from an ancestor, or from a familiar animal, plant, or natural feature. If a descent group is known as "Children of Abraham," there will be "Children of Abraham" generation after generation. Ditto for "Wolves," "Willow Trees," or "People of the Bamboo Houses." All of these are actual descent group names.

Attributes of Descent Groups

Descent groups frequently are exogamous: Exogamy means to marry outside one's own group. Members of a descent group must marry someone from another descent group. Often, descent group membership is determined at birth and is lifelong. Two common rules admit certain people as descent-group members while excluding others. With a rule of **patrilineal descent,** people automatically have lifetime membership in their father's group. The children of the group's men join the group, but the children of the group's women are excluded. With **matrilineal descent,** people join the mother's group automatically at birth and stay members throughout life. Matrilineal descent groups therefore include only the children of the group's women. (In Figures 7.1 and 7.2, which show patrilineal and matrilineal descent groups, respectively, the triangles stand for males and the circles for females.) Matrilineal and patrilineal descent are types of **unilineal descent.** That means they use only *one* line of descent, either the male or the female line. Patrilineal descent is much more common than matrilineal descent is. In a sample of 564 societies (Murdock 1957), patrilineal descent outnumbered matrilineal descent three to one (247 patrilineal to 84 matrilineal).

Members of any descent group, whether patrilineal or matrilineal, believe that they descend from the same *apical ancestor.* That person stands at the apex, or top, of their common genealogy. For example, Adam and Eve, according to the Bible,

FIGURE 7.1   A Patrilineage Five Generations Deep

Lineages are based on demonstrated descent from an apical ancestor. With patrilineal descent, children of the group's men (shaded) are included as descent-group members. Children of the group's women are excluded; they belong to *their* father's patrilineage. **Note:** In this and other kin charts, *triangles* represent *males*; *circles* are *females*; an *equals* sign indicates *marriage*; a *vertical* line shows *descent*; and a *horizontal* line denotes a *sibling* relationship.

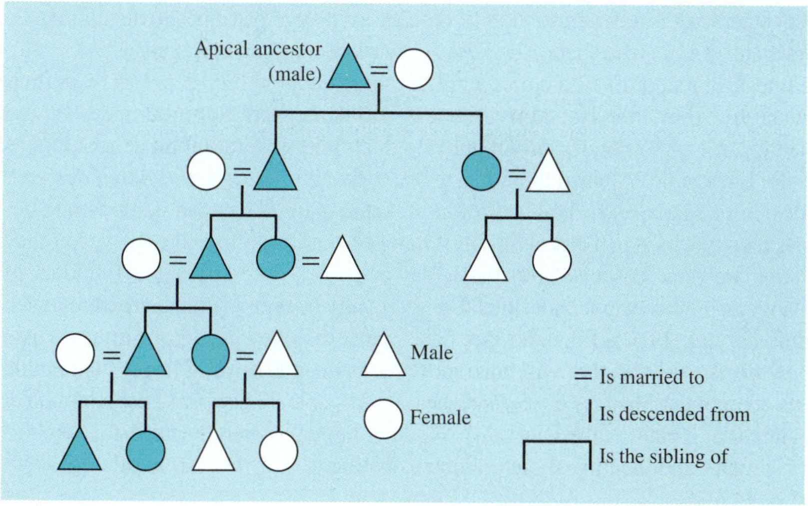

FIGURE 7.2 A Matrilineage Five Generations Deep

Matrilineages are based on demonstrated descent from a female ancestor. Only the children of the group's women (shaded) belong to the matrilineage. The children of the group's men are excluded; they belong to *their* mother's matrilineage.

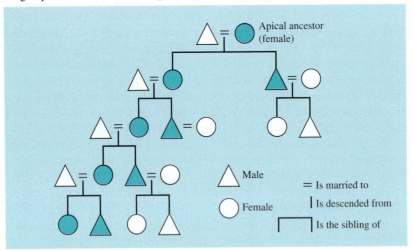

are the apical ancestors of all humanity. Since Eve is said to have come from Adam's rib, Adam stands as the original apical ancestor for the patrilineal genealogies laid out in the Bible.

Lineages and clans are two types of descent group. Clans tend to be larger than lineages and can include lineages. A **lineage** is a descent group based on *demonstrated descent*. Members can demonstrate how they descend from their common ancestor, by naming their forebears in each generation from the apical ancestor through the present. (This doesn't mean the genealogy is accurate, only that lineage members think it is.) In the Bible the litany of men who "begat" other men is a demonstration of descent for a large patrilineage that ultimately includes Jews and Arabs (who share Abraham as their last common apical ancestor).

Unlike lineages, members of a clan do not demonstrate how they descend from their common ancestor; they merely claim, assert, or *stipulate* their common ancestry and descent. They don't try to specify actual genealogical links generation by generation, as members of a lineage do. A **clan,** then, is a descent group based on *stipulated descent*.

The Betsileo of Madagascar have both lineages and clans. They can demonstrate descent for the most recent 8 to 10 generations. Going further back than that, however, they can only stipulate their descent from particular ancestors. The stipulated founders of Betsileo clans can include vaguely defined foreign royalty or even mythical creatures, such as mermaids (Kottak 1980). Like the Betsileo, many societies have both lineages and clans. When this is true, the clan will have more members and cover a larger geographic area than its component lineages do. Sometimes a clan's apical ancestor is not a human at all but an animal or a plant (called a *totem*). Whether human or not, the ancestor symbolizes the social unity and identity of the members, distinguishing them from other groups.

The economic types that usually have descent-group organization are horticulture, pastoralism, and agriculture. A given society usually has multiple descent groups. Any one of them may be confined to a single village, but they usually span more than one village. Any branch of a descent group that lives in one place is a *local descent group*. Two (or more) local branches of different descent groups may live in the same village.

Lineages, Clans, and Residence Rules

As we've seen, descent groups, unlike families, are permanent and enduring units, with new members added in every generation. Members have access to the lineage estate, where some of them must live, in order to benefit from and manage that estate across the generations. An easy way to keep members at home is to have a rule about who belongs to the descent group and where they should live after they get married. Patrilineal and matrilineal descent, and the postmarital residence rules that usually accompany them, ensure that about half the people born in each generation will spend their lives on the ancestral estate.

With patrilineal descent, the typical postmarital residence rule is **patrilocality:** Married couples reside in the husband's father's community, so that the children will grow up in their father's village. It makes sense for patrilineal societies to require patrilocal postmarital residence. If the group's male members are expected to exercise their rights in the ancestral estate, it's a good idea to raise them on that estate and to keep them there after they marry.

A less common postmarital residence rule, associated with matrilineal descent, is **matrilocality:** Married couples live in the wife's mother's community, and their children grow up in their mother's village. Together, patrilocality and matrilocality are known as *unilocal* rules of postmarital residence. Regardless of where one resides after marriage, one remains a member of one's original unilineal descent group for life. This means that a man residing in his wife's village in a matrilineal society keeps his membership in his own matrilineal descent group, and a woman residing in her husband's village is still a member of her own patrilineal descent group.

Defining Marriage

"Love and marriage," "marriage and the family": These familiar phrases show how we link the romantic love of two individuals to marriage, and how we link marriage to reproduction and family creation. But marriage is an institution with significant roles and functions in addition to reproduction. What is marriage, anyway?

Marriage is notoriously difficult to define because of the varied forms it can take in different societies. Consider the following definition from *Notes and Queries on Anthropology:*

> Marriage is a union between a man and a woman such that the children born to the woman are recognized as legitimate offspring of both partners. (Royal Anthropological Institute 1951, p. 111)

This definition isn't universally valid for several reasons. First, in many societies, marriage unites more than two spouses. Here we speak of *plural marriages,* as when

This "I love you" wall is on display in an open area of Monmartre, Paris, France. It shows how to say "I love you" in various languages. Is romantic love a cultural universal? ©Conrad P. Kottak

a man weds two (or more) women, or a woman weds a group of brothers—an arrangement called *fraternal polyandry* that is characteristic of certain Himalayan cultures.

Second, some societies recognize various kinds of same-sex marriages. In South Sudan, for example, a Nuer woman could take a wife if her father had no sons, who were necessary for the survival of his patrilineage. That father could ask his daughter to stand as a fictive son in order to take a bride. This daughter would become the socially recognized husband of another woman (her wife). This was a symbolic and social relationship rather than a sexual one. The "wife" had sex with a man or men (whom her female "husband" approved) until she became pregnant. The children born to the wife were accepted as the offspring of both the female husband and the wife. Although the female husband was not the actual *genitor*, the biological father of the children, she was their *pater*, or socially recognized father. What's important in this Nuer case is *social* rather than *biological paternity*. Kinship is socially constructed. The bride's children were considered the legitimate offspring of her female "husband," who was biologically a woman but socially a man, and the patrilineal descent line continued.

A third objection to the definition of marriage offered earlier is that it focuses exclusively on the role of marriage in establishing the legitimacy of children. Does this mean that people who marry after childbearing age, or who do not plan to have children, are not actually married (see also this chapter's "Anthropology Today")?

In fact, marriage has several roles in society besides legitimating children. The British anthropologist Edmund Leach (1955) observed that, depending on the society, several different kinds of rights are allocated by marriage. According to Leach, marriage can, but doesn't always, accomplish the following:

1. Establish legal parentage.
2. Give either or both spouses a monopoly on the sexuality of the other.
3. Give either or both spouses rights to the labor of the other.
4. Give either or both spouses rights over the other's property.
5. Establish a joint fund of property—a partnership—for the benefit of the children.
6. Establish a socially significant "relationship of affinity" between spouses and their relatives.

Exogamy and Incest

In nonindustrial societies, a person's social world includes two main categories—friends and strangers. Strangers are potential or actual enemies. Marriage is one of the primary ways of converting strangers into friends, of creating and maintaining personal and political alliances. **Exogamy**—the custom and practice of seeking a mate outside one's own group, has adaptive value, because it links people into a wider social network that nurtures, helps, and protects them in times of need. Incest restrictions (prohibitions on sex with relatives) reinforce exogamy by pushing people to seek their mates outside the local group. Most societies discourage sexual contact involving close relatives, especially members of the same nuclear family.

Incest refers to sexual contact with a relative, but cultures define their kin, and thus incest, differently. In other words, incest, like kinship, is socially constructed. Some U.S. states, for example, permit marriage, and therefore sex, with first cousins, while others ban it. The social construction of kinship, and of incest, is far from simple.

For example, when unilineal descent is very strongly developed, the parent who belongs to a different descent group from your own isn't considered a relative. Thus, with strict patrilineality, the mother is not a relative but a kind of in-law who has married a member of your own group—your father. With strict matrilineality, the father isn't a relative because he belongs to a different descent group.

The Lakher of Southeast Asia are strictly patrilineal (Leach 1961). Using the male ego (the reference point, the person in question) in Figure 7.3, let's suppose that ego's father and mother get divorced. Each remarries and has a daughter by a second marriage. A Lakher always belongs to his or her father's group, all of whose members (one's *agnates,* or patrikin) are considered relatives, because they belong to the same descent group. Ego cannot have sex with or marry his father's daughter by the second marriage, just as in contemporary North America it's illegal for half siblings to have sex and marry. However, unlike our society, where all half siblings are restricted, sex between our Lakher ego and his maternal half sister would be nonincestuous. She isn't ego's relative because she belongs to her own father's descent group rather than ego's. The Lakher illustrate very well that definitions of relatives, and therefore of incest, vary from culture to culture.

FIGURE 7.3 **Patrilineal Descent-Group Identity and Incest among the Lakher**

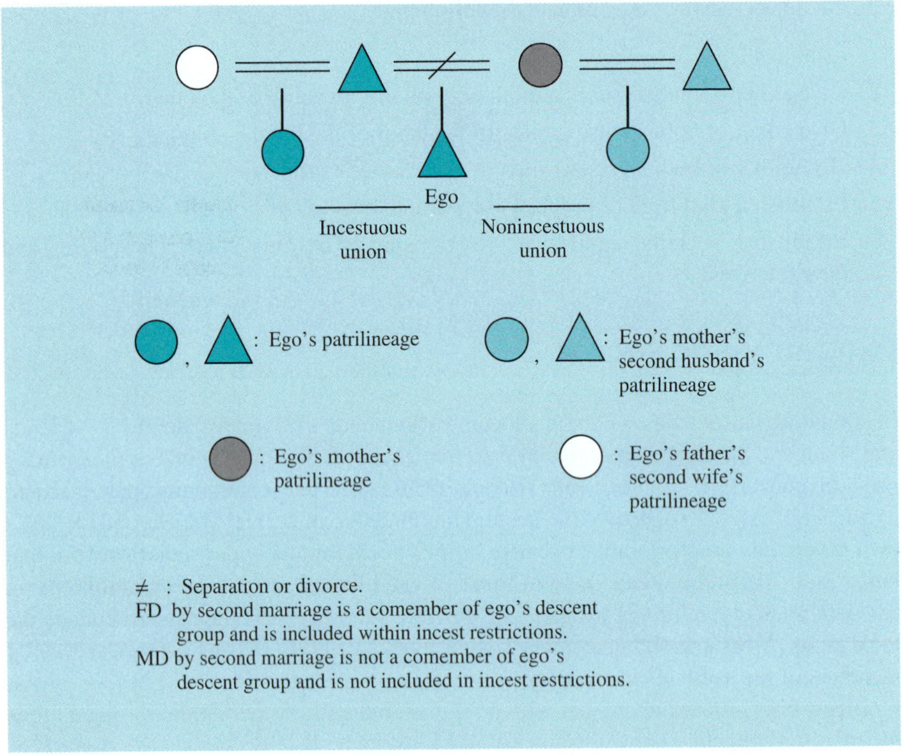

○ , ▲ : Ego's patrilineage

○ , ▲ : Ego's mother's second husband's patrilineage

● : Ego's mother's patrilineage

○ : Ego's father's second wife's patrilineage

≠ : Separation or divorce.
FD by second marriage is a comember of ego's descent group and is included within incest restrictions.
MD by second marriage is not a comember of ego's descent group and is not included in incest restrictions.

Incest and Its Avoidance

A century ago, early anthropologists speculated that incest restrictions reflect an instinctive horror of mating with close relatives (Hobhouse 1915; Lowie 1920/1961). But why, one wonders, if humans really do have an instinctive aversion to incest, would formal restrictions be necessary? No one would want to have sexual contact with a relative. Yet as social workers, judges, psychiatrists, and psychologists are well aware, incest is more common than we might suppose.

A cross-cultural study of 87 societies (Meigs and Barlow 2002) suggested that incest occurred in several of them. It's not clear, however, whether the authors of the study controlled for the social construction of incest. They report, for example, that incest occurs among the Yanomami, but they may be considering cross-cousin marriage to be incestuous, when it is not so considered by the Yanomami. Indeed, it is the preferred form of marriage, not just for the Yanomami but in many tribal societies. Another society in their sample is the Ashanti, for whom the ethnographer Meyer Fortes (1950) reports, "In the old days it [incest] was punished by death. Nowadays the culprits are heavily fined" (p. 257). This suggests that there really were violations of Ashanti incest restrictions and that such violations were punished. More strikingly, among 24 Ojibwa individuals from whom he obtained information about incest, A. Irving Hallowell (1955) found 8 cases of parent–child incest and 10 cases of brother–sister incest. Because reported cases of actual parent–child and sibling incest are rare in the ethnographic literature, questions about the possibility of social construction arise here again. In many cultures, including the Ojibwa, people use the same terms for their mother and their aunt, their father and their uncle, and their cousins and siblings. Could the siblings in the Ojibwa case actually have been cousins, and the parents and children uncles and nieces?

In ancient Egypt, sibling marriage apparently was allowed both for royalty and for commoners, in some districts at least. Based on official census records from Roman Egypt (first to third centuries C.E.), 24 percent of all documented marriages in the Arsinoites district were between "brothers" and "sisters." The rates were 37 percent for the city of Arsinoe and 19 percent for the surrounding villages. These figures are much higher than any other documented levels of inbreeding among humans (Scheidel 1997). Again one wonders if the relatives involved were as close biologically as the kin terms would imply.

According to Anna Meigs and Kathleen Barlow (2002), for Western societies with nuclear family organization, "father–daughter incest" is much more common with stepfathers than with biological fathers. But is it really incest if they aren't biological relatives? American culture is unclear on this matter. Incest also happens with biological fathers, especially those who were absent or did little caretaking of their daughters in childhood (Williams and Finkelhor 1995). In a carefully designed study, Linda M. Williams and David Finkelhor (1995) found father–daughter incest to be least likely when there was substantial paternal parenting of daughters. This experience enhanced the father's parenting skills and his feelings of nurturance, protectiveness, and identification with his daughter, thus reducing the chance of incest.

Endogamy

The practice of exogamy pushes social organization outward, establishing and preserving alliances among groups. In contrast, rules of **endogamy** dictate mating or marriage within a group to which one belongs. Endogamic rules are less common but are still familiar to anthropologists. Indeed, most cultures *are* endogamous units, although they usually do not need a formal rule requiring people to marry someone from their own society. In our society, classes and ethnic groups are quasi-endogamous groups. Members of an ethnic or religious group often want their children to marry within that group, although many of them do not do so. The outmarriage rate varies among such groups, with some more committed to endogamy than others.

An extreme example of endogamy is India's **caste system,** which was formally abolished in 1949, although its structure and effects linger. Castes are stratified groups in which lifelong membership is set at birth. Indian castes are grouped into five major categories, or *varna.* Each is ranked relative to the other four, and these categories extend throughout India. Each varna includes a large number of minor castes (*jati*), each of which includes people within a region who may intermarry. All the jati in a single varna in a given region are ranked, just as the varna themselves are ranked.

Occupational specialization often sets off one caste from another. A community may include castes of agricultural workers, merchants, artisans, priests, and sweepers. The untouchable varna, found throughout India, includes castes whose ancestry, ritual status, and occupations are considered so impure that higher-caste people consider even casual contact with untouchables to be defiling.

The belief that intercaste sex leads to ritual impurity for the higher-caste partner has been important in maintaining endogamy. A man who has sex with a lower-caste woman can restore his purity with a bath and a prayer. However, a woman who has intercourse with a man of a lower caste has no such recourse. Her defilement cannot be undone. Because women have the babies, these differences ensure the pure ancestry of high-caste children. Although Indian castes are endogamous groups, many of them are internally subdivided into exogamous lineages. Traditionally this meant that Indians had to marry a member of another descent group from the same caste. This shows that rules of exogamy and endogamy can coexist in the same society.

Same-Sex Marriage

What about same-sex marriage? Such unions, of various sorts, have been recognized in many different historical and cultural settings. We saw earlier that the Nuer of South Sudan allowed a woman whose father lacked sons to take a wife and be socially recognized as her husband and as the father (pater, although not genitor) of her children. In situations in which women, such as prominent market women in West Africa, are able to amass property and other forms of wealth, they may take a wife. Such marriages allow the prominent woman to strengthen her social status and the economic importance of her household (Amadiume 1987).

Sometimes, when same-sex marriage is allowed, one of the partners is of the same biological sex as the spouse but is considered to belong to a different, socially constructed gender. Several Native American groups had figures known as "Two-Spirit," representing a gender in addition to male or female (Murray and Roscoe 1998). Sometimes, the Two-Spirit was a biological man who assumed many of the mannerisms, behavior patterns, and tasks of women. Such a Two-Spirit might marry a man and fulfill the traditional wifely role. Also, in some Native American cultures, a marriage of a "manly hearted woman" (a third or fourth gender) to another woman brought the traditional male–female division of labor to their household. The manly woman hunted and did other male tasks, while the wife played the traditional female role.

As of this writing, same-sex marriage is legal in 23 countries: Argentina, Belgium, Brazil, Canada, Columbia, Denmark, England and Wales, Finland, France, Greenland, Iceland, Ireland, Luxembourg, the Netherlands, New Zealand, Norway, Portugal, Scotland, South Africa, Spain, Sweden, the United States, and Uruguay. Twenty-first-century North America has witnessed a rapid and dramatic shift in public and legal opinions about same-sex marriage.

The legalization of same-sex marriage throughout the United States in June 2015 was achieved despite considerable opposition. In 1996, the U.S. Congress approved the Defense of Marriage Act (DOMA), which denied federal recognition and benefits to

A same-sex couple "just married" in Scotland, where, on February 4, 2014, the law was changed to allow same-sex couples to marry legally.
©Mark Runnacles/Getty Images News/Getty Images

same-sex couples. Voters in at least 29 U.S. states passed measures defining marriage as an exclusively heterosexual union. On June 26, 2013, the U.S. Supreme Court struck down a key part of DOMA and granted to legally married same-sex couples the same federal rights and benefits received by any legally married couple. In June 2015, the Supreme Court upheld the legality of same-sex marriage throughout the United States. Although opposition continues (often on religious grounds), public opinion has followed the judicial shift toward approval of same-sex marriage. (This chapter's "Anthropology Today" discusses how anthropological knowledge could have informed the 2015 Supreme Court decision legalizing same-sex marriage.)

Marriage: A Group Affair

Outside industrial societies, marriage often is more a relationship between groups than one between individuals. In our society, we think of marriage as an individual matter. Although the bride and groom usually seek their parents' approval, the final choice (to live together, to marry, to divorce) lies with the couple. The idea of romantic love symbolizes this individual relationship.

In nonindustrial societies, although there can be romantic love (Goleman 1992), marriage is a group concern. People don't just take a spouse; they assume obligations to a group of in-laws. When residence is patrilocal, for example, a woman must leave the community where she was born. She faces the prospect of spending the rest of her life in her husband's village, with his relatives.

Gifts at Marriage

Gifts at marriage are widespread among the world's cultures. A marital gift known as **dowry** occurs when the bride's family or kin group provides substantial gifts when their daughter marries. Ernestine Friedl (1962) describes a form of dowry in rural Greece, in which the bride gets a wealth transfer from her mother, to serve as a kind of trust fund during her marriage. More commonly, however, the dowry goes to the husband's family, and the custom is correlated with low female status. In this form of dowry, best known from India, women are perceived as burdens. When a man and his family take a wife, they expect to be compensated for the added responsibility.

In many societies with patrilineal descent, it is customary for the husband's group to present a substantial gift—before, at, or soon after the wedding—to his bride's group. The BaThonga of Mozambique call such a gift *lobola*, and the custom of giving something like **lobola** is widespread in patrilineal societies (Radcliffe-Brown 1924/1952). This gift compensates the bride's group for the loss of her companionship and labor. More important, it makes the children born to the woman full members of her husband's descent group. In matrilineal societies, children are members of the mother's group, and there is no reason for a lobola-like gift.

Lobola-like gifts exist in many more cultures than dowry does, but the nature and quantity of transferred items differ. Among the BaThonga of Mozambique, whose name—lobola—I will extend for this widespread custom, the gift consists of cattle. Use of livestock (usually cattle in Africa, pigs in Papua New Guinea) for lobola is common, but the number of animals given varies from society to society. We can generalize, however, that the larger the gift, the more stable the marriage. Lobola is insurance against divorce.

Imagine a patrilineal society in which a marriage requires the transfer of about 25 cattle from the groom's descent group to the bride's. Michael, a member of descent group A, marries Sarah from group B. His relatives help him assemble the lobola. He gets the most help from his close patrikin—his older brother, father, father's brother, and closest patrilineal cousins. The distribution of the cattle once they reach Sarah's group mirrors the manner in which they were assembled. Sarah's father, or her oldest brother if the father is dead, receives her lobola. He keeps most of the cattle to use as lobola for his sons' marriages. However, a share also goes to everyone who will be expected to help when Sarah's brothers marry.

When Sarah's brother David gets married, many of the cattle go to a third group—C, which is David's wife's group. Thereafter, they may serve as lobola to still other groups. Men constantly use their sisters' lobola cattle to acquire their own wives. In a decade, the cattle given when Michael married Sarah will have been exchanged widely.

In such societies, marriage entails an agreement between descent groups. If Sarah and Michael try to make their marriage succeed but fail to do so, both groups may conclude that the marriage can't last. Here it becomes especially obvious that marriages are relationships between groups as well as between individuals. If Sarah has a younger sister or niece (her older brother's daughter, for example), the concerned parties may agree to Sarah's replacement by a kinswoman.

However, incompatibility isn't the main problem that threatens marriage in societies with lobola customs. Infertility is a more important concern. If Sarah has no children, she and her group have not fulfilled their part of the marriage agreement. If the relationship is to endure, Sarah's group must furnish another woman, perhaps her younger sister, who can have children. If this happens, Sarah may choose to stay in her husband's village as his wife. Perhaps she will someday have a child. If she does stay on, her husband will have established a plural marriage, with more than one wife.

Durable Alliances

It is possible to exemplify the group-alliance nature of marriage by examining still another common practice—continuation of marital alliances when one spouse dies.

Sororate

What happens if Sarah dies young? Michael's group will ask Sarah's group for a substitute, often her sister. This custom is known as the **sororate** (see Figure 7.4). If Sarah has no sister, or if all her sisters already are married, another woman from her group may be available. Michael marries her, there is no need to return the lobola, and the alliance continues.

The sororate exists in both matrilineal and patrilineal societies. In a matrilineal society with matrilocal postmarital residence, a widower may remain with his wife's group by marrying her sister or another female member of her matrilineage (see Figure 7.4).

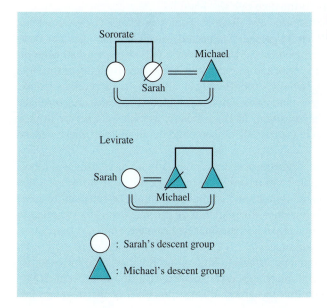

FIGURE 7.4
Sororate and Levirate

Levirate

What happens if the husband dies? In many societies, the widow may marry his brother. This custom is known as the **levirate** (see Figure 7.4). Like the sororate, it is a continuation marriage that maintains the alliance between descent groups, in this case by replacing the husband with another member of his group. The implications of the levirate vary with age. One study found that in African societies the levirate, although widely permitted, rarely involves cohabitation of the widow and her new husband. Furthermore, widows don't automatically marry the husband's brother just because they are allowed to. Often they prefer to make other arrangements.

Divorce

What factors work for and against divorce cross-culturally? As we've seen, marriages that are political alliances between groups are more difficult to dissolve than are marriages that are more individual affairs. We've seen that a substantial lobola gift may reduce the divorce rate for individuals; replacement marriages (levirate and sororate) also work to preserve group alliances. Divorce tends to be more common in matrilineal than in patrilineal societies. When residence is matrilocal (in the wife's home village), the wife may simply send off a man with whom she's incompatible, or he may choose to leave.

Among the Hopi of the American Southwest, houses were owned by matrilineal clans, with matrilocal postmarital residence. The household head was the senior woman of that household, which also included her daughters and their husbands and children. A son-in-law had no important role there; he returned to his own mother's home for his clan's social and religious activities. In this matrilineal society, women were socially and economically secure and the divorce rate was high.

In a study of the marital histories of 423 Hopi women in Oraibi (Orayvi) pueblo, Mischa Titiev (1992) found that 35 percent had been divorced at least once. For comparison, of all ever-married women in the United States, only 4 percent had been divorced in 1960, 10.7 percent in 1980, and 15 percent in 2013. The instability of the Hopi marital bond was due, at least partially, to conflicting loyalties to matrikin versus spouse. Jerome Levy (1992) generalizes that, cross-culturally, high divorce rates are correlated with a secure female economic position. In Hopi society, women were secure in their home and land ownership and in the custody of their children. In addition, there were no formal barriers to divorce.

Divorce is more difficult in a patrilineal society, especially when a substantial lobola gift would have to be reassembled and repaid if the marriage failed. A woman residing patrilocally (in her husband's household and community) might be reluctant to leave him. In patrilineal, patrilocal societies, the children of divorce would be expected to remain with their father, as members of his patrilineage. From the women's perspective, this is a strong impediment to divorce.

Divorce is fairly common among foragers. Among the Kalahari San, for example, between 25 and 40 percent of all marriages end in divorce (Blurton-Jones et al. 2000). Facilitating divorce is the fact that the group alliance functions of marriage are less important, because descent groups are less common among foragers than among food producers. Also facilitating divorce is the fact that marriages tend to last longer when a couple shares—and would have trouble dissolving—a significant joint fund of property. This usually is not the case among foragers, who have minimal material possessions. Marital stability is favored, however, when the nuclear family is a fairly autonomous year-round unit with a gender-based division of labor, particularly when the population is sparse, so that few alternative spouses are available.

In contemporary Western societies, we have the idea that romantic love is necessary for a good marriage (see Ingraham 2008). When romance fails, so may the marriage. Or it may not fail, if other benefits associated with marriage are compelling. Economic ties and obligations to children, along with other factors, such as concern about public opinion, or simple inertia, may keep marriages intact after sex, romance, or companionship fades. Also, even in modern societies, leaders and other elites may want to maintain politically strategic marriages at all costs.

Plural Marriages

Most nonindustrial food-producing societies, unlike most industrial nations, allow **plural marriages,** or **polygamy.** There are two varieties; one is common, and the other is very rare. The more common variant is **polygyny,** in which a man has more than one wife. The rare variant is **polyandry,** in which a woman has more than one husband. Polyandry is practiced in only a few societies, notably among certain groups in Tibet, Nepal, India, and Sri Lanka. In contemporary North America, where divorce is fairly easy and common, polygamy is against the law. North Americans are allowed, however, to practice *serial monogamy:* Individuals may have more than one spouse but never, legally, more than one at the same time.

Polygyny

We must distinguish between the social approval of plural marriage and its actual frequency. Many cultures approve of a man's having more than one wife. However, even when polygyny is allowed or encouraged, most men are monogamous, and polygyny characterizes only a fraction of the marriages.

What factors promote, and discourage, polygyny? Polygyny is much more common in patrilineal than in matrilineal societies. The relatively high status that women enjoy in matrilineal societies tends to grant them a degree of independence from men that makes polygyny less likely. Nor is polygyny characteristic of most foraging societies, where a married couple and nuclear family often function as an economically viable team. Most industrial nations have outlawed polygyny.

An equal sex ratio tends to work against polygyny if marriage is an expectation for both men and women. In the United States, about 105 males are born for every 100 females. In adulthood the ratio of men to women equalizes, and eventually it reverses. The average North American woman outlives the average man. In many nonindustrial societies as well, the male-biased sex ratio among children reverses in adulthood.

The custom of men marrying later than women promotes polygyny. Among Nigeria's Kanuri people (Cohen 1967), for example, men married between the ages of 18 and 30; women, between 12 and 14. The age difference between spouses meant there were more widows than widowers. Most of the widows remarried, some in polygynous unions. Among the Kanuri and in other polygynous societies, such as the Tiwi of northern Australia, widows made up a large number of the women involved in plural marriages (Hart, Pilling, and Goodale 1988). Polygyny is favored in situations in which having plural wives is an indicator of a man's household productivity, prestige, and social position. The more wives, the more workers. Increased productivity means more wealth. This wealth in turn attracts additional wives to the household. Wealth and wives bring greater prestige to the household and its head.

Polygyny also is supported when the existing spouses agree that another one should be added, especially if they are to share the same household. Sometimes, the first wife requests a second one to help with household chores. The second wife's status is lower than that of the first; they are senior and junior wives. The senior wife sometimes chooses the junior one from among her close kinswomen. Polygyny also can work when the cowives live apart. Among the Betsileo of Madagascar, the different wives always lived in different villages. A man's first (senior) wife, called "Big Wife," lived in the village where he cultivated his best rice field and spent most of his time. High-status Betsileo men with multiple rice fields could have a wife and households near each field. Those men spent most of their time with the senior wife, but they visited the others throughout the year.

Polygyny also can be politically advantageous. Plural wives can play important political roles in nonindustrial states. The king of the Merina, a populous society in the highlands of Madagascar, had palaces for each of his 12 wives in different provinces. He stayed with them when he traveled through the kingdom, and they acted as his local agents, overseeing and reporting on provincial matters. The king of Buganda, the major precolonial state of Uganda, took hundreds of wives, representing all the clans in his nation. Everyone in the kingdom became the king's in-law, and all the clans had a chance to provide the next ruler. This was a way of giving the common people a stake in the government.

We see that there is no single explanation for polygyny. Its context and function vary from society to society and even within the same society. Some men are polygynous because they have inherited a widow from a brother. Others have plural wives because they seek prestige or want to increase their household productivity. Men and women with political and economic ambitions cultivate marital alliances that serve their aims. In many societies, including the Betsileo of Madagascar and the Igbo of Nigeria, women arrange the marriages.

Polyandry

Polyandry is rare and is practiced under very specific conditions. Most of the world's polyandrous peoples live in South Asia—Tibet, Nepal, India, and Sri Lanka. In some of these areas, polyandry seems to be a cultural adaptation to mobility associated with customary male travel for trade, commerce, and military operations. Polyandry ensures there will be at least one man at home to accomplish male activities within a gender-based division of labor. Fraternal polyandry is also an effective strategy when resources are scarce. Brothers with limited resources (in land) pool their resources in expanded

Modern-day polygyny is illustrated by this photo (left) of South Africa's President Jacob Zuma and his three wives. In the United States as in South Africa, powerful men often have multiple wives, but legally not at the same time. U.S. President Donald Trump and his (third) wife Melania march in his inaugural day parade (right). (left): ©Mike Hutchings/AP Images; (right): ©Evan Vucci - Pool/ Getty Images News/Getty Images

(polyandrous) households. They take just one wife. Polyandry restricts the number of wives and heirs. Less competition among heirs means that land can be transmitted with minimal fragmentation.

The Online Marriage Market

People today shop for everything online, including romantic relationships, in what has been labeled the online "marriage market." There are huge differences in the marriage markets of industrial versus nonindustrial societies. In some of the latter, potential spouses may be limited to certain cousins or members of a specific descent group. Often, marriages are arranged by relatives. In almost all cases, however, there is some kind of preexisting social relationship between any two individuals who marry and their kin groups.

Potential mates still meet in person in modern nations. Sometimes, friends or relatives help arrange such meetings. Besides friends of friends, the marriage market also includes the workplace, bars, clubs, parties, churches, and hobby groups. Add the Internet, which has become a new place to seek out and develop "virtual" relationships, including romantic ones. As part of the "Me, My Spouse, and the Internet" project at the University of Oxford in England, Bernie Hogan, Nai Li, and William Dutton (2011) surveyed cohabiting couples in 18 countries (Table 7.2 lists those countries and the sample size for each). This study (conducted online) sampled 12,600 couples (25,200 individuals aged 18 and older), all with home Internet access. Respondents were asked about how they met their partners, their dating strategies, how they maintain their current relationships and social networks, and how they use the Internet.

The Oxford study found that people still seek and find partners in the old, familiar places, even as they look online as well. One-third of the respondents in the study had some experience with online dating, and about 15 percent were in a relationship that had started online. People who know someone who dates online are themselves more likely to date online and to approve of online dating. Like online banking and online shopping, Internet dating is an "experience technology" (Hogan et al. 2011): One's attitudes about that technology reflect

TABLE 7.2

Countries Sampled in the Oxford Internet Institute Project "Me, My Spouse, and the Internet"

Source: Hogan, Bernie, Nai Li, and William H. Dutton, *A Global Shift in the Social Relationships of Networked Individuals: Meeting and Dating Online Comes of Age.* Oxford, United Kingdom: Oxford Internet Institute, University of Oxford. 2011, Table 1.1, p. 5. Copyright © 2011.

Country	Sample Size	Percentage of Sample
Italy	3,515	13.9
France	2,970	11.8
Spain	2,673	10.6
Germany	2,638	10.5
United Kingdom	2,552	10.1
Brazil	2,438	9.7
Japan	2,084	8.3
Netherlands	1,491	5.9
Belgium	1,124	4.5
Sweden	794	3.1
Portugal	603	2.4
Finland	508	2.0
Ireland	368	1.5
Norway	317	1.3
Austria	309	1.2
Greece	297	1.2
Switzerland	278	1.1
Denmark	241	1.0
Total	25,200	100.0

one's experiences with it. People don't even need to have been successful at online dating to feel positive about it. Simply trying it enhances their view of the experience.

Who benefits most from the new technology? Is it young, tech-savvy people, who go online for virtually everything? Or might it be people who are socially isolated in the offline world, including divorced, older, and widowed people? Interestingly, the Oxford researchers found that older people were more likely than younger ones to use online dating to find their current partners. About 36 percent of people over 40 had done so, versus 23 percent of younger adults.

In Europe, the media-saturated nations of northern Europe were most likely to use online dating, which benefits from a critical mass of Internet connectivity (the more people online, the larger the pool of potential contacts). On the other hand, online Brazilians (who tend to be gregarious both on- and offline) were most likely to know someone who either began a relationship online or married someone first met online. Personal knowledge of an online romantic relationship was reported by 81 percent of the Brazilians in the study, versus only 40 percent of Germans.

The Internet reconfigures access to people in general. More of the respondents in the Oxford study reported making online friends or work connections than romantic liaisons. More than half (55 percent) of respondents (considering all 18 countries) had met someone new online (Hogan et al. 2011). The 2,438 Brazilians in the sample were the most likely to move from an online to a face-to-face contact. Fully 83 percent of Internet-enabled Brazilians reported meeting someone face-to-face after first meeting him or her online. Japanese respondents were least likely to meet in person after an online acquaintance. They also were least likely to engage in online dating.

Anthropology Today   *What Anthropologists Could Teach the Supreme Court about the Definition of Marriage*

A majority of Americans today, especially the younger ones, have no trouble accepting the practice and legalization of same-sex marriage. However, opinions on this issue have evolved rapidly. As recently as 2004, then-president George W. Bush was calling for a constitutional amendment banning gay marriage.

Eleven years later, on June 26, 2015, the U.S. Supreme Court issued one of its most socially significant rulings—legalizing same-sex marriage throughout the United States. In the landmark case *Obergefell v. Hodges,* the Court ruled, in a 5–4 decision, that the right to marry is guaranteed to same-sex couples by both the due process clause and the equal protection clause of the 14th Amendment to the U.S. Constitution.

In his strong dissent to that ruling, Chief Justice John Roberts asked, "Just who do we think we are?"—to so enlarge the definition of marriage. Roberts faulted the court for endorsing "the transformation of a social institution that has formed the basis of human society for millennia, for the Kalahari Bushmen and the Han Chinese, the Carthaginians and the Aztecs."

If Roberts knew more about anthropology, he would realize that these four societies don't really support his claim that marriage has universally been a union between one man and one woman. Although the "Kalahari Bushmen" (San peoples) do have exclusively heterosexual marriages, they also divorce and remarry at will. Nor, in Han period China, was marriage a lifetime union between one man and one woman. Han men were allowed to divorce, remarry, and consort with concubines. Within the Roman Empire, Carthaginian women who were Roman citizens were allowed to marry and divorce freely. Many members of the final society cited by Roberts—the

Aztecs—were polygamists. The Aztecs used matchmakers to arrange marriages and asked widows to marry a brother of their deceased husband (Joyce 2015). I doubt that Chief Justice Roberts intended to endorse frequent divorce, consorting with mistresses and concubines, and polygamy as aspects of "a social institution that has formed the basis of human society for millennia."

Roberts went on to argue that marriage "arose in the nature of things to meet a vital need: ensuring that children are conceived by a mother and father committed to raising them in the stable conditions of a lifetime relationship." Here the focus is on the role of marriage in procreation and raising children. As we have seen, however, marriage confers socially significant rights and obligations other than raising children. Nor is procreation necessary for or within marriage. Is a childless marriage any less legitimate than one with children? Is legal adoption of a child less legitimate than conception of the child by a married heterosexual couple? Every day in contemporary societies, men and women marry without expecting to conceive and raise children.

As John Borneman and Laurie Kain Hart (2015) observe, marriage is an elastic institution whose meaning and value vary from culture to culture and evolve over time. Consider the many examples of families, kinship groups, and marriage types considered in this chapter. From the Bosnian *zadruga* to the Nayar *tarawad* to matrilineal and patrilineal clans, lineages, local descent groups and extended families, children have been raised in, and have managed to survive and even flourish in, all kinds of kin groups. If we go back millennia, as Chief Justice Roberts would like to trace marriage, we would find "love, marriage, and the baby carriage" to be the

continued

Anthropology Today *continued*

exception rather than the rule. That is, the combination of romantic love, marriage, procreation, and raising children mainly, or even exclusively, within a nuclear family is a relatively recent—rather than a universal or ages-old—development.

Finally, consider the different forms of marriage that have been considered in this chapter: woman-marriage-to-a-woman among the Nuer, cousin marriage, Lakher

marriage to a half sibling, serial monogamy, and other forms that violate the idea that marriage is a lifetime union of one man and one woman.

I would hope, therefore, that the next time a member of the Supreme Court attempts to justify a practice using terms like "for millennia," "ages-old," "universal," or "basic human," he or she will first consult an anthropologist.

The Internet may enhance opportunities to meet people and to form personal relationships. but this accessibility also can be disruptive. It can spur jealousy, for example, when a partner makes new friends or reconnects to old ones—and with good reason. The Oxford researchers found that many people disclosed intimate personal details in online settings with someone other than their spouse or partner (Hogan et al. 2011; Oxford 2013). A future study might investigate whether the Internet plays a role in divorce as well as in dating and marriage.

Summary

1. Kinship and marriage organize social and political life in nonindustrial societies. One widespread kin group is the nuclear family, consisting of a married couple and their children. Other groups, such as extended families and descent groups, may assume functions usually associated with the nuclear family. Nuclear families tend to be especially important in foraging and industrial societies.

2. In contemporary North America, the nuclear family is the characteristic kin group for the middle class. Expanded households and sharing with extended family kin occur more frequently among the poor, who may pool their resources in dealing with poverty. Today, however, even in the American middle class, nuclear family households are declining as single-person households and other domestic arrangements increase.

3. The descent group is a basic kin group among nonindustrial food producers (farmers and herders). Unlike families, descent groups have perpetuity, lasting for generations. Descent-group members share and manage an estate. Lineages are based on demonstrated descent; clans, on stipulated descent. Unilineal (patrilineal and matrilineal) descent is associated with unilocal (patrilocal and matrilocal, respectively) postmarital residence.

4. Marriage, which usually is a form of domestic partnership, is difficult to define. Marriage conveys various rights. It establishes legal parentage, and it gives each spouse rights to the sexuality, labor, and property of the other. Marriage also establishes a "relationship of affinity" between each spouse and the other spouse's relatives.

5. Most societies have incest restrictions. Because kinship is socially constructed, such restrictions apply to different relatives in different societies. Exogamy extends social and political ties outward; endogamy does the reverse. Endogamic rules are common in stratified societies. One extreme example is India, where castes are the endogamous units.

6. In societies with descent groups, marriages are relationships between groups as well as between spouses. With lobola, the groom and his relatives transfer wealth to the bride and her relatives. As the value of the lobola gift increases, the divorce rate declines. Lobola customs show that marriages among nonindustrial food producers create and maintain group alliances. So does the sororate, by which a man marries the sister of his deceased wife, and the levirate, by which a woman marries the brother of her deceased husband.

7. The ease and frequency of divorce vary across cultures. When marriage is a matter of intergroup alliance, as is typically true in societies with descent groups, divorce is less common. A large fund of joint property also complicates divorce.

8. Many societies permit plural marriages. The two kinds of polygamy are polygyny and polyandry. The former involves multiple wives; the latter, multiple husbands. Polygyny is much more common than polyandry.

9. The Internet, which reconfigures social relations and networks more generally, is an important addition to the marriage market in contemporary nations.

Think Like an Anthropologist

1. Although the nuclear family may remain a cultural ideal for many Americans, other domestic arrangements now outnumber the "traditional" American household by more than five to one. What are some reasons for this shift? How do the media, including TV sitcoms, reflect changing ideas about family form and function?

2. Depending on the society, several different kinds of rights are allocated by marriage. What are those rights? Which among those rights do you consider more fundamental than others in your definition of marriage? Which ones can you do without? Why?

Key Terms

caste system, *149*
clan, *144*
descent group, *142*
dowry, *152*
endogamy, *149*
exogamy, *147*
expanded family
  household, *140*
extended family
  household, *140*
family, *137*

family of
  orientation, *138*
family of
  procreation, *138*
incest, *147*
levirate, *154*
lineage, *144*
lobola, *152*
matrilineal
  descent, *143*
matrilocality, *145*

neolocality, *139*
patrilineal
  descent, *143*
patrilocality, *145*
plural marriages
  (polygamy), *155*
polyandry, *155*
polygyny, *155*
sororate, *153*
unilineal
  descent, *143*

Chapter  8

Gender

Sex and Gender

Because anthropologists study biology, society, and culture, they are in a unique position to comment on nature (biological predispositions) and nurture (environment) as determinants of human behavior. Human attitudes, values, and behavior are limited not only by our genetic predispositions—which often are difficult to identify—but also by our experiences during enculturation. Our attributes as adults are determined both by our genes and by our environment during growth and development.

Questions about nature and nurture emerge in the discussion of human sex–gender roles and sexuality. Men and women differ genetically. Women have two X chromosomes, and men have an X and a Y. The father determines a baby's sex because only he has the Y chromosome to transmit. The mother always provides an X chromosome.

The chromosomal difference is expressed in hormonal and physiological contrasts. Humans are sexually dimorphic, more so than some primates, such as gibbons (small, tree-living Asiatic apes) and less so than others, such as gorillas and orangutans. **Sexual dimorphism** refers to differences in male and female biology besides the contrasts in breasts and genitals. Women and men differ not just in primary (genitalia and reproductive organs) and secondary (breasts, voice, hair distribution) sexual characteristics, but also in average weight, height, strength, and longevity. Women tend to live longer than men and have excellent endurance capabilities. In a given population, men tend to be taller and to weigh more than women do. Of course, there is a considerable overlap between the sexes in terms of height, weight, and physical strength, and there has been a pronounced reduction in sexual dimorphism during human biological evolution.

Just how far, however, do such genetically and physiologically determined differences go? What effects do they have on the way men and women act and are treated in different societies? Anthropologists have discovered both similarities and differences in the roles of men and women in different cultures. The predominant anthropological position on sex–gender roles and biology may be stated as follows:

> The biological nature of men and women [should be seen] not as a narrow enclosure limiting the human organism, but rather as a broad base upon which a variety of structures can be built. (Friedl 1975, p. 6)

Sex differences are biological, but gender encompasses all the traits that a culture assigns to and inculcates in males and females. *Gender,* in other words, refers to the cultural construction of whether one is female, male, or something else. Given the "rich and various constructions of gender" within the realm of cultural diversity, Susan Bourque and Kay Warren (1987) note that the same images of masculinity and femininity do not always apply. Margaret Mead did an early ethnographic study of variation in gender roles. Her book *Sex and Temperament in Three Primitive Societies* (1935/1950) was based on fieldwork in three societies in Papua New Guinea: the Arapesh, Mundugumor, and Tchambuli. The extent of personality variation in men and women in those three societies on the same island amazed Mead. She found that Arapesh men and women both acted as Americans have traditionally expected women to act: in a mild, parental, responsive way. Mundugumor men and women both, in contrast, acted as she believed we expect men to act: fiercely and aggressively. Finally, Tchambuli men were "catty," wore curls, and went shopping, but Tchambuli women were energetic and managerial and placed less emphasis on personal adornment than did the men. (Drawing on their case study of the Tchambuli, whom they call the Chambri, Errington and Gewertz [1987], while recognizing gender malleability, have disputed the specifics of Mead's account.)

There is a well-established field of feminist scholarship within anthropology (Lewin and Silverstein 2016; Rosaldo 1980b; Strathern 1988). Anthropologists have gathered systematic ethnographic data about similarities and differences involving gender in many cultural settings (Brettell and Sargent 2012; Burn 2011; Kimmel 2013; Mascia-Lees 2010; Ward and Edelstein 2013). Before we examine the cross-cultural data, some definitions are in order.

Gender roles are the tasks and activities a culture assigns by gender. Related to gender roles are **gender stereotypes,** which are oversimplified but strongly held ideas about the characteristics of males and females. **Gender stratification** describes an unequal distribution of rewards (socially valued resources, power, prestige, human rights, and personal freedom) between men and women, reflecting their different positions in a social hierarchy.

In stateless societies, gender stratification often is more obvious in regard to prestige than it is in regard to wealth. In her study of the Ilongots of northern Luzon in the Philippines, Michelle Rosaldo (1980a) described gender differences related to the positive cultural value placed on adventure, travel, and knowledge of the external world.

The realm of cultural diversity contains richly varied expressions of gender roles. In Niger, this Wodaabe man prepares for the annual Gerewol celebration, in which young bachelors paint their faces, dress elaborately, and gather in lines to dance and sing, vying for the attentions of marriageable young women. ©Robert Harding World Imagery/Alamy Stock Photo

More often than women, Ilongot men, as headhunters, visited distant places. They acquired knowledge of the external world, amassed experiences there, and returned to express their knowledge, adventures, and feelings in public oratory. They received acclaim as a result. Ilongot women had inferior prestige because they lacked external experiences on which to base knowledge and dramatic expression. We must distinguish between prestige systems and actual power in a given society (Ong 1989). High male prestige does not necessarily entail economic or political power held by men over their families. (For more on Rosaldo's contributions to gender studies, see Lugo and Maurer 2000.)

Recurrent Gender Patterns

You probably had chores when you were growing up. Was there any gender bias in what you were asked to do, compared with your brother or sister? If you were raised by two parents, did any tension arise over your parents' division of labor? Based on cross-cultural data from 185 societies worldwide, Table 8.1 lists activities that are generally male, generally female, or swing (either male or female). Before you look at that table, see if you can assign the following to one gender or the other (M or F): hunting large animals ( ), gathering wild vegetable foods ( ), tending crops ( ), fishing ( ), cooking ( ), fetching water ( ), making baskets ( ), making drinks ( ). Now consult Table 8.1 and see

TABLE 8.1   **Generalities in the Division of Labor by Gender, Based on Data from 185 Societies**

Source: Murdock, G.P. and C. Provost, "Factors in the Division of Labor by Sex: A Cross-Cultural Analysis," *Ethnology* vol. 12, no., p. 202–225. © 1973.

Generally Male Activities	Swing (Male or Female) Activities	Generally Female Activities
Hunting large aquatic animals (e.g., whales, walrus)	Making fire	Gathering fuel (e.g., firewood)
Smelting ores	Body mutilation	Making drinks
Metalworking	Preparing skins	Gathering wild vegetal foods
Lumbering	Gathering small land animals	Dairy production (e.g., churning)
Hunting large land animals	Planting crops	Spinning
Working wood	Making leather products	Doing the laundry
Hunting fowl	Harvesting	Fetching water
Making musical instruments	Tending crops	Cooking
Trapping	Milking	Preparing vegetal food (e.g., processing cereal grains)
Building boats	Making baskets	
Working stone	Carrying burdens	
Working bone, horn, and shell	Making mats	
Mining and quarrying	Caring for small animals	
Setting bones	Preserving meat and fish	
Butchering*	Loom weaving	
Collecting wild honey	Gathering small aquatic animals	
Clearing land	Manufacturing clothing	
Fishing	Making pottery	
Tending large herd animals		
Building houses		
Preparing the soil		
Making nets		
Making rope		

*All the activities above "butchering" are almost always done by men; those from "butchering" through "making rope" are usually done by men.

how you did. Reflect on your results. Is what's true cross-culturally still true of the division of labor by gender in today's world, including the United States?

The data in Table 8.1 on the division of labor by gender illustrate cross-cultural generalities rather than universals. For example, the table reports a general tendency for men to build boats, but there are societies that contradict the rule. One was the Hidatsa, a Native American group in which the women made the boats used to cross the Missouri River. (Traditionally, the Hidatsa were village farmers and bison hunters on the North American Plains; they now live in North Dakota.) Another exception is that Pawnee women worked wood; this is the only Native American group that assigned this activity to women. (The Pawnee, also traditionally Plains farmers and bison hunters, originally lived in what is now central Nebraska and central Kansas; they now live on a reservation in north central Oklahoma.)

Exceptions to cross-cultural generalizations may involve societies or individuals. That is, a society like the Hidatsa can contradict the cross-cultural generalization that men build boats by assigning that task to women. Or, in a society where men usually build boats, a particular woman or women can contradict that expectation by doing the male activity. Table 8.1 shows that in a sample of 185 societies, certain activities ("swing activities") are assigned to either or both men and women. Among the most important of these swing activities are planting, tending, and harvesting crops. Some societies customarily assign more farming chores to women, whereas others make men the primary farmers. Among the tasks almost always assigned to men, some (e.g., hunting large animals on land and sea) seem clearly related to the greater average size and strength of males. Others, such as working wood and making musical instruments, seem more arbitrary. Women, of course, are not exempt from arduous and time-consuming physical labor, such as gathering firewood and fetching water. In Arembepe, Bahia, Brazil, women routinely transported water in 5-gallon tins, balanced on their heads, from wells and lagoons located long distances from their homes.

The original coding of the data in Table 8.1 probably illustrates a male bias in that extradomestic activities received much more prominence than domestic activities did. Think about how female domestic activities could have been specified in greater detail. One wonders whether collecting wild honey (listed in Table 8.1) is more necessary or time-consuming than nursing a baby (absent from the table). Also, notice that the table does not mention trade and market activity, in which either or both men and women are active.

Both women and men have to fit their activities into 24-hour days. Turn now to Table 8.2, which shows that the time and effort spent in subsistence activities by men and women tend to be about equal. If anything, women do slightly more subsistence work than men do. In domestic activities and child care, however, female labor predominates. In about half the societies studied, men did virtually no domestic work. Even in societies where men did domestic chores, the bulk of such work was done by women. Adding together their subsistence activities and their domestic work, women tend to work more hours than men do. Furthermore, women had primary responsibility for young children in two-thirds of the societies studied.

TABLE 8.2 **Time and Effort Expended on Subsistence Activities by Men and Women (percent)***

Source: Whyte, M.F. "Cross-Cultural Codes Dealing with the Relative Status of Women," *Ethnology,* vol.17, no.2, p.211–239. Copyright © 1978.

More by men	16
Roughly equal	61
More by women	23

*Percentage of 88 randomly selected societies for which information was available on this variable.

TABLE 8.3   **Does the Society Allow Multiple Spouses? (percent)***

Source: Whyte, M.F. "Cross-Cultural Codes Dealing with the Relative Status of Women," *Ethnology,* vol.17, no.2, p.211–239. Copyright © 1978.

For males only (polygyny)	77
For both, but more commonly for males	4
For neither (monogamy)	16
For both, but more commonly for females (polyandry)	2

*Percentage of 92 randomly selected societies for which information was available on this variable.

What about access to mates? Table 8.3 shows that polygyny (multiple wives) is much more common than polyandry (multiple husbands). Furthermore, concerning premarital and extramarital sex, men tend to be less restricted than women are, although the restrictions were equal in about half the societies studied (Whyte 1978). Double standards that limit women more than men are one illustration of gender stratification, which we now examine more systematically.

Gender Roles and Gender Stratification

Economic roles affect gender stratification (the *unequal* distribution of social value by gender). In one cross-cultural study, Sanday (1974) found that gender stratification decreased when men and women made roughly equal contributions to subsistence. She found that gender stratification was greatest when the women contributed either much more or much less than the men did.

In foraging societies, gender stratification was most marked when men contributed much *more* to the diet than women did. This was true among the Inuit and other northern hunters and fishers. Among tropical and semitropical foragers, by contrast, gathering usually supplies more food than hunting and fishing do. Gathering is generally women's work. Men usually hunt and fish, but women also do some fishing and may hunt small animals, as is true among the Agta of the Philippines (Griffin and Estioko-Griffin 1985). Gender status tends to be more equal when gathering is prominent than it is when hunting and fishing are the main subsistence activities.

Gender status also is more equal when the domestic and public spheres aren't sharply separated. (**Domestic** means within or pertaining to the home.) Strong differentiation between the home and the outside world is called the **domestic–public dichotomy,** or the *private–public contrast*. The outside world can include politics, trade, warfare, or work. Often when domestic and public spheres are clearly separated, public activities have greater prestige than domestic ones do. This can promote gender stratification, because men are more likely to be active in the public domain than women are.

Reduced Gender Stratification: Matrilineal–Matrilocal Societies

Cross-cultural variation in gender status also is related to rules of descent and postmarital residence. With matrilineal descent and *matrilocality* (residence after marriage with the wife's relatives), female status tends to be high. Matriliny and matrilocality disperse related males, rather than consolidating them. By contrast, patriliny and *patrilocality* (residence after marriage with the husband's kin) keep male relatives together. Matrilineal–matrilocal systems tend to occur in societies where population pressure on strategic resources is minimal and warfare is infrequent.

Women tend to have high status in matrilineal–matrilocal societies for several reasons. Descent-group membership, succession to political positions, allocation of land, and overall social identity all come through female links. Among the matrilineal Malays of Negeri Sembilan, Malaysia (Peletz 1988), matriliny gave women sole inheritance of ancestral rice fields. Matrilocality created solidary clusters of female kin. These Malay women had considerable influence beyond the household. In such matrilineal contexts, women are the basis of the entire social structure. Although public authority may be assigned nominally to the men, much of the power and decision making may belong to the senior women.

Matriarchy

If a patriarchy is a political system ruled by men, is a matriarchy necessarily a political system *ruled* by women? Or might we apply the term *matriarchy,* as anthropologist Peggy Reeves Sanday (2002) does, to a political system in which women play a much more prominent role than men do in social and political organization? One example would be the Minangkabau of West Sumatra, Indonesia, whom Sanday (2002) has studied for decades. Sanday considers the Minangkabau a matriarchy because women are the center, origin, and foundation of the social order. The oldest village in a cluster is called the "mother village." In ceremonies, women are addressed by the term used for their mythical Queen Mother. Women control land inheritance, and couples reside matrilocally. In the wedding ceremony, the wife collects her husband from his household and, with her female kin, escorts him to hers. If there is a divorce, the husband simply takes his things and leaves. Yet despite the special position of women, the Minangkabau matriarchy is not the equivalent of female rule, given the Minangkabau belief that all decision making should be by consensus.

Increased Gender Stratification: Patrilineal–Patrilocal Societies

Martin and Voorhies (1975) link the decline of matriliny and the spread of the **patrilineal–patrilocal complex** (consisting of patrilineality, patrilocality, warfare, and male supremacy) to pressure on resources. Faced with scarce resources, patrilineal–patrilocal cultivators such as the Yanomami often raid other villages. This warfare favors patrilocality and patriliny, customs that keep related men together in the same village, where they make strong allies in battle.

The patrilineal–patrilocal complex also characterizes many societies in highland Papua New Guinea. Women work hard growing and processing subsistence crops, raising and tending pigs (the main domesticated animal and a favorite food), and doing domestic cooking, but they are isolated from the public domain, which men control. Men grow and distribute prestige crops, prepare food for feasts, and arrange marriages. The men even get to trade the pigs and control their use in ritual.

A Minangkabau bride and groom in West Sumatra, Indonesia, where anthropologist Peggy Reeves Sanday has conducted several years of ethnographic fieldwork. ©Lindsay Hebberd/Corbis

In densely populated areas of the Papua New Guinea highlands, male–female avoidance is associated with strong pressure on resources (Lindenbaum 1972). Men fear all female contact, including sexual acts. They think that sexual contact with women will weaken them. Indeed, men see everything female as dangerous and polluting. They segregate themselves in men's houses and hide their precious ritual objects from women. They delay marriage, and some never marry. By contrast, the sparsely populated areas of Papua New Guinea, such as recently settled areas, lack taboos on male–female contacts. The image of woman as polluter fades, men and women mingle together, and reproductive rates are high.

Patriarchy and Violence

Patriarchy describes a political system ruled by men in which women have inferior social and political status, including basic human rights. Barbara Miller (1997), in a study of systematic neglect of females, describes women in rural northern India as "the endangered sex." Societies that feature a full-fledged patrilineal–patrilocal complex, replete with warfare and intervillage raiding, also typify patriarchy. Such practices as dowry murders, female infanticide, and clitoridectomy exemplify patriarchy, which extends from tribal societies such as the Yanomami to state societies such as India and Pakistan.

In some parts of Papua New Guinea, the patrilineal–patrilocal complex has extreme social repercussions. Regarding females as dangerous and polluting, men may segregate themselves in men's houses (such as this one, located near the Sepik River), where they hide their precious ritual objects from women. Are there places like this in your society? ©George Holton/Science Source

The gender inequality spawned by patriarchy and violence, which continues into the 21st century, can be deadly. Anyone who follows current events will have heard of recent cases of blatant abuse of women and girls, particularly in the context of warfare and terrorism, for example, in Bosnia, Syria, and Nigeria. In all of these places, rape has been used as a weapon of war or as punishment for transgressions committed by the victim's male relatives. In Afghanistan, Pakistan, and elsewhere, girls have been prevented from, or punished for, attending school. In 2014, Boko Haram, a jihadist rebel group in northern Nigeria, which also opposes female education, kidnapped nearly 300 schoolgirls, whom they subjected to abuse and forced marriages.

Sometimes, thankfully, such abuse fails in its attempt to silence female voices. Consider Malala Yousafzai (born in 1997 in northern Pakistan), who at the early age of 9 years embarked on her ongoing career as a forceful and persuasive advocate for female education. Her courageous early work, including public speaking and a blog for the BBC (started when she was 11), criticized the Taliban for its efforts to block girls' education and prompted the Taliban to issue a death threat against her. In October 2012, a gunman shot Malala (then age 14) three times on a school bus as she was traveling home from school. She survived and has continued to speak out about the importance of education for girls. In 2014 she became the youngest person ever to receive the Nobel Peace Prize.

Family violence and domestic abuse of women are also widespread problems. Domestic violence occurs in nuclear family settings, such as Canada and the United States, as well as in more blatantly patriarchal contexts. Cities, with their impersonality and isolation from extended kin networks, are breeding grounds for domestic violence, as may be certain rural areas where women lead isolated lives.

In many societies, especially patriarchal ones, women experience, and fear, intimidation as they increasingly enter the public sphere, especially in impersonal, urban settings. "Ladies Only" lines like this one at the Golden Temple in Amritsar, Punjab, India, are designed to help women feel safer and more comfortable in public areas. ©Conrad P. Kottak

When a woman lives in her own birth village, she has kin nearby to protect her interests. Even in patrilocal polygynous settings, women often count on the support of their cowives and sons in disputes with potentially abusive husbands. Unfortunately, settings in which women have a readily available support network are disappearing from today's world. Patrilineal social forms and isolated families have spread at the expense of matriliny. Many nations have declared polygyny illegal. More and more women, and men, find themselves cut off from their families and extended kin.

With the spread of the women's rights and human rights movements, attention to abuse of women has increased. Laws have been passed, and mediating institutions established. Brazil's female-run police stations for battered women provide an example, as do shelters for victims of domestic abuse in the United States and Canada. A series of "Ladies Only" facilities, including trains and entry lines, can be found throughout India. But patriarchal institutions do persist in what should be a more enlightened world.

Gender in Industrial Societies

The economic roles of men and women have changed and changed again over the course of American history. Nineteenth-century pioneer women worked productively in farming and home industry. As production shifted from home to factory, some women, particularly those who were poor or unmarried, turned to factory employment. Young White women typically worked outside the home only for a time, until they married and had children. The experience was different for African American women, many of whom, after abolition, continued working as field hands and domestic workers.

Changes in Gendered Work

Changing attitudes about women's work have reflected economic conditions and world events. In the United States, for example, the "traditional" idea that "a woman's place is in the home" developed as industrialism spread after 1900. One reason for this change was an influx of European immigrants, providing a male workforce willing to accept low wages for jobs, including factory work, that women previously might have held. Eventually, machine tools and mass production further reduced the need for female labor.

Anthropologist Maxine Margolis (2000) describes how gendered work, attitudes, and beliefs have varied in response to American economic needs. For example, when men are off fighting wars, work outside the home has been presented as women's patriotic duty, and the notion that women are biologically unfit for hard physical labor has faded.

The rapid population growth and business expansion that followed World War II created a demand for women to fill jobs in clerical work, public school teaching, and nursing (traditionally defined as female occupations). Inflation and the culture of consumption also have spurred female employment. When demand and/or prices rise, multiple paychecks help maintain family living standards.

During the world wars the notion that women were biologically unfit for hard physical labor faded. Shown here is World War II's famous Rosie the Riveter. Is there a comparable poster woman today? What does her image say about modern gender roles? Source: National Archives and Records Administration

Economic changes after World War II also set the stage for the contemporary women's movement, marked by the publication of Betty Friedan's influential book *The Feminine Mystique* in 1963 and the founding of NOW, the National Organization for Women, in 1966. Among other things, the movement promoted expanded work opportunities for women, including the goal (as yet unrealized) of equal pay for equal work. Between 1970 and 2015, the female percentage of the American workforce rose from 38 to 47 percent. About 77 million women now have paid employment, compared with about 86 million men. Women fill more than half (52 percent) of all management and professional jobs (Bureau of Labor Statistics 2014). And it's not mainly single women working, as once was the case. Table 8.4 presents figures on the generally increasing extradomestic labor of American wives and mothers, including those with young children.

TABLE 8.4   **Workforce Participation Rates of American Mothers, Wives, and Husbands, 1960–2015***

Source: Proctor, B. D., J. L. Semega, and M. A. Kollar, 2016, "Income and Poverty in the United States: 2015." U.S. Census Bureau, *Current Population Reports,* P60–256. p. 11, 2016.

Year	Percentage of Married Women, Husband Present with Children under 6	Percentage of All Married Women[†]	Percentage of All Married Men[‡]
1960	19	32	89
1970	30	40	86
1980	45	50	81
1990	59	58	79
2010	62	61	76
2015	60	61	74

*Civilian population 16 years of age and older.
†Husband present.
‡Wife present.

Note in Table 8.4 that the cash employment of American married men has been falling while that of American married women has been rising. In 1960, 89 percent of all married men worked, compared with just 32 percent of married women—a gap of 57 percent. That gap had narrowed to 13 percent by 2015, as cash employment of husbands declined to 74 percent, while that of wives rose to 61 percent. The median income of American women working full time in 2015 was 80 percent that of a comparably employed male, up from 68 percent in 1989 (Entmacher et al. 2013; Proctor, Semega, and Kollar 2016).

As women increasingly work outside the home, ideas about the gender roles of males and females have changed. Compare your grandparents and your parents. Chances are you have an employed mother, but your grandmother is more likely to have been a stay-at-home mom. Your grandfather is more likely than your father to have worked in manufacturing and to have belonged to a union. Your father is more likely than your grandfather to have participated significantly in child care and housework.

Thanks to automation and robotics, jobs have become less demanding in terms of physical labor. With machines to do the heavy work, the smaller average body size and lesser average strength of women are no longer significant impediments to blue-collar employment. But the main reason we don't see more modern-day Rosies working alongside male riveters is that the U.S. workforce itself has been abandoning heavy-goods manufacture. In the 1950s, two-thirds of American jobs were blue-collar, compared with fewer than 15 percent today. The location of those jobs has shifted within the world capitalist economy. Third World countries, with their cheaper labor costs, produce steel, automobiles, and other heavy goods less expensively than the United States can, but the United States excels at services. The American mass education system has many deficiencies, but it does train millions of people for service and information-oriented jobs.

Another important change since the 1960s is the increasing levels of education and professional employment among women. In the United States today, more women than men attend and graduate from college. Women will soon comprise the majority of college-educated workers in the U.S. labor force. Back in 1968, women made up less than 10 percent of the entering classes of MD (medicine), JD (law), and MBA (business) programs. The proportion of female students in those programs has risen to about 50 percent. Nowadays, female college graduates aged 30 to 34 are just as likely to be doctors, dentists, lawyers, professors, managers, and scientists as they are to be working in traditionally female professions as teachers, nurses, librarians, secretaries, or social workers. In the 1960s, women were seven times more likely to be in the latter than in the former series of professions.

Despite the many gains, female employment continues to lag noticeably in certain highly paid professions. In computer science and engineering, the percentage of female graduates has declined, to about 20 percent from 37 percent in 1980. By midcareer, twice the number of women as men leave their jobs in computer science, often because they perceive an uncomfortable and unsupportive workplace environment. Nearly 40 percent of women who left science, engineering, and technology jobs cited a "hostile macho culture" as their primary reason for doing so, versus only 27 percent who cited compensation (Council of Economic Advisers Report 2014).

Work and Family: Reality and Stereotypes

People everywhere have work and family obligations, but ideas about how to balance those responsibilities have changed considerably in recent years. Both men and women increasingly question the cultural assumption that the man should be the breadwinner while the woman assumes domestic and child-care responsibilities. Over 40 percent of American mothers are their household's primary or sole breadwinner. This includes both single mothers and married mothers. Fathers increasingly are assuming caregiving activities traditionally done by mothers. Seven percent of American families with children are father-only families. In general, American fathers spend significantly more time on child care and housework today than they did in the past. American fathers now do 4.6 more hours of child care, and 4.4 more hours of housework, per week than they did in 1965.

However, just as barriers remain to women's progress in the workplace, there are lingering obstacles—both material and cultural—to men's success at home. Women still do much more domestic work than men do, and the average man still works longer hours outside the home and earns more money than the average woman does. There is a cultural lag as well. A persistent stereotype is that of the incompetent male homemaker. For decades, clueless husbands and inept fathers have been a staple of television sitcoms—especially those produced after large numbers of women began to enter the workforce. Women still tend to think of themselves as better homemakers than their husbands are. Former Princeton professor Anne-Marie Slaughter (2013, 2015) cites examples of American women who maintain deeply entrenched stereotypes about men's (lack of) domestic capabilities—from kids to kitchens (Slaughter 2013).

Slaughter discusses how, even when men want to play a prominent domestic role, women may resist. The same woman who says she wants her husband to do more at home may then criticize him for not "doing things right" when he does pitch in. As Slaughter points out, "Doing things right" means doing things the woman's way. Practice, of course, does make perfect, and women still do a disproportionate share of housework and child care in 21st-century America. If the woman is the one who usually does the domestic work, and if she assumes she can do it better and faster than her husband, she probably will do so. A stereotype can become a self-fulfilling prophecy, often reinforced by material reality.

When women ask their husbands for "help" around the house or with the kids, they are affirming the feminine role as primary homemaker and child-care provider. The husband is viewed as merely a helper rather than as an equal partner. Slaughter (2013, 2015) argues that men and women need to commit to and value a larger male domestic role, and employers need to make it easier for their employees to balance work and family responsibilities.

Both fathers and mothers increasingly are seeking jobs that offer flexibility, require less travel, and include paid parental leave (including paternity leave). The United States lags behind other developed nations in providing such benefits, which help workers build long-term careers as they also fulfill family responsibilities. Although a few states and local governments do offer paid parental leave to their employees, only about 11 percent of American private-sector employers offer paid leave specifically for family reasons. Americans, both men and women, increasingly report that work interferes with family—not the other way around. Some 46 percent of working men and women report that job demands sometimes or often interfere with their family lives, up from 41 percent 15 years ago (Parker and Livingston 2016).

A quarter of American workers report actual or threatened job loss because of an illness- or family-related absence. The work–family balancing act is particularly challenging for low-wage workers. They tend to have the least workplace flexibility, the most uncertain work hours, and the fewest benefits, and they can least afford to take unpaid leave. The toll is especially hard on single mothers.

The Feminization of Poverty

Alongside the economic gains of many American women, especially the college educated, stands an opposite extreme: the feminization of poverty. This refers to the increasing representation of women (and their children) among America's poorest people. The 2015 median income of married-couple families ($84,626) was substantially more than twice that of families maintained by a single woman ($37,797) (Proctor et al. 2016).

The feminization of poverty isn't just a North American phenomenon. The percentage of single-parent (usually female-headed) households has been increasing worldwide. The figure ranges from about 10 percent in Japan, to between 10 and 20 percent in certain South Asian and Southeast Asian countries, to almost 50 percent in certain African countries and the Caribbean. Among the developed Western nations, the United States maintains the largest percentage of single-parent households (around 30 percent), followed by the United Kingdom, Canada, Ireland, and Denmark (over 20 percent in each). Globally, households headed by women tend to be poorer than those headed by men. In the United States in 2015, the poverty rate for female-headed families with no husband present was 28.2 percent, compared with 5.4 percent for married-couple families (Proctor et al. 2016). More than half the poor children in the United States live in families headed by women (Entmacher et al. 2013).

One way to improve the situation of poor women is to encourage them to organize. Membership in a group can help women gain confidence and mobilize resources (Dunham 2009). New women's groups can in some cases revive or replace traditional forms of social organization that have been disrupted (Buvinic 1995; Gunewardena and Kingsolver 2007).

Work and Happiness

Table 8.5 lists the 13 countries in which female labor-force participation was greatest in 2015. The highest rate, 86 percent, was in Iceland; the lowest rate among the 13 was in the United States, at 67 percent. Turkey is also included in the table as an example of a low-participation country, with a rate of 35 percent.

A relationship appears to exist between a country's rate of female labor-force participation and its citizens' feelings of well-being. The *World Happiness Report,* which has been published annually since 2012, is an attempt to measure well-being and happiness in 155 countries. Its measurements are based on a set of six key variables, and a series of lesser ones. The six variables that are related most strongly to a country's sense of well-being are its per-capita gross domestic product (GDP, an indicator of its economic strength), social support, healthy life expectancy, freedom to make life choices, generosity in giving, and perceptions of corruption. The first five are positive variables.

TABLE 8.5
Female Labor Force Participation and Well-Being by Country, 2015–2017

Source: Organization for Economic Cooperation and Development, 2016; Helliwell, John, Richard Layard and Jeffrey Sachs, 2016.

Country	Percentage of Women in Labor Force (2015)	Rank among World's "Happiest Countries" (2017)
Iceland	86	3
Switzerland	80	4
Sweden	80	10
Norway	76	1
Denmark	75	2
Netherlands	75	6
New Zealand	74	8
Canada	74	7
Finland	74	5
Germany	73	16
United Kingdom	73	19
Australia	71	9
United States	67	14
Turkey (lowest in table)	35	69

As they increase, so does the sense of well-being. The last one, perceptions of corruption, is a negative variable. That is, the less people perceive corruption, the happier they are. The 2017 *World Happiness Report* is issued by the Sustainable Development Solutions Network at Columbia University.

Norway was the world's happiest country in 2017, followed by Denmark, Iceland, and Switzerland. Canada came in seventh; and the United States, 14th. All but two of the countries with the highest female employment (Germany and the United Kingdom) also were among the world's 14 happiest. Correlations, of course, are not causes, and one wonders exactly why, as more women work outside the home, citizens might feel a greater sense of well-being. The greater financial security associated with dual-earner households may be part of the explanation. The world's happiest countries not only have more employed women, but they also have a higher living standard and a more secure government safety net. Can you think of other factors that might explain a relationship between happiness and work outside the home?

Beyond Male and Female

Gender is socially constructed, and societies may recognize more than two genders (see Nanda 2014). The contemporary United States, for example, includes individuals who may self-identify using such labels as "transgender," "intersex," "gender fluid," and "transsexual." Such persons contradict dominant male/female gender distinctions by being part male and female, or neither male nor female. Because people who self-identify as transgender are increasingly visible, we must be careful about seeing masculine and feminine as absolute and binary categories.

Sex, we have seen, is biological, whereas gender is socially constructed. Transgender is a social category that includes individuals who *may or may not* contrast biologically with ordinary males and females. Within the transgender category, intersex people usually contrast biologically with ordinary males and females, but *transgender also includes people whose gender identity has no apparent biological roots*. The distinction between the terms *intersex* and *transgender* is like the distinction between sex and gender. *Intersex* refers to biology, while *transgender* refers to an identity that is socially constructed and individually performed (Butler 1988, 1990, 2015).

The term **intersex** encompasses a variety of conditions involving a discrepancy between the external genitals (penis, vagina, etc.) and the internal genitals (testes, ovaries, etc.). The causes of intersex are varied and complex (Kaneshiro 2009): (1) An XX intersex person has the chromosomes of a woman (XX) and normal ovaries, uterus, and fallopian tubes, but the external genitals appear male. Usually this results from a female fetus having been exposed to an excess of male hormones before birth. (2) An XY intersex person has the chromosomes of a man (XY), but the external genitals are incompletely formed, ambiguous, or female. The testes may be normal, malformed, or absent. (3) A true gonadal intersex person has both ovarian and testicular tissue. The external genitals may be ambiguous or may appear to be female or male. (4) Intersex also can result from an unusual chromosome combination, such as X0 (only one X chromosome, and no Y chromosome), XXY, XYY, and XXX. In the last three cases there is an extra sex chromosome, either an X or a Y.

These chromosomal combinations don't typically produce a discrepancy between internal and external genitalia, but there may be problems with sex hormone levels and overall sexual development. The XXY configuration, known as *Klinefelter syndrome,* is the most common of these chromosomal combinations and the second most common condition (after Down syndrome) caused by the presence of extra chromosomes in humans. Effects of Klinefelter occur in about 1 of every 1,000 males. One in every 500 males has an extra X chromosome but lacks the main symptoms—small testicles and reduced fertility. With XXX, or *triple X syndrome,* there is an extra X chromosome in each cell of a human female. Triple X occurs in about 1 of every 1,000 female births. There usually is no physically distinguishable difference between triple X women and other women. The same is true of XYY compared with other males.

Turner syndrome encompasses several conditions, of which X0 (absence of one sex chromosome) is most common. In this case, all or part of one of the sex chromosomes is absent. Girls with Turner syndrome typically are sterile because of nonworking ovaries and amenorrhea (absence of a menstrual cycle).

Biology isn't destiny; people construct their identities in society. Many individuals affected by one of the biological conditions just described see themselves simply as male or female, rather than transgender. Individuals may become **transgender** when their gender identity contradicts their biological sex at birth and the gender identity that society assigned to them in infancy. Feeling that their previous gender assignment was incorrect, they assert or seek to achieve a new one. The transgender category is diverse. Some transgender individuals lean toward male; some, female; some, toward neither of the dominant genders.

The anthropological record attests that gender diversity beyond male and female exists in many societies and has taken many forms across societies and cultures (see Nanda 2014; Peletz 2009). Consider, for example, the eunuch, or "perfect servant" (a castrated man who served as a safe attendant to harems in Byzantium [Tougher 2008]). Hijras, who live mainly in northern India, are culturally defined as "neither men nor women," or as men who become women by undergoing castration and adopting women's dress and behavior. Hijras identify with the Indian mother goddess and are believed to channel her power. They are known for their ritualized performances at births and marriages, where they dance and sing, conferring the mother goddess's blessing on the child or the married couple. Although culturally defined as celibate, some hijras now engage in prostitution, in which their role is as women with men (Nanda 1996, 1998). Hijra social movements have campaigned for recognition as a third gender, and in 2005, Indian passport application forms were updated with three gender options: M, F, and E (for male, female, and eunuch [i.e, hijra], respectively) (*Telegraph* 2005).

Several Native American tribes, including the Zuni of the American Southwest, included gender-variant individuals, described by the term "Two-Spirit." Depending on the society, as many as four genders might be recognized: feminine women, masculine women, feminine men, and masculine men. The Zuni Two-Spirit was a male who

Neither men nor women, hijras constitute India's third gender. Many hijras get their income from performing at ceremonies, begging, or prostitution. The beauty contest shown here was organized by an AIDS prevention and relief organization that works with the local hijra community. ©Maciej Dakowicz/Alamy Stock Photo

adopted social roles traditionally assigned to women and, through performance of a third gender, contributed to the social and spiritual well-being of the community (Roscoe 1991, 1998). Some Balkan societies included "sworn virgins," born females who assumed male gender roles and activities to meet societal needs when there was a shortage of men (Gremaux 1993).

Among the Gheg tribes of North Albania, "virginal transvestites" were biologically female, but locals considered them "honorary men" (Shryock 1988). Some Albanian adolescent girls have chosen to become men, remain celibate, and live among men, with the support of their families and villagers (Young 2000). And consider Polynesia. In Tonga the term *fakaleitis* describes males who behave as women do, thereby contrasting with mainstream Tongan men. Similar to Tonga's *fakaleitis*, Samoan *fa'afafine* and Hawaiian *mahu* are men who adopt feminine attributes, behaviors, and visual markers.

Transgender individuals are increasingly visible in the media and our everyday lives. The Amazon television series *Transparent,* whose principal character is a transgender woman, has received several awards. The emergence of Caitlyn Jenner as a transgender woman received considerable media attention in 2015. Facebook now offers more than 50 gender options (Miller 2015). There have been various recent attempts to estimate the transgender population of the United States. The U.S. Census Bureau attempted such an estimate based on census records of people whose name change suggested a gender switch (Miller 2015). Of Americans who participated in the 2010 census, about 90,000 had changed their names to one of the opposite gender. Another estimate examined survey data and estimated that 0.3 percent of the American population, or 700,000 adults, were likely transgender (see Miller 2015).

In the contemporary West, the category *transgender* encompasses varied individuals whose gender performance and identity enlarge an otherwise binary gender structure. The lesbian and gay rights movement has expanded to include bisexual and transgender individuals. This lesbian, gay, bisexual, and transgender (LGBT) community works to promote government policies and social practices that protect its members' civil and human rights. In recent years, the LGBT movement and its supporters have achieved many successes, including the repeal of the Don't Ask, Don't Tell (DADT) policy of the U.S. armed services and, most notably, legalization of same-sex marriage throughout the United States. With reference specifically to transgender rights, states that legally prohibit discrimination based on sexual identity (e.g., Washington, Oregon, and Vermont) have larger shares of transgender people than do states without such laws (Miller 2015). As of this writing, one unresolved issue affecting the rights of transgender Americans is whether public restroom and locker room access should be based on gender at birth or current gender identity.

Sexual Orientation

Gender identity refers to whether a person feels, acts, and is regarded as male, female, or something else. One's gender identity does not dictate one's sexual orientation. Men who have no doubt about their masculinity can be sexually attracted to women or to other men, as can women with regard to female gender identity and variable sexual attraction. **Sexual orientation,** to which we now turn, refers to a person's sexual attraction to, and habitual sexual activities with, persons of the opposite sex (*heterosexuality*), the same sex (*homosexuality*), or both sexes (*bisexuality*). *Asexuality,* indifference toward or lack of attraction to either sex, also is a sexual orientation. All four of these forms are found throughout the world. But each type of desire and experience holds different meanings for individuals and groups. For example, male–male sexual activity may be a private affair in Mexico, rather than public, socially sanctioned, and encouraged, as it is among the Etoro and several other groups in Papua New Guinea (see also Blackwood 2010; Herdt and Polen 2013; Hyde and DeLamater 2016; Lyons and Lyons 2011; Nanda 2014).

Recently in the United States there has been a tendency to see sexual orientation as fixed and biologically based. There is not enough information at this time to determine the extent to which sexual orientation is based on biology. What we can say is that all human activities and preferences, including erotic expression, are at least partially constructed and influenced by culture.

In any society, individuals will differ in the nature, range, and intensity of their sexual interests and urges. No one knows for sure why such individual sexual differences exist. Part of the answer probably is biological, reflecting genes or hormones. Another part may have to do with experiences during growth and development.

But whatever the reasons for individual variation, culture always plays a role in molding individual sexual urges toward a collective norm. And such sexual norms vary from culture to culture.

What do we know about variation in sexual norms from society to society and over time? A classic cross-cultural study of 76 societies (Ford and Beach 1951) found wide variation in attitudes about forms of sexual activity. In a single society, such as the United States, attitudes about sex differ over time and with socioeconomic status, region, and rural versus urban residence. However, even in the 1950s, prior to the "age of sexual permissiveness" (the pre-HIV period from the mid-1960s through the 1970s), research showed that almost all American men (92 percent) and more than half of American women (54 percent) admitted to masturbation. In the famous Kinsey report (Kinsey, Pomeroy, and Martin 1948), 37 percent of the men surveyed admitted having had at least one sexual experience leading to orgasm with another male. In a later study of 1,200 unmarried women, 26 percent reported same-sex sexual activities. (Because Kinsey's research relied on nonrandom samples, it should be considered merely illustrative, rather than a statistically accurate representation, of sexual behavior at the time.)

In almost two-thirds (63 percent) of the 76 societies in the Ford and Beach study, various forms of same-sex sexual activity were acceptable. Occasionally sexual relations between people of the same sex involved transvestism on the part of one of the partners (see Kulick 1998). Transvestism did not characterize male–male sex among the Sudanese Azande, who valued the warrior role (Evans-Pritchard 1970). Prospective warriors—young men aged 12 to 20—left their families and shared quarters with adult fighting men, who paid lobola for, and had sex with, them. During this apprenticeship, the young men did the domestic duties of women. Upon reaching warrior status, these young men took their own younger male brides. Later, retiring from the warrior role, Azande men married women. Flexible in their sexual expression, Azande males had no difficulty shifting from sex with older men (as male brides) to sex with younger men (as warriors) to sex with women (as husbands) (see Murray and Roscoe 1998).

Consider also the Etoro (Kelly 1976), a group of 400 people who subsisted by hunting and horticulture in the Trans-Fly region of Papua New Guinea. The Etoro illustrate the power of culture in molding human sexuality. The following account, based on ethnographic fieldwork by Raymond C. Kelly in the late 1960s, applies only to Etoro males and their beliefs. Etoro cultural norms prevented the male anthropologist who studied them from gathering comparable information about female attitudes and behavior. Note also that the activities described have been discouraged by missionaries. Because there has been no restudy of the Etoro specifically focusing on these activities, the extent to which these practices continue today is unknown. For this reason, I'll use the past tense in describing them.

Etoro opinions about sexuality were linked to their beliefs about the cycle of birth, physical growth, maturity, old age, and death. Etoro men believed that semen was necessary to give life force to a fetus, which was, they believed, implanted in a woman by an ancestral spirit. A man was required to have sexual intercourse with his wife during her pregnancy to nourish the growing fetus. The Etoro believed, however, that men had a limited lifetime supply of semen. Any sex act leading to ejaculation was seen as draining that supply, and as sapping a man's virility and vitality. The birth of children, nurtured by semen, symbolized a necessary sacrifice that would lead to the husband's eventual death. Male–female sexual intercourse, required for reproduction, was otherwise discouraged. Women who wanted too much sex were viewed as witches, hazardous to their husbands' health. Furthermore, Etoro culture allowed male–female intercourse only about 100 days a year. The rest of the time it was tabooed. Seasonal birth clustering shows that the taboo was respected.

So objectionable was male–female sex that it was removed from community life. It could occur neither in sleeping quarters nor in the fields. Coitus could happen only in the woods, where it was risky because poisonous snakes, the Etoro believed, were attracted by the sounds and smells of male–female sex.

Although coitus was discouraged, sex acts between males were viewed as essential. Etoro believed that boys would not produce semen on their own. To grow into men and eventually give life force to their children, boys had to acquire semen orally from older men. From the age of 10 until adulthood, boys were inseminated by older men. No taboos were attached to this. This oral insemination could proceed in the sleeping area or garden. Every three years, a group of boys around the age of 20 were formally initiated into manhood. They went to a secluded mountain lodge, where they were visited and inseminated by several older men.

A code of propriety governed male–male sex among the Etoro. Although sexual relations between older and younger males were considered culturally essential, those between boys of the same age were discouraged. A boy who took semen from other youths was believed to be sapping their life force and stunting their growth. A boy's rapid physical development could suggest he was getting semen from other boys. Like a sex-hungry wife, he could be shunned as a witch.

The sexual practices described in this section rested not on hormones or genes but on cultural beliefs and traditions. The Etoro shared a cultural pattern, which Gilbert Herdt (1984, 2006) calls "ritualized homosexuality," with some 50 other tribes in a particular region of Papua New Guinea. These societies illustrate one extreme of a male–female avoidance pattern that has been widespread in Papua New Guinea, and in patrilineal–patrilocal societies more generally.

Flexibility in sexual expression seems to be an aspect of our primate heritage. Both masturbation and same-sex sexual activity exist among chimpanzees and other primates. Male bonobos (pygmy chimps) regularly engage in a form of mutual masturbation that has been called "penis fencing." Females get sexual pleasure from rubbing their genitals against those of other females (De Waal 1997). Our primate sexual potential is molded by culture, the environment, and reproductive necessity. Male–female coitus is practiced in all human societies—which, after all, must reproduce themselves—but alternatives also are widespread (Lyons and Lyons 2011; Rathus, Nevid, and Fichner-Rathus 2014). Like our gender roles, the sexual component of human personality and identity—the ways in which we express our "natural," or biological, sexual urges—is a matter that culture and environment influence and limit.

Anthropology Today *Gender, Ethnicity, and a Gold Medal for Fiji*

On August 11, 2016, in Rio de Janeiro, Brazil, the island nation of Fiji won its first-ever Olympic medal. That gold medal, in men's rugby sevens, was awarded after Fiji trounced Great Britain, its former colonial master, by a score of 43 to 7. In Fiji, a Southwest Pacific nation of some 900,000 people, rugby is immensely popular. Specifically, Fijians excel at rugby sevens, a rapid game played by seven participants per side in just 14 minutes.

The addition of rugby to the roster of Olympic sports for the Rio summer games offered Fijians an opportunity to excel in a venue where previously Fiji had been woefully unrepresented. Only two Fijian athletes had qualified to participate in the games between 1956, when Fiji officially entered the Olympics, and 2016, when it won its gold medal.

Rugby is the national sport of Fiji, where its fans include men, women, and Fijians of all ethnic backgrounds. There are, however, dramatic differences in rugby participation between men and women, and between Fiji's two main ethnic groups: indigenous Fijians and Indo-Fijians. The latter are the descendants of Indian immigrants who came to the island as indentured servants or free migrants during the 19th and 20th centuries, when both Fiji and India were British colonies. As anthropologist Niko Besnier, who has conducted fieldwork in Fiji since 1980, notes, participation in rugby is mainly by men who are indigenous Fijians.

In contrast to the success of the men's rugby team, the Fijian women's team—the Fijiana—managed only an eighth place finish out of 11 teams participating. This less-than-stellar result is not surprising given Fijian attitudes toward female players. Besnier and Brownell (2016) report that many Fijians view female rugby players as

Fijiana player Rusila Nagasau rushes to score against Colombia during a women's rugby match on Day 2 (August 7) of the 2016 summer Olympic Games in Rio de Janeiro, Brazil. ©David Rogers/Getty Images Sport/ Getty Images

continued

Anthropology Today   *continued*

"tomboys"—women who act too masculine by being independent, aggressive, and loud, and who often are assumed to be lesbians. Besnier heard stories of female players who had been beaten by their fathers or expelled from their family homes—an especially unhappy fate in a kin-based society. The Fijiana also receive little official support, with few corporate sponsors, unlike the men's team, which enjoys the sponsorship of the country's major companies. When Besnier visited the Fijiana at their training camp in March 2016, he found the women put up in a Christian camp, five people to a room, while the men's team was lodged at a luxury resort. Prior to the Olympic Games, there was even an attempt to replace some of the actual Fijiana national team with women from netball, who were more "feminine acting" even though they knew little about rugby (Besnier and Brownell 2016).

Women aren't the only Fijians who are discouraged from rugby. Indo-Fijians also face multiple barriers to participation in the sport. Indigenous Fijians contend that Indo-Fijians have slight physiques that make them unsuitable for rugby's roughness. Even Indo-Fijian parents discourage their sons from playing, fearing injury by the larger and rougher indigenous Fijians. In this ostensibly multicultural society, it is not uncommon for indigenous Fijians (57 percent of the population) to resent the Indian-derived minority (38 percent) because of its business success. Indo-Fijians fear physical expressions of this resentment on the playing field. Can you think of comparable barriers to sports participation and success based on gender and ethnic differences in other societies, including your own? Are these barriers physical, cultural, or a combination of the two?

Summary

1. *Gender roles* are the tasks and activities that a culture assigns to each sex. *Gender stereotypes* are oversimplified ideas about attributes of males and females. *Gender stratification* describes an unequal distribution of rewards by gender, reflecting different positions in a social hierarchy. Cross-cultural comparison reveals some recurrent patterns involving the division of labor by gender. Gender roles and gender stratification also vary with environment, economy, adaptive strategy, level of social complexity, and degree of participation in the world economy.

2. When gathering is prominent, gender status is more equal than when hunting or fishing dominates a foraging economy. Gender status also is more equal when the domestic and public spheres aren't sharply separated.

3. Gender stratification also is linked to descent and residence. Women's status in matrilineal societies tends to be high because overall social identity comes through female links. Women in many societies, especially matrilineal ones, wield power and make decisions. Scarcity of resources promotes intervillage warfare, patriliny, and patrilocality. The localization of related males is adaptive for military solidarity. Men may use their warrior role to symbolize and reinforce the social devaluation

and oppression of women. Patriarchy describes a political system ruled by men in which women have inferior social and political status, including basic human rights.

4. Americans' attitudes toward gender vary with class and region. When the need for female labor declines, the idea that women are unfit for many jobs increases, and vice versa. Factors such as war, falling wages, and inflation help explain female cash employment and Americans' attitudes toward it. The need for flexible employment, permitting a proper balance of work and family responsibilities, is increasingly important to both male and female workers. Despite the increased participation by women in the labor force and higher education, and by men in the domestic realm, including child care, barriers to full equality remain. Countering the economic gains of many American women is the feminization of poverty. This has become a global phenomenon, as impoverished female-headed households have increased worldwide.

5. Societies may recognize more than two genders. The term *intersex* describes a group of conditions, including chromosomal configurations, that may produce a discrepancy between external and internal genitals. Transgender individuals may or may not contrast biologically with ordinary males and females. Self-identified transgender people tend to be individuals whose gender identity contradicts their biological sex at birth and the gender identity that society assigned to them in infancy.

6. *Gender identity* refers to whether a person feels, and is regarded as, male, female, or something else. One's gender identity does not dictate one's sexual orientation. *Sexual orientation* stands for a person's habitual sexual attraction to, and activities with, persons of the opposite sex (heterosexuality), the same sex (homosexuality), or both sexes (bisexuality). Sexual norms and practices vary widely from culture to culture.

Think Like an Anthropologist

1. How are sex, gender, and sexual orientation related to one another? What are the differences among these three concepts? Provide an argument about why anthropologists are uniquely positioned to study the relationships among the three.

2. Using your own society, give an example of a gender role, a gender stereotype, and gender stratification. Are these examples likely to apply cross-culturally?

Key Terms

domestic, *167*	gender	sexual
domestic–public	stratification, *163*	dimorphism, *162*
dichotomy, *167*	intersex, *177*	sexual
gender identity, *180*	patriarchy, *169*	orientation, *180*
gender roles, *163*	patrilineal–	transgender, *178*
gender	patrilocal	
stereotypes, *163*	complex, *168*	

Chapter

Religion

What Is Religion?

In his book *Religion: An Anthropological View,* Anthony F. C. Wallace (1966) defined **religion** as "belief and ritual concerned with supernatural beings, powers, and forces" (p. 5). By "supernatural," Wallace was referring to a nonmaterial realm beyond (but believed to impinge on) the observable world. The supernatural cannot be verified or falsified empirically and is inexplicable in ordinary terms. It must be accepted "on faith." Supernatural *beings* (e.g., deities, ghosts, demons, souls, spirits) dwell outside our material world, which they may visit from time to time. There also are supernatural or sacred *forces,* some of them wielded by deities and spirits, others that simply exist. In many societies, people believe they can benefit from, become imbued with, or manipulate such forces (see Bielo 2015; Bowen 2014; Hicks 2010; Lambek 2008; Stein and Stein 2011; Warms, Garber, and McGee 2009).

Wallace's definition of religion focuses on beings, powers, and forces within the supernatural realm. Émile Durkheim (1912/2001), one of the founders of the anthropology of religion, focused on the distinction between the sacred (the domain of religion)
and the profane (the everyday world). Like the supernatural for Wallace, Durkheim's
"sacred" was a domain set off from the ordinary, or the mundane (he preferred the word
profane). For Durkheim, although every society recognized a sacred domain, the specifics of that domain varied from society to society. In other words, he saw religion as a
cultural universal, while recognizing that specific religious beliefs and practices would
vary from society to society. Durkheim believed that Native Australian societies had
retained the most elementary, or basic, forms of religion. He noted that their most sacred
objects, including plants and animals that served as totems, were not supernatural at all.
Rather, they were "real-world" entities (e.g., kangaroos, grubs) that had acquired religious meaning and became sacred objects for the social groups that "worshipped" them.
Durkheim saw totemism as the most elementary or basic form of religion.

Durkheim (1912/2001) focused on groups of people—congregants—who gather together for worship, such as a group of Native Australians worshiping a particular totem.
He stressed the collective, social, and shared nature of religion; the meanings it embod-
ies; and the emotions it generates. He highlighted religious *effervescence*, the bubbling
up of collective emotional intensity generated by worship. As Michael Lambek (2008)
remarks, "good anthropology understands that religious worlds are real, vivid, and significant to those who construct and inhabit them" (p. 5).

Congregants who worship together share certain beliefs; they have accepted a particular set of doctrines concerning the sacred and its relationship to human beings. The
word *religion* derives from the Latin *religare*—"to tie, to bind"—but it is not necessary
for all members of a given religion to meet together as a common body. Subgroups meet
regularly at local congregation sites. They may attend occasional meetings with

Participation in a collective religious act, such as singing in this choir, can
strengthen social bonds among congregants, while promoting feelings of
spiritual effervescence. ©Radius Images/Alamy Stock Photo RF

adherents representing a wider region. And they may form an imagined community with people of similar faith throughout the world.

Verbal manifestations of religious beliefs include prayers, chants, myths, texts, and statements about ethics and morality (see Hicks 2010; Moro and Meyers 2012; Stein and Stein 2011; Winzeler 2012). Other aspects of religion include notions about purity and pollution (including taboos involving diet and physical contact), sacrifice, initiation, rites of passage, vision quests, pilgrimages, spirit possession, prophecy, study, devotion, and moral actions (Lambek 2008, p. 9).

Like ethnicity and language, religion is associated with social divisions within and between societies and nations. Religion both unites and divides. Participation in common rites may affirm, and thus maintain, the solidarity of a group of adherents. As we know from daily headlines, however, religious difference also may be associated with bitter enmity. Contacts and confrontations have increased between so-called world religions, such as Christianity and Islam, and the more localized forms of religion that missionaries typically lump together under the disparaging term "paganism." Increasingly, ethnic, regional, and class conflicts come to be framed in religious terms. Contemporary examples of religion as a social and political force include the rise of the religious right in the United States, the worldwide spread of Pentecostalism, and various Islamic movements (see Lindquist and Handelman 2013).

Long ago, Edward Sapir (1928/1956) argued for a distinction between "a religion" and "religion." The former term would apply only to a formally organized religion, such as the world religions just mentioned. The latter—"religion"—is universal; it refers to religious beliefs and behavior, which exist in all societies, even if they don't stand out as a separate and clearly demarcated sphere. Anthropologists agree that religion exists in all human societies; it is a cultural universal. However, we'll see that it isn't always easy to distinguish the sacred from the profane and that different societies conceptualize divinity, the sacred, the supernatural, and ultimate realities very differently.

Expressions of Religion

How and when did religion begin? No one knows for sure. There are suggestions of religion in Neandertal burials and on European cave walls, where painted stick figures may represent **shamans,** early religious specialists. Nevertheless, any statement about when, where, why, and how religion arose, or any description of its original nature, can only be speculative. Although such speculations are inconclusive, many have revealed important functions and effects of religious behavior. Several theories will be examined in this section.

Spiritual Beings

Another founder (along with Durkheim) of the anthropology of religion was the Englishman Sir Edward Burnett Tylor (1871/1958). Religion arose, Tylor thought, as people tried to understand phenomena they could not explain by reference to daily experience. Tylor believed that ancient humans—and contemporary nonindustrial peoples—were particularly intrigued with death, dreaming, and trance. People see images they may remember when they wake up or come out of a trance state. Tylor concluded that attempts to explain dreams and trances led early humans to believe that two entities inhabit the body. One is active during the day, and the other—a double, or soul—is active during sleep and in trance states. When the double leaves the body permanently, the person dies. Death is departure of the soul. From the Latin for soul, *anima,* Tylor named this belief **animism.** The soul was one sort of spiritual entity; people remembered various other entities from their dreams and trances—other spirits. For Tylor, animism, the earliest form of religion, was a belief in spiritual beings.

Tylor proposed that religion evolved through stages, beginning with animism. **Polytheism** (the belief in multiple gods) and then **monotheism** (the belief in a single, all-powerful deity) developed later. Because religion originated to explain things, Tylor thought it would decline as science offered better explanations. To an extent, he was right. We now have scientific explanations for many things that religion once elucidated (see Salazar and Bestard 2015). Of course, many of the "faithful" reject such secular explanations, preferring the nonscientific, religious ones instead. Nevertheless, because religion persists even among those who accept science, it must do something more than explain. It must, and does, have other functions and meanings.

Powers and Forces

In addition to animism—and sometimes coexisting with it in the same society—is a view of the supernatural as a domain of impersonal power, or force, which people can control under certain conditions. (You'd be right to think of *Star Wars.*) Such a conception has been particularly prominent in Melanesia, the area of the South Pacific that includes Papua New Guinea and adjacent islands. Melanesians traditionally believed in **mana,** a sacred impersonal force existing in the universe. Mana could reside in people, animals, plants, and objects.

Melanesian mana was similar to our notion of luck. Objects with mana could change someone's luck. For example, a charm or an amulet belonging to a successful hunter could transmit that hunter's mana to the next person who held or wore it. A woman could put a rock in her garden, see her yields improve, and attribute the change to the force contained in the rock.

Beliefs in manalike forces have been widespread, although the specifics of the religious doctrines have varied. Consider the contrast between mana in Melanesia and Polynesia (the islands included in a triangular area marked by Hawaii to the north, Easter Island to the east, and New Zealand to the southwest). In Melanesia, anyone could acquire mana by chance, or by working hard to get it. In Polynesia, however, mana wasn't potentially available to everyone but was attached to political offices. Chiefs and nobles had more mana than ordinary people did.

So charged with mana were the highest chiefs that contact with them was dangerous to commoners. The mana of chiefs flowed out of their bodies. It could infect the ground, making it dangerous for others to walk in the chief's footsteps. It could permeate the containers and utensils chiefs used in eating. Because high chiefs had so much mana, their bodies and possessions were **taboo** (set apart as sacred and off-limits to ordinary people). Because ordinary people couldn't bear as much sacred current as royalty could, when commoners were accidentally exposed, purification rites were necessary.

As Horton (1993) and Lambek (2008) point out, there are universals in human thought and experience, common conditions and situations that call out for explanation. One of these universal questions is what happens in sleep and trance, and with death. Another is the question of why some people prosper, while others fail. A religious explanation might blame unequal success or fortune on such nonmaterial factors as luck, mana, sorcery, or being one of "God's chosen."

The beliefs in spiritual beings (e.g., animism) and supernatural forces (e.g., mana) fit within Wallace's definition of religion given at the beginning of this chapter. Most religions include both spirits and forces. Likewise, the supernatural beliefs of contemporary North Americans include beings (gods, saints, souls, demons) and forces (charms, talismans, crystals, and sacred objects).

Magic and Religion

Magic refers to supernatural techniques intended to accomplish specific goals. Those techniques include actions, offerings, spells, formulas, and incantations used with deities or with impersonal forces. Magicians might employ *imitative magic* to produce a desired effect by imitating it. For example, if magicians wish to harm someone, they may imitate that effect on an image of the victim. Sticking pins in "voodoo dolls" is an example. With *contagious magic,* whatever is done to an object is believed to affect a person who has, or once had, contact with it. Sometimes practitioners of contagious magic use body products from prospective victims—their nails or hair, for example. The spell performed on the body product is believed eventually to reach the person. Magic exists in societies with diverse religious beliefs, including animism, mana, polytheism, and monotheism.

Uncertainty, Anxiety, Solace

Religion and magic serve emotional needs as well as cognitive (e.g., explanatory) ones. Religion can help people face death and endure life crises. Magical techniques can be used when outcomes are beyond human control. According to Malinowski, when people face uncertainty and danger, they often turn to magic. The Trobriand Islanders, whom Malinowski studied, used magic during sailing—a hazardous activity in which people lacked control over wind and weather (Malinowski 1931/1978). Only in situations they could not control did Trobrianders, out of psychological stress, turn to magic.

Despite our improving technical skills, we still cannot control every outcome, so magic persists in contemporary societies. Most of us still draw on magic and ritual in situations of uncertainty, such as before a test or perhaps a plane ride. To enhance their success magically, athletes use personal rituals in many sports, with baseball magic particularly noteworthy. The anthropologist George Gmelch (1978, 2006) describes a series of rituals, taboos, and sacred objects used in the sport. Like Trobriand sailing magic, these behaviors reduce psychological stress, creating an illusion of magical control when real control is lacking. Baseball magic is especially prevalent in pitching and batting.

Rituals

Several features distinguish **rituals** from other kinds of behavior (Rappaport 1974, 1999). Rituals are formal—stylized, repetitive, and stereotyped. People perform them in special places and at set times. Rituals include liturgical orders—sequences of words and actions invented prior to the current performance of the ritual in which they occur.

These features link rituals to plays, but there are important differences. Actors merely portray something, but ritual performers—who make up congregations—are in earnest. Rituals convey information about the participants and their traditions. Repeated year after year, generation after generation, rituals translate enduring messages, values, and sentiments into action.

Rituals are social acts. Inevitably, some participants are more committed than others are to the beliefs that lie behind the rites. However, just by taking part in a joint public act, the performers signal that they accept a common social and moral order, one that transcends their status as individuals.

Rites of Passage

Magic and religion, as Malinowski noted, can reduce anxiety, allay fears, and help people deal with life crises. Ironically, beliefs and rituals also can create anxiety and a sense of insecurity and danger (Radcliffe-Brown 1952/1965). Anxiety may arise because a ritual exists. Indeed, participation in a collective ritual (e.g., circumcision of early teen boys, common among East African pastoralists) can produce considerable stress, whose common relief, once the ritual is completed, enhances the solidarity of the participants. Collective circumcision is an example of a ritual, or rite, of passage, as participants transition from one stage of life to another.

Rites of passage (rituals associated with the transition from one place, or stage of life, to another) can be individual or collective. The traditional vision quests of Native Americans, particularly the Plains Indians, illustrate individual rites of passage. To move from boyhood to manhood, a youth would temporarily separate from his community. After a period of isolation in the wilderness, often featuring fasting and drug consumption, the young man would see a vision, which would become his guardian spirit. He would return then to his community as an adult.

Contemporary rituals or rites of passage include confirmations, baptisms, bar and bat mitzvahs, initiations, weddings, and application for Medicare. Passage rites involve changes in social status, such as from boyhood to manhood, or from nonmember to sorority sister. More generally, a rite of passage may mark any change in place, condition, social position, or age.

All rites of passage have three phases: separation, liminality, and incorporation. In the first phase, people withdraw from ordinary society. In the third phase, they reenter society, having completed a ritual that changes their status. The second, or liminal, phase is the most interesting. It is the limbo, or "time-out," during which people have left one status but haven't yet entered or joined the next (Turner 1967/1974).

Liminality always has certain characteristics. Liminal people exist apart from ordinary distinctions and expectations; they are living in a time out of time. A series of contrasts set liminality apart from normal social life. For example, among the Ndembu of Zambia, a new chief underwent a rite of passage before taking office. During the liminal period, his past and future positions in society were ignored, even reversed. He was subjected to a variety of insults, orders, and humiliations.

Often, rites of passage are collective. Several individuals—boys being circumcised, fraternity or sorority initiates, men at military boot camps, football players in summer training camps, women becoming nuns—pass through the rites together as a group. Table 9.1 summarizes the contrasts, or oppositions, between liminality and normal

TABLE 9.1   **Oppositions between Liminality and Normal Social Life**

Source: Turner, Victor, *The Ritual Process*. London, United Kingdom: Routledge. Copyright ©1969

Liminality	Normal Social Structure
transition	state
homogeneity	heterogeneity
communitas	structure
equality	inequality
anonymity	names
absence of property	property
absence of status	status
nakedness or uniform dress	dress distinctions
sexual continence or excess	sexuality
minimization of sex distinctions	maximization of sex distinctions
absence of rank	rank
humility	pride
disregard of personal appearance	care for personal appearance
unselfishness	selfishness
total obedience	obedience only to superior rank
sacredness	secularity
sacred instruction	technical knowledge
silence	speech
simplicity	complexity
acceptance of pain and suffering	avoidance of pain and suffering

social life. Most notable is the social aspect of collective liminality called **communitas** (Turner 1967/1974), an intense community spirit, a feeling of great social solidarity, equality, and togetherness. Liminal people experience the same treatment and conditions and must act alike. Liminality may be marked ritually and symbolically by reversals of ordinary behavior. For example, sexual taboos may be intensified; conversely, sexual excess may be encouraged. Liminal symbols, such as special clothing or body paint, mark the condition as extraordinary—beyond ordinary society and everyday life.

Liminality is basic to all rites of passage. Furthermore, in certain societies, including our own, liminal symbols may be used to set off one (religious) group from another and from society as a whole. Such "permanent liminal groups" (e.g., sects, brotherhoods, and cults) are found most characteristically in nation-states. Such liminal features as humility, poverty, equality, obedience, sexual abstinence, and silence (see Table 9.1) may be required for all sect or cult members. Those who join such a group agree to its rules. As if they were undergoing a passage rite—but in this case a never-ending one—they may have to abandon their previous possessions and social ties, including those with family members. Is liminality compatible with Facebook?

Members of a sect or cult often wear uniform clothing. They may adopt a common hairstyle (shaved head, short hair, or long hair). Liminal groups submerge the individual in the collective. This may be one reason Americans, whose core values include individuality and individualism, are so fearful and suspicious of "cults."

Passage rites are often collective. A group—such as these Maasai initiates in Kenya or these navy trainees in San Diego—passes through the rites as a unit. Such liminal people experience the same treatment and conditions and must act alike. They share communitas, an intense community spirit, a feeling of great social solidarity or togetherness. (top): ©John Warburton-Lee Photography/Alamy Stock Photo; (bottom): ©Joe McNally/Hulton Archive/Getty Images

Not all collective rituals are rites of passage. Most societies observe occasions on which people come together to worship or celebrate and, in doing so, affirm and reinforce their solidarity. Rituals such as the totemic ceremonies described in the next section are *rites of intensification:* They intensify social solidarity. The ritual creates communitas and produces emotions—the collective spiritual effervescence described by Durkheim (1912/2001)—that enhance social solidarity.

Totemism

Totemism was a key ingredient in the religions of the Native Australians. **Totems** could be animals, plants, or geographic features. In each tribe, groups of people had particular totems. Members of each totemic group believed themselves to be descendants of their totem, which they customarily neither killed nor ate. However, this taboo was suspended once a year, when people assembled for ceremonies dedicated to the totem. Only on that occasion were they allowed to kill and eat their totem. These annual rites were believed to be necessary for the totem's survival and reproduction.

Totemism uses nature as a model for society. The totems usually are animals and plants, which are part of nature. People relate to nature through their totemic association with natural species. Because each group has a different totem, social differences mirror natural contrasts. Diversity in the natural order becomes a model for diversity in the social order. However, although totemic plants and animals occupy different niches in nature, on another level they are united because they all are part of nature. The unity of the human social order is enhanced by symbolic association with and imitation of the natural order (Durkheim 1912/2001; Lévi-Strauss 1963; Radcliffe-Brown 1952/1965).

Totems are sacred emblems symbolizing common identity. This is true not just among Native Australians but also among Native American groups of the North Pacific Coast of North America, whose totem poles are well known. Their totemic carvings, which commemorated and told visual stories about ancestors, animals, and spirits, were also associated with ceremonies. In totemic rituals, people gather together to honor their totem. In so doing, they use ritual to maintain the social oneness that the totem symbolizes.

Totemic principles continue to demarcate groups, including clubs, teams, and universities, in modern societies. Think of familiar team mascots and symbols. Badgers, wolverines, and gators are animals, and buckeye nuts come from the buckeye tree. Differences between natural species (e.g., lions, tigers, and bears) distinguish sports teams and even political parties (donkeys and elephants). Although the modern context is more secular, one can still witness, in intense college football rivalries, some of the effervescence Durkheim noted in Australian totemic religion and other rites of intensification.

Social Control

Religion means a lot to people. It helps them cope with uncertainty, adversity, fear, and tragedy. It offers hope that things will get better. Lives can be transformed through spiritual healing. Sinners can repent and be saved—or they can go on sinning and be damned. If the faithful truly internalize a system of religious rewards and punishments, their religion becomes a powerful influence on their attitudes and behavior, as well as on what they teach their children.

Many people engage in religious activity because it works for them. Prayers get answered. Faith healers heal. Many Native American people in southwestern Oklahoma use faith healers at high monetary cost, not just because it makes them feel better but also because they believe it works (Lassiter 1998). Each year legions of Brazilians visit a church, Nosso Senhor do Bonfim, in the city of Salvador, Bahia. They vow to repay "Our Lord" (Nosso Senhor) if healing happens. Showing that the vows work, and are repaid, are the thousands of *ex votos,* plastic impressions of every conceivable body part, that adorn the church, along with photos of people who have been cured.

Religion can work by getting inside people and mobilizing their emotions—their joy, their wrath, their certainty, their righteousness. People can feel a deep sense of shared joy, meaning, experience, communion, belonging, and commitment to their religion. The power of religion affects action. When religions meet, they can coexist peacefully, or their differences can be a basis for enmity and disharmony, even battle. Throughout history, political leaders have used religion to promote and justify their views and policies.

How may leaders mobilize communities and, in so doing, gain support for their own policies? One way is by persuasion; another is by fomenting hatred or fear. Consider witchcraft accusations. Witch hunts can be powerful means of social control by creating a climate of danger and insecurity that affects everyone. No one wants to seem deviant, to be accused of being a witch. Witch hunts often take aim at socially marginal people who can be accused and punished with the least chance of retaliation. During the great

Witchcraft accusations persist in today's world, with women disproportionately targeted. Hundreds of alleged witches, including these women, are confined to five isolated "witch camps" in northern Ghana. Witchcraft accusations there tend to follow disputes over inheritance rights, or a husband's death that leaves a widow perceived to be a burden on her husband's family or her own. ©Markus Matzel/ullstein bild via Getty Images

European witch craze of the 15th, 16th, and 17th centuries (Harris 1974), most accusations and convictions were against poor women with little social support.

Accusations of witchcraft are ethnographic as well as historical facts. Witchcraft beliefs are common in village and peasant societies, where people live close together and have limited mobility. Such societies often have what anthropologist George Foster (1965) called an "image of limited good"—the idea that resources are limited, so that one person can profit disproportionately only at the expense of others. In this context, the threat of witchcraft accusations can serve as a leveling mechanism if it motivates wealthier villagers to be especially generous or else face shunning and social ostracism. Similarly, in the chapter "Gender," we saw that Etoro women who wanted too much sex, as well as boys who grew too rapidly, could be shunned as witches who were depleting a man's limited lifetime supply of semen.

To ensure proper behavior, religions offer rewards (e.g., the fellowship of the religious community) and punishments (e.g., the threat of being cast out or excommunicated). Religions, especially the formal, organized ones typically found in state societies, often prescribe a code of ethics and morality to guide behavior. Moral codes are ways of maintaining order and stability that are reinforced continually in religious sermons, catechisms, and the like. They become internalized psychologically. They guide behavior and produce regret, guilt, shame, and the need for forgiveness, expiation, and absolution when they are not followed.

Kinds of Religion

Although religion is a cultural universal, religions exist in particular societies, and cultural differences show up systematically in religious beliefs and practices. For example, the religions of stratified, state societies differ from those of societies with less marked social contrasts—societies without kings, lords, and subjects. Churches, temples, and other full-time religious establishments, with their monumental structures and hierarchies of officials, must be supported in some consistent way, such as by tithes and taxes. What kinds of societies can support such hierarchies and architecture?

All societies have religious figures—those believed capable of mediating between humans and the supernatural. More generally, all societies have medico-magico-religious specialists. Modern societies can support both priesthoods and health care professionals. Lacking the resources for such specialization, foraging societies typically have only part-time specialists, who often have both religious and healing roles. *Shaman* is a general term that encompasses curers, mediums, spiritualists, astrologers, palm readers, and other independent diviners. In foraging societies, shamans are usually part-time; that is, they also hunt or gather.

Societies with productive economies (based on agriculture and trade) and large, dense populations (nation-states) can support full-time religious specialists—professional priesthoods. Like the state itself, priesthoods are hierarchically and bureaucratically organized. Anthony Wallace (1966) describes the religions of such stratified societies as "ecclesiastical" (pertaining to an established church and its hierarchy of officials) and "Olympian," after Mount Olympus, home of the classical Greek gods. In such religions, powerful anthropomorphic gods have specialized functions, for example, gods of love, war, the sea, and death. Such *pantheons* (collections of deities) were prominent in the religions of many nonindustrial nation-states, including the Aztecs of Mexico, several African and Asian kingdoms, and classical Greece and Rome. Greco-Roman religions were polytheistic, featuring many deities. In monotheism, all supernatural phenomena are believed to be manifestations of, or under the control of, a single eternal, omniscient, omnipotent, and omnipresent being. In the ecclesiastical monotheistic religion known as Christianity, a single supreme being is manifest in a trinity (see Bellah 2011).

Protestant Values and Capitalism

Notions of salvation and the afterlife dominate Christian ideologies. However, most varieties of Protestantism lack the hierarchical structure of earlier monotheistic religions, including Roman Catholicism. With a diminished role for the priest (minister), salvation is directly available to individuals, who have unmediated access to the supernatural.

In his influential book *The Protestant Ethic and the Spirit of Capitalism* (1904/1958), the social theorist Max Weber linked the spread of capitalism to the values preached by early Protestant leaders. He saw Protestants as more successful financially than Catholics and attributed this difference to the values stressed by their religions. Weber viewed Protestants as more entrepreneurial and future-oriented than Catholics. Protestantism placed a premium on hard work, an ascetic life, and profit seeking. Early Protestants saw success on Earth as a sign of divine favor and probable salvation.

Weber also argued that rational business organization required the removal of production from the home. Protestantism made such a separation possible by emphasizing individualism: Individuals, not families or households, would be saved or not. Today, of course, in North America as throughout the world, people of many religions and with diverse worldviews are successful capitalists. Furthermore, traditional Protestant values often have little to do with today's economic maneuvering. Still, there is no denying that the individualistic focus of Protestantism was compatible with the severance of ties to land and kin that industrialism demanded.

World Religions

Information on the world's major religions in 2010 and projected for 2050 is provided in Figure 9.1, based on recent comprehensive studies by the Pew Research Center (2012a, 2015b). Considering data from more than 230 countries, researchers estimated that the world contained about 5.8 billion religiously affiliated people—84 percent of its population of 6.9 billion in 2010.

There were approximately 2.2 billion Christians (31.4 percent of the world's population), 1.6 billion Muslims (23.2 percent), 1 billion Hindus (15 percent), nearly 500 million Buddhists (7.1 percent), and 14 million Jews (0.2 percent). In addition, more than 400 million people (5.9 percent) practiced folk or traditional religions of various sorts. Some 58 million people, a bit less than 1 percent of the world's population, belonged to

FIGURE 9.1 **Major World Religions by Percentage of World Population, 2010, and Projected for 2050**

Source: *The Future of World Religions: Population Growth Projections, 2010–2050.* Washington, DC: Pew Research Center, April 2, 2015. Copyright ©2015.

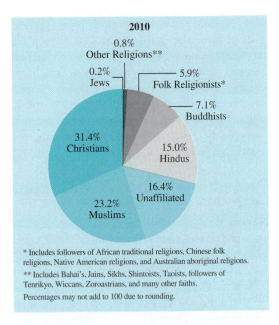

2010

0.8% Other Religions**
0.2% Jews
5.9% Folk Religionists*
7.1% Buddhists
31.4% Christians
15.0% Hindus
16.4% Unaffiliated
23.2% Muslims

* Includes followers of African traditional religions, Chinese folk religions, Native American religions, and Australian aboriginal religions.
** Includes Bahai's, Jains, Sikhs, Shintoists, Taoists, followers of Tenrikyo, Wiccans, Zoroastrians, and many other faiths.
Percentages may not add to 100 due to rounding.

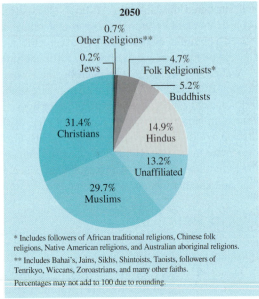

2050

0.7% Other Religions**
0.2% Jews
4.7% Folk Religionists*
5.2% Buddhists
31.4% Christians
14.9% Hindus
13.2% Unaffiliated
29.7% Muslims

* Includes followers of African traditional religions, Chinese folk religions, Native American religions, and Australian aboriginal religions.
** Includes Bahai's, Jains, Sikhs, Shintoists, Taoists, followers of Tenrikyo, Wiccans, Zoroastrians, and many other faiths.
Percentages may not add to 100 due to rounding.

other religions, including Baha'i, Jainism, Sikhism, Shintoism, Taoism, Tenrikyo, Wicca, and Zoroastrianism.

About 1.1 billion people—16.4 percent of the world's population—lacked any religious affiliation. The unaffiliated therefore constitute the third-largest group worldwide with respect to religious affiliation, behind Christians and Muslims. There are about as many unaffiliated people as Roman Catholics in the world. Many of the unaffiliated actually hold some religious or spiritual beliefs, even if they don't identify with a particular religion (Pew Research Center 2012b, 2015b).

Worldwide, Islam is growing at a rate of about 2.9 percent annually, compared with 2.3 percent for Christianity. Within Christianity, the growth rate for "born-again" Christians (e.g., Evangelicals/Pentecostals) is much higher than for either Catholics or mainline Protestants. Recent demographic projections by the Pew Research Center (2015b) suggest that by 2050 there will be almost as many Muslims (29.7 percent) as Christians (31.4 percent) in the world (see Figure 9.1). In Europe, Muslims will constitute about 10 percent of the population, compared with about 6 percent today. This chapter's "Anthropology Today" documents recent religious changes in the United States, including the growth of non-Christian religions and of the unaffiliated—religious "nones."

Religion and Change

Like political organization, religion helps maintain social order. And like political mobilization, religious energy can be harnessed not just for change but also for revolution. Reacting to conquest or to actual or perceived foreign domination, for instance, religious leaders may seek to alter or revitalize their society.

Revitalization Movements and Cargo Cults

Revitalization movements are social movements that occur in times of change, in which religious leaders emerge and undertake to alter or revitalize a society. Christianity originated as a revitalization movement. Jesus was one of several prophets who preached new religious doctrines while the Middle East was under Roman rule. It was a time of social unrest, when a foreign power ruled the land. Jesus inspired a new, enduring, and major religion. His contemporaries were not so successful.

Revitalization movements known as **cargo cults** have arisen in colonial situations in which local people have regular contact with outsiders but lack their wealth, technology, and living standards. Cargo cults attempt to explain European domination and wealth and to achieve similar success magically by mimicking European behavior and manipulating symbols of the desired lifestyle. The cargo cults of Melanesia and Papua New Guinea are hybrid creations that weave Christian doctrine with indigenous beliefs. They take their name from their focus on cargo—European goods of the sort natives have seen unloaded from the cargo holds of ships and airplanes.

In one early cult, members believed that the spirits of the dead would arrive in a ship. Those ghosts would bring manufactured goods for the natives and would kill all the Whites. Later cargo cults replaced ships with airplanes (Worsley 1959/1985). Many cults have used elements of European culture as sacred objects. The rationale is that Europeans use these objects, have wealth, and therefore must know the "secret of cargo." By mimicking how Europeans use or treat objects, natives hope to come upon the secret knowledge needed to get cargo for themselves.

For example, having seen Europeans' reverent treatment of flags and flagpoles, the members of one cult began to worship flagpoles. They believed the flagpoles were sacred towers that could transmit messages between the living and the dead. Other natives built airstrips to entice planes bearing canned goods, portable radios, clothing, wristwatches, and motorcycles. Some cargo cult prophets proclaimed that success would come through a reversal of European domination and native subjugation. The day was near, they preached, when natives—aided by God, Jesus, or native ancestors—would turn the tables. Native skins would turn white, and those of Europeans would turn brown; Europeans would die or be killed.

Cargo cults blend Aboriginal and Christian beliefs. Melanesian myths told of ancestors shedding their skins and changing into powerful beings and of dead people returning to life. Christian missionaries also preached resurrection. The cults' preoccupation with cargo is related to traditional Melanesian big-man systems. In the chapter "Political Systems," we saw that a Melanesian big man had to be generous. People worked for the big man, helping him amass wealth, but eventually he had to give a feast and give away all that wealth.

Because of their experience with big-man systems, Melanesians believed that all wealthy people eventually had to give away their wealth. For decades they had attended Christian missions and worked on plantations. All the while they expected Europeans to return the fruits of their labor as their own big men did. When the Europeans refused to distribute the wealth or even to let natives know the secret of its production and distribution, cargo cults developed.

Like arrogant big men, Europeans would be leveled, by death if necessary. However, natives lacked the physical means of doing what their traditions said they should do. Thwarted by well-armed colonial forces, natives resorted to magical leveling. They called on supernatural beings to intercede, to kill or otherwise deflate the European big men and redistribute their wealth.

On the island of Tanna, in Vanuatu, Melanesia, members of the John Frum cargo cult stage a military parade. The young men, who carry fake guns and have "USA" painted on their bodies, see themselves as an elite force within the American army.
©Thierry Falise/LightRocket via Getty Images

Cargo cults are religious responses to the expansion of the world capitalist economy. However, this religious mobilization had political and economic results. Cult participation gave Melanesians a basis for common interests and activities and thus helped pave the way for political parties and economic interest organizations. Previously separated by geography, language, and customs, Melanesians started forming larger groups as members of the same cults and followers of the same prophets. The cargo cults paved the way for political action through which the indigenous peoples eventually regained their autonomy.

New and Alternative Religious Movements

This chapter's "Anthropology Today" describes changing patterns of religious affiliation in the United States, including significant growth in the number of Americans who affiliate with no organized religion. This trend toward nonaffiliation, whether as atheist, agnostic, or "nothing in particular" can also be detected in Canada, Western Europe, China, and Japan. In addition to increasing nonaffiliation, contemporary industrial societies also feature new religious trends and forms of spiritualism. The New Age movement, which emerged in the 1980s, draws on and blends cultural elements from multiple traditions. It advocates change through individual personal transformation. In the United States and Australia, respectively, some people who are not Native Americans or Native Australians have appropriated the symbols, settings, and purported religious practices of Native Americans and Native Australians for New Age religions. Native American activists decry the appropriation and commercialization of their spiritual beliefs and rituals, as when "sweat lodge" ceremonies are held on cruise ships, with wine and cheese served. They see the appropriation of their ceremonies and traditions as theft. Some Hindus feel similarly about the popularization of yoga.

Many contemporary nations contain unofficial religions. One example is "Yoruba religion," a term applied to perhaps 15 million adherents in Africa as well as to millions of practitioners of *syncretic,* or blended, religions (with elements of Catholicism and spiritism) in the Western Hemisphere . Forms of Yoruba religion include *santería* (in the Spanish Caribbean and the United States), *candomblé* (in Brazil), and *vodoun* (in the French Caribbean). Yoruba religion, with roots in precolonial nation-states of West Africa, has spread far beyond its region of origin, as part of the African diaspora. It remains an influential, identifiable religion today, despite suppression, such as by Cuba's communist government. There are perhaps 3 million practitioners of santería in Cuba, plus another 800,000 in the United States (Ontario Consultants 2007). Between 5 and 10 million Brazilians participate in candomblé, also known as *macumba* (Garcia-Navarro 2013). Voodoo (*vodoun*) has between 2.8 and 3.2 million practitioners (Ontario Consultants 2011), many (perhaps most) of whom would name something else, such as Catholicism, as their religion.

Religion and Cultural Globalization

Evangelical Protestantism and Pentecostalism

The rapid and ongoing spread of Evangelical Protestantism represents a highly successful form of contemporary cultural globalization. A century ago, more than 90 percent of the 80 million Evangelicals in the world at that time lived in Europe and North America (Pew Research Center 2011). Today, there are as many as 1 billion Evangelicals worldwide. Most now live in Latin America, Asia, sub-Saharan Africa, and the Middle East and North Africa.

The growth of Evangelical Protestantism has been particularly explosive in Brazil—traditionally (and still) the world's most Catholic nation. In 1980, when Pope John Paul II visited the country, 89 percent of Brazilians claimed to be Roman Catholics. Since then, the growth rate of Evangelical Protestantism has skyrocketed. Protestants accounted for less than 5 percent of Brazil's population through the 1960s. By 2000, Evangelicals comprised more than 15 percent of Brazilians affiliated with a church. The current estimate of the Evangelical share of Brazil's population is between 20 and 25 percent and growing—mainly at the expense of Catholicism. Among the factors that have worked against Catholicism are these: a declining and mainly foreign priesthood, sharply contrasting political agendas of many of its clerics, and its reputation as mainly a women's religion.

Evangelical Protestantism stresses conservative morality, biblical authority, and a personal ("born-again") conversion experience. Most Brazilian Evangelicals are Pentecostals, who also embrace glossolalia (speaking in tongues) and beliefs in faith healing, spirits, exorcism, and miracles. In its focus on ecstatic and exuberant worship, Pentecostalism has been heavily influenced by—and shares features with—African American Protestantism. In Brazil it shares features with candomblé, which also features chanting and spirit possession (Casanova 2001; Meyer 1999).

Peter Berger (2010) suggests that modern Pentecostalism may be the fastest-growing religion in human history and focuses on its social dimensions to explain why. According to Berger, Pentecostalism promotes strong communities while offering practical and psychological support to people whose circumstances are changing. My own experience in Brazil supports Berger's hypothesis; most new Pentecostals I encountered came from underprivileged, poor, and otherwise marginalized groups in areas undergoing rapid social change.

The British sociologist David Martin (1990) argues that Pentecostalism is spreading so rapidly because its adherents embody Max Weber's Protestant ethic—valuing self-discipline, hard work, and thrift. Others see Pentecostalism as a kind of cargo cult, built on the belief that magic and ritual activity can promote material success (Freston 2008; Meyer 1999). Berger (2010) thinks that today's Pentecostals probably include both types—Weberian Protestants working to produce material wealth as a sign of their salvation, along with people who believe that magic and ritual will bring them good fortune.

Converts to Pentecostalism are expected to separate themselves both from their pasts and from the secular social world that surrounds them. In Arembepe, Brazil, for example, the *crentes* ("true believers," as members of the local Pentecostal community are called) set themselves apart by their beliefs, behavior, and lifestyle (Kottak 2006). They worship, chant, and pray. They dress simply and forgo such worldly temptations (seen as vices) as tobacco, alcohol, gambling, and extramarital sexuality, along with dancing, movies, and other forms of popular culture.

Pentecostalism strengthens family and household through a moral code that respects marriage and prohibits adultery, gambling, drinking, and fighting. These activities were

In São Paulo, Brazil, evangelicals pray inside the Bola de Neve Church. Popular with youths, this church sponsors activities such as surfing, skating, and rock 'n' roll and reggae music with religious lyrics. ©REUTERS/Alamy Stock Photo

valued mainly by men in preconversion culture. Pentecostalism has appeal for men, however, because it solidifies their authority within the household. Although Pentecostal ideology is strongly patriarchal, with women expected to subordinate themselves to men, women tend to be more active church members than are men. Pentecostalism promotes services and prayer groups by and for women. In such settings women develop leadership skills, as they also extend their social-support network beyond family and kin (Burdick 1998).

Homogenization, Indigenization, or Hybridization?

Any cultural form that spreads from one society to another—be it a Starbucks, a McDonald's, or a form of religion—has to fit into the country and culture it enters. We can use the rapid spread of Pentecostalism as a case study of the process of adaptation of foreign cultural forms to local settings.

Joel Robbins (2004) has examined the extent to which what he calls Pentecostal/charismatic Christianity preserves its basic form and core beliefs as it spreads and adapts to various national and local cultures. Pentecostalism is a Western invention: Its beliefs, doctrines, organizational features, and rituals originated in the United States, following the European rise and spread of Protestantism. The core doctrines of acceptance of Jesus as one's savior, baptism with the Holy Spirit, faith healing, and belief in the second coming of Jesus have spread across nations and cultures without losing their basic shape.

Scholars have argued about whether the global spread of Pentecostalism is best understood as (1) a process of Western cultural domination and homogenization (perhaps supported by a right-wing political agenda) or (2) one in which imported cultural forms respond to local needs and are differentiated and indigenized. Robbins (2004) takes a middle-ground position, viewing the spread of Pentecostalism as a form of cultural hybridization. He argues that global and local features appear with equal intensity within these Pentecostal cultures. Churches retain certain core Pentecostal beliefs and behaviors while also responding to the local culture and being organized at the local level.

Reviewing the literature, Robbins (2004) finds little evidence that a Western political agenda is propelling the global spread of Pentecostalism. It is true that foreigners (including American pastors and televangelists) have helped introduce Pentecostalism to countries outside North America. There is little evidence, however, that overseas churches are largely funded and ideologically shaped from North America. Pentecostal churches typically are staffed with locals, who run them as organizations that are attentive and responsive to local situations. Conversion is typically a key feature of that agenda. Once converted, a Pentecostal is expected to be an active evangelist, seeking to bring in new members. This evangelization is one of the most important activities in Pentecostal culture and certainly aids its expansion.

Pentecostalism spreads as other forces of globalization displace people and disrupt local lives. To people who feel socially adrift, Pentecostal evangelists offer tightly knit communities and a weblike structure of personal connections within and between Pentecostal communities. Such networks can facilitate access to health care, job placement, educational services, and other resources.

Unlike Catholicism, which is hierarchical, Pentecostalism is egalitarian. Adherents need no special education—only spiritual inspiration—to preach or to run a church. Based on his research in Brazil, John Burdick (1993) notes that many Afro-Brazilians are drawn to the Pentecostal community because others who are socially and racially like them are in the congregation, some serving as preachers. Opportunities for participation and leadership are abundant, for example, as lay preachers, deacons, and leaders of various men's, women's, and youth groups. The churches fund outreach to the needy and other locally relevant social services.

The Spread of Islam

Islam—whose 1.6 billion followers constitute over a fifth of the world's population—is another rapidly spreading global religion that can be used to illustrate cultural globalization. The globalization of Islam also illustrates cultural hybridization. Islam has adapted successfully to the many nations and cultures it has entered, adopting architectural styles, linguistic practices, and even religious beliefs from host cultures.

For example, although mosques (Islamic houses of worship) all share certain characteristics (e.g., they face Mecca and have some common architectural features), they also incorporate architectural and decorative elements from their national settings. Arabic is Islam's liturgical language, used for prayer, but most Muslims' discussion of their faith occurs in their local language. In China, Islamic concepts have been influenced by Confucianism. In India and Bangladesh, the Islamic idea of the prophet has blended with the Hindu notion of the avatar, a deity who takes mortal form and descends to Earth to fight evil and guide the righteous. Islam entered Indonesia by means of Muslim merchants who devised devotional exercises that fit in with preexisting religions—Hinduism and Buddhism in Java and Sumatra and animism in the eastern islands, which eventually became Christian. In Bali, Hinduism survived as the dominant religion.

Outside the French embassy in London, a group known as "Muslims against Crusades" protests France's introduction of a burka ban. What role have such bans played, either in reducing or in increasing, recent religious radicalization?
©Cliff Hide News/Alamy Stock Photo

Both Pentecostalism and Islam, we have learned, hybridize and become locally relevant as they spread globally. Although certain core features endure, local people always assign their own meanings to the messages and social forms they receive from outside, including religion. Such meanings reflect their cultural backgrounds, experiences, and prior belief systems. We must consider the processes of hybridization and indigenization in examining and understanding any form of cultural diffusion or globalization.

Antimodernism and Fundamentalism

Antimodernism is the rejection of the modern in favor of what is perceived as an earlier, purer, and better way of life. This viewpoint first arose out of disillusionment with the Industrial Revolution and with subsequent developments in science, technology, and consumption patterns. Antimodernists consider the use of modern technology to be misguided or think that technology should have a lower priority than religious and cultural values.

Religious *fundamentalism* describes antimodernist movements in various religions, including Christianity, Islam, and Judaism. Not only do fundamentalists feel strongly alienated from modern secular culture, but they also have separated from a larger religious group, whose founding principles, they believe, have been corrupted or abandoned. Fundamentalists advocate return and strict fidelity to the "true" (fundamental) religious principles of the larger religion.

Exemplifying their antimodernism, fundamentalists also seek to rescue religion from absorption into modern, Western culture. In Christianity, fundamentalists are "born-again Christians" as opposed to "mainline Protestants." In Islam, they are jamaat (in Arabic, communities based on close fellowship) engaged in jihad (struggle) against a Western culture hostile to Islam and the God-given (shariah) way of life. In Judaism, they are Haredi, "Torah-true" Jews. All these fundamentalists see a sharp divide between themselves and other religions, as well as between their own "sacred" view of life and the modern "secular" world (see Antoun 2008).

Both Pentecostalism and Christian fundamentalism preach ascetic morality, the duty to convert others, and respect for the Bible. Fundamentalists, however, tend to cite their success in living a moral life as proof of their salvation, whereas Pentecostals find assurance of their salvation in exuberant, ecstatic experience. Fundamentalists also seek to remake the political sphere along religious lines, whereas Pentecostals tend to have less interest in politics (Robbins 2004).

Religious Radicalization Today

What radicalizes people today? What motivates them to join militant groups like al Qaeda and the Islamic State (also known as IS, ISIS, ISIL, and Daesh)? The growth of such extremist groups is part of a process of political globalization that has accompanied economic globalization. Political globalization reflects the need, in a fragmented world, for some form of attachment to a larger community. Among those most likely to feel this need are displaced and alienated people. Among them are refugees, migrants, and marginalized groups—individuals who feel adrift and apart from, perhaps even despised by, the society or nation-state that surrounds them. One French militant whom anthropologist Scott Atran interviewed traced his radicalization to a childhood incident in which a Frenchman spat at his sister and called her a "dirty Arab" (Atran quoted in Reardon 2015).

Atran is the foremost anthropologist working on the topic of religious radicalization. He and his multinational team of researchers have interviewed members of radical movements in several countries, including members of ISIS in Kirkuk, Iraq, and potential members in Barcelona, Spain, and Paris, France. Atran's team also worked in Morocco, in two neighborhoods in Casablanca sympathetic to militant jihad. One of those neighborhoods had produced five of the seven 2004 Madrid train bombers. The other had sent dozens of volunteers, including suicide bombers, to Iraq and Syria. The researchers got to know the families and friends of the militants, learning how they lived and gaining insight into their beliefs.

Atran argues that militants and terrorists are "devoted actors" (Atran 2016; Atran et al. 2014)—individuals who are willing to kill and die for values and beliefs they consider to be sacred and unquestionable. One key value of ISIS is the need to establish a caliphate ruled by sharia law and led by a successor to the prophet Mohammed. Devoted actors will sacrifice themselves, their families, and all else for their cause. Commitment will be strongest when sacred values are shared, cementing a group identity (Atran 2016). The researchers found that militants, almost always young men, tend to form groups of three to four like-minded friends who forge themselves into a family-like unit, becoming a "band of brothers" in arms, devoted to one another. Like members of a cult, they share a collective sense of righteousness and special destiny. As potential martyrs, they require strong inspiration. Their commitment to a common cause, combined with family-like relationships, provides that inspiration.

Although most recruits to ISIS and al Qaeda are Muslims, many have little prior knowledge of the religious teachings of Islam. What inspires them is not so much religious doctrine as the wish to pursue a thrilling cause—one that promises glory, esteem, respect, and remembrance. In the minds of some youth, ISIS has become "cool." It even attracts "jihad tourists"—people who visit Syria over school breaks or holidays seeking a brief adventure and then return to their routine jobs in the West. These militants are not part of an organized global network based on top-down control. Rather, their groups remain decentralized and self-organizing. These locally dispersed groups can, however, connect via the Internet to form a more global community of alienated youth seeking heroic sacrifice.

Atran suggests that attempts to defeat ISIS militarily or by trying to buy off its members will probably fail (Atran et al. 2014). He argues that sacred values are fought most successfully with other sacred values, or by undermining the social networks that are held together by those values. He also suggests that the armed forces and sacred ideals needed to defeat ISIS will probably have to come from the Muslim communities threatened by ISIS.

Secular Rituals

In concluding this chapter on religion, we may recognize some problems with the definitions of religion given at the beginning of this chapter. The first problem: If we define religion with reference to the sacred and/or supernatural beings, powers, and forces, how do we classify ritual-like behaviors that occur in secular contexts? Some anthropologists believe there are both sacred and secular rituals. Secular rituals include formal, invariant, stereotyped, earnest, repetitive behavior and rites of passage that take place in nonreligious settings.

A second problem: If the distinction between the supernatural and the natural is not consistently made in a society, how can we tell what is religion and what isn't? The Betsileo of Madagascar, for example, view witches and dead ancestors as real people who play roles in ordinary life. However, their occult powers are not empirically demonstrable.

A third problem: The behavior considered appropriate for religious occasions varies tremendously from culture to culture. One society may consider drunken frenzy the surest sign of faith, whereas another may inculcate quiet reverence. Who is to say which is "more religious"?

Apparently secular settings, things, and events can acquire intense meaning for individuals who have grown up in their presence. Identities and loyalties based on fandom can be powerful indeed. Italians, Brazilians, and several other nationalities are rarely, if ever, as nationally focused and emotionally unified as they are when their teams are playing soccer in the World Cup. The collective effervescence that Durkheim (1912/2001) found so characteristic of religion can equally well describe what Brazilians experience when their country wins a World Cup.

In the context of comparative religion, the idea that the secular can become sacred isn't surprising. Long ago, Durkheim (1912/2001) pointed out that the distinction between sacred and profane doesn't depend on the intrinsic qualities of the sacred

Anthropology Today   *Newtime Religion*

Because the U.S. Census doesn't gather information about religion, there are no official government statistics on Americans' religious affiliations. To help fill this gap, the Pew Research Center, based in Washington, D.C., carried out "Religious Landscape Studies" in 2007 and 2014. These comprehensive surveys of more than 35,000 adults provide a basis for systematic comparison, enabling us to assess changes in the religious affiliations of Americans between 2007 and 2014 (see Pew Research Center 2015a).

Although the United States continues to have the world's largest Christian population, the number and percentage of Americans affiliated with a Christian church have been declining. Between 2007 and 2014, the Christian share of the U.S. population fell almost 8 points, from 78.4 percent to 70.6 percent. This change was due primarily to declines among Catholics and mainline Protestants, each of which shrank by about three percentage points. Table 9.2 provides percentages of

TABLE 9.2   **Religious Affiliations of Americans, 2007 and 2014**

Source: "Religion and Public Life.". *America's Changing Religious Landscape*. Washington, DC: Pew Research Center. May 12, 2015, p. 3. Copyright ©2015.

Affiliation	2007	2014	Change (Percentage Points)
Christian	78.4%	70.6%	−7.8
Protestant	51.3%	46.5%	−4.8
Evangelical	26.3%	25.4%	−0.9
Mainline	18.1%	14.7%	−3.4
Historically Black	6.9%	6.5%	−0.4
Catholic	23.9%	20.8%	−3.1
Orthodox Christian	0.6%	0.5%	−0.1
Mormon	1.7%	1.6%	−0.1
Jehovah's Witness	0.7%	0.8%	0.1
Other Christian	0.3%	0.4%	0.1
Non-Christian faiths	4.7%	5.9%	1.2
Jewish	1.7%	1.9%	0.2
Muslim	0.4%	0.9%	0.5
Buddhist	0.7%	0.7%	0.0
Hindu	0.4%	0.7%	0.3
Other world religions*	0.3%	0.3%	0.0
Other faiths**	1.2%	1.5%	0.3
Unaffiliated	16.1%	22.8%	6.7
Atheist	1.6%	3.1%	1.5
Agnostic	2.4%	4.0%	1.6
Nothing in particular	12.1%	15.8%	3.7
Don't know/refused	0.8%	0.6%	−0.2

All percentages are of total sample.
*Includes Sikhs, Baha'is, Taoists, Jains, etc.
**Includes Unitarians, New Age religions, Native American religions, etc.

change between 2007 and 2014 for all religious categories.

Of the 85 percent of Americans who were raised as Christians, nearly a quarter no longer follow that faith. Former Christians now represent about 19 percent of all U.S. adults. Catholicism has experienced a particularly steep decline. Of the 32 percent of Americans who were raised Catholic, 41 percent no longer practice. Catholics are declining in terms of both percentages and absolute numbers. There were 51 million American Catholics in 2014, 3 million fewer than in 2007.

The absolute number of mainline Protestants—Methodists, Baptists, Lutherans, Presbyterians, and Episcopalians—also fell, from 41 million in 2007 to 36 million in 2014. However, the number of Americans participating in historically Black Protestant churches has remained fairly stable in recent years, at around 16 million people. Evangelicals represent the only group of Protestants whose numbers have been increasing, even as their share of the U.S. population has declined by a percentage point. Evangelicals now number around 62 million American adults, an increase of about 2 million since 2007.

As the Christian share of the population has been declining, the percentage of Americans belonging to non-Christian faiths has been rising. Between 2007 and 2014, this percentage rose from 4.7 percent to 5.9 percent, with growth especially strong for Muslims and Hindus.

The most notable increase, however—from 16.1 percent to 22.8 percent—has been in the unaffiliated category—Americans with no religious affiliation. These religious "nones" include people who identify as atheists, agnostics, or "nothing in particular." Almost a third

(31 percent) of them admit to being atheists or agnostics; they represent 7 percent of the American population overall. Religious nones, at 56 million, now outnumber both Catholics and mainline Protestants. These unaffiliated Americans tend to be young, with a median age of 36 years, compared with 46 years for the U.S. population as a whole, and 52 years for mainline Protestants. The unaffiliated percentage is highest in the West, followed (in order) by the Northeast, Midwest, and South. In the West, the unaffiliated, at 28 percent, outnumber all religious groups. Among ethnic groups, non-Hispanic Whites are most likely to be unaffiliated: 24 percent, versus 20 percent for Latinos and 18 percent for African Americans. Men are much more likely than women to be unaffiliated—27 percent to 19 percent.

How might we explain the growth of the unaffiliated category? One factor may be the decrease in religious in-marriage or endogamy. Of the Americans who have wed since 2010, 39 percent were in a religiously mixed marriage, compared with just 19 percent of Americans who married before 1960. When parents have different religions, or when one is affiliated while the other is not, it may be easier to raise children unaffiliated than to choose between faiths.

It has also becoming increasingly common—and accepted—for people to switch between religions, or to no religion at all. Just over one-third (34 percent) of Americans have a religious identity (or lack thereof) different from the one in which they were raised. If switching from one Protestant church to another, for example, from mainline to Evangelical, is also included, this figure rises to 42 percent. Those raised without any religious affiliations as children are even more likely to

continued

Anthropology Today *continued*

switch to a new category in adulthood. About half of the 9 percent of Americans raised in a nonreligious household claim a religious affiliation as adults.

We see that diversity in religious beliefs and practices is on the rise in the United States. Furthermore, the established religions themselves are becoming more racially and ethnically diverse in membership. Minorities now constitute 41 percent of American Catholics, 24 percent of Evangelicals, and 14 percent of mainline Protestants. There is every reason to believe that these trends involving religious affiliation, or lack thereof, will continue in the United States.

symbol. In Australian totemic religion, for example, sacred beings include such humble creatures as ducks, frogs, rabbits, and grubs, whose inherent qualities could hardly have given rise to the religious sentiment they inspire.

Madagascar's tomb-centered ceremonies are times when the living and the dead are joyously reunited, when people get drunk, gorge themselves, and have sexual license. Perhaps the gray, sober, ascetic, and moralistic aspects of many official religious events, in taking the fun out of religion, force some, indeed many, people to find religion (i.e., truth, beauty, meaning, passionate involvement) in fun.

Summary

1. Given the varied and worldwide scope of beliefs and behavior labeled "religious," anthropologists recognize the difficulty of defining religion. Religion, a cultural universal, consists of beliefs and behavior concerned with supernatural beings, powers, and forces. Religion also encompasses the feelings, meanings, and congregations associated with such beliefs and behavior. Religious worlds are real, vivid, and significant to those who construct and inhabit them. Anthropological studies have revealed many forms, expressions, and functions of religion.

2. Tylor considered animism—the belief in spirits or souls—to be religion's earliest and most basic form. He focused on religion's explanatory role, arguing that religion would eventually disappear as science provided better explanations. Besides animism, another view of the supernatural also occurs in nonindustrial societies, seeing the supernatural as a domain of raw, impersonal power or force (called mana in Polynesia and Melanesia). People can manipulate and control mana under certain conditions.

3. When ordinary technical and rational means of doing things fail, people may turn to magic. Often they use magic when they lack control over outcomes. Religion offers comfort and psychological security at times of crisis. On the other hand, rites can also create anxiety. Rituals are formal, invariant, stylized, earnest acts in which

people subordinate their beliefs to a social collectivity. Rites of passage have three stages: separation, liminality, and incorporation. Such rites can mark any change in social status, age, place, or social condition. Collective rites are often cemented by communitas, a feeling of intense solidarity.

4. Religion establishes and maintains social control through a series of moral and ethical beliefs and real and imagined rewards and punishments, internalized in individuals. Religion also achieves social control by mobilizing its members for collective action.

5. Religions exist in particular societies, and cultural differences show up systematically in religious beliefs and practices. The ecclesiastical and monotheistic religions of stratified, state societies, for example, differ from those of societies that lack hierarchies and specialized officials. The world's major religions vary in their growth rates, with Islam expanding more rapidly than Christianity.

6. Religion helps maintain social order, but it also can promote change. Cargo cults are revitalization movements that hybridize beliefs and that have helped people adapt to changing conditions. Among contemporary "new" religious movements, some have been influenced by Christianity, others by Eastern (Asian) religions, still others by mysticism and spiritualism or by science and technology.

7. The spread of Evangelical/Pentecostal Protestantism worldwide illustrates contemporary cultural globalization. Evangelical Protestantism stresses conservative morality, the authority of the Bible, and a personal ("born-again") conversion experience. To people who feel socially adrift, Pentecostalism offers tightly knit communities and a weblike structure of personal connections. The rapid spread of Islam also illustrates cultural globalization and hybridization. Although certain core features endure, local people always assign their own meanings to the messages and social forms they receive from outside, including religion. Antimodernism is the rejection of the modern, including globalization, in favor of what is perceived as an earlier, purer, and better way of life. Religious fundamentalism describes antimodernist movements in Christianity, Islam, and Judaism. Militant extremism in the name of religion also appeals to people, primarily young men, who feel alienated from, or despised by, the society that surrounds them. These radicals form "bands of brothers" united by common values and willing to kill and die for a cause.

8. There are secular as well as religious rituals. It is possible for apparently secular settings, things, and events to acquire intense meaning for individuals who have grown up in their presence.

Think Like an Anthropologist

1. Describe a rite of passage you (or a friend) have been through. How did it fit the three-phase model given in the text? Now consider a move you have made, such as going away to college. Did it fit the three-phase model? In both cases, describe your experiences with liminality.

2. This chapter notes that many Americans see recreation (e.g., sports) and religion as separate domains. Based on my fieldwork in Brazil and Madagascar and my reading about other societies, I believe that this separation is both ethnocentric and false. Do you agree with me about this? What has been your own experience?

Key Terms

animism, *189*

cargo cults, *199*

communitas, *192*

liminality, *191*

magic, *190*

mana, *189*

monotheism, *189*

polytheism, *189*

religion, *186*

revitalization
   movements, *199*

rites of passage, *191*

rituals, *190*

shaman, *188*

taboo, *189*

totem, *194*

Chapter 10

Ethnicity and Race

Ethnic Groups and Ethnicity

Ethnicity is based on cultural similarities (shared with members of the same ethnic group) and differences (between that group and others). Ethnic groups must deal with other such groups in the nation or region they inhabit. Interethnic relations are important in the study of any nation or region—especially so because of the ongoing transnational movement of migrants and refugees (see Marger 2015; Parrillo 2016). Table 10.1 lists American ethnic groups, based on the most recent U.S. Census Bureau estimates available as of this writing.

Members of an **ethnic group** *share* certain beliefs, values, habits, customs, and norms because of their common background. They define themselves as different and special because of cultural features. This distinction may arise from language, religion,

TABLE 10.1   **Racial/Ethnic Identification in the United States, 2015**

Source: Kaiser Family Foundation estimates based on the Census Bureau's March 2016 Current Population Survey (CPS: Annual Social and Economic Supplement). Copyright © 2016.

Claimed Identity	Number (millions)	Percentage
White (non-Hispanic)	195.9	61.4
Hispanic	57.1	17.9
Black	39.2	12.3
Asian	17.8	5.6
Other*	8.9	2.8
Total population	318.9	100.0

* Includes American Indian, Alaska Native, and Two or More Races.

historical experience, geographic placement, kinship, or "race" (see Spickard 2012). Markers of an ethnic group may include a collective name, belief in common descent, a sense of solidarity, and an association with a specific territory, which the group may or may not currently inhabit.

Ethnicity means identification with, and feeling part of, an ethnic group and exclusion from certain other groups because of this affiliation. Ethnic feelings and associated behavior vary in intensity within ethnic groups and countries and over time. A change in the degree of importance attached to an ethnic identity may reflect political changes (Soviet rule ends—ethnic feeling rises) or individual life-cycle changes (old people relinquish, or young people reclaim, an ethnic background).

Status and Identity

Ethnicity is only one basis for group identity. Cultural differences also are associated with class, region, religion, and other social variables (see Warne 2015). Individuals often have more than one group identity, and in modern nations, people continually negotiate their social identities. All of us "wear different hats," presenting ourselves sometimes as one thing, sometimes as another.

These different social identities are known as statuses. In daily conversation, we hear the term *status* used as a synonym for *prestige*. In this context, "She's got a lot of status" means she's got a lot of prestige; people look up to her. Among social scientists, that's not the only meaning of *status*. Social scientists use **status** more neutrally—for any position, no matter what the prestige, that someone occupies in society. Parent is a social status. So are professor, student, factory worker, Republican, salesperson, homeless person, labor leader, ethnic-group member, and thousands of others. People always occupy multiple statuses (e.g., Hispanic, Catholic, infant, brother). Among the statuses we occupy, particular ones dominate in particular settings, such as son or daughter at home and student in the classroom.

Some statuses are **ascribed:** People have limited choice about occupying them. Age is an ascribed status. We can't choose not to age, although many people, especially wealthy ones, use cultural means, such as plastic surgery, to try to disguise the biological aging process. Race and gender usually are ascribed; most people are born members of a given race or gender and remain so all their lives. **Achieved statuses,** by contrast, aren't automatic; they come through choices, actions, efforts, talents, or accomplishments and may be positive or negative. Examples of achieved statuses include physician, senator, convicted felon, salesperson, union member, father, and college student.

From the media, you will be familiar with recent cases in which gender and race have become achieved rather than ascribed statuses. Transgender individuals modify the gender status they were assigned at birth or during childhood. People who were born members of one race have chosen to adopt another. In some cases, individuals who were born African American have passed as White, Hispanic, or Native American. In a case widely reported in 2015, a woman known as Rachel Dolezal, who was born White, changed her racial identity to Black or African American as an adult. In doing this, she modified her phenotype by changing her hairstyle to better fit her new identity. Given what culture can do to biology, few statuses are absolutely ascribed.

Often status is contextual: One identity is used in certain settings, another in different ones. We call this the *situational negotiation of social identity* (Leman 2001; Spickard 2013; Warne 2015). Members of an ethnic group may shift their ethnic identities. Hispanics, for example, may use different ethnic labels (e.g., *Cuban* or *Latino*) to describe themselves depending on context. In one study, half (51 percent) of American Hispanics surveyed preferred to identify using their family's country of origin (as in *Mexican, Cuban,* or *Dominican*) rather than *Hispanic* or *Latino.* Just one-quarter (24 percent) chose one of those two pan-ethnic terms, while 21 percent said they use the term *American* most often (Taylor et al. 2012).

Latinos who have different national origins may mobilize around issues of general interest to Hispanics, such as a path to citizenship for, or the possible deportation of, undocumented immigrants, while acting as separate interest groups in other contexts. Among Hispanics, Cuban Americans are older and richer on average than Mexican Americans and Puerto Ricans, and their class interests and voting patterns differ. Cuban Americans are more likely to vote Republican than are Puerto Ricans and Mexican Americans. Some Mexican Americans whose families have lived in the United States for generations have little in common with new Hispanic immigrants, such as those from Central America.

Hispanics are the fastest-growing ethnic group in the United States, increasing by 62 percent between 2000 and 2015—from 35.3 million to 57.1 million. *Hispanic* is a category based mainly on language. It includes Whites, Blacks, and "racially" mixed Spanish speakers and their ethnically conscious descendants. The label *Hispanic* lumps together people of diverse geographic origin—Mexico, Puerto Rico, El Salvador, Cuba, the Dominican Republic, Guatemala, and other Spanish-speaking countries of Central and South America and the Caribbean. *Latino* is a broader category, which also can include Brazilians (who speak Portuguese). Mexicans constitute about two-thirds of American Hispanics. Next come Puerto Ricans, at around 9 percent. Salvadorans, Cubans, Dominicans, and Guatemalans living in the United States all number more than 1 million people per nationality. Of the major racial and ethnic groups in the United States, Hispanics are by far the youngest. At 27 years, their median age is a decade younger than that of the U.S. population overall (Krogstad 2014).

Hispanic and *Latino* are ethnic categories that cross-cut "racial" contrasts such as between *Black* and *White*. Note the physical diversity among these children in Trinidad, Cuba. ©Paul Bucknall/Alamy Stock Photo

Minority Groups and Stratification

Minority groups are so called because they occupy subordinate (lower) positions within a social hierarchy. They have inferior power and less secure access to resources than do *majority groups*. Minority groups are obvious features of stratification in the United States. The 2015 poverty rate was 9 percent for non-Hispanic Whites, 11 percent for Asian Americans, 21 percent for Hispanics, and 24 percent for African Americans (Proctor et al. 2016). Inequality shows up consistently in unemployment figures as well as in income and wealth. Median household incomes in 2015 were as follows: $77,166 for Asian Americans, $62,950 for non-Hispanic Whites, $45,148 for Hispanics, and $36,898 for African Americans (Proctor et al. 2016). The median wealth of White households in 2013 was 13 times that of Black households—its highest point since 1989, when Whites had 17 times the wealth of Black households (Kochhar and Fry 2014).

Human Biological Diversity and the Race Concept

When an ethnic group is assumed to have a biological basis (distinctively shared "blood" or genes), it is called a **race** (see Mukhopadhyay et al. 2014; Wade 2015). Discrimination against such a group is called **racism** (Gotkowitz 2011; Scupin 2012). Race, like ethnicity in general, is a cultural category rather than a biological reality. That is, ethnic groups, including "races," derive from contrasts perceived and perpetuated in particular societies, rather than from scientific classifications based on common genes.

Historically, scientists have approached the study of human biological diversity in two main ways: (1) racial classification (now largely abandoned) versus (2) the current explanatory approach, which focuses on understanding specific differences. *Biological differences are real, important, and apparent to us all.* Modern scientists find it most productive to seek explanations for these differences, rather than trying to pigeonhole people into categories called races. First we'll consider problems with **racial classification** (the attempt to assign humans to discrete categories—races—based on common ancestry). Then we'll offer some explanations for specific aspects of human biological diversity.

In theory, a biological race is a geographically isolated subdivision of a species. Such a population is capable of interbreeding with other populations of the same species, but it does not do so because of its isolation. Some biologists also use *race* to refer to breeds, as of dogs or roses. Thus, a pit bull and a Chihuahua would be different races of dogs. Such domesticated races have been bred by humans for generations. Humanity (*Homo sapiens*) lacks distinct races because human populations have not been isolated enough from one another to develop into such separate groups. Nor have humans experienced controlled breeding like that which has created the various kinds of dogs and roses.

Although races are supposedly based on shared genetic material (inherited from a common ancestor), early scholars instead used phenotypical traits (usually skin color) for racial classification. **Phenotype** refers to an organism's evident traits, its "manifest biology"—anatomy and physiology. Humans display hundreds of evident (detectable) physical traits. They range from skin color, hair form, eye color, and facial features (which are visible) to blood groups, color blindness, and enzyme production (which become evident through testing) (see Anemone 2011).

Racial classifications based on phenotype raise the problem of deciding which trait(s) should be primary. Should races be defined by height, weight, body shape, facial features, teeth, skull form, or skin color? Like their fellow citizens, early European and American scientists gave priority to skin color. Many schoolbooks and encyclopedias still proclaim the existence of three great races: the White, the Black, and the Yellow. This overly simplistic classification was compatible with the political use of race during the colonial period of the late 19th and early 20th centuries. Such a tripartite scheme kept White Europeans neatly separate from their African, Asian, and Native American subjects. Colonial empires began to break up, and scientists began to question established racial categories, after World War II (see Tattersall and DeSalle 2011).

Races Are Not Biologically Distinct

History and politics aside, one obvious problem with classifying people by skin color is that the terms "White," "Black," and "Yellow" do not accurately describe human skin colors. So-called "White" people are more pink, beige, or tan than white. "Black" people are various shades of brown, and "Yellow" people are tan or beige. It does not make the tripartite division of human races any more accurate when we use the more scientific-*sounding* synonyms—Caucasoid, Negroid, and Mongoloid—rather than White, Black, and Yellow.

Another problem with classifying people by skin color is that many populations don't fit neatly into any one of the three "great races." For example, where would one put the

Polynesians? *Polynesia* is a triangle of South Pacific islands formed by Hawaii to the north, Easter Island to the east, and New Zealand to the southwest. Does the "bronze" skin color of Polynesians connect them to the Caucasoids or to the Mongoloids? Some scientists, recognizing this problem, enlarged the original tripartite scheme to include the Polynesian "race." Native Americans presented a similar problem. Were they Red or Yellow? Some scientists added a fifth race—the "Red," or Amerindian—to the major racial groups.

Many people in southern India have dark skin, but scientists have been reluctant to classify them with "Black" Africans because of their Caucasoid facial features and hair form. Some, therefore, have created a separate race for these people. What about the Australian Aborigines, hunters and gatherers native to what has been, throughout human history, the most isolated continent? By skin color, one might place some Native Australians in the same race as tropical Africans. However, similarities to Europeans in hair color (light or reddish) and facial features have led some scientists to classify them as Caucasoids. There is no evidence, however, that Australians are closer genetically to Europeans or Africans than they are to Asians. Recognizing this problem, scientists often regard Native Australians as a separate race.

Finally, consider the San ("Bushmen") of the Kalahari Desert in southern Africa. Scientists have perceived their skin color as varying from brown to yellow. Some who regard San skin as "yellow" have suggested an Asian connection. There is no evidence, however, for close common ancestry between San and Asians. Somewhat more reasonably, some scholars assign the San to the Capoid race (from the Cape of Good Hope), which is seen as being different from other groups inhabiting tropical Africa.

Similar problems arise when any single trait is used as a basis for racial classification. An attempt to use facial features, height, weight, or any other phenotypical trait is fraught with difficulties. For example, consider the Nilotes, natives of the upper Nile region of Uganda and South Sudan. Nilotes tend to be tall and to have long, narrow noses. Certain Scandinavians also are tall, with similar noses. Given the distance between their homelands, to classify them as members of the same race makes little sense. There is no reason to assume that Nilotes and Scandinavians are more closely related to each other than either is to shorter and nearer populations with different kinds of noses.

Would racial classifications be better if we based them on a combination of physical traits rather than a single trait such as skin color, height, or nose form? To do so would avoid some of the problems raised using a single trait, but other problems would arise. The main problem is that physical features do not go together in a coherent and consistent bundle. Some tall people have dark skin; others are lighter. Some short people have curly hair; others have straight hair. Imagine the various possible combinations of skin color, stature, and skull form. Add to that facial features such as nose form, eye shape, and lip thickness. People with dark skin may be tall or short and have hair ranging from straight to very curly. Dark-haired populations may have light or dark skin, along with various skull forms, facial features, and body sizes and shapes. The number of combinations is very large, and the amount that heredity (versus environment) contributes to such phenotypical traits is often unclear (see also Anemone 2011; Beall 2014). Using a combination of physical characteristics would not solve the problem of constructing an accurate racial classification scheme.

The photos in this chapter illustrate only a small part of the range of human biological diversity. Shown here is a Bai minority woman from Shapin, in China's Yunnan province. ©Paul Grebliunas/The Image Bank/Getty Images.

A Quechua woman in Macha, Bolivia. ©Leonid Plotkin/Alamy Stock Photo

A boy at the Pushkar livestock fair, Rajasthan, India.©Conrad P. Kottak

A Polynesian boy from Bora Bora, Society Islands, French Polynesia. ©Tom Cockrem/Lonely Planet Images/Getty Images

A Native Australian man from Cloncurry, Queensland, Australia. ©Holger Leue/Lonely Planet Images/Getty Images

The phenotypical features of contemporary humans aren't precisely or even necessarily correlated with genetic relationships. Because of environmental changes that affect humans during growth and development, the range of phenotypes characteristic of a population may change without any genetic change whatsoever. There are several examples. In the early 20th century, the anthropologist Franz Boas (1940/1966) described changes in skull form (e.g., toward rounder heads) among the children of Europeans who had migrated to North America. The reason for this was not a change in genes, for the European immigrants tended to marry among themselves. Also, some of their children had been born in Europe and merely raised in the United States. Something in the environment, probably in the diet, was producing this change. Changes in average height and weight produced by dietary differences in a few generations are common and may have nothing to do with race or genetics.

Explaining Skin Color

Traditional racial classification assumed that biological characteristics such as skin color were determined by heredity and that they were stable (immutable) over many generations. We now know that a biological similarity doesn't necessarily indicate recent common ancestry. Dark skin color, for example, can be shared by tropical Africans, southern Indians, and indigenous Australians for reasons other than common heredity. Scientists have made considerable progress in explaining variation in human skin color, along with many other aspects of human biological diversity. We shift now from classification to explanation, in which natural selection plays a key role.

Natural selection is the process by which the forms most fit to survive and reproduce in a given environment do so. Over the generations, the less fit organisms die out, and the favored types survive by producing more offspring. The role of natural selection in producing variation in skin color will illustrate the explanatory approach to human biological diversity. Comparable explanations have been provided for other aspects of human biological variation.

Skin color is a complex biological trait—influenced by several genes. *Melanin,* the primary determinant of human skin color, is a chemical substance manufactured in the epidermis, or outer skin layer. The melanin cells of darker-skinned people produce more and larger granules of melanin than do those of lighter-skinned people. By screening out ultraviolet (UV) radiation from the sun, melanin offers protection against a variety of maladies, including sunburn and skin cancer. It is advantageous to have lots of melanin if one lives in the tropics, where UV radiation is intense.

Before the 16th century, most of the world's very dark-skinned peoples did live in the *tropics,* a belt extending about 23 degrees north and south of the equator, between the Tropic of Cancer and the Tropic of Capricorn. The association between dark skin color and a tropical habitat existed throughout the Old World, where humans and their ancestors have lived for millions of years. The darkest populations of Africa evolved not in shady equatorial forests but in sunny, open grassland, or savanna, country.

Outside the tropics, skin color tends to be lighter. Moving north in Africa, for example, there is a gradual transition from dark to medium brown. Skin color continues to lighten as one moves through the Middle East, into southern Europe, through central Europe, and to the north. South of the Old World tropics, skin color also is lighter. In the

Princess Madeleine of Sweden at the wedding of Sweden's Crown Princess Victoria and Daniel Westling at the Stockholm Cathedral. Very light skin color, illustrated in this photo, maximizes absorption of ultraviolet radiation by those few parts of the body exposed to direct sunlight during northern winters. ©Antony Jones/Julian Parker/Mark Cuthbert/UK Press via Getty Images

Before the 16th century, almost all the very dark-skinned populations of the world lived in the tropics, as does this Samburu woman from Kenya. ©Jan Spieczny/Photolibrary/Getty Images

Americas, however, tropical populations do not have very dark skin. This is true because the settlement of the New World by light-skinned Asian ancestors of Native Americans was relatively recent, dating back no more than 20,000 years.

How, aside from recent migrations, can we explain the geographic distribution of human skin color? Natural selection provides an answer. In the tropics, intense UV radiation creates a series of hazards, including severe sunburn, which make light skin color an adaptive disadvantage (Table 10.2 summarizes those threats). By damaging sweat glands, sunburn reduces the body's ability to perspire and thus to regulate its own temperature. Sunburn also can increase susceptibility to disease. Yet another disadvantage of having light skin color in the tropics is that exposure to UV radiation can cause skin cancer. Melanin, nature's own sunscreen, confers a selective advantage (i.e., a better chance to survive and reproduce) on darker-skinned people living in the tropics. Outside the tropics, however, melanin's role in blocking UV radiation can become a selective disadvantage.

Years ago, W. F. Loomis (1967) focused on the role of UV radiation in stimulating the manufacture of vitamin D by the human body. The unclothed human body can produce its own vitamin D when exposed to sufficient sunlight. However, in a cloudy environment that also is so cold that people have to wear clothing much of the year (such as northern Europe, where very light skin color evolved), clouds and clothing impede the body's

TABLE 10.2 **Advantages and Disadvantages (Depending on Environment) of Dark and Light Skin Color**

Also shown are cultural alternatives that can make up for biological disadvantages and examples of natural selection (NS) operating today in relation to skin color.

		Cultural Alternatives	NS in Action Today
DARK SKIN COLOR			
Advantage	Melanin is natural sunscreen.		
	In tropics: screens out UV. Reduces susceptibility to folate destruction and thus to neural tube defects (NTDs), including spina bifida. Prevents sunburn and thus enhances sweating and temperature regulation. Reduces disease susceptibility. Reduces risk of skin cancer.		
Disadvantage	Outside tropics: reduces UV absorption. Increases susceptibility to rickets, osteoporosis.	Foods, vitamin D supplements	East Asians in northern U.K.; Inuit with modern diets
LIGHT SKIN COLOR			
Advantage	No natural sunscreen.		
	Outside tropics: admits UV. Body manufactures vitamin D and thus prevents rickets and osteoporosis.		
Disadvantage	Especially in tropics: increases susceptibility to folate destruction and thus to NTDs, including spina bifida.	Folic acid/folate supplements	Whites still have more NTDs.
	Increases susceptibility to sunburn and thus to impaired sweating and poor temperature regulation. Increases disease susceptibility. Increases susceptibility to skin cancer.	Shelter, sunscreens, lotions, etc.	

manufacture of vitamin D, as does having too much melanin in one's skin. Vitamin D deficiency reduces the absorption of calcium in the intestines. A nutritional disease known as *rickets,* which softens and deforms the bones, may develop. In women, deformation of the pelvic bones from rickets can interfere with childbirth. In cold northern areas, light skin color maximizes the absorption of UV radiation and the manufacture of vitamin D by the few parts of the body that are exposed to direct sunlight. There has been selection against dark skin color in northern areas because melanin screens out UV radiation.

This natural selection continues today: East Asians who have migrated recently to northern areas of the United Kingdom have a higher incidence of rickets and osteoporosis (also related to vitamin D and calcium deficiency) than the general British population. A related example involves Eskimos (Inuit) and other indigenous inhabitants of northern Alaska and northern Canada. According to Nina Jablonski (quoted in Iqbal 2002), "Looking at Alaska, one would think that the native people should be pale as ghosts" (to maximize their UV absorption and vitamin D). One reason they are not pale is that they haven't inhabited this region very long in terms of geological time. Even more important, their traditional diet, which is rich in fish oils, supplies sufficient vitamin D so as to make a reduction in pigmentation unnecessary. (This is another example of how a cultural alternative can help overcome a disadvantageous biological trait.) However, again illustrating natural selection at work today, "when these people don't eat their aboriginal diets of fish and marine mammals, they suffer tremendously high rates of vitamin D-deficiency diseases such as rickets in children and osteoporosis in adults" (Jablonski quoted in Iqbal 2002). Far from being immutable, skin color can become an evolutionary liability very quickly.

Yet another way in which natural selection has affected human skin color involves the destructive effects of UV radiation on folate, an essential nutrient that the human body manufactures from folic acid (see Jablonski and Chaplin 2000). Pregnant women require large amounts of folate to support rapid cell division in the embryo. Folate deficiency causes neural tube defects (NTDs) in human embryos. NTDs are marked by the incomplete closure of the neural tube, so the spine and spinal cord fail to develop completely. One NTD, anencephaly (with the brain an exposed mass), results in stillbirth, or death soon after delivery. With spina bifida, another NTD, survival rates are higher, but babies have severe disabilities, including paralysis. Today, women of reproductive age are advised to take folate supplements to prevent serious birth defects such as spina bifida.

UV radiation destroys folate in the human body. We have seen that melanin protects against various UV hazards, making dark skin coloration adaptive in the tropics. Now we learn that melanin also is adaptive because it helps conserve folate in the human body and thus protects against NTDs (Jablonski 2006; Jablonski and Chaplin 2000). Africans and African Americans rarely demonstrate severe folate deficiency, even among individuals with marginal nutritional status.

Today, of course, cultural alternatives to biological adaptation allow light-skinned people to survive in the tropics and darker-skinned people to live in the far north. Light-skinned people can clothe themselves, seek shelter from the sun, and use artificial sunscreens. Dark-skinned people living in the north can, indeed must, get vitamin D from their diet or take supplements. Today, pregnant women are routinely advised to take folic acid or folate supplements as a hedge against NTDs. Even so, light skin color still is correlated with a higher incidence of spina bifida.

Jablonski and Chaplin (2000) explain variation in human skin color as resulting from a balancing act between the evolutionary needs to (1) protect against all UV hazards (thus favoring dark skin in the tropics) and (2) have an adequate supply of vitamin D (thus favoring lighter skin outside the tropics). We see that common ancestry, the presumed basis of race, is not the only reason for biological similarities. Natural selection, still at work today, makes a major contribution to variations in human skin color, as well as to many other human biological differences and similarities.

Race and Ethnicity

In American culture, we hear the words *ethnicity* and *race* frequently, without clear distinctions made between them. For example, the term *race* often is used inappropriately to refer to Hispanics, who, in fact, can be of any race. The following example provides one illustration of the popular confusion about ethnicity and race in American culture. Eight years prior to her appointment to the U.S. Supreme Court, Sonia Sotomayor, then an appeals court judge, gave a talk titled "A Latina Judge's Voice," at the University of California, Berkeley, School of Law. As part of a much longer speech, Sotomayor declared:

> I would hope that a wise Latina woman with the richness of her experiences would more often than not reach a better conclusion than a white male who hasn't lived that life. (Sotomayor 2001/2009)

On hearing about that speech, conservatives, including former House Speaker Newt Gingrich and radio talk show host Rush Limbaugh, seized on this declaration as evidence that Sotomayor was a "racist" or a "reverse racist." Her critics ignored the fact that *Latina* is an ethnic (and gendered-female) rather than a racial category. I suspect that Sotomayor also was using "white male" as an ethnic-gender category, to refer to nonminority men. Our popular culture does not consistently distinguish between ethnicity and race (see Ansell 2013; Banton 2015).

The Social Construction of Race

Most Americans continue to believe (incorrectly) that their population includes *biologically based* races to which various labels are applied. Such *racial terms* include *White, Black, Yellow, Red, Caucasoid, Negroid, Mongoloid, Amerindian, Euro-American, African American, Asian American,* and *Native American."* We know, however, that races, while assumed to have a biological basis, actually are socially constructed in particular societies. Let's consider now several examples of the social construction of race, beginning with the United States.

Hypodescent: Race in the United States

Most Americans acquire their racial identity at birth, but race isn't based on biology or on simple ancestry. Take the case of the child of a "racially mixed" marriage involving one Black and one White parent. We know that 50 percent of the child's genes come

An international and multiethnic American family. Joakim Noah, center, is an All-Star professional basketball player, who played in college for the Florida Gators. Also shown are his mother, a former Miss Sweden, and father, a French singer and tennis player who won the French Open in 1983. Joakim's grandfather, Zacharie Noah, was a professional soccer player from the African nation of Cameroon. What is Joakim Noah's race?
©Matt Marton/AP Images

from one parent and 50 percent from the other. Still, American culture overlooks heredity and classifies this child as Black. This rule is arbitrary. On the basis of genotype (genetic composition), it would be just as logical to classify the child as White.

American rules for assigning racial status can be even more arbitrary. In some states, anyone known to have any Black ancestor, no matter how remote, is classified as a member of the Black race. This is a rule of **descent** (it assigns social identity on the basis of ancestry), but of a sort that is rare outside the contemporary United States. It is called **hypodescent** (Harris and Kottak 1963), because it automatically places the children of a union between members of different groups in the minority group (*hypo* means "lower"). Hypodescent divides American society into groups that have been unequal in their access to wealth, power, and prestige.

The rule of hypodescent affects Blacks, Asians, Native Americans, and Hispanics differently. It's easier to negotiate Native American or Hispanic identity than Black identity. The ascription rule isn't as definite, and the assumption of a biological basis isn't as strong. To be considered Native American, one ancestor out of eight (great-grandparents) or out of four (grandparents) may suffice. This depends on whether the assignment is by federal or state law or by a Native American tribal council. The child of a Hispanic may (or may not, depending on context) claim Hispanic identity. Many Americans with a Native American or Latino grandparent consider themselves White and lay no claim to minority group status.

Race in the Census

The U.S. Census Bureau has gathered data by race since 1790. Figure 10.1 shows that the most recent (2010) census asked about both race and Hispanic origin. What do you think of the racial categories included?

Attempts to add a "multiracial" category to the U.S. Census have been opposed by the National Association for the Advancement of Colored People (NAACP) and the National Council of La Raza (a Hispanic advocacy group). Racial classification is a political issue involving access to resources, including jobs, voting districts, and federal funding of programs aimed at minorities. The hypodescent rule results in all the

FIGURE 10.1   Questions on Race and Hispanic Origin from U.S. Census 2010

Source: U.S. Census Bureau, Census 2010 questionnaire.

5. **Is this person of Hispanic, Latino, or Spanish origin?**

☐ No, not of Hispanic, Latino, or Spanish origin

☐ Yes, Mexican, Mexican Am., Chicano

☐ Yes, Puerto Rican

☐ Yes, Cuban

☐ Yes, another Hispanic, Latino, or Spanish origin — *Print origin, for example, Argentinean, Colombian, Dominican, Nicaraguan, Salvadoran, Spaniard, and so on.* ↗

☐☐☐☐☐☐☐☐☐☐☐☐☐☐☐☐☐☐☐☐☐

6. **What is this person's race?** *Mark* ☒ *one or more boxes.*

☐ White

☐ Black, African Am., or Negro

☐ American Indian or Alaska Native — *Print name of enrolled or principal tribe.* ↗

☐☐☐☐☐☐☐☐☐☐☐☐☐☐☐☐☐☐☐☐☐

☐ Asian Indian   ☐ Japanese   ☐ Native Hawaiian

☐ Chinese   ☐ Korean   ☐ Guamanian or Chamorro

☐ Filipino   ☐ Vietnamese   ☐ Samoan

☐ Other Asian — *Print race, for*   ☐ Other Pacific Islander — *Print*
example, Hmong, Laotian, Thai,   *race, for example, Fijian, Tongan,*
Pakistani, Cambodian, and so on. ↗   *and so on.* ↗

☐☐☐☐☐☐☐☐☐☐☐☐☐☐☐☐☐☐☐☐☐

☐ Some other race — *Print race.* ↗

☐☐☐☐☐☐☐☐☐☐☐☐☐☐☐☐☐☐☐☐☐

population growth being attributed to the minority category. Minorities fear their political clout will decline if their numbers go down.

But things are changing. Choice of "some other race" in the U.S. Census tripled between 1980 (6.8 million) and 2010 (over 19 million)—suggesting imprecision in and dissatisfaction with the existing categories. In the 2000 census, 2.4 percent of Americans—almost 7 million people—chose a first-ever option of identifying themselves as belonging to two or more races. This figure rose to 2.9 percent in the 2010 census. The number of interracial marriages and children is increasing, with implications for the traditional system of American racial classification. "Interracial," "biracial," or "multiracial" children who grow up with both parents undoubtedly identify with

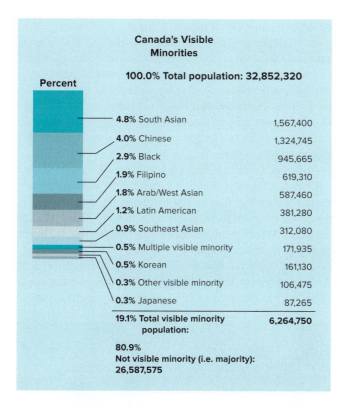

Canada's Visible Minorities

100.0% Total population: 32,852,320

Percent

4.8% South Asian	1,567,400
4.0% Chinese	1,324,745
2.9% Black	945,665
1.9% Filipino	619,310
1.8% Arab/West Asian	587,460
1.2% Latin American	381,280
0.9% Southeast Asian	312,080
0.5% Multiple visible minority	171,935
0.5% Korean	161,130
0.3% Other visible minority	106,475
0.3% Japanese	87,265
19.1% Total visible minority population:	**6,264,750**

**80.9%
Not visible minority (i.e. majority):
26,587,575**

FIGURE 10.2

Visible Minority Population of Canada, 2011 National Household Survey

Source: Statistics Canada, 2011 National Household Survey. http://www12.statcan.gc.ca/nhs-enm/2011/as-sa/99-010-x/99-010-x2011001-eng.cfm#a4.

particular qualities of either parent. It is troubling for many of them to have so important an identity as race dictated by the arbitrary rule of hypodescent.

Rather than race, the Canadian census asks about "visible minorities." That country's Employment Equity Act defines such groups as "persons, other than Aboriginal peoples [First Nations in Canada], who are non-Caucasian in race or non-white in colour" (Statistics Canada 2001). "South Asian" and "Chinese" are Canada's largest visible minorities (see Figure 10.2). Canada's visible minority population of 19 percent in 2011 (up from 11 percent in 1996) contrasts with a figure of about 39 percent for the United States today (up from 25 percent in 2000).

As in the United States, Canada's visible minority population has been growing much faster than the country's overall population. In 1981, visible minorities accounted for just 4.7 percent of the Canadian population, versus 19.1 percent in 2011 (the most recent data available as of this writing). Between 2006 and 2011, Canada's total population increased 5 percent, while visible minorities rose 24 percent. If recent immigration trends continue, visible minorities will comprise almost one-third (31 percent) of the Canadian population by 2031 (Statistics Canada 2010).

Not Us: Race in Japan

Japan presents itself and is commonly viewed as a nation that is homogeneous in race, ethnicity, language, and culture. Although Japan's population really is less diverse than those of most nations, it does contain significant minority groups (see Graburn 2008; Weiner 2009). Constituting about 10 percent of Japan's total population, those groups include aboriginal Ainu, annexed Okinawans, outcast *burakumin,* children of mixed marriages, and immigrant nationalities, especially Koreans, who number more than 700,000 (Lie 2001; Ryang and Lie 2009). The (majority) Japanese define themselves by opposition to others, whether minority groups in their own nation or outsiders—anyone who is "not us." The "not us" should stay that way; assimilation generally is discouraged. Cultural mechanisms, especially residential segregation and taboos on "interracial" marriage, work to keep minorities "in their place."

To describe racial attitudes in Japan, Jennifer Robertson (1992) used Kwame Anthony Appiah's (1990) term "intrinsic racism"—the belief that a (perceived) racial difference is a sufficient reason to value one person less than another. In Japan the valued group is majority ("pure") Japanese, who are believed to share "the same blood." Thus, the caption to a printed photo of a Japanese American model reads: "She was born in Japan but raised in Hawaii. Her nationality is American but no foreign blood flows in her veins" (Robertson 1992, p. 5). Something like hypodescent also operates in Japan, but less precisely than in the United States, where mixed offspring automatically become members of the minority group. The children of mixed marriages between majority Japanese

Ariana Miyamoto, the daughter of a Japanese woman and an African American man, was crowned Miss Universe Japan in March 2015. Soon thereafter, complaints emerged on social media that she did not look "Japanese enough" to represent Japan in an international beauty competition. Over 3 percent of new marriages in Japan each year are now international, and almost 2 percent of children born in Japan are biracial. ©Kyodo via AP Images

and others (including Euro-Americans) may not get the same "racial" label as their minority parent, but they are still stigmatized for their non-Japanese ancestry (De Vos and Wagatsuma 1966).

In its construction of race, Japanese culture regards certain ethnic groups as having a biological basis, when there is no evidence that they do. The best example is the burakumin, a stigmatized group of some 3 million outcasts, sometimes compared to India's untouchables. The burakumin are physically and genetically indistinguishable from other Japanese. Many of them "pass" as (and marry) majority Japanese, but a deceptive marriage can end in divorce if burakumin identity is discovered (Amos 2011).

Burakumin are perceived as standing apart from majority Japanese. Based on their ancestry (and thus, it is assumed, their "blood" or genetics), burakumin are considered "not us." Majority Japanese try to keep their lineage pure by discouraging mixing. The burakumin are residentially segregated in neighborhoods (rural or urban) called *buraku,* from which the racial label is derived. Compared with majority Japanese, the burakumin are less likely to attend high school and college. When burakumin attend the same schools as majority Japanese, they face discrimination. Majority children and teachers may refuse to eat with them, because burakumin are considered unclean.

In applying for university admission or a job and in dealing with the government, Japanese must list their address, which becomes part of a household or family registry. This list makes residence in a buraku, and likely burakumin social status, evident. Schools and companies use this information to discriminate. (The best way to pass is to move so often that the buraku address eventually disappears from the registry.) Majority Japanese also limit "race" mixture by hiring marriage mediators to check out the family histories of prospective spouses. They are especially careful to check for burakumin ancestry (Amos 2011).

Traditionally, the burakumin performed such "unclean" jobs as animal slaughter and disposal of the dead. Burakumin still do similar jobs, including work with leather and other animal products. They are more likely than majority Japanese to do manual labor (including farm work) and to belong to the national lower class. Burakumin and other Japanese minorities also are more likely to have careers in crime, prostitution, entertainment, and sports.

The burakumin are internally stratified. In other words, there are class contrasts within the group. Because certain jobs are reserved for the burakumin, people who are successful in those occupations (e.g., shoe factory owners) can be wealthy. Burakumin also have found jobs as government bureaucrats. Successful burakumin can temporarily escape their stigmatized status by travel, including foreign travel.

Discrimination against the burakumin is similar to the discrimination that Blacks have experienced in the United States. The burakumin often live in villages and neighborhoods with poor housing and sanitation. They have limited access to education, jobs, amenities, and health facilities. In response to burakumin political mobilization, Japan has dismantled the legal structure of discrimination against burakumin and has worked to improve conditions in the buraku. (The Buraku Liberation and Human Rights Research Institute provides the most recent information about the burakumin liberation movement.) However, discrimination against nonmajority Japanese is still practiced in companies. Some employers say that hiring burakumin would give their company an unclean image and thus create a disadvantage in competing with other businesses.

Phenotype and Fluidity: Race in Brazil

There are more flexible, less exclusionary ways of socially constructing race than those used in the United States and Japan. Along with the rest of Latin America, Brazil has less exclusionary categories, which permit individuals to alter their racial classification. Brazil shares a history of slavery with the United States, but it lacks the hypodescent rule.

Brazilians use many more racial labels—over 500 were once reported (Harris 1970)—than Americans or Japanese do. In northeastern Brazil, I found 40 different racial terms in use in Arembepe, then a village of only 750 people (Kottak 2006). Through their traditional classification system, Brazilians recognize and attempt to describe the physical variation that exists in their population. The system used in the United States, by recognizing only a few races, blinds Americans to an equivalent range of evident physical contrasts.

In the United States, one's race is assigned automatically by hypodescent and usually doesn't change. In Brazil, racial identity is more flexible, more of an achieved status. Brazilian racial classification pays attention to phenotype. A Brazilian's phenotype and racial label may change because of environmental factors, such as the tanning rays of the sun or the effects of humidity on the hair. A Brazilian can change his or her "race" (say, from "Indian" to "mixed") by changing his or her manner of dress, language, location (e.g., rural to urban), and even attitude (e.g., by adopting urban behavior). Two racial/ethnic labels used in Brazil are *indio* (indigenous, Native American) and *cabôclo* (someone who "looks *indio*" but wears modern clothing and participates in Brazilian culture, rather than living in an indigenous community). The perception of biological race is influenced not just by the physical phenotype but also by how one dresses and behaves.

Furthermore, racial differences in Brazil may be so insignificant in structuring community life that people may forget the terms they have applied to others. Sometimes they even forget the ones they've used for themselves. In Arembepe, I made it a habit to ask the same person on different days to tell me the races of others in the village (and my own). In the United States, I am always "White" or "Euro-American," but in Arembepe, I got lots of terms besides *branco* ("White"). I could be *claro* ("light"), *louro* ("blond"), *sarará* ("light-skinned redhead"), *mulato claro* ("light mulatto"), or *mulato* ("mulatto"). The racial term used to describe me or anyone else varied from person to person, week to week, even day to day. My best informant, a man with very dark skin color, changed the term he used for himself all the time—from *escuro* ("dark") to *preto* ("Black") to *moreno escuro* ("dark brunet").

For centuries the United States and Brazil have had mixed populations, with ancestors from Native America, Europe, Africa, and Asia. Although races have mixed in both countries, Brazilian and American cultures have constructed the results differently. The historical reasons for this contrast lie mainly in the different characteristics of the settlers of the two countries. The mainly English early settlers of the United States came as women, men, and families, but Brazil's Portuguese colonizers were mainly men—merchants and adventurers. Many of these Portuguese men married Native American women and recognized their racially mixed children as their heirs. Like their North American counterparts, Brazilian plantation owners had sexual relations with their slaves. But the Brazilian landlords more often freed the children that resulted—for demographic and economic reasons. (Sometimes these were their only children.) Freed

These photos, taken by the author in Brazil, give just a glimpse of the spectrum of phenotypical diversity encountered among contemporary Brazilians. ©Conrad P. Kottak

offspring of master and slave became plantation overseers and foremen and filled many intermediate positions in the emerging Brazilian economy. They were not classed with the slaves but were allowed to join a new intermediate category. No hypodescent rule developed in Brazil to ensure that Whites and Blacks remained separate (see Degler 1970; Harris 1964).

In today's world system, Brazil's system of racial classification has been changing in the context of international identity politics and rights movements. Just as more and more Brazilians claim indigenous (Native Brazilian) identities, an increasing number now assert their Blackness and self-conscious membership in the African diaspora. Particularly in such northeastern Brazilian states as Bahia, where African demographic and cultural influence is strong, public universities have instituted affirmative action programs aimed at indigenous peoples and especially at Blacks. Racial identities firm up in the context of international (e.g., pan-African and pan-Indian) mobilization and access to strategic resources based on race.

Ethnic Groups, Nations, and Nationalities

The term **nation** once was synonymous with *tribe* or *ethnic group*. All three of these terms have been used to refer to a single culture sharing a single language, religion, history, territory, ancestry, and kinship. Thus, one could speak interchangeably of the Seneca (Native American) nation, tribe, or ethnic group. Now *nation* has come to mean state—an independent, centrally organized political unit, or a government. *Nation* and *state* have become synonymous. Combined in **nation-state,** they refer to an autonomous political entity, a country.

Because of migration, conquest, and colonialism, most nation-states are not ethnically homogeneous. James Fearon (2003) found that about 70 percent of all countries have an ethnic group that forms an absolute majority of the population; the average population share of such groups is 65 percent. The average size of the *second* largest group, or largest ethnic minority, is 17 percent. Only 18 percent of all countries, including Brazil and Japan, have a single ethnic group that accounts for 90 percent or more of its population.

Ethnic Diversity by Region

There is substantial regional variation in countries' ethnic structures. Strong states, particularly in Europe (e.g., France), have deliberately and actively worked to homogenize their diverse premodern populations to a common national identity and culture. Although countries with no ethnic majority are fairly rare in the rest of the world, this is the norm in Africa. The average African country has a plurality group of about 22 percent, with the second largest slightly less than this. Rwanda, Burundi, Lesotho, Swaziland, and Zimbabwe are exceptions; each has a large majority group and a minority that makes up almost all the rest of the population. Botswana has a large majority (the Tswana) and a set of smaller minorities (Fearon 2003).

Most Latin American and Caribbean countries contain a majority group (speaking a European language, such as Portuguese in Brazil, Spanish in Argentina) and a single minority group—"indigenous peoples." "Indigenous peoples" is a catch-all category encompassing several small Native American tribes or remnants. Exceptions are Guatemala and the Andean countries of Bolivia, Peru, and Ecuador, with large indigenous populations (see Gotkowitz 2011; Wade 2010).

Most countries in Asia and the Middle East/North Africa have ethnic majorities. The Asian countries of Myanmar, Laos, Vietnam, and Thailand contain a large lowland majority edged by more fragmented mountain folk. Several oil-producing countries in the Middle East, including Saudi Arabia, Bahrain, United Arab Emirates, Oman, and Kuwait, contain an ethnically homogeneous group of citizens who form either a plurality or a bare majority; the rest of the population consists of ethnically diverse noncitizen workers. Several countries in the Middle East/North Africa contain two principal ethnic or ethnoreligious groups: Arabs and Berbers in Morocco, Algeria, Libya, and Tunisia; Muslims and Copts in Egypt; Turks and Kurds in Turkey; Greeks and Turks in Cyprus; and Palestinians and Transjordan Arabs in Jordan (Fearon 2003).

Nationalities without Nations

Benedict Anderson (1991/2006) traces Western European *nationalism* (the feeling of belonging to a nation), back to the 18th century. He stresses the crucial role of the printed word in the growth of national consciousness in England, France, and Spain. The novel and the newspaper were "two forms of imagining" communities (consisting of all the people who read the same sources and thus witnessed the same events) that flowered in the 18th century (Anderson 1991/2006, pp. 24–25). Groups that have, once had, or wish to have or regain, political autonomy (their own country) are called **nationalities.** As a result of political upheavals, wars, and migration, many nationalities have been split and placed in separate nation-states. For example, the German and Korean homelands were artificially divided after wars, according to communist and capitalist ideologies. World War I dispersed the Kurds, who form a majority in no state but exist as minority groups in Turkey, Iran, Iraq, and Syria.

Colonialism—the foreign domination of a territory—established a series of multitribal and multiethnic states. The new national boundaries that were created under colonialism often corresponded poorly with preexisting cultural divisions. However, colonial institutions also helped forge new identities that extended beyond nations and nationalities. A good example is the idea of *négritude* ("Black identity") developed by African intellectuals in Francophone (French-speaking) West Africa. Négritude can be traced to the association and common experience in colonial times of youths from Guinea, Mali, the Ivory Coast, and Senegal at the William Ponty School in Dakar, Senegal (Anderson 1991/2006, pp. 123–124).

Ethnic Tolerance and Accommodation

Ethnic diversity may be associated either with positive group interaction and coexistence or with conflict. There are nation-states, including some of the "less-developed countries," in which multiple cultural groups live together in reasonable harmony.

Assimilation

Assimilation describes the process of change that members of ethnic groups may experience when they move to a country where another culture dominates. In assimilating, ethnic group members adopt the patterns and norms of the host culture. They are incorporated into the dominant culture to the point that their ethnic group no longer exists as a separate cultural unit. Some countries, such as Brazil, are more assimilationist than others. Germans, Italians, Japanese, Middle Easterners, and East Europeans started migrating to Brazil late in the 19th century. These immigrants have assimilated to a common Brazilian culture, which has Portuguese, African, and Native American roots. The descendants of these immigrants speak the national language (Portuguese) and participate in the national culture. (During World War II, Brazil, which was on the Allied side, forced assimilation by banning instruction in any language other than Portuguese—especially in German.) The United States was much more assimilationist during the early 20th century than it is today, as the multicultural model has become more prominent (see the section "Multiculturalism").

The Plural Society

Assimilation isn't inevitable, and there can be ethnic harmony without it. Ethnic distinctions can persist despite generations of interethnic contact. Through a study of three ethnic groups in Swat, Pakistan, Fredrik Barth (1958/1968) challenged an old idea that interaction always leads to assimilation. He showed that ethnic groups can be in contact for generations without assimilating. Barth (1958/1968, p. 324) defines **plural society** as a society combining ethnic contrasts, ecological specialization (i.e., use of different environmental resources by each ethnic group), and the economic interdependence of those groups.

In Barth's view, ethnic boundaries are most stable and enduring when the groups occupy different ecological niches. That is, they make their living in different ways and don't compete. Ideally, they should depend on each other's activities and exchange with one another. When different ethnic groups exploit the *same* ecological niche, the militarily more powerful group will typically replace the weaker one. If they exploit more or less the same niche, but the weaker group is better able to use marginal environments, they also may coexist (Barth 1958/1968, p. 331). Given such niche specialization, ethnic boundaries and interdependence can be maintained, although the specific cultural features of each group may change. By shifting the analytic focus from individual cultures or ethnic groups to *relationships* between cultures or ethnic groups, Barth (1958/1968, 1969) has made important contributions to ethnic studies (see also Kamrava 2013).

Multiculturalism

The view of cultural diversity in a country as something good and desirable is called **multiculturalism** (see Kottak and Kozaitis 2012). The multicultural model is the opposite of the assimilationist model, in which minorities are expected to abandon their cultural traditions and values, replacing them with those of the majority population. The multicultural view encourages the practice of cultural–ethnic traditions. A multicultural society socializes individuals not only into the dominant (national) culture but also into an ethnic culture. Thus, in the United States today millions of people speak both English and another language, eat both "American" foods (apple pie, steak, hamburgers) and "ethnic" dishes, and celebrate both national (July 4, Thanksgiving) and ethnic–religious holidays.

Multiculturalism seeks ways for people to understand and interact that don't depend on sameness but rather on respect for differences. Multiculturalism stresses the interaction of ethnic groups and their contribution to the country. It assumes that each group has something to offer to and learn from the others. The United States and Canada have become increasingly multicultural, focusing on their internal diversity. Rather than as "melting pots," they are better described as ethnic "salads" (each ingredient remains distinct, although in the same bowl and with the same dressing).

Several forces have propelled North America away from the assimilationist model toward multiculturalism. First, multiculturalism reflects the fact of recent large-scale migration, particularly from the less-developed countries. The global scale of modern migration introduces unparalleled ethnic variety to host nations (see Marger 2015; Parrillo 2016). Multiculturalism is related to globalization. People use modern means of transportation to migrate to nations whose lifestyles they learn about through the media and from tourists who increasingly visit their own countries.

Migration also is fueled by rapid population growth, coupled with insufficient jobs (both for educated and uneducated people), in the less-developed countries. As traditional rural economies decline or mechanize, displaced farmers move to cities, where they and their children often are unable to find jobs. As people in the less-developed countries get better educations, they seek more skilled employment. They hope to partake of an international culture of consumption that includes such modern amenities as refrigerators, televisions, and automobiles.

Changing Demographics in the United States

In October 2006, the population of the United States reached 300 million people, just 39 years after reaching 200 million and 91 years after reaching the 100 million mark (in 1915). Consider how much the country's ethnic composition has changed in the past 50 or so years. The 1970 census, the first to attempt an official count of Hispanics, found they represented no more than 4.7 percent of the American population. By 2015 this figure had risen to 17.9 percent—over 57 million Hispanics. The number of African Americans grew from 11.1 percent in 1967 to 12.3 percent in 2015, while (non-Hispanic) Whites ("Anglos") declined from 83 percent to 61.4 percent. In 1967 fewer than 10 million people in the United States (5 percent of the population) had been born elsewhere, compared with more than 41 million foreign born today (13 percent) (all data from U.S. Census Bureau). In 2011, for the first time in American history, minorities (including Hispanics, Blacks, Asians, Native Americans, and those of mixed race) accounted for more than half (50.4 percent) of all births in the United States (Tavernise 2012).

In 1973, 78 percent of the students in American public schools were White, and 22 percent were minorities. By 2004, only 57 percent of public school students were White. In fall 2014, for the first time, the overall number of Latino, African American, and Asian students in public K–12 classrooms surpassed the number of non-Hispanic Whites.

The Gray and the Brown

Drawing on a Brookings Institution (2010) report titled *State of Metropolitan America: On the Front Lines of Demographic Transformation,* Ronald Brownstein (2010) analyzes an intensifying confrontation between groups he describes as "the gray and the brown." Brownstein and demographer William Frey, an author of the Brookings report, focus on two key U.S. demographic trends:

1. Ethnic/racial diversity is increasing, especially among the young.
2. The country is aging, and most of the senior population is White.

Frey (in Brookings Institution 2010, pp. 26, 63) sees these trends as creating a "cultural generation gap"—a sharp contrast in the attitudes, priorities, and political leanings of younger and older Americans. Whites now constitute 80 percent of older Americans but less than 55 percent of children.

Politically the two groups—the gray (older) and the brown (younger)—are poles apart. The aging White population appears increasingly resistant to taxes and public spending, while younger people and minorities value government support of education, health, and social welfare. In recent presidential elections, young people, especially minorities, have strongly supported the Democratic candidates, Barack Obama (2008 and 2012) and Hillary Clinton (2016), while White seniors voted solidly for Republicans John McCain, Mitt Romney, and Donald Trump.

The gray and the brown are more interdependent economically than either usually realizes. Minority children may benefit disproportionately from public education today, but minority workers will pay a growing share of the payroll taxes needed to sustain Social Security and Medicare in the future. These are government programs that most directly benefit old White people.

The history of U.S. national immigration policy helps us understand how the gap between the gray and the brown arose. Federal policies established in the 1920s severely

In this recent American photo, contrast the visible ethnic diversity in the line of children with the racially more uniform line of older people. ©James Marshall/Corbis

curtailed immigration from areas other than northern Europe. In 1965, Congress loosened restrictions—resulting in an eventual influx of immigrants from southern Europe, Asia, Africa, the Caribbean, and Latin America (see Vigil 2012).

Non-Hispanic Whites constituted the overwhelming majority of Americans through the mid-20th century, including the post–World War II baby boom (1946–1964). Most baby boomers grew up and have lived much of their lives in White suburbs, residentially isolated from minorities (Brownstein 2010). As they age and retire, many older White Americans are reconstituting such communities in racially homogeneous enclaves in the Southeast and Southwest.

In such communities, except for their yard and construction workers and house cleaners, older White people live apart from multicultural America and the minorities who represent a growing share of the national population. Since 1965, expanded immigration and higher fertility rates among minorities have transformed American society. As recently as 1980, minorities made up only 20 percent of the total population (versus almost 40 percent today). If recent demographic trends continue, the ethnic composition of the United States will change even more dramatically (see Figure 10.3). Similar trends are evident in western Europe and are everyday expressions of globalization.

FIGURE 10.3   **Ethnic Composition of the United States**
The proportion of the American population that is White and non-Hispanic is declining. The projection for 2050 shown here comes from a 2008 U.S. Census Bureau report. Note especially the dramatic rise in the Hispanic portion of the American population between 2015 and 2050.

Source: 2015 data from the Henry W. Kaiser Family Foundation, http://kff.org/other/state-indicator/distribution-by-raceethnicity/; 2050 projection from a 2008 projection by the U.S. Census Bureau, http://www.census.gov/population/www/ projections/analytical-document09.pdf, Table 1, p. 17.

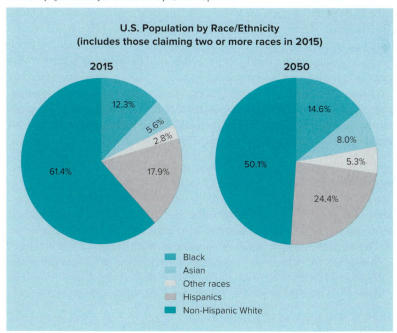

The Backlash to Multiculturalism

When Barack Obama was first elected president of the United States in 2008, it seemed to many commentators that the United States had entered a postracial era. It was taken as a sign of progress in racial and ethnic relations that an African American man could be elected to the highest office in the land. The backlash began soon after Obama's election, culminating in Donald Trump's election as president in 2016. The period between 2008 and 2010 saw the growth of the Tea Party wing of the Republican Party and a dramatic reduction in the power of Democrats after the 2010 election. A similar coalition of young people, women, and minorities that backed Obama in 2008 and 2012 enabled Hillary Clinton to win the popular vote in 2016 but was insufficient to propel her to an Electoral College victory and the presidency.

One of the rallying cries of Tea Party voters has been to "take our country back." A similar sentiment was prominent in the 2016 presidential campaign. Businessman and reality TV star Donald Trump rose to prominence as a Republican presidential candidate by promising to "make America great again." Prominent in his campaign was open *ethno-nationalism,* the idea of an association between ethnicity—traditionally and predominantly European derived and Christian—and the right to rule the United States. Trump advocated deportation of undocumented immigrants, focusing on Mexicans. He also proposed a temporary ban on admission of Muslims to the United States, initially in response to a shooting by jihadist terrorists in San Bernardino, California, and perceived threats from the Islamic State and Syrian refugees. Trump was promising to purge the United States of ethnic groups here illegally and to protect the country from members of what is in the United States a minority religion.

Most of Trump's rivals for the Republican nomination joined him in urging deportation but did not support his call for a ban on Muslims. All, however, faulted President Obama, like President George W. Bush before him, for avoiding the term *Radical Islam* when he spoke of terrorists and enemies. Trump and other Republican candidates also railed against "political correctness," which they saw as excessive caution about using language and labels that might offend particular groups. Trump, in particular, used the claim of hyper-sensitive political correctness to justify his stereotyping of Mexicans, Muslims, and Syrian refugees. Anyone who complained about insults was "overreacting"—just being hyper-sensitive. Trump's successful candidacy harnessed and expressed the backlash against the multicultural model of ethnic relations that has been gaining ground in the United States for the past few decades. Rarely, if ever, does cultural change occur without opposition.

Ethnic Conflict

Ethnic differences can exist harmoniously, for example, in plural societies or through multiculturalism. However, ethnic differences also can lead to confrontation and discrimination. Why are ethnic differences often associated with conflict and violence? An ethnic group may react if it perceives prejudice or discrimination by another group, or society as a whole, or if it feels otherwise devalued or disadvantaged (see the section "Black Lives Matter"). An ethnic group can resent the actual or perceived privileges of other groups (see Donham 2011; Friedman 2003).

Sectarian Violence

Much of the ethnic unrest in today's world has a religious component—whether between Christians and Muslims, Muslims and Jews, or different sects within one of the major religions. The Iraqi dictator Saddam Hussein, who was deposed in 2003, favored his own Sunni Muslim sect while fostering discrimination against others (Shiites and Kurds). Under Saddam, Sunnis, although a numeric minority within Iraq's population, enjoyed privileged access to power, prestige, and position. After the elections of 2005, which many Sunnis chose to boycott, Shiites gained political control over Iraq and retaliated quickly against prior Sunni favoritism. A civil war soon developed out of *sectarian violence* (conflicts among sects of the same religion) as Sunnis (and their foreign supporters) fueled an insurgency against the new government and its foreign supporters, including the United States. Shiites then retaliated further against Sunni attacks and a history of Sunni privilege. The Sunnis, lacking power in the new Iraqi government, eventually helped form the so-called Islamic State (IS), also known as ISIS, ISIL, and Daesh, which, as of this writing, controls portions of Iraq and adjacent areas of Syria.

Iraq and Syria each contain substantial Muslim populations of Shiites, Sunnis, and Kurds (along with various ethno-religious minorities). Syria's president, Bashar al-Assad, like his father and predecessor in office, Hafez al-Assad (who ruled from 1971 to 2000), has favored his own minority Muslim group (Alawites—allied with the Shiites) over his country's Sunni majority. Syria has witnessed escalating internal warfare since 2011, when, as in other parts of the Middle East, a series of uprisings known collectively as the Arab Spring occurred in opposition to authoritarian governments. The Assad regime fanned the flames of civil war by its violent repression of the protesters and eventual rebels.

The parties to the ongoing conflict in Syria include (among others) the Assad government and its foreign allies, including Russia, Shiite Iran, and the Lebanese militia Hezbollah. Sunni-led ISIS maintains a significant presence in northern and eastern Syria, adjacent to and extending into Iraq. A third group consists of "moderate" rebels, presumably including Sunnis opposed to both Assad and ISIS. These rebels, whose numbers and effectiveness are currently unclear, have been supported by the United States and other Sunni-majority countries of the Middle East. Finally, the Kurds, also supported by the United States, are assisting in the war against ISIS.

The conflict in Syria has displaced about half of that nation's population of 23 million. Some 6.6 million people have been displaced internally, while about 4.6 million others have fled Syria as refugees. The latter have sought refuge primarily in other Middle Eastern countries, including Turkey, Lebanon, Jordan, Iraq, and Egypt. Others have traveled by boat across the Aegean Sea to the Greek islands and mainland, and from there into Europe via the Balkans. Others have crossed the Mediterranean into Italy, and some have crossed from North Africa to Spain. Sweden and, particularly, Germany have been the most welcoming European countries, with Germany pledging to accept up to 800,000 Syrian refugees. In Syria itself, if Assad eventually vacates the presidency, Sunni reprisals are likely against Alawites and other religious minorities, including Christians and Shiite Muslims (see Adams 2012).

Prejudice and Discrimination

Members of an ethnic group may be the targets of prejudice (negative attitudes and judgments) or discrimination (punitive action). **Prejudice** means devaluing (looking

On December 19, 2016, Syrians wait to be evacuated from the eastern part of the war-ravaged city of Aleppo, as buses and ambulances await them. ©Mohammed Seyh/Anadolu Agency/Getty Images

down on) a group because of its assumed behavior, values, capabilities, or attributes. People are prejudiced when they hold stereotypes about groups and apply them to individuals. (**Stereotypes** are fixed ideas—often unfavorable—about what the members of a group are like.) Prejudiced people assume that members of the group will act as they are "supposed to act" (according to the stereotype) and interpret a wide range of individual behaviors as evidence of the stereotype. They use this behavior to confirm their stereotype (and low opinion) of the group.

Discrimination refers to policies and practices that harm a group and its members. Discrimination may be legally sanctioned—*de jure* (part of the law) or it may be *de facto* (practiced, but not legally sanctioned). An example of de facto discrimination is the harsher treatment that American minorities (compared with other Americans) tend to get from the police and the judicial system. This unequal treatment isn't legal, but it happens, anyway, as the following section documents.

Black Lives Matter

Anyone who follows the news regularly will be familiar with a series of cases in which young African American men have been shot dead by White police officers. The "Black Lives Matter" movement has arisen in the United States in response to these and other incidents in which Black lives have not seemed to matter much to local officials. As described by Elizabeth Day (2015), the movement originated in July 2013, when an African American woman named Alicia Garza reacted to the acquittal of George Zimmerman, a neighborhood watch volunteer, in the shooting of Trayvon Martin, an unarmed Black teenager, in Sanford, Florida. Stunned by Zimmerman's acquittal on charges of second-degree murder and manslaughter, Garza posted the following message on Facebook "Black people. I love you. I love us. Our lives matter."

Garza's friend, Patrisse Cullors, adopted Garza's words and began to post them online using the hashtag #blacklivesmatter. The two women wanted to raise public awareness about the apparent devaluation of Black lives in the American judicial and enforcement systems. Garza and Cullors used social media to encourage users to share stories of why #blacklivesmatter. In August 2014, another unarmed African American teenager, 18-year-old Michael Brown, was killed by 12 rounds of ammunition from the gun of a White police officer in Ferguson, Missouri. Garza helped organize a "Freedom Ride" to Ferguson that brought some 500 people to the St. Louis suburb. On arrival, she was astonished to see her own phrase being shouted by protesters and written on their banners. There were additional protests in Ferguson after a grand jury failed to indict the police officer. Thereafter, with a series of additional cases in which unarmed Black men were shot by White police officers, the slogan "Black Lives Matter" rose to national prominence. The American Dialect Society even named #blacklivesmatter as their word of the year for 2015. By 2016, Black Lives Matter chapters had opened throughout the country (Day 2015).

The movement has grown not only in response to police shootings and brutality but also following the mass murder on June 17, 2015, of nine African American churchgoers in Charleston, South Carolina, by a White supremacist domestic terrorist. That tragic event prompted the governor to call for and achieve the removal of a contentious and racially charged symbol, the Confederate battle flag, from prominent display in the state capital, Columbia.

Social media continue to be prominent in linking and organizing the #blacklivesmatter movement. Activists have been able to respond quickly to an ongoing series of widely reported incidents (e.g., in Cleveland, Baltimore, North Charleston, Chicago, and elsewhere) in which Black people have been killed by police or died in police custody. Critics of the movement contend that not only "Black lives" but "all lives" should matter, as indeed they should. However, this criticism ignores, and would diminish needed attention to, the disproportionate likelihood of arrest, incarceration, and mistreatment by police that African Americans, in particular, face. Americans have not heard in recent years a series of reports about unarmed White men being shot to death by police officers. Discrimination against American minorities may no longer be *de jure*, but it certainly remains *de facto*.

The third day of protests against police brutality, which followed the release of security camera footage contradicting the NYPD account of the death of Delrawn Small, a young African-American man. ©Erik McGregor/Pacific Press/LightRocket via Getty Images

Anti-Ethnic Discrimination

This section considers some of the more extreme forms of anti-ethnic discrimination, including genocide, forced assimilation, ethnocide, ethnic expulsion, and cultural colonialism. The most extreme form is **genocide,** the deliberate elimination of a group (such as Jews in Nazi Germany, Muslims in Bosnia, or Tutsi in Rwanda) through mass murder (see Hinton and O'Neill 2009). More recently, in the Darfur region of western Sudan, government-supported Arab militias, called the *Janjaweed,* have forced Black Africans off their land. The militias are accused of genocide, of killing up to 30,000 darker-skinned Africans.

Ethnocide is the deliberate suppression or destruction of an ethnic culture by a dominant group. One way of implementing a policy of ethnocide is through *forced assimilation*, in which the dominant group forces an ethnic group to adopt the dominant culture. Many countries have penalized or banned the language and customs of an ethnic group (including its religious observances). One example of forced assimilation is the anti-Basque campaign that the dictator Francisco Franco (who ruled between 1939 and 1975) waged in Spain. Franco banned Basque books, journals, newspapers, signs, sermons, and tombstones and imposed fines for using the Basque language in schools. In reaction to his policies, nationalist sentiment strengthened in the Basque region, and a Basque terrorist group took shape.

A policy of *ethnic expulsion* aims at removing groups that are culturally different from a country. There are many examples, including Bosnia-Herzegovina in the 1990s. Uganda expelled 74,000 Asians in 1972. The neofascist parties of contemporary Western Europe advocate repatriation (expulsion) of immigrant workers, such as Algerians in France and Turks in Germany. As of this writing (2017), the United States contains approximately 11 million undocumented immigrants. They are here without documents because they overstayed their visas or work permits, entered unofficially, or were smuggled in. Millions of them work, pay taxes, and have children born in the United States, who are American citizens. What are their prospects? The future of undocumented immigrants became a particularly contentious political issue during the 2016 presidential election, with multiple Republican presidential candidates advocating their mass deportation. Such deportation would be a form of forced expulsion, although America's undocumented immigrants come from many countries and lack legal documents granting them the right to remain in the United States.

When members of an ethnic group are expelled, they often become **refugees**—people who have been forced (involuntary refugees) or who have chosen (voluntary refugees) to flee a country, to escape persecution or war. A government policy of ethnic expulsion is only one source of refugees. Recent Syrian refugees have been driven from their homes by civil war and reprisals by various factions and their foreign allies. They were not, by and large, voluntary refugees, but they were not forced out by a government policy of ethnic expulsion.

Cultural colonialism refers to the internal domination by one group and its culture or ideology over others. One example is how the Russian people, language, and culture and the communist ideology dominated the former Soviet empire. In cultural colonialism, the dominant culture makes itself the official culture. This is reflected in schools, the media, and public interaction. Under Soviet rule, ethnic minorities had very limited self-rule in republics and regions controlled by Moscow. All the republics and their peoples were to be united by the oneness of "socialist internationalism." A common

Anthropology Today   *Why Are the Greens So White?*
Race and Ethnicity in Golf

How do race and ethnicity figure in the world of golf, a sport whose popularity has been growing not only in the United States, but also in Europe, Asia, and Australia? More than 20 million Americans play golf, an industry that also supports about 400,000 workers. For decades, golf has been the preferred sport of business tycoons and politicians—mainly White. President Dwight D. Eisenhower (1953–1960), whose love for golf was well known, etched a lasting (and accurate) image of golf as a Republican sport (despite the fact that former presidents Bill Clinton and Barack Obama also play the game). A recent survey found that only 2 of the top 125 PGA touring pros identified as Democrats. The most recent Republican President, Donald Trump, is both a business tycoon and an avid golfer.

A glance at golfers in any televised game reveals a remarkable lack of variation in skin color. American golf was the nation's last major sport to desegregate, and minorities traditionally have been relegated to supporting roles. Latinos maintain golf's greens and physical infrastructure. Until the motorized golf cart replaced them, African Americans had significant opportunities to observe and learn the game by caddying. Indeed, there once was a tradition of African American caddies becoming excellent golfers.

The best example of this trajectory is Dr. Charlie Sifford (1922–2015), who, in 1961, broke the color barrier in American professional golf. Sifford began his golf career as a caddie for White golfers. He went on to dominate the all-Black United Golfers Association, winning five straight national titles, but he wanted to play with the world's best golfers. At the age of 39, Sifford successfully challenged—and ended—the White-only policy of the Professional Golfers' Association (PGA), becoming its first African American member.

Sifford, who had to endure phone threats, racial slurs, and other indignities at the beginning of his PGA career, went on to win the Greater Hartford Open in 1967, the Los Angeles Open in 1969, and the 1975 Senior PGA Championship. In 2004 he became the first African American inducted into the World Golf Hall of Fame. His major regret was that he never got to play in a Masters Tournament. That event, held annually in Augusta, Georgia, did not invite its first Black player until Lee Elder in 1975. Sifford's bitterness about his own exclusion from the Masters was tempered somewhat by his pleasure when Tiger Woods, another African American golfer, won the first of his four green Masters jackets in 1997.

In terms of diversity, golf has actually regressed since the 1970s, when 11 African Americans played on the PGA Tour. If we consider multiracial players to be African American, there currently is only 1 African American (Tiger Woods) among the 125 top players on the PGA Tour. In Britain, only 2 percent of an estimated 850,000 regular golfers are non-White. Economic factors continue to limit minority access to golf. Prospective golfers need money for instruction, equipment, access to top-notch courses, and travel to tournaments. Asian Americans, who enjoy a relatively high socioeconomic status, are the only minority group in the United States with a growing representation in golf, for both men and women.

Tiger Woods is currently a single exceptional non-White individual in this mainly White, affluent, Republican sport. Woods became one of America's most celebrated and popular athletes by combining golfing success with a carefully cultivated reputation as a family man. He presented himself as the hard-working and achievement-oriented son of an Asian mother and an African

continued

Anthropology Today *continued*

American father, and as a devoted husband and father (with a Scandinavian wife and two photogenic children). Woods's fall from grace began late in 2009, as a flood of media reports converted his image from family man into serial philanderer. Although his marriage did not survive his transgressions, his golfing career did.

Woods gradually reintegrated into the world of golf, even receiving the 2013 PGA Tour Player of the Year Award. He had won 5 of the 16 tournaments he played that year and placed in the top 10 in three others. Woods planned to return to competition after being sidelined with back injuries and surgeries in 2015–2017. His 79 PGA Tour victories and 14 major titles rank second to the all-time records held by Sam Snead and Jack Nicklaus, respectively. Although no longer the untarnished hero of yesteryear, Tiger Woods remains the world's most prominent and celebrated African American golfer. What role, if any, do you think race, ethnicity, racism, and racial stereotyping have played in the rise, fall, and reintegration of Tiger Woods?

Source: Ferguson (2015); Riach (2013); Starn (2011).

---

technique in cultural colonialism is to flood ethnic areas with members of the dominant ethnic group. In the former Soviet Union, ethnic Russian colonists were sent to many areas, to diminish the cohesion and clout of the local people.

For example, when Ukraine belonged to the Soviet Union, Moscow promoted a policy of Russian in-migration and Ukrainian out-migration, so that ethnic Ukrainians' share of the population of Ukraine declined from 77 percent in 1959 to 73 percent in 1991. That trend reversed after Ukraine gained independence, so that, by the turn of the 21st century, ethnic Ukrainians made up more than three-fourths of their country's population. Russians still constitute Ukraine's largest minority, but they now represent less than one-fifth of the population. They are concentrated in eastern Ukraine, where ethnic Russians have rebelled against Ukraine's pro-Western government. Eastern Ukraine, especially those provinces dominated by the Russian language and ethnicity, is considered a potential target of Russian annexation. In 2014, Russia did annex Crimea, where ethnic Russians (composing over 60 percent of the Crimean population) and the Russian language dominate.

The fall of the Soviet Union in 1991 was accompanied by a resurgence of ethnic feeling among formerly dominated groups. The ethnic groups and nationalities once controlled by Moscow have sought, and continue to seek, to forge their own separate and viable nation-states. This celebration of autonomy is part of an ethnic awakening that has flourished since the late 20th century. The new assertiveness of long-resident ethnic groups extends to the Welsh and Scots in the United Kingdom, Bretons and Corsicans in France, and Basques and Catalans in Spain.

Summary

1. An ethnic group consists of members of a particular culture in a nation or region that contains others. Ethnicity is based on actual, perceived, or assumed cultural similarities (among members of the same ethnic group) and differences (between that group and others). Ethnic distinctions can be based on language, religion,

history, geography, kinship, or race. A race is an ethnic group assumed to have a biological basis. Usually, race and ethnicity are ascribed statuses; people are born members of a group and remain so all their lives.

2. Because of a range of problems involved in classifying humans into racial categories, the study of human biological diversity now focuses on specific differences and attempts to explain them. *Homo sapiens* has not evolved distinct races. Biological similarities between human groups may reflect—rather than common ancestry—similar but independent adaptations to similar natural selective forces, such as degrees of ultraviolet radiation from the sun, in the case of skin color.

3. Human races are cultural rather than biological categories. Such races derive from contrasts perceived in particular societies, rather than from scientific classifications based on common genes. In the United States, racial labels such as *White* and *Black* designate socially constructed categories defined by American culture. American racial classification, governed by the rule of hypodescent, is based neither on phenotype nor on genes. Children of mixed unions, no matter what their appearance, are classified with the minority group parent.

4. Racial attitudes in Japan illustrate intrinsic racism—the belief that a perceived racial difference is a sufficient reason to value one person less than another. The valued group is majority (pure) Japanese, who are believed to share the same blood. Majority Japanese define themselves by opposition to others, such as Koreans and burakumin. These may be minority groups in Japan or outsiders—anyone who is "not us."

5. Such exclusionary racial systems are not inevitable. Although Brazil shares a history of slavery with the United States, it lacks the hypodescent rule. Brazilian racial identity is more of an achieved status. It can change during someone's lifetime, reflecting phenotypical changes.

6. The term *nation* once was synonymous with *ethnic group*. Now *nation* has come to mean a state—a centrally organized political unit. Because of migration, conquest, and colonialism, most nation-states are not ethnically homogeneous. Ethnic groups that seek autonomous political status (their own country) are nationalities. Political upheavals, wars, and migrations have divided many nationalities.

7. Assimilation describes the process of change members of an ethnic group may experience when they move to a country where another culture dominates. By assimilating, the minority adopts the patterns and norms of the host culture. Assimilation isn't inevitable, and there can be ethnic harmony without it. A plural society combines ethnic contrasts and economic interdependence between ethnic groups. The view of cultural diversity in a nation-state as good and desirable is multiculturalism. A multicultural society socializes individuals not only into the dominant (national) culture but also into an ethnic one. The 2016 U.S. presidential campaign and election illustrate a backlash to multiculturalism.

8. In the United States, ethnic/racial diversity is increasing, especially among the young. Simultaneously, the country is aging, and most of the senior population is White. These trends are associated with contrasting attitudes, priorities, and political leanings of younger and older Americans. Minorities now constitute almost 40 percent of the total U.S. population.

9. Ethnicity can be expressed either in peaceful multiculturalism or in discrimination or violent confrontation. Ethnic conflict often arises in reaction to prejudice (attitudes and judgments) or discrimination (action). The most extreme form of ethnic discrimination is genocide, the deliberate elimination of a group through mass murder. A dominant group may try to destroy certain ethnic practices (ethnocide), or to force ethnic group members to adopt the dominant culture (forced assimilation). A policy of ethnic expulsion may create refugees. Cultural colonialism is internal domination—by one group and its culture or ideology over others.

Think Like an Anthropologist

1. What's the difference between a culture and an ethnic group? In what culture(s) do you participate? To what ethnic group(s) do you belong? What is the basis of your primary cultural identity? Do others readily recognize this basis and identity? Why or why not?

2. Name five social statuses you currently occupy. To what extent are these statuses achieved? Are any of them mutually exclusive? Which are contextual?

3. Consider the "American Anthropological Association Statement on Race". What is its main argument? If race is a problematic concept when applied to humans, what has replaced, or should replace, it?

Key Terms

achieved status, *215*
ascribed status, *214*
assimilation, *234*
colonialism, *233*
cultural
   colonialism, *242*
descent, *225*
discrimination, *240*
ethnic group, *213*
ethnicity, *214*

ethnocide, *242*
genocide, *242*
hypodescent, *225*
multiculturalism, *234*
nation, *232*
nation-state, *232*
nationalities, *233*
natural
   selection, *220*

phenotype, *217*
plural society, *234*
prejudice, *239*
race, *216*
racial
   classification, *217*
racism, *216*
refugees, *242*
status, *214*
stereotypes, *240*

Chapter 11

Applying Anthropology

What Is Applied Anthropology?

Applied anthropology is the use of anthropological data, perspectives, theory, and methods to identify, assess, and solve contemporary problems (see Ervin 2005; Nolan 2013; Wasson, Butler, and Copeland-Carson 2012). Applied anthropologists help make anthropology relevant and useful to the world beyond anthropology. Medical anthropologists, for instance, have worked as cultural interpreters in public health programs, helping such programs fit into local culture. Development anthropologists work for or with international development agencies, such as the World Bank and the U.S. Agency for International Development (USAID). The findings of garbology, the archaeological study of waste, are relevant to the Environmental Protection Agency, the paper industry, and packaging and trade associations. Archaeology also is applied in cultural resource management and historic preservation. Biological anthropologists apply their expertise in programs aimed at public health, nutrition, genetic counseling, aging, substance abuse, and mental health. Forensic anthropologists work with the police, medical examiners, the courts, and international organizations to identify victims of crimes, accidents, wars, and terrorism. Linguistic anthropologists study physician–patient communication and show how speech differences influence classroom learning. Most applied anthropologists seek humane and effective ways of helping people.

The ethnographic method is a particularly valuable tool in applying anthropology. Remember that ethnographers study societies firsthand, living with, observing, and learning from ordinary people. Nonanthropologists working in social-change programs often are content to converse with officials, read reports, and copy statistics. However, the applied anthropologist's likely early request is some variant of "take me to the local people." Anthropologists know that people must play an active role in the changes that affect them and that "the people" have information that "the experts" lack (see Field and Fox 2009).

The Role of the Applied Anthropologist

Early Applications

Anthropology is, and has long been, the primary academic discipline that focuses on non-Western cultures. One example is the role that anthropologists played as advisers to, and even agents of, colonial regimes during the first half of the 20th century. Under colonialism, some anthropologists worked as administrators in the colonies or held lower-level positions as government agents, researchers, or advisers. The main European colonial powers at that time—Britain, France, Portugal, and the Netherlands—all employed anthropologists. When those colonial empires began to collapse after World War II, as the former colonies gained independence, many anthropologists continued to offer advice to government agencies about the areas and cultures they knew the best.

In the United States, American anthropologists have worked extensively with the subjugated Native American populations within its borders. The 19th-century American anthropologist Lewis Henry Morgan studied the Seneca Iroquois tribe, Native Americans living in New York state, not far from his home in Rochester. Morgan was also a lawyer who represented the Iroquois in their disputes with a company that wanted to seize some of their land. Just as Morgan worked on behalf of the Seneca, there are anthropologists today who work on behalf of the non-Western groups they have studied. Other anthropologists, working as government employees and agents, have helped to establish and enforce policies developed by ruling classes and aimed at local populations.

Bronislaw Malinowski, a Polish-born scholar who spent most of his career teaching in England, was one of the most prominent cultural anthropologists of the early 20th century. Malinowski is well known for his ethnographic fieldwork with the Trobriand Islanders of the South Pacific and for his role in establishing ethnographic field methods. He also is recognized as one of the founders of applied anthropology, which he called "practical anthropology" (Malinowski 1929). Like many other anthropologists of his time, Malinowski worked *with* colonial regimes, rather than opposing the European subjugation of non-Western peoples.

Malinowski, who focused on Britain's African colonies, intended his "practical anthropology" to support and facilitate colonial rule. He believed that anthropologists could help European colonial officials to effectively administer non-Western societies. Anthropologists could help answer questions like the following: How much taxation and forced labor could "the natives" tolerate without resisting? How was contact with European settlers and colonial officials affecting tribal societies? Anthropologists could study local land ownership and use in order to determine how much of their own land "natives" could keep and how much Europeans could take from them. Malinowski did not question the right of Europeans to rule the societies they had conquered. For him, the anthropologist's job was not to question colonial rule, but to make it work as harmoniously as possible. Other colonial-era anthropologists offered similar advice to the French, Portuguese, and Dutch regimes (see also Duffield and Hewitt 2009; Lange 2009).

During World War II, American anthropologists applied anthropology by trying to gain insights about the motivations and behavior of the enemies of the United States—principally Germany and Japan. Margaret Mead (1977) estimated that during the 1940s, 95 percent of U.S. anthropologists were involved in the war effort. For example, Ruth Benedict (1946) wrote an influential study of Japanese national culture not by doing fieldwork in Japan, but by studying Japanese literature, movies, and other cultural products and by interviewing Japanese in the United States. She called her approach "the study of culture at a distance." After World War II, American anthropologists worked to promote local-level cooperation with American policies on several Pacific islands that had been under Japanese control and were now administered by the United States.

Many of the early applications of anthropology described in this section were problematic because they aided and abetted the subjugation and control of non-Western cultures by militarily stronger societies. Most applied anthropologists today see their work as radically removed from colonial-era applied anthropology. Applied anthropologists today usually see their work as a helping profession, designed to assist local people.

Academic and Applied Anthropology

The U.S. baby boom, which began in 1946 and peaked in 1957, fueled a tremendous expansion of the American educational system. New junior, community, and four-year colleges opened, and anthropology became a standard part of the curriculum. During the 1950s and 1960s, most American anthropologists were college professors, although some still worked in agencies and museums.

The growth of academic anthropology continued through the early 1970s. Especially during the Vietnam War, undergraduates flocked to anthropology classes to learn about other cultures. Students were especially interested in Southeast Asia, whose indigenous societies were being disrupted by war. Many anthropologists protested the superpowers' apparent disregard for non-Western lives, values, customs, and social systems.

Most anthropologists still worked in colleges and museums during the 1970s and 1980s. However, an increasing number of anthropologists were finding jobs in international organizations, governments, businesses, hospitals, and schools. The AAA estimates that nowadays more than half of anthropology PhDs seek nonacademic employment. This shift toward application has benefited the profession. It has forced anthropologists to consider the wider social value and implications of their research.

Applied Anthropology Today

According to Barbara Rylko-Bauer, Merrill Singer, and John van Willigen (2006), modern applied anthropology uses theories, concepts, and methods from anthropology to confront human problems, such as poverty, that often contribute to profound social suffering.

Archaeologists Tim Griffith, left, and Ginny Hatfield of Fort Hood's (Texas) Cultural Resources Management Program, sift through sediment collected from an archaeological site. This CRM program manages resources representing more than 10,000 years of occupation of the land around Fort Hood. ©Scott Gaulin/Temple Daily Telegram/AP Images

However, applied anthropologists also have clients who are neither poor nor powerless. An applied anthropologist working as a market researcher may be concerned with discovering how to increase sales of a particular product. Such commercial goals can pose ethical dilemmas, which also may arise in cultural resource management (CRM). The CRM anthropologist helps decide how to preserve significant remains when development threatens sites. The client that hires a CRM firm may be seeking to build a road or a factory. That client may have a strong interest in a CRM finding that no sites need protection, and the client may pressure the CRM firm in that direction. Among the ethical questions that arise in applied anthropology are these: To whom does the researcher owe loyalty? What problems are involved in sticking to the truth? What happens when applied anthropologists don't make the policies they have to implement? How does one criticize programs in which one has participated? Anthropology's professional organizations have addressed such questions by establishing codes of ethics and ethics committees.

Anthropologists study, understand, and respect diverse cultural values. Because of this knowledge of human problems and social change, anthropologists are highly qualified to suggest, plan, and implement policies affecting people. Proper roles for applied anthropologists include (1) identifying needs for change that local people perceive, (2) collaborating with those people to design culturally appropriate and socially sensitive change, and (3) working to protect local people from harmful policies and projects that may threaten them.

For decades, applied anthropologists have collaborated directly with communities to achieve community-directed change. Applied anthropologists not only work collaboratively with local people, but they may even be hired by such communities to advocate on their behalf. One example is Barbara Rose Johnston's (2005) research on behalf of Guatemalan communities that were adversely affected by the construction of a dam. Johnston's reports document the dam's long-term impact on these communities. She also offered recommendations and a plan for reparations.

Development Anthropology

Development anthropology is the branch of applied anthropology that focuses on social issues in, and the cultural dimension of, economic development (see Crewe and Axelby 2013). Development anthropologists don't just carry out development policies planned by others; they also plan and guide policy. (For more detailed discussions of issues in development anthropology, see Edelman and Haugerud 2005; Escobar 2012; Nolan 2002.)

Still, ethical dilemmas often confront development anthropologists (Escobar 2012; Venkatesan and Yarrow 2014). Foreign aid, including funds for economic development, usually does not go where need and suffering are greatest. Rather, such aid tends to support political, economic, and strategic priorities that are set by international donors, political leaders, and powerful interest groups. The goals and interests of the planners may ignore or conflict with the best interests of the local people. Although the stated aim of most development projects is to enhance the quality of life, living standards often decline in the affected area.

Equity

An important stated goal of recent development projects has been to promote equity. **Increased equity** entails (1) reducing poverty and (2) evening out the distribution of wealth. Projects should not benefit only the "haves," but also the "have nots." If people who are already doing well get most of the benefits of a project, then it has not increased equity.

If projects are to increase equity, they must have the support of reform-minded governments. Wealthy and powerful people typically resist projects that offer more to the "have nots" than to the "haves." Often, they will actively oppose a project that threatens the status quo.

Negative Equity Impact

Some projects not only fail to increase equity; they actually widen the gap between the "haves" and "have nots." When this happens, we say they have had a *negative equity impact*. I observed firsthand an example of negative equity impact in Arembepe, Bahia, Brazil, a fishing community on the Atlantic Ocean (see Kottak 2006). A development initiative there offered loans to buy motors for fishing boats, but only people who already owned boats ("haves") could get these loans. Nonowners ("have nots") did not qualify. After getting the loans, the boat owners, in order to repay them, increased the percentage

A mix of boats harbored in Pucusana, a fishing village in Peru. A boat owner gets a loan to buy a motor. To repay it, he increases the share of the catch he takes from his crew. Later, he uses his rising profits to buy a more expensive boat and takes even more from his crew. Can a more equitable solution be found? ©Sean Sprague/The Image Works

of the catch they took from the men who fished in their boats. Their rising profits allowed them to eventually buy larger and more expensive boats. They cited their increased capital expense as a reason to pay their workers less. Over the years, the gap between "haves" and "have nots" widened substantially. The eventual result was socioeconomic stratification—the creation of social classes in a community that had been egalitarian. In the past, Arembepe's fishing boats had been simple sailboats, relying only on wind power, and any enterprising young fisher could hope eventually to own one of his own. In the new economy, a fishing boat became so expensive that ambitious young men, who once would have sought careers in fishing, no longer could afford to buy a boat of their own. They sought wage labor on land instead. To avoid this kind of negative equity impact, credit-granting agencies must seek out and invest in enterprising young fishers, rather than giving loans only to owners and established businesspeople. A lesson here is that the stated goal of increased equity is easier said than done. Because the "haves" tend to have better connections than the "have nots," they are more likely to find out about and take advantage of new programs. They also tend to have more clout with government officials, who often decide who will benefit from a particular program.

Strategies for Innovation

Development anthropologists should work collaboratively and proactively with local people, especially the "have nots," to assess, and help them realize, their own wishes and needs for change. Too many true local needs cry out for a solution to waste money funding projects in area A that are inappropriate there but needed in area B, or that are unnecessary anywhere. Development anthropology can help sort out the needs of the As and Bs and fit projects accordingly. Projects that put people first by consulting with them and responding to their expressed needs must be identified (Cernea 1991). To maximize social and economic benefits, projects must (1) be culturally compatible, (2) respond to locally perceived needs, (3) involve men and women in planning and carrying out the changes that affect them, (4) harness traditional organizations, and (5) be flexible (see Kottak 1990b, 1991).

Consider a recent example of a development initiative that failed because it ignored local culture. Working in Afghanistan after the fall of the Taliban, ethnographer Noah Coburn (2011) studied Istalif, a village of potters. During his fieldwork there, Coburn discovered that an NGO had spent $20,000 on an electric kiln that could have greatly enhanced the productivity of local potters. The only problem was that the kiln was donated to a women's center that men could not enter. The misguided donors ignored the fact that Istalif's men did the work—pot-making and firing—that a kiln could facilitate. Women's role in pottery came later—in glazing and decorating.

Overinnovation

Development projects are most likely to succeed when they avoid the fallacy of **overinnovation** (too much change). People usually are willing to change just enough to maintain, or slightly improve on, what they already have. Motivation to change comes from the traditional culture and the small concerns of ordinary life. Peasants' values are not such abstract ones as "learning a better way," "progressing," "increasing technical know-how," "improving efficiency," or "adopting modern techniques." People want to grow and harvest their crops, amass resources for a ceremony, get a child through school, or have enough cash to pay bills. The goals and values of people who farm and fish for their own subsistence differ from those of people who work for cash, just as they differ from those of development planners.

Development projects that fail usually do so because they are either economically or culturally incompatible (or both). For example, one South Asian project tried to get farmers to start growing onions and peppers, expecting those cash crops to fit into the existing system of rice cultivation—the main local subsistence crop. It turned out, however, that the labor peaks for the new cash crops coincided with those for rice, to which the farmers naturally gave priority. This project failed because it promoted too much change, introducing unfamiliar crops that conflicted with, rather than building on and complementing, an existing system. The planners should have realized that cultivation of the new crops would conflict with that of the main subsistence crop in the area. A good anthropologist could have told them as much.

Recent development efforts in Afghanistan also illustrate the problematic nature of overinnovation. Reporting on social change efforts in Afghanistan after the fall of the Taliban, anthropologists Noah Coburn (2011) and Thomas Barfield (2010) criticize various top-down initiatives that proved incompatible with local culture. Coburn suggests that the best strategy to maintain peace in the Afghan countryside is to work with existing resources, drawing on local beliefs and social organization. To be avoided are overinnovative plans from outside, whether from the national government or foreign donors. Destined for failure, according to Coburn, are attempts to create impersonal bureaucracies based on merit. Also doomed are attempts to impose liberal beliefs about gender at the village level. These are Western ideas that are particularly incompatible in rural areas. Barfield also cites the futility of direct attempts to change rural Afghans' beliefs about such entrenched matters as religion and gender equality. A better strategy, he suggests, is for change agents to work first in urban areas, where innovation is more welcome, and then let those changes spread gradually to the countryside.

Barfield also faults Western powers for trying to impose an autocratic system (the Karzai regime, which ended in 2014) on a country where autocracy is politically unsustainable. In 2014, Afghanistan elected an anthropologist as its president. Ashraf Ghani, who received his doctorate in anthropology from Columbia University in New York, had worked for the World Bank as a development anthropologist. Let us hope that Ghani's background in anthropology and development will eventually lead to more effective development strategies in the conflict-ridden nation he now leads.

Indigenous Models

Many governments are not genuinely, or realistically, committed to improving the lives of their citizens. Interference by major powers also has kept governments from enacting needed reforms. Occasionally, however, a government does act as an agent of and for its people. One historic example is Madagascar, whose people, the Malagasy, were organized into descent groups prior to indigenous state formation in the 18th century. The Merina, creators of the major precolonial state of Madagascar, wove descent groups into its structure, making members of important groups advisers to rulers—thus giving them authority in government. The Merina state collected taxes and organized labor for public works projects. In return, it redistributed resources to peasants in need. It also granted them some protection against war and slave raids and allowed them to cultivate their rice fields in peace. The government maintained the water works for rice cultivation. It opened to ambitious peasant boys the chance of becoming state bureaucrats, through hard work and study.

Throughout the history of the Merina state—and continuing to some extent in postcolonial Madagascar—there have been strong relationships between the individual, the descent group, and the state. Local Malagasy communities, where residence is based on descent, are more cohesive and homogeneous than are communities in Latin America or North America. Madagascar gained political independence from France in 1960. Its new government had an economic development policy aimed at increasing the ability of the Malagasy to feed themselves. Government policy emphasized increased production of rice, a subsistence crop, rather than cash crops. Furthermore, local communities, with their traditional cooperative patterns and solidarity based on kinship and descent, were treated as partners in, not obstacles to, the development process.

In a sense, the descent group is preadapted to equitable national development. In Madagascar, descent groups pooled their resources to educate their most ambitious and talented members. Once educated, those men and women gained economically secure positions in the nation. They then shared the advantages of their new positions with their kin. For example, they gave room and board to rural cousins attending school and helped them find jobs.

This Madagascar example suggests that when government officials are of "the people" (rather than the elites) and have strong personal ties to common folk, they are more likely to promote democratic reform. In Latin America, by contrast, leaders and followers too often have been from different social classes, with no connections based on kinship, descent, marriage, or common background. When elites rule, elites usually prosper. Recently, however, Latin America has elected some nonelite leaders. Brazil's lower class (indeed the entire nation) benefited socioeconomically when one of its own was elected president. Luiz Inácio da Silva, or Lula, a former factory worker with only a fourth-grade education, served two terms (ending in 2011) as one of the Western Hemisphere's most popular leaders.

Anthropology and Education

Attention to culture also is fundamental to **anthropology and education,** a field whose research extends from classrooms into homes, neighborhoods, and communities (see Anderson-Levitt 2012; Levinson and Pollock 2011; Spindler and Hammond 2006). In classrooms, anthropologists have observed interactions among teachers, students, parents, and visitors. Anthropologists view children as total, cultural creatures whose enculturation and attitudes toward education belong to a context that includes family and peers (see also Kontopodis et al. 2011; Reyhner et al. 2013).

The NGO Shidhulai Swanirvar Sangstha operates a multi-vessel fleet of floating one-room elementary schools in flood-prone areas of Bangladesh. Here we see a teacher and students in one of those classrooms. Each schoolboat docks each day to pick-up and let off about 30 students. The boats have solar panels that power an internet-linked laptop, library, and electronic resources.
©Jonas Gratzer/LightRocket via Getty Images

Sociolinguists and cultural anthropologists have worked side by side in education research. In one classic study of Puerto Rican seventh-graders in the urban Midwest, anthropologists uncovered some key misconceptions held by teachers (Hill-Burnett 1978). The teachers mistakenly had assumed that Puerto Rican parents valued education less than did non-Hispanics, but in-depth interviews revealed that the Puerto Rican parents valued it more. The anthropologists also identified certain practices that were preventing Hispanics from being adequately educated. For example, the teachers' union and the board of education had agreed to teach "English as a foreign language." However, they had provided no bilingual teachers to work with Spanish-speaking students. The school was assigning all students (including non-Hispanics) with low reading scores and behavior problems to the English-as-a-foreign-language classroom. This educational disaster brought together in the classroom a teacher who spoke no Spanish, children who barely spoke English, and a group of English-speaking students with reading and behavior problems. The Spanish speakers were falling behind not just in reading but in all subjects. They could at least have kept up in the other subjects if a Spanish speaker had been teaching them science, social studies, and math until they were ready for English-language instruction in those areas.

Urban Anthropology

In today's world, media-transmitted images and information play an important role in attracting people to cities. Often, people move to cities for economic reasons, because jobs are scarce at home. Cities also attract people who want to be where the action is. Rural Brazilians routinely cite *movimento,* urban activity and excitement, as something to be valued. International migrants tend to settle in large cities, where a lot is going on and where they can feel at home in ethnic enclaves. Consider Canada, which, after Australia, is the country with the highest percentage of foreign-born population. Three-quarters of immigrants to Canada settle in Toronto, Vancouver, or Montreal. It is estimated that by 2031 nearly one-half (46 percent) of Canadians aged 15 and over will be foreign born or will have at least one foreign-born parent, up from 39 percent in 2006 (Statistics Canada 2010).

More than half of Earth's people live in cities—53 percent in 2014. That figure first surpassed 50 percent in 2008, and it is projected to rise to 70 percent by 2050 (Handwerk 2008). Only about 3 percent of people were city dwellers in 1800, compared with 13 percent in 1900, 40 percent in 1980, and 53 percent today. The degree of urbanization (about 30 percent) in the less-developed countries (LDCs) is well below the world average (50 percent). Even in the LDCs, however, the urban growth rate now exceeds the rural growth rate. By 2030, the percentage of city dwellers in the LDCs is projected to rise to 41 percent. In Africa and Asia alone, a million people a week migrate to cities. The world had only 16 cities with more than a million people in 1900, versus over 400 such cities today.

Over 1 billion people now live in urban slums, mostly without reliable water, sanitation, public services, and legal security. If current trends continue, urban population increase and the concentration of people in slums will continue to be accompanied by

One-sixth of the Earth's population lives in urban slums. Roçinha (shown here) is a populous shantytown city within the city of Rio de Janeiro, Brazil. How might anthropologists study slums?
©Caio Leal/AFP/Getty Images

rising rates of crime, along with water, air, and noise pollution (see Dürr and Jaffe 2010). These problems will be most severe in the LDCs.

For centuries, cities have been influenced by global forces, including world capitalism and colonialism (Zukin et al. 2015). However, the roles of cities in the world system have changed recently because of the time–space compression made possible by modern transportation and communication systems. That is, everything appears closer today because contact and movement are so much easier.

As industrialization and urbanization spread globally, anthropologists increasingly study these processes and the social problems they create. **Urban anthropology,** which has theoretical (basic research) and applied dimensions, is the cross-cultural and ethnographic study of urbanization and life in cities (see Nononi 2014; Pardo and Prato 2012; Zukin et al. 2015). The United States and Canada have become popular arenas for urban anthropological research on topics such as immigration, ethnicity, poverty, class, and urban violence (Vigil 2010).

An early student of urbanization, the anthropologist Robert Redfield, contrasted rural communities, where social relations are on a face-to-face basis, with cities, where impersonality reigns. Redfield (1941) proposed that urbanization be studied along a rural–urban continuum. He described differences in values and social relations in four sites that spanned such a continuum. In Mexico's Yucatán peninsula, Redfield compared an isolated Mayan-speaking Indian community, a rural peasant village, a small provincial city, and a large capital. Several studies in Africa (Little 1971) and Asia were influenced by Redfield's view that cities are centers through which cultural innovations spread to rural and tribal areas.

In any nation, urban and rural represent different social systems. However, cultural diffusion or borrowing occurs as people, products, images, and messages move from one to the other. Migrants take rural practices and beliefs to cities and bring urban patterns back home. The experiences and social forms of the rural area affect adaptation to city life. City folk also develop new institutions to meet specific urban needs.

An applied anthropology approach to urban planning starts by identifying key social groups in specific urban contexts. After identifying those groups, the anthropologist tries to elicit their wishes for change, convey those needs to funding agencies, and work with agencies and local people to realize those goals. In Africa, relevant groups might include ethnic associations, occupational groups, social clubs, religious groups, and burial societies. The groups provide cash support and lodging for their rural relatives. Sometimes such groups think of themselves as a gigantic kin group that includes urban and rural members. Members may call one another "brother" and "sister." As in an extended family, richer members help their poorer relatives. A member's improper behavior, however, can lead to expulsion—an unhappy fate for a migrant in a large, ethnically heterogeneous city.

Medical Anthropology

Medical anthropology is a biocultural field that studies variation in health care systems, including disease, illness, health standards, and disease theories. All societies have **health care systems** consisting of beliefs, customs, specialists, and techniques aimed at ensuring health and diagnosing and curing illness. Medical anthropology is both academic and applied and includes anthropologists from all four subfields (see Brown and Barrett 2010; Joralemon 2010; Singer 2012; Wiley and Allen 2012). Medical anthropologists examine such questions as which diseases and health conditions affect particular populations (and why) and how illness is socially constructed, diagnosed, managed, and treated in various societies.

Disease refers to a scientifically identified health threat caused by genetics or a bacterium, virus, fungus, parasite, or other pathogen. **Illness** is a condition of poor health perceived or felt by an individual (Inhorn and Brown 1990). Perceptions of good and bad health are culturally constructed. Particular cultures and ethnic groups recognize different illnesses, symptoms, and causes and have developed different health care systems and treatment strategies (Womack 2010).

The incidence and severity of *disease* vary as well (see Baer, Singer, and Susser 2013). Group differences are evident in the United States. Consider, for example, health status indicators in relation to U.S. census categories: White, Black, Hispanic, American Indian or Alaska Native, and Asian or Pacific Islander. African Americans' rates for six indicators (total mortality, heart disease, lung cancer, breast cancer, stroke, and homicide) range from 2.5 to 10 times greater than those of the other groups. Other ethnic groups have higher rates for suicide (White Americans) and motor vehicle accidents

(American Indians and Alaskan Natives). Overall, Asians have the longest lifespans (see Dressler, Oths, and Gravlee 2005).

Reviewing the health conditions of the world's surviving indigenous populations (about 400 million people), anthropologists Claudia Vallegia and Josh Snodgrass (2015) found their health risks to be uniformly high. Compared with nonindigenous people, indigenous groups tend to have shorter and riskier lives. Mothers are more likely to die in childbirth; infants and children have lower survival chances. Malnutrition stunts their growth, and they suffer more from infectious diseases. Reflecting their increasing exposure to global forces, they have rising rates of cardiovascular and other chronic diseases, as well as depression and substance abuse. They also have limited access to medical care. An increasing number of anthropologists are working in global health programs at academic and research institutions. This presence, no doubt, will increase understanding of the health concerns of indigenous peoples—but more is needed. Vallegia and Snodgrass (2015) urge medical anthropologists to involve themselves more in community outreach, which could help bring better health care to indigenous populations.

In many areas, the world system and colonialism worsened the health of indigenous peoples by spreading diseases, warfare, servitude, and other stressors. Traditionally and in ancient times, hunter-gatherers, because of their small numbers, mobility, and relative isolation from other groups, lacked most of the epidemic infectious diseases that affect agrarian and urban societies (Cohen and Armelagos 2013; Singer 2015). Epidemic diseases such as cholera, typhoid, and bubonic plague thrive in dense populations, and thus among farmers and city dwellers. The spread of malaria has been linked to population growth and deforestation associated with food production.

Disease Theory Systems

The kinds and incidence of disease vary among human populations, and cultures perceive and treat illness differently (see Lupton 2012). Still, all societies have what George Foster and Barbara Anderson (1978) call "disease theory systems" to identify, classify, and explain illness. Foster and Anderson identified three basic theories about the causes of illness: personalistic, naturalistic, and emotionalistic. Personalistic disease theories blame illness on agents, such as sorcerers, witches, ghosts, or ancestral spirits.

Naturalistic disease theories explain illness in impersonal terms. One example is Western medicine, or biomedicine, which aims to link illness to scientifically demonstrated agents that bear no personal malice toward their victims. Thus, Western medicine attributes illness to organisms (e.g., bacteria, viruses, fungi, or parasites), accidents, toxic materials, or genes. Other naturalistic systems blame poor health on unbalanced body fluids. Many Latin cultures classify food, drink, and environmental conditions as "hot" or "cold." People believe their health suffers when they eat or drink hot or cold substances together or under inappropriate conditions. For example, one shouldn't drink something cold after a hot bath or eat a pineapple (a "cold" fruit) when one is menstruating (a "hot" condition).

Emotionalistic disease theories assume that emotional experiences cause illness. For example, Latin Americans may develop *susto,* an illness brought on by anxiety, fright, or tragic news. Its symptoms (lethargy, vagueness, distraction) are similar to those of "soul loss," a diagnosis of similar symptoms made by people in Madagascar.

A society's illness-causation theory is important for treatment. When illness has a personalistic cause, magicoreligious specialists may be effective curers. They draw on varied techniques (occult and practical), which constitute their special expertise. A shaman may cure soul loss by enticing the spirit back into the body. Shamans may ease difficult childbirths by asking spirits to travel up the birth canal to guide the baby out (Lévi-Strauss 1967). A shaman may cure a cough by counteracting a curse or removing a substance introduced by a sorcerer.

If there is a "world's oldest profession" besides hunter and gatherer, it is **curer,** often a shaman. The curer's role has some universal features (Foster and Anderson 1978). Thus, a curer emerges through a culturally defined process of selection (parental prodding, inheritance of the role, visions, dream instructions) and training (apprentice shamanship, medical school). Eventually, the curer is certified by older practitioners and acquires a professional image. Patients believe in the skills of the curer, whom they consult and compensate. Health interventions always have to fit into local cultures. When Western medicine is introduced, people usually preserve many of their old methods while also accepting new ones. Native curers may go on treating certain conditions (e.g., spirit possession), while physicians deal with others. The native curer may get as much credit as the physician for a cure.

Scientific Medicine versus Western Medicine

We should not lose sight, ethnocentrically, of the difference between scientific medicine and Western medicine per se. **Scientific medicine** relies on advances in technology, genomics, molecular biology, pathology, surgery, diagnostics, and applications. Scientific medicine surpasses tribal treatment in many ways. Although medicines such as quinine, coca, opium, ephedrine, and rauwolfia were discovered in nonindustrial societies, thousands of effective drugs are available today to treat myriad diseases. Today's surgical procedures are much safer and more effective than those of traditional societies. These are strong benefits of scientific medicine.

Western medicine refers to the practice of medicine in a particular modern Western nation, such as the United States. Of course, the practice of medicine and the quality and availability of heath care vary among Western nations. Some make free or low-cost health care available to all citizens, while other countries are not so generous. Millions of Americans, for example, remain uninsured. Western medicine has both "pros" and "cons." The strongest "pro" of Western medicine is that it incorporates scientific medicine and its many benefits. "Cons" associated with Western medicine include overprescription of drugs, unnecessary surgeries and procedures, and the impersonality and inequality of the physician–patient relationship. In addition, overuse of antibiotics seems to be triggering an explosion of resistant microorganisms. Another "con" associated with Western medicine is that it tends to draw a rigid line between biomedical and psychological causation. Non-Western theories usually lack this sharp distinction, recognizing that poor health has intertwined physical, emotional, and social causes (see also Brown and Barrett 2010; Joralemon 2010; Strathern and Stewart 2010).

Treatment strategies that emulate the much more personal non-Western curer–patient–community relationship might benefit Western systems. Physician–patient encounters too often are rushed and truncated. Those who perform a surgical procedure or diagnose a condition often include specialists (e.g., radiologists and lab technicians) that the patient will never see. Surgeons are not renowned for their "bedside manner." Efforts are being made to improve physician–patient relationships. A recent trend in the United States is the rise of "concierge medicine," in which a physician charges an annual fee to each patient, limits the practice to a certain number of patients, and has ample time to spend with each patient because of the reduced case-load. To an extent, the Internet has empowered patients, who now have access to all kinds of medical information that used to be the sole property of physicians. This access, however, has its drawbacks. Information can make patients more informed as health care consumers, but it also prompts more questions than a physician usually can answer during a brief appointment.

Industrialization, Globalization, and Health

Despite the advances in scientific medicine, industrialization and globalization have spawned many significant health problems. Certain diseases, and physical conditions such as obesity, have spread with economic development and globalization (Inhorn and Wentzell 2012). Schistosomiasis, or bilharzia (liver flukes), is one of the fastest-spreading and most dangerous parasitic infections now known. People get schistosomia-sis from snails living in ponds, lakes, and waterways, usually ones created by irrigation projects. The applied anthropology approach to reducing such diseases is to see if local people perceive a connection between the vector (e.g., snails in the water) and the dis-ease. If not, local organizations, schools, and the media, including social media, can help spread the relevant information.

HIV/AIDS has been spread through international travel within the modern world system. The world's highest rates of HIV infection and AIDS-related deaths are in Africa, especially southern Africa (Mazzeo, Rödlach, and Brenton 2011). Sexually transmitted infections are spread through prostitution as young men from rural areas seek wage work in cities, labor camps, and mines, often across national borders. When

This tapestry by South African artist Jane Makhubele promotes condom use as a method of AIDS prevention Courtesy Melville J. Herskovits Library of African Studies, Northwestern University

the men return home, they infect their wives (see Baer et al. 2013). By killing productive adults, AIDS leaves behind dependent children and seniors. Cultural factors affect the spread of HIV, which is less likely to spread when men are circumcised.

Other problems associated with industrialization and globalization include the following: poor nutrition; dangerous machinery; impersonal work; isolation; poverty; homelessness; substance abuse; and noise, air, and water pollution (see McElroy and Townsend 2014). With industrialization and globalization, people turn from subsistence work, usually alongside family and neighbors, to cash employment in more impersonal settings such as factories. Rather than living in villages where everyone knows everyone else, people increasingly live in cities—and often in slums, where they tend to have poorer diets, more exposure to pathogens, poor sanitation, and polluted air. We all remember the scares caused by Ebola, H1N1, and other emergent viruses. Such pathogens, however, are not the only, or perhaps even the primary, cause of health problems associated with industrialization and globalization. Other stressors that endanger our health are economic (e.g., poverty), social (e.g., crowding, homelessness), political (e.g., terrorism), and cultural (e.g., ethnic conflict). Poverty contributes to many illnesses, including arthritis, heart conditions, back problems, and hearing and vision impairment.

In the United States and other developed countries, good health has become something of an ethical imperative (Foucault 1990). Individuals are expected to regulate their behavior so as to achieve bodies in keeping with new medical knowledge. Those who do so acquire the status of sanitary citizens—people with modern understanding of the body, health, and illness. Such citizens practice hygiene and look to health care professionals when they are sick. People who act differently (e.g., smokers, overeaters, those who avoid doctors) are stigmatized and blamed for their own health problems (Briggs 2005; Foucault 1990).

Nowadays, even getting an epidemic disease such as cholera may be viewed as a moral failure, because people did not take proper precautions. It's assumed that people who act rationally can avoid "preventable" diseases. Individuals are expected to follow scientifically based imperatives (e.g., "boil water," "don't smoke"). People (e.g., gay men, smokers, veterans) can become objects of avoidance and discrimination simply by belonging to a group seen as having a greater risk of poor health.

Medical anthropology also studies the impact of new scientific and medical techniques on ideas about life, death, and personhood (what it means to be a person). For decades, disagreements about personhood—such as about when life begins and ends—have been part of political and religious discussions of contraception, abortion, and assisted suicide. Recent technological and scientific advances have raised new debates about personhood associated with stem cells, "harvested" embryos, assisted reproduction, genetic screening, cloning, and life-prolonging medical treatments.

Kaufman and Morgan (2005) emphasize the contrast between what they call low-tech and high-tech births and deaths. A desperately poor young mother dies of AIDS in Africa, while half a world away an American child of privilege is born as the result of a $50,000 in-vitro fertilization procedure. Medical anthropologists increasingly are concerned with how the boundaries of life and death are being questioned and negotiated in our globalized world.

Anthropology and Business

For decades, anthropologists have used ethnographic procedures to understand organizations and other business settings (Briody and Trotter 2008; Cefkin 2009; A. Jordan 2013; B. Jordan 2013). Ethnographic research in an automobile factory, for example, might view workers, managers, and executives as different social categories participating in a common system. Each group has its own characteristic attitudes and behavior patterns. The free-ranging nature of ethnography allows the anthropologist to move across levels and microcultures—from worker through management and back. Having learned the entire system by crossing and recrossing its internal boundaries, the anthropologist can become an effective "cultural broker," translating managers' goals or workers' concerns to the other group (see Ferraro and Briody 2013). A free-ranging ethnographer can be a perceptive oddball in settings where information and decisions typically move through a rigid hierarchy. When allowed to converse freely with, and observe, all types and levels of personnel, the anthropologist gains a unique perspective on organizational conditions and problems.

Business executives, like public policy makers, run organizations that provide goods and services for people. For people! The field of market research, which employs an increasing number of anthropologists, is based on the need to know what actual and potential customers do, think, and want. Smart planners study and listen to people to understand what they desire in a product or service and how they use it—the meaningful role it plays in their lives.

Ethnographers can help a business to rethink faulty preconceptions and assumptions about their clients' purchasing habits or service needs, and to *discover* what those clients really are seeking (see Graber and Atkinson 2012). Ethnography relies on in-depth observation of people as they lead their everyday lives. Applying ethnographic techniques, business anthropologists shadow people—actual and potential customers—at home and at work. Researchers observe how those people interact with other people and products. They take notes and video-record behavior and interactions. Eventually, they draw conclusions and make recommendations (see Ha n.d.).

Let's consider now a few case studies illustrating the value of anthropology to business. In advertising, we hear phrases like "all new" and "new and improved" a lot more often than "old reliable." The new, however, isn't always improved. The Coca-Cola Company (TCCC) learned this painful lesson in 1985 when it changed the formula of its premier soft drink, Coca-Cola, and introduced "New Coke." That change provoked a national brouhaha, as hordes of customers protested. TCCC soon brought back old, familiar, reliable Coke under the name "Coca-Cola Classic," which thrives today. New Coke, now history, offers a classic case of how not to treat consumers. TCCC tried a *top-down change* (a change initiated at the top of a hierarchy rather than inspired by the people most affected by the change). Customers didn't ask TCCC to change its product; executives made that decision, and customers rebelled.

In an article titled "An Anthropologist Walks into a Bar," Christian Madsbjerg and Mikkel Rasmussen (2014) describe a study commissioned by a beer company, which they call BeerCo. A team of anthropologists studied a dozen bars in Finland and the

United Kingdom. The researchers immersed themselves in the life of each bar or pub, observing and getting to know owners, staff, and regulars. The team analyzed 150 hours of video, thousands of still photographs, and massive field notes. Their findings convinced BeerCo to abandon its previous "one-size-fits-all" approach and to launch a more differentiated and targeted campaign. BeerCo started customizing its promotional materials for different types of bars and bar owners. It trained its salesforce to understand and treat each bar owner as an individual. It enhanced loyalty to the brand by offering taxi service for wait staff who had to work late. BeerCo's pub and bar sales rebounded. This case illustrates once again the value of knowing the local culture, and for businesses, of targeting products and services accordingly. (This chapter's "Anthropology Today" provides yet another example of the value of cultural understanding for business expansion.)

Paco Underhill (2009) is a retail anthropologist whose influential book *Why We Buy: The Science of Shopping* has been translated into 27 languages. His market research company, Envirosell, specializes in the study of shopping habits (see Green 1999). Researchers follow shoppers around stores, recording their interactions with merchandise. Underhill's team noted that Americans, on entering a store, tend to gravitate to the right, replicating a pattern used in driving and walking. Australians and Britons, who drive on the left, do the opposite. Based on this observation, Underhill recommended that North American stores place their best merchandise on the right side of the store. He also recommended that stores and departments that cater primarily to women need to give men a place to sit and something to do. (I would add the additional recommendation that Wi-Fi should be easily available, since nowadays "something to do" typically involves a smartphone.) Another Underhill recommendation is that products designed for older people should be placed above the bottom shelf, which gets harder to reach as customers age. Finally, he stresses the key role of the dressing room, as the place where most buying decisions are finalized. Dressing rooms should be clean and well-lit, with places to sit and for children to play (see Green 1999).

One common approach in market research is to assemble a focus group (a small group of people guided by a researcher as they discuss a topic). A limitation of focus groups, surveys, and other common market research techniques is that they elicit only what people *say,* report, or write down, rather than observing real-time, real-life behavior, as anthropologists do. Focus groups also face the danger of group think, when one or two very vocal members unduly influence the entire group. When answering a set of survey questions, people want to answer as quickly as possible. They have limited patience and imperfect recall. Their answers will be more accurate and complete when they are interviewed in person and probed for additional information.

The ethnographic market research firm Ethnographic Solutions provides qualitative research, including a variety of ethnographic approaches, that has benefited numerous pharmaceutical, biotech, and medical device companies. The firm's website describes the value of several techniques, including *physician–patient dialogue research.* The goal is to understand how physicians and patients decide together to initiate and navigate a course of treatment, including the products to be used. Conducted in physicians' offices, physician–patient dialogue research combines on-site interviewing and observation with later analysis of field notes and video-recorded interactions.

Business anthropology in action: At the Intel Corporation in Hillsboro, Oregon, anthropologist Alexandra Zafiroglu displays a blanket with a huge photograph of the contents of one automobile. Zafiroglu works on a team directed by anthropologist Genevieve Bell (Intel's Director of User Experience Research) studying objects stored in cars. This research provides insights about how drivers use hand-held mobile devices in conjunction with technology built into their cars. ©Leah Nash/The New York Times/Redux

The resulting perspective goes beyond traditional market research, which typically takes place in an artificial setting, such as a research facility or via a survey, and which relies on imperfect recall.

Public and Applied Anthropology

Many academic anthropologists, myself included, have worked occasionally as applied anthropologists. Often our role is to advise and consult about the direction of change in places where we originally did "academic" research. In my case, this has meant policy-relevant work on environmental preservation in Madagascar and poverty reduction in northeastern Brazil.

Other academics, while not doing applied anthropology per se, have urged anthropologists to engage more in what they call **public anthropology** (Borofsky 2000; Beck and Maida 2015) or *public interest anthropology* (Sanday 2003). Suggested ways of making anthropology more visible and relevant to the public include nonacademic publishing; testifying at government hearings; consulting; acting as an expert witness; and engaging in citizen activism, electoral campaigns, and political administrations (Sanjek 2004). Public anthropologists work to oppose policies that promote injustice and to reframe discussions of key social issues in the media and by public officials. As Barbara Rylko-Bauer and her colleagues (2006) point out, there is also a long tradition of work guided by such goals in applied anthropology (see also Beck and Maida 2013).

New media are helping to disseminate anthropological knowledge to a wider public. The world of cyberspace, including the blogosphere, constantly grows richer in the resources and communication opportunities available to anthropologists. Some of the most widely read anthropological blogs include Savage Minds, a group blog; Living Anthropologically, by Jason Antrosio and Neuroanthropology, by Greg Downey and Daniel Lende. Also see this detailed list of anthropology blogs, as updated for 2016: http://anthropologyreport.com/anthropology-blogs-2016/. Anthropologists participate as well in various listservs and networking groups (e.g., on LinkedIn and Research Gate). A bit of googling on your part will take you to anthropologists' personal web-sites, as well as research project websites.

Careers and Anthropology

Many college students find anthropology interesting and consider majoring in it. However, their parents or friends may discourage them by asking, "What kind of job are you going to get with an anthropology degree?" The first step in answering that question is to consider the more general question "What do you do with any college major?" The answer is "Not much, without a good bit of effort, thought, and planning." One survey of graduates of the University of Michigan's College of Literature, Science, and the Arts (LS&A) showed that few had jobs that were obviously linked to their majors. Most professions, including medicine and law, require advanced degrees. Although many colleges offer bachelor's degrees in engineering, business, accounting, and social work, master's degrees often are needed to get the best jobs in those fields. Anthropologists, too, need an advanced degree, almost always a PhD, to find gainful employment in academic, museum, or applied anthropology.

A broad college education, and even a major in anthropology, can be an excellent foundation for success in many fields. One survey of women executives showed that most had not majored in business but in the social sciences or humanities. Only after graduating from college did they study business, leading to a master's degree in business administration (MBA). Those executives felt that the breadth of their college educations had contributed to their business careers. Anthropology majors go on to medical, law, and business schools and find success in many professions that often have little explicit connection to anthropology.

Anthropology's breadth provides knowledge and an outlook on the world that are useful in many kinds of work. For example, an anthropology major combined with a master's degree in business is excellent preparation for work in international business. Breadth is anthropology's hallmark. Anthropologists study people biologically, culturally, socially, and linguistically, across time and space, in various countries, in simple and complex settings. Most colleges offer anthropology courses that compare cultures, along with others that focus on particular world areas, such as Latin America, Asia, Africa, the Middle East, and Eastern Europe. The knowledge of foreign areas

Anthropology Today *Culturally Appropriate Marketing*

Innovation succeeds best when it is culturally appropriate. This axiom of applied anthropology could guide the international spread not only of development projects but also of businesses, such as fast food. Each time McDonald's or Burger King expands to a new nation, it must devise a culturally appropriate strategy for fitting into the new setting.

McDonald's has been very successful internationally. Almost 70 percent of its current annual revenue comes from sales outside the United States. As the world's most successful restaurant chain, McDonald's has more than 36,000 restaurants in some 120 countries. One place where McDonald's has expanded successfully is Brazil, where 100 million middle-class people, most living in densely packed cities, provide a concentrated market for a fast-food chain. Still, it took McDonald's some time to find the right marketing strategy for Brazil.

In 1980 when I visited Brazil after a seven-year absence, I first noticed, as a manifestation of Brazil's growing participation in the world economy, the appearance of two McDonald's restaurants in Rio de Janeiro. There wasn't much difference between the Brazilian McDonald's and an American one. The restaurants looked alike. The menus were more or less the same, as was the taste of the quarter-pounders. I picked up an artifact, a white paper bag with yellow lettering, exactly like the take-out bags then used in American McDonald's. An advertising device, it carried several messages about how Brazilians could bring McDonald's into their lives. However, it seemed to me that McDonald's Brazilian ad campaign was missing some important points about how fast food should be marketed in a culture that valued large, leisurely lunches.

The bag proclaimed, "You're going to enjoy the [McDonald's] difference," and listed several "favorite places where you can enjoy McDonald's products." This list confirmed that the marketing people were trying to adapt to Brazilian middle-class culture, but they were making some mistakes. "When you go out in the car with the kids" transferred the uniquely developed North American cultural combination of highways, affordable cars, and suburban living to the very different context of urban Brazil. A similar suggestion was "traveling to the country place." Even Brazilians who owned country places could not find McDonald's, still confined to the cities then, on the road. The ad creator had apparently never attempted to drive up to a fast-food restaurant in a neighborhood with no parking spaces.

Several other suggestions pointed customers toward the beach, where *cariocas* (Rio natives) do spend much of their leisure time. One could eat McDonald's products "after a dip in the ocean," "at a picnic at the beach," or "watching the surfers." These suggestions ignored the Brazilian custom of consuming cold things, such as beer, soft drinks, ice cream, and ham and cheese sandwiches, on the beach. Brazilians don't consider a hot, greasy hamburger proper beach food. They view the sea as "cold" and hamburgers as "hot"; they avoid "hot" foods at the beach.

Also culturally dubious was the suggestion to eat McDonald's hamburgers "lunching at the office." Brazilians prefer their main meal at midday, often eating at a leisurely pace with business associates. Many firms serve ample lunches to their employees. Other workers take advantage of a two-hour lunch break to go home to eat with the spouse and children.

continued

Anthropology Today continued

Nor did it make sense to suggest that children should eat hamburgers for lunch, since most kids attend school for half-day sessions and have lunch at home. Two other suggestions—"waiting for the bus" and "in the beauty parlor"—did describe common aspects of daily life in a Brazilian city. However, these settings have not proved especially inviting to hamburgers or fish fillets.

The homes of Brazilians who can afford McDonald's products often have cooks and maids to do many of the things that fast-food restaurants do in the United States. The suggestion that McDonald's products be eaten "while watching your favorite television program" is culturally appropriate, because Brazilians watch TV a lot. However, Brazil's consuming classes can ask the cook to make a snack when hunger strikes. Indeed, much televiewing occurs during the light dinner served when the husband gets home from the office.

Most appropriate to the Brazilian lifestyle was the suggestion to enjoy McDonald's "on the cook's day off." Throughout Brazil, Sunday is that day. The Sunday pattern for middle-class families who live on the coast is a trip to the beach, liters of beer, a full midday meal around 3:00 P.M., and a light evening snack. McDonald's found its niche in the Sunday evening meal, when families flock to the fast-food restaurant.

McDonald's has expanded rapidly in Brazil, where, as in North America, young appetites have fueled the fast-food explosion. McDonald's outlets now dot urban neighborhoods throughout Brazil, and the cost of hiring in-home help has skyrocketed. Given these changes, Brazilian teenagers increasingly use McDonald's for after-school snacks, and whole families have evening meals there. As an anthropologist could have predicted, the fast-food industry has not revolutionized Brazilian food and meal customs. Rather, McDonald's is succeeding because it has adapted to preexisting Brazilian cultural patterns. Once McDonald's realized that more money could be made by fitting in with, rather than trying to Americanize, Brazilian meal habits, it started aiming its advertising at that goal. As of this writing (2017), McDonald's has about 900 outlets in Brazil.

acquired in such courses can be useful in many jobs. Anthropology's comparative outlook and its focus on diverse lifestyles combine to provide an excellent foundation for overseas employment (see Ellick and Watkins 2011; Omohundro 2001).

For work in contemporary North America as well, anthropology's focus on culture and diversity is increasingly relevant. Every day we hear about cultural differences and about problems whose solutions require an ability to recognize and reconcile differences related to social variables such as race, ethnicity, gender, and class. Government, schools, hospitals, and businesses constantly deal with people from different social classes, ethnic groups, and cultural backgrounds. Physicians, attorneys, social workers, police officers, judges, teachers, and students can all do a better job if they understand cultural differences in a nation that is one of the most ethnically diverse in history.

Knowledge of the traditions and beliefs of the groups that make up a modern nation is important in planning and carrying out programs that affect those groups. Experience in planned social change—whether community organization in North America or economic development overseas—shows that a proper social study should be done before a project or policy is implemented. When local people want the change and it fits their lifestyle and traditions, it has a better chance of being successful, beneficial, and cost effective.

People with anthropology backgrounds do well in many fields (see https://savageminds.org/2014/05/05/who-majors-in-anthropology/ for some famous people who have studied anthropology). Even if one's job has little or nothing to do with anthropology in a formal or obvious sense, a background in anthropology provides a useful orientation when we work with our fellow human beings. For most of us, this means every day of our lives.

Summary

1. Applied anthropology uses anthropological perspectives, theory, methods, and data to identify, assess, and solve problems. Applied anthropologists have a range of employers. Examples are government agencies; development organizations; NGOs; tribal, ethnic, and interest groups; businesses; hospitals; social services; and educational agencies. Applied anthropologists come from all four subfields. Ethnography is one of applied anthropology's most valuable research tools.

2. Development anthropology focuses on social issues in, and the cultural dimension of, economic development. Not all governments seek to increase equality and end poverty. Resistance by elites to reform is typical. At the same time, local people rarely cooperate with projects requiring major and risky changes in their daily lives. Many projects seek to impose inappropriate property notions and incompatible social units on their intended beneficiaries. The best strategy for change is to base the social design for innovation on traditional social forms in each target area.

3. Anthropology and education researchers work in classrooms, homes, and other settings relevant to education and make policy recommendations based on their findings. Both academic and applied anthropologists study migration from rural areas to cities and across national boundaries. North America has become a popular arena for urban anthropological research on migration, ethnicity, poverty, and related topics. Although rural and urban are different social systems, there is cultural diffusion from one to the other.

4. Medical anthropology is a biocultural field that studies variation in health care systems, including disease, illness, health standards, and disease theories. In a given setting, the characteristic diseases reflect diet, population density, economy, and social complexity. Native theories of illness may be personalistic, naturalistic, or emotionalistic. In applying anthropology to business, the key features are (1) ethnography and observation as ways of gathering data, (2) a focus on diversity, and (3) cross-cultural expertise. Public anthropology attempts to extend anthropological knowledge of social problems and issues to a wider and more influential audience.

5. A broad college education, including anthropology and foreign-area courses, offers an excellent background for many fields. Anthropology's comparative, cross-cultural outlook provides an excellent basis for overseas employment. Even for

work in North America, a focus on culture and cultural diversity is valuable. Anthropology majors attend medical, law, and business schools and succeed in many fields, some of which have little explicit connection with anthropology.

Think Like an Anthropologist

1. This chapter uses the association between early anthropology and colonialism to illustrate some of the dangers of early applied anthropology. We also learn how American anthropologists studied Japanese "culture at a distance" to predict the behavior of the enemies of the United States during World War II. Political and military conflicts continue today. What role, if any, could and/or should applied anthropologists play in these conflicts?

2. This chapter describes some of the applications of anthropology in educational settings. Think back to your grade school or high school classroom. Were there any social issues that might have interested an anthropologist? Were there any problems that an applied anthropologist might have been able to help solve? How so?

3. Indicate your career plans, if known, and describe how you might apply the knowledge learned through introductory anthropology in your future vocation. If you have not yet chosen a career, pick one of the following: economist, engineer, diplomat, architect, or elementary school teacher. Why is it important to understand the culture and social organization of the people who will be affected by your work?

Key Terms

anthropology and
  education, *255*
curer, *260*
development
  anthropology, *251*
disease, *258*
health care
  systems, *258*

illness, *258*
increased
  equity, *251*
medical
  anthropology, *258*
overinnovation, *253*
public
  anthropology, *265*

scientific
  medicine, *260*
urban
  anthropology, *257*

Chapter

12

The World System, Colonialism, and Inequality

The World System

Although fieldwork in small communities has been anthropology's hallmark, isolated groups are impossible to find today. Truly isolated human societies probably never have existed. For thousands of years, human groups have been in contact with one another. Local societies always have participated in a larger system, which today has global

Illustrating the contemporary global spread of capitalism is this photo of Hong Kong's perpetually crowded Sai Yeung Choi Street, where throngs of people shop, sightsee, and search for restaurants. What international brands (an important component of today's world capitalist economy) can you identify in the photo? ©Alex Woo. All rights reserved./ Getty Images RF

dimensions. We call it the *modern world system,* by which we mean a world in which nations are economically and politically interdependent.

A huge increase in international trade during and after the 15th century led to the **capitalist world economy** (Wallerstein 1982, 2004), a single world system committed to production for sale or exchange, with the object of maximizing profits rather than supplying domestic needs. The world system and the relations among the countries within it are shaped by the capitalist world economy. **Capital** refers to wealth or resources invested in business, with the intent of generating further wealth—making a profit.

World-System Theory

World-system theory can be traced to the French social historian Fernand Braudel. In his three-volume work *Civilization and Capitalism, 15th–18th Century* (1981, 1982, 1992), Braudel argued that societies consist of interrelated parts assembled into a system. Societies themselves are subsystems of larger systems, with the world system the largest. The key claim of **world-system theory** is that all the countries of the world belong to a global system that is marked by differences in wealth and power. This world system, based on capitalism, has existed at least since the 16th century, when the Old World established regular contact with the Americas.

World-system theory assigns particular countries to one of three different positions, based on their economic and political clout: core, semiperiphery, and periphery. The **core** consists of the strongest and most powerful nations, which have the most productive economies and the greatest concentration of capital. The core monopolizes the most profitable activities, especially the control of world finance (Arrighi 2010). The **semiperiphery** is intermediate between the core and the

Jobs continue to migrate from core nations to places in the semiperiphery, such as this call center in India. ©Fredrik Renander/Alamy Stock Photo

periphery. Contemporary nations of the semiperiphery are industrialized. Like core nations, they produce and export both industrial goods and commodities, but they lack the power and economic dominance of core nations. Thus, Brazil, a semiperiphery nation, exports automobiles to Nigeria (a periphery nation) and auto engines, orange juice extract, coffee, and shrimp to the United States (a core nation). The **periphery** includes the world's poorest and least privileged countries. Economic activities there are less mechanized than in the semiperiphery, although some degree of industrialization has reached even periphery nations. The periphery produces mainly raw materials, agricultural commodities, and, increasingly, human labor for export to the core and the semiperiphery.

In the United States and Western Europe today, immigration—documented and undocumented—from the periphery and semiperiphery supplies cheap labor, especially for agriculture, construction, and paid domestic labor. U.S. states as distant as California, Michigan, and South Carolina make significant use of farm labor from Mexico. The availability of relatively cheap workers from noncore nations such as Mexico (in the United States) and Turkey (in Germany) benefits farmers and business owners in core countries while supplying remittances to families in the semiperiphery and periphery. As a result of 21st-century telecommunications technology, cheap labor doesn't even need to migrate to the United States. Thousands of families in India are being supported as American companies outsource jobs—from telephone assistance to software engineering—to nations outside the core (see Nadeem 2011).

The Emergence of the World System

International trade is much older than the capitalist world economy. As early as 600 B.C.E., the Phoenicians/Carthaginians sailed around Britain on regular trade routes and circumnavigated Africa. Likewise, Indonesia, the Middle East, and Africa have been linked in Indian Ocean trade for at least 2,000 years. By the 15th century, advances in navigation, mapmaking, and shipbuilding fueled the geographic expansion of trading networks. Europe established regular contact with Asia, Africa, and eventually the New World (the Caribbean and the Americas). Christopher Columbus's first voyage from Spain to the Bahamas and the Caribbean in 1492 was soon followed by additional voyages. These journeys opened the way for a major exchange of people, resources, products, ideas, and diseases, as the Old and New Worlds were forever linked (Crosby 2003; Diamond 2005; Mann 2011; Marks 2015). The *Columbian exchange* is the term for the spread of people, resources, products, ideas, and diseases between Eastern and Western Hemispheres after contact.

Previously in Europe, as throughout the world, rural people had produced mainly for their own needs, growing their own food and making clothing, furniture, and tools from local products. People produced beyond their immediate needs in order to pay taxes and to purchase trade items such as salt and iron. As late as 1650, the English diet was based on locally grown starches. In the 200 years that followed, however, the English became extraordinary consumers of imported goods. One of the earliest and most popular of those goods was sugar (Mintz 1985).

Sugarcane, originally domesticated in Papua New Guinea, was first processed in India. Reaching Europe via the eastern Mediterranean, it was carried to the Americas by Columbus (Mintz 1985). The climate of Brazil and the Caribbean proved ideal for growing sugarcane, and Europeans built plantations there to supply the growing demand for sugar. This led to the development in the 17th century of a plantation economy based on a single cash crop—a system known as *monocrop* production.

The demand for sugar spurred the development of the transatlantic slave trade and New World plantation economies based on slave labor. By the 18th century, an increased English demand for raw cotton led to rapid settlement of what is now the southeastern United States and the emergence there of another slave-based monocrop production system. Like sugar, cotton was a key trade item that fueled the growth of the world system.

Industrialization

By the 18th century the stage had been set for the **Industrial Revolution**—the historical transformation (in Europe after 1750) of "traditional" into "modern" societies through industrialization. The Industrial Revolution began, in Europe, around 1750. However, the seeds of industrial society had been planted well before then (Gimpel 1988). For example, a knitting machine invented in England in 1589 was so far ahead of its time that it played a profitable role in factories two and three centuries later.

The Industrial Revolution required capital for investment, and that capital came from the established system of transoceanic commerce, which generated enormous profits.

In the home-handicraft, or domestic, system of production, an organizer supplied raw materials to workers in their homes and collected their products. Family life and work were intertwined, as in this English scene. Is there a modern equivalent to the domestic system of production?

Source: Library of Congress prints and Photographs Division [LC-USZ62-4801]

Wealthy people invested in machines and engines to drive machines. New technology and techniques increased production in both farming and manufacturing.

European industrialization eventually replaced the *domestic system* of production, also known as the home-handicraft system. In this system, an organizer-entrepreneur supplied raw materials to workers in their homes and collected finished products from them. This entrepreneur, whose sphere of operations might span several villages, owned the materials, paid for the work, and arranged the distribution of the finished product.

Causes of the Industrial Revolution

The Industrial Revolution began with machines that manufactured cotton products, iron, and pottery. These were widely used items whose manufacture could be broken down into simple routine motions that machines could perform. When manufacturing moved from homes to factories, where machinery replaced handwork, agrarian societies evolved into industrial ones. As factories produced cheap staple goods, the Industrial Revolution led to a dramatic increase in production. Industrialization fueled urban growth and created a new kind of city, with factories crowded together in places where coal and labor were cheap.

The Industrial Revolution began in England, for several reasons. More than other nations, England needed to innovate in order to meet a demand for staples—at home and from its far-flung colonies. As industrialization proceeded, Britain's population began to increase dramatically. It doubled during the 18th century (especially after 1750) and did so again between 1800 and 1850. This demographic explosion fueled consumption, but British entrepreneurs could not meet the increased demand with traditional production methods. This spurred experimentation, innovation, further industrialization, and rapid technological change.

Also supporting early English industrialization were Britain's advantages in natural resources. Britain was rich in coal and iron ore and had navigable coasts and waterways.

It was a seafaring island-nation located at the crossroads of international trade. These features gave Britain a favored position for importing raw materials and exporting manufactured goods. Another factor in England's industrial growth was the fact that much of its 18th-century colonial empire was occupied by English settler families, who looked to the mother country as they tried to replicate European civilization abroad. These colonies bought large quantities of English staples.

It also has been argued that particular cultural and religious factors contributed to industrialization. Many members of the emerging English middle class were Protestants, whose beliefs and values encouraged industry, thrift, the dissemination of new knowledge, inventiveness, and willingness to accept change (Weber 1904/1958). These cultural values were eminently compatible with the spirit of entrepreneurial innovation that propelled the Industrial Revolution.

Socioeconomic Changes Associated with the Industrial Revolution

The socioeconomic changes that accompanied industrialization were mixed. English national income tripled between 1700 and 1815 and increased 30 times more by 1939. Standards of comfort rose, but prosperity was uneven. Initially, factory workers got decent wages, until owners started recruiting workers in areas where labor (including that of women and children) was cheap. By the 19th century, cities were polluted by factory smoke, and housing was crowded and unsanitary. People faced disease outbreaks and rising death rates. This was the world of Ebenezer Scrooge, Bob Cratchit, Tiny Tim—and Karl Marx.

Industrial Stratification

The Industrial Revolution created a new class system—a new form of socioeconomic stratification. Based on his observations of 19th-century industrial capitalism in England, Karl Marx saw this stratification as a sharp and simple division between two opposed classes: the bourgeoisie (capitalists) and the proletariat (propertyless workers) (Marx and Engels 1848/1976). The bourgeoisie traced its origins to overseas commerce, which had created a wealthy commercial class (White 2009).

Industrialization had shifted production from farms and cottages to mills and factories, where mechanical power was available and where workers could be assembled to operate heavy machinery. The **bourgeoisie** owned the factories, mines, estates, and other means of production. Members of the **working class,** *or* **proletariat,** had to sell their labor to survive.

By promoting rural-to-urban migration, industrialization hastened the process of *proletarianization*—the separation of workers from the means of production. The bourgeoisie controlled not only factories but also schools, the press, and other key institutions. *Class consciousness* (personal identification and solidarity with one's economic group) was a vital part of Marx's view of class. He saw bourgeoisie and proletariat as having radically opposed interests. Marx viewed classes as powerful collective forces that could mobilize human energies to influence the course of history. Based on their common experience and interests, workers, he thought, would develop class consciousness, which could lead to revolutionary change.

Although England never experienced a proletarian revolution, workers did organize to protect their interests and increase their share of industrial profits. During the 19th century, trade unions and socialist parties emerged, expressing a rising anticapitalist spirit. This early English labor movement worked to remove young children from factories and limit the hours during which women and children could work. The profile of stratification in industrial core nations gradually took shape. Capitalists controlled production, but labor was organizing for better wages and working conditions. By 1900, many governments had factory regulation and social-welfare programs. Mass living standards in core nations rose as population grew.

Today, the existence of publicly traded companies complicates the division between capitalists and workers. Through pension plans and personal investments, some workers have become part-owners rather than propertyless workers. Today's key capitalist isn't the factory owner, who may have been replaced by stockholders, but the CEO or the chair of the board of directors, neither of whom may actually own the corporation.

The social theorist Max Weber faulted Karl Marx for an overly simple and exclusively economic view of stratification. Weber (1922/1968) looked beyond class and identified three (separate but correlated) dimensions of social stratification: wealth, power, and prestige. Weber also believed that social identities based on nationality, ethnicity, and religion could take priority over class (social identity based on economic status). In fact, the modern world system *is* cross-cut by collective identities based on nationality, ethnicity, and religion. Class conflicts tend to occur within nations, and nationalism has impeded global class solidarity, particularly of proletarians.

Although the capitalist class dominates politically in most countries, growing wealth has made it easier for core nations to benefit their workers. However, the improvement in core workers' living standards wouldn't have occurred without the world system. The wealth that flows from periphery and semiperiphery to core has helped core capitalists maintain their profits while satisfying the demands of core workers. In the periphery and semiperiphery, wages and living standards are lower. The current *world stratification system* features a substantial contrast between both capitalists and workers in the core nations, on the one hand, and workers on the periphery, on the other.

The Persistence of Inequality

Modern stratification systems aren't simple and dichotomous. They include (particularly in core and semiperiphery nations) a middle class of skilled and professional workers. Gerhard Lenski (1966) argued that social equality tends to increase in advanced industrial societies. The masses improve their access to economic benefits and political power. In Lenski's scheme, the shift of political power to the masses reflects the growth of the middle class, which reduces the polarization between owning and working classes. The proliferation of middle-class occupations creates opportunities for social mobility and a more complex stratification system (Giddens 1973; Kerbo 2012).

TABLE 12.1
U.S. National Income by Quintile, 2015

Source: Proctor, Bernadette D., Jessica L. Semega, and Melissa A. Kollar, 2016, "Income and Poverty in the United States: 2015". U.S. Census Bureau, *Current Population Reports, P60-256.* Washington, DC: U.S. Government Printing Office. Copyright, 2016

Segment of Population	% Share of National Income	Mean Household Income
Top 5 percent	22.1	$350,870
Top 20 percent	51.1	202,366
Second 20 percent	23.2	92,031
Third 20 percent	14.3	56,832
Fourth 20 percent	8.2	32,631
Bottom 20 percent	3.1	12,457

Wealth Distribution in the United States

Most contemporary Americans claim to belong to the middle class, which they tend to perceive as a vast, undifferentiated group. There are, however, significant, and growing, socioeconomic contrasts within the middle class, and especially between the richest and the poorest Americans. Table 12.1 shows how income varied from the top to the bottom fifths (quintiles) of American households in 2015. In that table, we see that the top fifth earned more than half of all income generated in the United States, 16 times the share of the bottom fifth. This 2015 ratio of 16:1 compares with 14:1 in 2000 and 11:1 in 1970. Figure 12.1 examines changes in mean (average) income over time—from 1967

FIGURE 12.1   Mean (Average) Household Income by Quintile and Top 5 Percent, 1967–2014

Source: DeNavas-Walt, C., and B. D. Proctor, "Table H-3: Mean Household Income Received by Each Fifth and Top 5 Percent, All Races: 1967–2014." Income and Poverty in the United States: 2014. U.S. Census Bureau, *Current Population Reports, P60-252.* Washington, DC: U.S. Government Printing Office, 2015

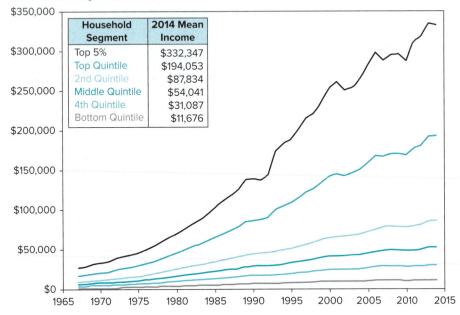

Household Segment	2014 Mean Income
Top 5%	$332,347
Top Quintile	$194,053
2nd Quintile	$87,834
Middle Quintile	$54,041
4th Quintile	$31,087
Bottom Quintile	$11,676

The presidential candidacy of "Democratic Socialist" Bernie Sanders (shown here at a 2016 rally at Philadelphia's Temple University) critiqued a system advantaging "millionaires and billionaires" and advocated a "political revolution." Did that happen? What demographic groups made up Sanders's constituency?
©Dominick Reuter/AFP/Getty Images

to 2014—for the five quintiles and top 5 percent of American households. Notice the much greater rise for the top quintile, and especially for the top 5 percent, compared with the bottom quintiles.

The top 1 percent have been especially favored, receiving about 95 percent of the income gains since the Great Recession of 2007–2009 ended. Higher stock prices, home values, and corporate profits propelled the recovery among affluent Americans, while blue- and white-collar workers continued to feel the effects of high unemployment and stagnant wages (Lowrey 2013).

When we consider wealth (investments, property, possessions, and the like) rather than income, the contrast is even more striking. Figure 12.2 shows that the top 1 percent of American families hold 39.8 percent of the nation's wealth (Coy 2014; Saez and Zucman 2014). The combined assets of the 16,000 ultra-rich families who comprise the top 0.01 percent hold assets equal to the total wealth of the bottom two-thirds of American families. Figure 12.2 also shows that the bottom 90 percent of American households hold barely a quarter (25.6 percent) of the nation's total wealth. Recognition of such disparities, and that the rich have been getting richer and the poor, poorer, led to the Occupy movement of 2011 and fueled Bernie Sanders's 2016 presidential campaign. Both the Occupy movement and the Sanders campaign drew attention to the lagging economic recovery for a majority of Americans.

Environmental Risks on the American Periphery

The nations on the periphery of the world system have the least economic development and political clout. Furthermore, within any given nation, certain regions and communities

FIGURE 12.2 **U.S. Distribution of Wealth, with a Breakdown of the Top 1 Percent into Three Groups—Rich, Very Rich, and Ultra-Rich**

See also Coy (2014) and Saez and Zucman (2014).

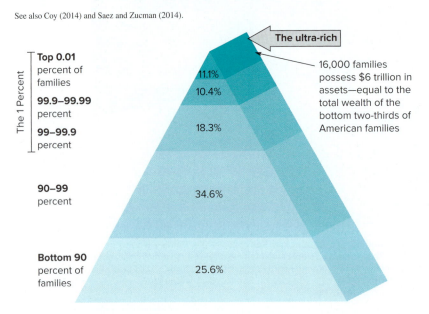

are similarly disadvantaged. One expression of this inequality is exposure to pollution and environmental hazards. Communities that are poorer and predominantly minority are more likely to be the victims of toxic waste exposure than are more affluent or even average (middle-class) communities.

News reports in 2015 and 2016 highlighted the plight of Flint, Michigan, whose water supply was seriously contaminated following a 2014 cost-cutting switch in its water source. The state of Michigan, which had seized control of Flint's city administration and budget from locally elected officials during a financial emergency, temporarily switched Flint's water source from Lake Huron and the Detroit River to the Flint River. The switch, which took place in April 2014, was to last until completion, in an estimated three years, of a new supply line from Lake Huron. The Flint River had a reputation for nastiness, and, soon after the switch, residents complained their water looked, smelled, and tasted funny (McLaughlin 2016).

Residents complained about myriad health problems, including skin rashes, hair loss, nausea, dizziness, and pain. A local pediatrician found that lead levels in Flint toddlers had doubled, and in some cases tripled, since the switch. After a research team confirmed the toxicity of Flint's water supply, officials finally abandoned the Flint River (Kozlowski 2016), switching back to the Detroit River and Lake Huron in October 2015. By this time, however, irreparable damage had been done not only to public health but also to the lead water pipes. The state responded by handing out filters and bottled water (McLaughlin 2016). Arguments erupted about who should fund the replacement of Flint's corroded water pipes. On January 5, 2016, Michigan governor Rick Snyder declared Flint to be in a state of emergency. Soon thereafter, President Barack Obama declared the city to be in a federal state of emergency, authorizing additional help from FEMA (the Federal Emergency Management Agency) and the Department of Homeland Security. As of this writing, residents of Flint have filed more than a dozen lawsuits, faulting various agencies and individuals, including the city of Flint, the state's Department of Environmental Quality, and Governor Snyder, for violating the U.S. Safe Drinking Water Act.

That this story of toxic endangerment happened in one of Michigan's least affluent cities is no accident. Throughout the United States (as in many other nations), environmental hazards disproportionately endanger poor and minority communities. Flint's population is 57 percent African American. Over 40 percent of its residents live below the poverty line, compared with state and national rates of 17 percent and 15 percent, respectively. One doubts that similar events would have played out in one of Michigan's affluent communities.

Research demonstrates that industries typically target minority and low-income neighborhoods when deciding where to locate polluting facilities (Erickson 2016). Environmental researchers Paul Mohai and Robin Saha (2015) analyzed 30 years of data on the placement of hazardous waste facilities in the United States. Their sample included 319 commercial hazardous waste treatment, storage, and disposal facilities built between 1966 and 1995. Their analysis revealed a clear pattern of racial and socioeconomic bias in the location of environmental hazards. Polluting facilities and other locally unwanted land uses were, and still are, located disproportionately in non-White and poor neighborhoods. These communities have fewer resources and political clout to oppose the location of such facilities. Flint's story has garnered headlines, but there are hundreds more stories waiting to be told about environmental threats on the American periphery.

Colonialism and Imperialism

The major forces influencing cultural interactions during the past 500 years have been commercial expansion, capitalism, and the dominance of colonial and core nations (Wallerstein 2004; Wolf 1982). **Colonialism** is the political, social, economic, and cultural domination of a territory and its people by a foreign power for an extended time. The colonial power establishes and maintains a presence in the dominated territory, in the form of colonists and administrative personnel (see Stoler, McGranahan, and Perdue 2007). **Imperialism** refers to a conscious policy of extending the rule of a country or an empire over foreign nations and of taking and holding foreign colonies (see Burbank and Cooper 2010). Imperialism goes back to early states, including Egypt in the Old World and the Incas in the New. A Greek empire was forged by Alexander the Great, and Julius Caesar and his successors spread the Roman empire. More recent examples include the British, French, and Soviet empires (see Burbank and Cooper 2010).

If imperialism is almost as old as the state, then colonialism can be traced back to the Phoenicians, who established colonies along the eastern Mediterranean 3,000 years ago. The ancient Greeks and Romans were avid colonizers as well as empire builders (see Pagden 2015; Stearns 2016).

The First Phase of European Colonialism: Spain and Portugal

The first phase of modern colonialism began with the European "Age of Discovery"—of the Americas and of a sea route to the Far East. During the 16th century, Spain, having conquered Mexico (the Aztec empire) and Peru-Bolivia (the Incas), explored and colonized widely in the Caribbean, the southern portions of what was to become the United States, and Central and South America. In the Pacific, Spain extended its rule to the Philippines and Guam. The Portuguese colonial empire included Brazil, South America's largest colonial territory; Angola and Mozambique in Africa; and Goa in South Asia. Rebellions and wars aimed at independence ended the first phase of European colonialism by the early 19th century. Brazil declared independence from Portugal in 1822. By 1825 most of Spain's colonies had gained their political independence. Spain held on to Cuba and the Philippines until 1898 but otherwise withdrew from the colonial field. During the first phase of colonialism, Spain and Portugal, along with Britain and France, were the major colonizing nations (see Herzog 2015). The last two (Britain and France) dominated the second phase of colonialism.

Commercial Expansion and European Imperialism

At an accelerating pace during the 19th century, European business interests sought markets overseas. This drive for commercial expansion led to European imperialism in Africa, Asia, and Oceania. During the second half of the 19th century, European imperial expansion was aided by improved transportation, which facilitated the colonization of vast areas of sparsely settled lands in Australia and the interior of North and South America. The new colonies purchased goods from the industrial centers and shipped back wheat, cotton, wool, mutton, beef, and leather. The first phase of European colonialism had been the exploration and exploitation of the Americas and the Caribbean, after Columbus. A second phase began as European nations competed for colonies between 1875 and 1914.

The British Colonial Empire

Like several other European nations, Britain had two stages of colonialism (see Darwin 2013). The first began with the Elizabethan voyages of the 16th century. During the 17th century, Britain acquired most of the eastern coast of North America, Canada's St. Lawrence basin, islands in the Caribbean, slave stations in Africa, and interests in India.

The British shared the exploration and early settlement of the New World with the Spanish, Portuguese, French, and Dutch. The British by and large left Mexico, along with Central and South America, to the Spanish and the Portuguese. The end of the Seven Years' War in 1763 forced a French retreat from most of Canada and India, where France previously had competed with Britain (Cody 1998). The American Revolution ended the first stage of British colonialism. India, Canada, and various Caribbean islands remained under British control.

The second stage of British colonialism—the British empire, on which the "sun never set," rose from the ashes of the first (see Black 2015). Beginning in 1788, but intensifying after 1815, the British settled Australia. Britain had acquired Dutch South Africa by 1815. By 1819 Singapore anchored a British trade network that extended to much of South Asia and along the coast of China. By this time, the empires of Britain's traditional rivals, particularly Spain, had been severely diminished in scope. Britain's position as imperial power and the world's leading industrial nation was unchallenged.

Britain's colonial expansion continued during the Victorian Era (1837–1901). Queen Victoria's prime minister Benjamin Disraeli guided a foreign policy justified by a view of imperialism as shouldering "the white man's burden"—a phrase coined by the poet Rudyard Kipling. People in the empire were seen as incapable of governing, so British guidance was needed to civilize and Christianize them. This paternalistic and racist doctrine was used to legitimize Britain's acquisition and control of parts of central Africa and Asia (Cooper 2014).

The British empire reached its maximum extent around 1914, when it covered a fifth of the world's land surface and ruled a fourth of its population (see Figure 12.3). After World War II, the British empire began to fall apart, with the rise of nationalist movements for independence. India gained its independence in 1947, as did the Republic of Ireland in 1949. The independence movement accelerated in Africa and Asia during the late 1950s (see Buettner 2016). Today, the ties that remain between Britain and its former colonies are mainly linguistic or cultural rather than political (Cody 1998).

French Colonialism

French colonialism also had two phases. The first began with the explorations of the early 1600s. Prior to the French revolution in 1789, missionaries, explorers, and traders carved out niches for France in Canada, the Louisiana territory, several Caribbean islands, and parts of India, which were lost along with Canada to Great Britain in 1763 (Harvey 1980).

FIGURE 12.3   **Map of the British Empire in 1765 and 1914**

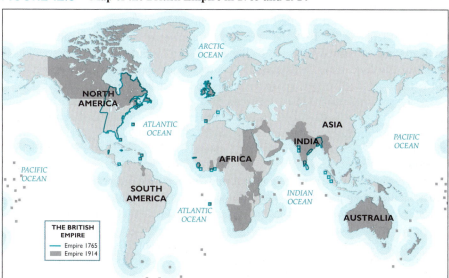

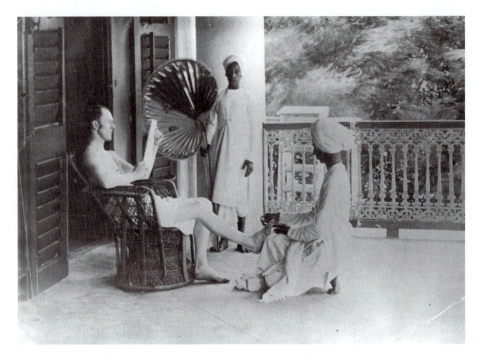

On January 1, 1900, a British officer in India receives a pedicure from a servant. What does this photo say to you about colonialism? Who gives pedicures in your society? ©Hulton Archive/ Getty Images

The foundations of the second French empire were established between 1830 and 1870. In Great Britain the drive for profit led expansion, but French colonialism was spurred more by the state, church, and armed forces than by pure business interests. France acquired Algeria and part of what eventually became Indochina (Cambodia, Laos, and Vietnam). By 1914 the French empire covered 4 million square miles and included some 60 million people (see Figure 12.4). By 1893, French rule had been fully established in Indochina. Tunisia and Morocco became French protectorates in 1883 and 1912, respectively (see Conklin, Fishman, and Zaretsky 2015).

To be sure, the French, like the British, had substantial business interests in their colonies, but they also sought, again like the British, international glory and prestige. The French promulgated a *mission civilisatrice,* their equivalent of Britain's "white man's burden." The goal was to implant French culture and language throughout the colonies.

The French used two forms of colonial rule: *indirect rule,* governing through native leaders and existing political structures, in areas with long histories of state organization, such as Morocco and Tunisia; and *direct rule* by French officials in many areas of Africa, where the French imposed new government structures to control diverse societies, many of them previously stateless. Like the British empire, the French empire began to disintegrate after World War II. France fought long—and ultimately futile—wars to keep its empire intact in Indochina and Algeria.

FIGURE 12.4   **Map of the French Empire at Its Height around 1914**

Source: Coy, Peter, "The Richest Rich Are in a Class By Theselves" *Bloomberg News,* April 3, 2014. Copyright © 2014 Bloomberg News.

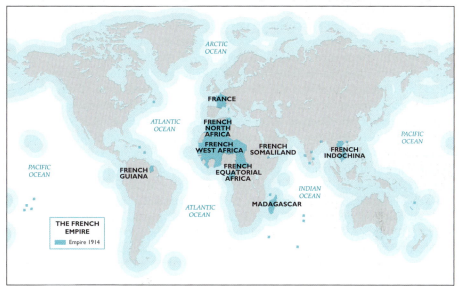

Colonialism and Identity

Many geopolitical labels in the news today had no equivalent meaning before colonialism. Whole countries, along with social groups and divisions within them, were colonial inventions. In West Africa, for example, by geographic logic, several adjacent countries could be one (Togo, Ghana, Ivory Coast, Guinea, Guinea-Bissau, Sierra Leone, Liberia). Instead, they are separated by linguistic, political, and economic contrasts promoted under colonialism.

Hundreds of ethnic groups and "tribes" are colonial constructions (see Ranger 1996). The Sukuma of Tanzania, for instance, were first registered as a single tribe by the colonial administration. Then missionaries standardized a series of dialects into a single Sukuma language, into which they translated the Bible and other religious texts, and which they taught in missionary schools. Over time this standardized the Sukuma language and ethnicity (Finnstrom 1997).

In the East African countries of Rwanda and Burundi, farmers and herders live in the same areas and speak the same language. Historically they have shared the same social world, although their social organization is "extremely hierarchical," almost "castelike" (Malkki 1995, p. 24). There has been a tendency to see the pastoral Tutsis as superior to the agricultural Hutus. Tutsis have been presented as nobles, Hutus as commoners. Yet when distributing identity cards in Rwanda, the Belgian colonizers simply identified all people with more than 10 head of cattle as Tutsi. Owners of fewer cattle were registered as Hutus (Bjuremalm 1997). Years later, these arbitrary colonial registers were used systematically for "ethnic" identification during the mass killings (genocide) that took place in Rwanda in 1994 (see Totten and Ubaldo 2011).

Postcolonial Studies

In anthropology, history, and literature, the field of postcolonial studies has gained prominence since the 1970s (see Ashcroft, Griffiths, and Tiffin 2013; Nayar 2016; Stoler, McGranahan, and Perdue 2013). **Postcolonial** studies focus on the past and present interactions between European nations and the societies they colonized (mainly after 1800). In 1914, European empires ruled more than 85 percent of the world (see Streets-Salter and Getz 2016). The term *postcolonial* also has been used to describe the second half of the 20th century in general, the period following colonialism. Even more generally, *postcolonial* may be used to signify a position against colonialism, imperialism, and Eurocentrism (Buettner 2016; Petraglia-Bahri 1996; Stoler et al. 2013).

The former colonies (*postcolonies*) can be divided into settler, nonsettler, and mixed (Petraglia-Bahri 1996). The settler countries, with large numbers of European colonists and sparser native populations, include Australia and Canada. Examples of nonsettler countries include India, Pakistan, Bangladesh, Sri Lanka, Malaysia, Indonesia, Nigeria, Senegal, Madagascar, and Jamaica. All these had substantial native populations and relatively few European settlers. Mixed countries include South Africa, Zimbabwe, Kenya, and Algeria. Such countries had significant European settlement despite having sizable native populations.

Given the varied experiences of such countries, *postcolonial* has to be a loose term. The United States, for instance, was colonized by Europeans and fought a war for independence from Britain. Is the United States a postcolony? It usually isn't perceived as such, given its current world power position, its treatment of Native Americans (sometimes called internal colonialism), and its annexation of other parts of the world. Research in postcolonial studies is growing, permitting a wide-ranging investigation of power relations in varied contexts. Broad topics in the field include the formation of empires, the impact of colonization, and the state of the postcolony today.

Development

During the Industrial Revolution, a strong current of thought viewed industrialization as a beneficial process of organic development and progress. Many economists still assume that industrialization increases production and income. They seek to create in today's "developing" countries a process like the one that first occurred spontaneously in 18th-century Great Britain.

We have seen that Britain used the notion of "the white man's burden" to justify its imperialist expansion and that France claimed to be engaged in a *mission civilisatrice,* a civilizing mission, in its colonies. Both these ideas illustrate an **intervention philosophy,** an ideological justification for outsiders to guide native peoples in specific directions. Economic development plans also have intervention philosophies. John Bodley (2012) argues that the basic belief behind interventions—whether by colonialists, missionaries, governments, or development planners—has been the same for more than one hundred years. This belief is that industrialization, Westernization, and individualism are desirable evolutionary advances that will bring long-term benefits to local people.

Neoliberalism

One currently influential intervention philosophy is neoliberalism. This term encompasses a set of assumptions that have become widespread during the past 30 years. Neoliberal policies are being implemented in developing nations, including postsocialist societies (e.g., those of the former Soviet Union). **Neoliberalism** is the current form of the classic economic liberalism laid out in Adam Smith's famous capitalist manifesto, *The Wealth of Nations,* published in 1776, soon after the Industrial Revolution. Smith advocated laissez-faire (hands-off) economics as the basis of capitalism: The government should stay out of its nation's economic affairs. Free, unregulated trade, Smith argued, is the best way for a nation's economy to develop. There should be no restrictions on manufacturing, no barriers to commerce, and no tariffs. This philosophy is called "liberalism" because it aims at liberating, or freeing, the economy from government controls. Economic liberalism encouraged "free" enterprise and competition, with the goal of generating profits. (Ironically, Adam Smith's liberalism is similar to today's capitalist "conservatism.")

Economic liberalism prevailed in the United States until President Franklin Roosevelt's New Deal during the 1930s. The Great Depression produced a turn to Keynesian economics, which challenged liberalism. John Maynard Keynes (1927, 1936) insisted that full employment was necessary for capitalism to grow, that governments and central banks should intervene to increase employment, and that government should promote the common good.

Especially since the fall of Communism (1989–1991), there has been a revival of neoliberalism, which has been spreading globally. Around the world, neoliberal policies have been imposed by powerful financial institutions such as the International Monetary Fund (IMF), the World Bank, and the Inter-American Development Bank (see Edelman and Haugerud 2005). Neoliberalism entails open (tariff- and barrier-free) international trade and investment. Profits are sought through the lowering of costs, whether through improving productivity, automating, laying off workers, or seeking workers who accept lower wages. In exchange for loans, the governments of postsocialist and developing nations have been required to accept the neoliberal premise that deregulation leads to economic growth, which will eventually benefit everyone through a process sometimes called "trickle down." Accompanying the belief in free markets and the idea of cutting costs is a tendency to impose austerity measures that cut government expenses. This can entail reduced public spending on education, health care, and other social services.

Neoliberalism and NAFTA's Economic Refugees

Most Americans are aware that there has been large-scale Mexican migration to the United States since the 1990s. Most are unaware, however, that the migratory balance has shifted in recent years. Between 2009 and 2014, the number of Mexicans returning to Mexico actually exceeded the number entering the United States (Gonzalez-Barrera 2015). Americans also are familiar with rhetoric (especially during and after the 2016 presidential campaigns) about negative effects of trade agreements on American workers. Much less common is knowledge about how the North American Free Trade Agreement (NAFTA) has been harmful to Mexico. Anthropologist Ana Aurelia López (2011) argues convincingly that international forces, including new technologies and NAFTA,

Demonstrators in Mexico City protest NAFTA's removal of import tariffs on farm goods entering Mexico from the United States and Canada. ©Eduardo Verdugo/AP Images

have destroyed traditional Mexican farming systems, degraded agricultural land, and displaced Mexican farmers and small-business people—thereby fueling the migration of millions of undocumented Mexicans to the United States. The following account is a synopsis of her findings.

For thousands of years, Mexican farmers grew corn (maize) in a sustainable manner. Generation after generation, farmers selected diverse strains of corn well adapted to a huge variety of specific microclimates. Mexico became a repository of corn genetic diversity for the world. When corn grown elsewhere developed disease or pest susceptibility or was of poor quality, Mexico provided other countries with genetically superior plants.

Before NAFTA, Mexico supported its farmers by buying a portion of their harvest each year at an elevated cost through price supports. This corn went to a countrywide chain of successful CONASUPO (Compañía Nacional de Subsistencias Populares) stores, which sold corn and other staple foodstuffs below market price to the urban and rural poor. Tariffs protected Mexican farmers from the entrance of foreign corn, such as that grown in the United States.

The first assault on Mexico's sustainable farming culture began in the 1940s when "Green Revolution" technologies were introduced, including seeds that required chemical inputs (e.g., fertilizers). The Mexican government encouraged farmers to replace their traditional, genetically diverse *maíz crillo* ("creole corn") with the genetically homogenized *maíz mejorado* ("improved corn"), a hybrid from the United States. Agrochemical companies initially supplied the required chemical inputs free of charge.

Company representatives visited rural villages and offered free samples of seeds and agrochemicals to a few farmers. As news of unusually large first-year crops spread, other farmers abandoned their traditional corn strains for the "improved," chemically dependent corn. As the transition accelerated, the price of both the new seeds and the associated chemical inputs began to rise and kept on rising. Eventually farmers no longer could afford either the seeds or the required agrochemicals. When cash-strapped farmers tried to return to planting their former *maíz criollo* seeds, the plants would grow but corn would not appear. Only the hybrid seeds from the United States would produce corn on the chemically altered soils. Today over 60 percent of Mexico's farmland is degraded due to the spread of agrochemicals—chemical fertilizers and pesticides. (This chapter's "Anthropology Today" describes another case of environmental degradation due to chemical pollution, with mining as the culprit.)

NAFTA, the "free trade" agreement that went into effect in 1994, produced another major assault on traditional Mexican farming. Loan agreements needed to implement NAFTA forced Mexico to restructure its economy along neoliberal lines. The government had to end its price supports for corn grown by small-scale farmers. Also ended were Mexico's CONASUPO food stores, which had benefited the rural and urban poor.

These terminations caused considerable harm to Mexico's farmers and its urban and rural poor. American agricultural industries, by contrast, have benefited from NAFTA. The U.S. government continues to subsidize its own corn farmers, who otherwise would go out of business. Prior to NAFTA, Mexico's tariffs made the sale of U.S. corn in Mexico unprofitable. Under NAFTA, Mexico's corn tariffs were phased out, and corn from the United States began flooding the Mexican markets.

The NAFTA economy offers Mexico's small-scale corn farmers few options: (1) stay in rural Mexico and suffer, (2) look for work in a Mexican city, or (3) migrate to the United States in search of work. NAFTA did not create a common labor market (i.e., the ability of Mexicans, Americans, and Canadians to move freely across each country's borders and work legally anywhere in North America). Nor did NAFTA make provisions for the predicted 15 million Mexican corn farmers who would be forced off the land as a result of the trade agreement. As could have been expected (and planned for), millions of Mexicans migrated to the United States.

Because of NAFTA, Mexican corn farmers have fled the countryside, and U.S.-subsidized corn has flooded the Mexican market. A declining number of traditional farmers remain to plant and conserve Mexico's unique corn varieties. Between one-third and one-half of Mexico's corn now is imported from the United States, much of it by U.S.-based Archer-Daniels-Midland, the world's largest corporate corn exporter. NAFTA also has facilitated the entrance of other giant U.S. corporations into Mexico: Walmart, Dow Agribusiness, Monsanto, Marlboro, and Coca-Cola. These multinationals, in turn, have displaced many small Mexican businesses, creating yet another wave of immigrants—former shopkeepers and their employees—to the United States.

We can summarize the impact of NAFTA on the Mexican economy: destroying traditional small-scale farming, degrading farmland, displacing farmers and small-business people, and fueling massive migration to the United States. In migrating, these millions of economic refugees have faced daunting challenges, including separation from their families and homeland, dangerous border crossings, and the ever-present possibility of deportation from the United States. As of this writing, under American President, Donald J. Trump, their fate has become even more uncertain.

Within today's world system, comparable effects of neoliberal policies extend well beyond Mexico. As contemporary forces of globalization transform rural landscapes worldwide, rural–urban and transnational migration have become global phenomena. Over and over again, Green Revolution technologies have transformed subsistence into cash economies, fueling a need for money to acquire foreign inputs while hooking the land on chemicals, reducing genetic diversity and sustainability, and forcing the poorest farmers off the land. Few Americans are aware, specifically, of NAFTA's role in ending a 7,000-year-old sustainable farming culture and displacing millions of Mexicans and, more generally, that comparable developments are happening all over the world.

Communism, Socialism, and Postsocialism

The labels *First World, Second World,* and *Third World* represent a common, although ethnocentric, way of categorizing nations. The *First World* refers to the "democratic West"—traditionally conceived in opposition to a *Second World* ruled by Communism. The *Second World* refers to the former Soviet Union and the socialist and once-socialist countries of Eastern Europe and Asia. Proceeding with this classification, the "less-developed countries," or "developing nations," make up the *Third World.*

Communism

The two meanings of communism involve how it is written, whether with a lowercase (small) or an uppercase (large) *c.* Small-*c* **communism** describes a social system in which property is owned by the community and in which people work for the common good. Large-*C* **Communism** was a political movement and doctrine seeking to overthrow capitalism and to establish a form of communism such as that which prevailed in the Soviet Union (USSR) from 1917 to 1991. The heyday of Communism was a 40-year period from 1949 to 1989, when more Communist regimes existed than at any time before or after. Today only 5 Communist states remain—China, Cuba, Laos, North Korea, and Vietnam, compared with 23 in 1985.

Communism, which originated with Russia's Bolshevik Revolution in 1917 and took its inspiration from Karl Marx and Friedrich Engels, was not uniform over time or among countries. All Communist systems were *authoritarian* (promoting obedience to authority rather than individual freedom). Many were *totalitarian* (banning rival parties and demanding total submission of the individual to the state). The Communist Party monopolized power in every Communist state, and relations within the party were highly centralized and strictly disciplined. Communist nations had state ownership, rather than private ownership, of the means of production. Finally, all Communist regimes, with the goal of advancing communism, cultivated a sense of belonging to an international movement (Brown 2001).

Postsocialist Transitions

Socialism is a sociopolitical organization and economic system in which the means of production are owned and controlled by the government, rather than by individuals or corporations. Because of their state ownership, Communist nations were also socialist, and their successors are referred to as postsocialist. Neoliberal economists assumed that dismantling and privatizing the Soviet Union's planned economy would raise gross domestic product (GDP) and living standards. The goal was to enhance production by substituting a free market system and providing incentives through privatization. In October 1991, Boris Yeltsin, who had been elected president of Russia that June, announced a program of radical market-oriented reform, pursuing a postsocialist changeover to capitalism. Yeltsin's program of "shock therapy" cut subsidies to farms and industries and ended price controls. During the 1990s, postsocialist Russia endured a series of disruptions, leading to declines in its GDP, average life expectancy, and birthrate, as well as increased poverty. In 2008–2009, Russia shared in the global recession after 10 years of economic growth, but its economy recuperated rapidly and was growing again by 2010, as were its birthrate and average life expectancy. The poverty rate has fallen substantially since the late 1990s but recently has been on the rise—even as Moscow is home to more billionaires than New York City or London (Rapoza 2012). The 2014 Russian poverty rate of 13.4 percent was a bit below the American rate of 14.8 percent the same year.

The World System Today

The spread of industrialization continues today, although nations have shifted their positions within the world system. By 1900, the United States had become a core nation, having overtaken Great Britain in iron, coal, and cotton production. In a few decades (1868–1900), Japan changed from a medieval handicraft economy to an industrial one, joining the semiperiphery by 1900 and moving to the core between 1945 and 1970. India and China have joined Brazil as leaders of the semiperiphery. The map in Figure 12.5 shows the world system today.

Twentieth-century industrialization added hundreds of new industries and millions of new jobs. Production increased, often beyond immediate demand, spurring strategies, such as advertising, to sell everything industry could churn out. Mass production gave rise to a culture of consumption, which valued acquisitiveness and conspicuous consumption.

How do things stand today? Worldwide, young people are abandoning traditional subsistence pursuits and seeking cash. A popular song once queried "How're you gonna keep 'em down on the farm after they've seen Paree?" Nowadays most people *have* seen Paree—Paris, that is—along with other world capitals, maybe not in person but in print or on-screen. Young people today are better educated and wiser in the ways of the world than ever before. Increasingly they are exposed to the material and cultural promises of a better life away from the farm. They seek paying jobs, but work is scarce, spurring migration within and across national boundaries. If they can't get cash legally, they seek it illegally.

Recently, job opportunities have diminished in core nations, including the United States and Western Europe. As the United States struggled to emerge from the recession of 2007–2009, its stock market tripled, from a low of 6,443 on March 6, 2009, to over 20,000 as of this writing. In what many observers saw as a "jobless recovery," corporations held on to their profits, rather than using them to hire new workers. In a global economy, profitability doesn't necessarily come from hiring workers who are fellow

FIGURE 12.5 **The World System Today**

Source: Kottak, Conrad, *Anthropology,* 10th ed. New York, NY: McGraw-Hill Education, 2004, fig 23.5, p. 660. Copyright © 2004. Used with permission of McGraw-Hill Education.

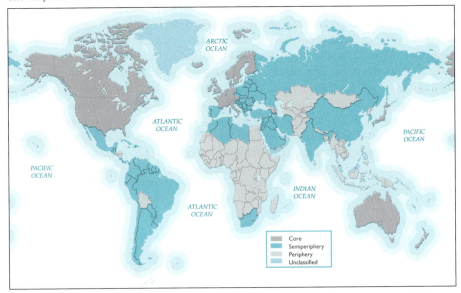

citizens. Jobs continue to be outsourced. Machines and information technology continue to replace people. Corporations, from airlines to banks, offer their customers incentives to bypass humans. Even outside the industrial world, but especially within it, the Internet allows an increasing number of people to buy plane tickets, print boarding passes, rent cars, reserve hotel rooms, move money, or pay bills online. Amazon has become a virtual department store that threatens to send not only "mom and pop" shops but even national chains such as Barnes and Noble, Office Depot, Radio Shack, and Sears into oblivion. Nowadays, when one does manage to speak by phone to a human, that person is as likely to be in Mumbai or Manila as Minneapolis or Miami.

Companies claim, with some justification, that labor unions limit their flexibility, adaptability, and profitability. American corporations (and the politicians who represent them) have become more ideologically opposed to unions and more aggressive in discouraging unionization. Unions still bring benefits to their workers. Median weekly earnings for union members—$1004 in 2016—remain higher than those of nonunion workers—$802 (U.S. Bureau of Labor Statistics 2017). Still, union membership in the United States has fallen to its lowest point in more than 70 years. The unionized percentage of the American workforce fell to 10.7 percent in 2016, compared with 20.1 percent in 1983 and a high of 35 percent during the mid-1950s. The number of unionized private-sector workers increased from 7.1 million in 2010 to 7.4 million in 2016, while the number of public-sector union members declined from 7.6 million to 7.1 million. This mainly reflected growth in private-sector jobs, while jobs in the public sector were being reduced (U.S. Bureau of Labor Statistics 2017). What jobs do you know that are unionized? How likely is it that you will join a union?

Anthropology Today   *Mining Giant Compatible with Sustainability Institute?*

The spread of industrialization has contributed to the destruction of indigenous economies, ecologies, and populations. Riverine discharges from the Ok Tedi mine, described here, have severely harmed about 50,000 people living in more than 100 villages downstream. Today, multinational corporations, along with the governments of nations such as Papua New Guinea (PNG), are accelerating the process of resource depletion that began with the Industrial Revolution. Fortunately, however, today's world also contains environmental watchdogs, including concerned anthropologists, lawyers, and NGOs. Described here is a conundrum faced by a major public university. Are multinational corporations whose operations have destroyed the landscapes and livelihoods of indigenous peoples proper advisers for an institute devoted to ecological sustainability?

In the 1990s, the giant mining company now known as BHP Billiton drew worldwide condemnation for the environmental damage caused by its copper and gold mine in Papua New Guinea. Its mining practices destroyed the way of life of thousands of farming and fishing families who lived along and subsisted on the rivers polluted by the mine, and it was only after being sued in a landmark class-action case that the company agreed to compensate them.

Today several activists and academics who work on behalf of indigenous people around the world say the company continues to dodge responsibility for the problems its mines create. . . .

Yet at the University of Michigan at Ann Arbor, BHP Billiton . . . is one of 14 corporate members of an External Advisory Board for the university's new Graham Environmental Sustainability Institute.

Critics at and outside the university contend that Michigan's decision to enlist BHP Billiton as an adviser to an institute devoted to sustainability reflects badly on the institution and allows the company to claim [an undeserved] mantle of environmental and social responsibility. . . .

The arguments echo the discussions about corporate "greenwashing" that have arisen at Stanford University and the University of California at Berkeley over major research grants from ExxonMobil and BP, respectively. . . .

For one BHP Billiton critic at Michigan, the issue is personal. Stuart Kirsch, a professor of anthropology, has spent most of his academic career documenting the damage caused by BHP Billiton's Ok Tedi mine in Papua New Guinea. . . .

Mr. Kirsch, who first visited some of the affected communities as a young ethnographer in 1987, became involved in the class-action lawsuit brought against the company and helped villagers participate in the 1996 legal settlement. "I put my career on hold while being an activist," he says.

He subsequently published several papers related to his work with the Yonggom people as they fought for recognition and compensation from mine operators—scholarship that helped him win tenure. . . . He remains involved with the network of activists and academics who follow mining and its impact on undeveloped communities around the world. . . .

The company's practices polluted the Ok Tedi and Fly Rivers and caused thousands of people to leave their homes because the mining-induced flooding made

continued

Anthropology Today *continued*

it impossible for them to grow food to feed themselves, says Mr. Kirsch.

BHP Billiton, based in Australia, later acknowledged that the mine was "not compatible with our environmental values," and spun it off to an independent company that pays all of its mining royalties to the government of Papua New Guinea.

But Mr. Kirsch says that in doing so, the company skirted responsibility for ameliorating the damage it caused. BHP Billiton says it would have preferred to close the mine, but the Papua New Guinea government, in need of the mine revenues, pressed to keep it open. The deal freed BHP Billiton from any future liabilities for environmental damage. . . .

Illtud Harri, a BHP Billiton spokesman, says the company regrets its past with Ok Tedi but considers its pullout from the mine "a responsible exit" that left in place a system that supports educational, agricultural, and social programs for the people of the community. . . .

BHP Billiton, a company formed from the 2001 merger of the Australian mining enterprise Broken Hill Proprietary Company with London-based Billiton, is now the world's largest mining company, with more than 100 operations in 25 countries. . . .

The BHP Billiton charter includes a statement that the company has "an overriding commitment to health, safety, environmental responsibility, and sustainable development." But its critics say the company continues to play a key role in mining projects with questionable records on environmental and human rights, even though in many of those cases, it is not directly responsible. . . .

BHP Billiton has the resources to present itself as the "golden boy," but, says Mr. Kirsch, "it's much harder to see the people on the Ok Tedi and Fly rivers."

A forum could help to right that imbalance, he says. "Let the students and faculty decide whether this is an appropriate company to advise the University of Michigan," says Mr. Kirsch. "It would be an educational process for everyone involved."

Update: As of this writing (2017), BHP Billiton no longer is listed as a member of the advisory board of Michigan's Graham Institute. And in Papua New Guinea, after BHP Billiton transferred its ownership of the mine to Ok Tedi Mining Limited, that independent company has spent more than a billion dollars on environmental remediation. The 1996 settlement decreed that BHP would be spared future legal claims in return for giving all its shares to the people of PNG. Those shares are now held in trust (valued at over $1 billion, and growing) in a Singapore-based entity, PNG Sustainable Development Program Limited. The mission of that trust is to promote development in PNG's Western Province, where the mine is located, and across PNG. Today, the provincial and national governments of PNG and the PNG Sustainable Development Program are the only shareholders of Ok Tedi Mining Limited, which pays all its royalties to the PNG government. For hundreds of miles down the Fly River, fishers and farmers still complain about the destruction of their habitat, even as the Ok Tedi mine supplies about 16 percent of PNG's national revenue.

Sources: Goldie Blumenstyk, "Mining Company Involved in Environmental Disaster Now Advises Sustainability Institute at U. of Michigan," *Chronicle of Higher Education,* December 7, 2007. Copyright © 2007, The Chronicle of Higher Education. Reprinted with permission; http://www.radioaustralia.net.au/pacific/radio/program/pacific-beat/documentary-special-ok-tedi/1069558; Stuart Kirsch (personal communication).

Summary

1. Local societies increasingly participate in wider systems—regional, national, and global. The capitalist world economy depends on production for sale, with the goal of maximizing profits. The key claim of world-system theory is that an identifiable social system, based on wealth and power differentials, extends beyond individual countries. That system is formed by a set of economic and political relations that has characterized much of the globe since the 16th century. World capitalism has political and economic specialization at the core, semiperiphery, and periphery.

2. Columbus's voyages opened the way for a major exchange between the Old and New Worlds. Seventeenth-century plantation economies in the Caribbean and Brazil were based on sugar. In the 18th century, plantation economies based on cotton arose in the southeastern United States.

3. The Industrial Revolution began in England around 1760. Transoceanic commerce supplied capital for industrial investment. Industrialization hastened the separation of workers from the means of production. Marx saw a sharp division between the bourgeoisie and the proletariat. Class consciousness was a key feature of Marx's view of this stratification. Weber believed that social solidarity based on ethnicity, religion, race, or nationality could take priority over class. Today's capitalist world economy maintains the contrast between those who own the means of production and those who don't, but the division is now worldwide. There is a substantial contrast between not only capitalists but workers in the core nations and workers on the periphery.

4. Inequality in measures of income and wealth has been increasing in the United States. Another aspect of inequality is in exposure to environmental risks such as pollution and hazardous waste facilities. Communities that are poorer and predominantly minority, such as Flint, Michigan, are most likely to be the victims of toxic waste exposure.

5. Imperialism is the conscious policy of extending the rule of a nation or an empire over other nations and of taking and holding foreign colonies. Colonialism is the domination of a territory and its people by a foreign power for an extended time. European colonialism had two main phases. The first started in 1492 and lasted through 1825. For Britain this phase ended with the American Revolution. For France it ended when Britain won the Seven Years' War, forcing the French to abandon Canada and India. For Spain, it ended with Latin American independence. The second phase of European colonialism extended approximately from 1850 to 1950. The British and French empires were at their height around 1914, when European empires controlled 85 percent of the world. Britain and France had colonies in Africa, Asia, Oceania, and the New World.

6. Many geopolitical labels and identities were created under colonialism that had little or nothing to do with existing social demarcations. The new ethnic or national divisions were colonial inventions, sometimes aggravating conflicts.

7. Like colonialism, economic development has an intervention philosophy that provides a justification for outsiders to guide native peoples toward particular goals.

Development usually is justified by the idea that industrialization and modernization are desirable evolutionary advances. Neoliberalism revives and extends classic economic liberalism: the idea that governments should not regulate private enterprise and that free market forces should rule. This intervention philosophy currently dominates aid agreements with postsocialist and developing nations.

8. Spelled with a lowercase *c*, *communism* describes a social system in which property is owned by the community and in which people work for the common good. Spelled with an uppercase *C*, *Communism* indicates a political movement and doctrine seeking to overthrow capitalism and to establish a form of communism such as that which prevailed in the Soviet Union from 1917 to 1991. The heyday of Communism was between 1949 and 1989. The fall of Communism can be traced to 1989–1990 in Eastern Europe and 1991 in the Soviet Union. Postsocialist states have followed the neoliberal agenda, through privatization, deregulation, and democratization.

9. By 1900 the United States had become a core nation. Mass production gave rise to a culture that valued acquisitiveness and conspicuous consumption. As subsistence economies yield increasingly to cash, job seeking and unemployment have become global problems. One effect of industrialization has been an accelerated rate of resource depletion.

Think Like an Anthropologist

1. According to world-system theory, societies are subsystems of bigger systems, with the world system as the largest. What are the various systems, at different levels, in which you participate?

2. To what extent is the following statement still true: "The wealth that flows from periphery and semi-periphery to core has helped core capitalists maintain their profits while satisfying the demands of core workers." Are core workers still satisfied? What factors might diminish their level of satisfaction?

Key Terms

bourgeoisie, *276*
capital, *272*
capitalist world
    economy, *272*
colonialism, *281*
communism, *290*
Communism, *290*
core, *272*

imperialism, *281*
Industrial
    Revolution, *274*
intervention
    philosophy, *286*
neoliberalism, *287*
periphery, *273*
postcolonial, *286*

semiperiphery, *272*
socialism, *290*
working class, or
    proletariat, *276*
world-system
    theory, *272*

Chapter 13

Anthropology's Role in a Globalizing World

Globalization: Its Meanings and Its Nature

This chapter applies an anthropological perspective to contemporary global issues. Let's begin by reviewing two different meanings of the term *globalization.* As used in this book, the primary meaning of globalization is *worldwide connectedness.* Modern systems of production, distribution, consumption, finance, transportation, and communication are global in scope. A second meaning of globalization is political; it has to do with ideology, policy, and neoliberalism (see Kotz 2015). In this more limited sense, globalization refers to efforts by international financial powers to create a global *free market* for goods and services. This second, political meaning of globalization has generated and continues to generate significant opposition. In this book, *globalization* is a neutral term for the fact of global connectedness and linkages, rather than any kind of political position (see also Eriksen 2014; Ervin 2014).

This connectedness generates policies, practices, and risks that have global implications. After a discussion of today's global economy, we turn to a discussion of energy consumption and environmental degradation, including climate change, or global warming. Also considered in this chapter are the threats that deforestation and emerging diseases pose to global biodiversity and human life. The second half of this chapter turns from economy and ecology to the contemporary flows of people, technology, information, messages, images, and ideology that contribute to a global culture of consumption. Part of globalization is intercultural communication, through the media (including the Internet), travel, and migration, which increasingly bring people from different societies into direct contact. Finally, we'll consider how such contacts and external linkages affect indigenous peoples, as well as how those groups have organized to confront and deal with national and global issues.

Our Global Economy

Economic systems (as we saw in the chapter "Making a Living," are based on production, distribution, and consumption. All these processes now have global, and increasingly impersonal, dimensions. The products, images, and information we consume each day can come from anywhere. How likely is it that the item you last bought from a website, an outlet, or a retail store was made in the United States, rather than Canada, Mexico, Peru, or China? The national has become international. Consider just a few of the familiar "American" brands that now have foreign ownership: Budweiser, Good Humor, Ben and Jerry's, Burger King, Caribou Coffee, Church's Chicken, Holiday Inn, 7-Eleven,

A scene from an Amazon warehouse on a Cyber Monday, the busiest day of the year for online shoppers. This warehouse could be in a lot of places, but it happens to be in Great Britain.
©Geoffrey Robinson/Alamy Stock Photo

Gerber, Purina, Adidas, Frigidaire, and Firestone. Half of the U.S. national debt now belongs to outsiders, compared with a mere 5 percent in 1970 (Bartlett 2010).

The Internet is a vital organ in our 21st-century global economy. All kinds of products—music, movies, clothing, appliances, this book, you name it—are produced, distributed, and consumed via the Internet. Economic functions that are spatially dispersed (perhaps continents apart) are coordinated online in real time. Activities that once involved face-to-face contact are now conducted impersonally, often across vast distances. When you order something via the Internet, the only human being you might speak to is the delivery driver. However, even that human contact may be replaced by a drone. The computers that take and process your order from Amazon can be on different continents. The products you order can come from a warehouse anywhere in the world (see Kennedy 2010).

Multinationals attempt to forge beneficial alliances with politicians and government officials, especially those who are most concerned with world trade. With the globalization of finance, nations have less control over their own economies. Institutions such as the World Bank, the International Monetary Fund, the European Union, and the European Central Bank routinely constrain and dictate national economic policies. Ask Greeks how they feel about austerity measures imposed by outsiders.

As capitalism has spread globally, the gap between rich and poor has widened both within and between nations (see Hirai 2015). The difference in per-capita income between the world's richest nation (Qatar) and the poorest nation (Central African Republic) was 233 to 1 in 2015, versus around 5 to 1 when the Industrial Revolution began (Pasquali 2016).

Energy Consumption and Industrial Degradation

Industrialization entailed a shift from reliance on renewable resources to the use of fossil fuels. Earth's supply of oil, gas, and coal is being depleted to support a previously unknown level of consumption. Americans are the world's foremost consumers of nonrenewable energy. The average American consumes about 35 times more energy than the average forager or tribesperson (Bodley 2015).

Table 13.1 compares energy consumption, total and per-capita, in the United States and selected other countries—the top 10 consumers of energy. Overall the United States, which ranks second among the countries, represents about 16 percent of the world's annual energy consumption. China ranks first, accounting for 23 percent of global energy consumption. However, North Americans—Canadians and Americans—rank first and second in per-capita consumption. The average American consumes three times the energy used by the average Chinese and nine times the energy used by the average inhabitant of India. Consumption has been rising in China and India, while declining a bit in the United States and Canada, and more dramatically in Europe.

Many contemporary nations are repeating—at an accelerated rate—the process of resource depletion that began in Europe and the United States during the Industrial Revolution. Fortunately, however, today's world has some environmental watchdogs that did not exist during the Industrial Revolution. Given the appropriate political will,

	Total	Per Capita
World	13,423	1.8
China	3,101	2.2
United States	2,196	6.7
India	882	.7
Russia	718	5.2
Japan	435	3.4
Germany	305	3.7
Brazil	299	1.4
South Korea	280	5.7
Canada	251	7.2
France	246	4.0

TABLE 13.1
Total Energy Consumption, 2015, Top Ten Countries (in MTOE—Million Tons of Oil Equivalent)

Source: *Global Energy Statistical Yearbook,* © 2016 Enerdata.

leading to national and international cooperation and sanctions, the modern world may benefit from the lessons of the past (see Hornborg, McNeill, and Martinez-Alier 2007).

There are, however, new dangers in today's world, some of which have become worldwide in scope. Accompanying globalization are significant risks that can spread rapidly beyond individual countries. Thanks to modern transportation systems, diseases that break out in one part of the world can quickly become global threats. Who can forget the Ebola threat of 2014, or Zika in 2015–2016? Furthermore, along with the actual threat that a disease might go global is the heightened risk perception, augmented by the media, that makes people think that anyone anywhere might succumb to a disease that is confined almost entirely to a particular region. Another global threat, which can spread even faster than a disease, is a cyberattack. We should fear cyber viruses as well as real viruses. We have become so reliant on the Internet that anything that might seriously impede the flow of information in cyberspace would have worldwide repercussions. Dangers that can affect people anywhere and everywhere on the planet are part of a *globalization of risk*. Risks are no longer merely local, like the Flint, Michigan, water crisis, or regional, like the California drought. They have become global in scope. People tend to worry more about short-term threats, such as toxic water or Ebola, and middle-term dangers, such as terrorism, than about long-term threats such as global climate change.

Global Climate Change

Each consumer of fossil fuels makes his or her individual contribution (that consumer's "carbon footprint") to global climate change. The fact that there are now about 7.5 billion of those "footprints" has major global significance. The year 2016 surpassed 2015 as the world's hottest year on record (Patel 2017). One reason for the heat was an unusually large El Niño weather pattern, which pumped a substantial amount of heat into the atmosphere. Even more significant has been the long-term planetary warming caused by human emissions of greenhouse gases (Gillis 2016b).

The **greenhouse effect** is a natural phenomenon that keeps the Earth's surface warm. The greenhouse gases include water vapor (H_2O), carbon dioxide (CO_2), methane (CH_4), nitrous oxide (N_2O), halocarbons, and ozone (O_3). Without those gases, life as we know it wouldn't exist. Like a greenhouse window, those gases allow sunlight to enter the atmosphere and then trap heat, preventing it from escaping.

The amount of carbon dioxide in the atmosphere has fluctuated naturally in the past. Every time it increases, the Earth heats up, ice melts, and sea levels rise. Since the Industrial Revolution, humans have been pumping carbon dioxide into the air faster than nature ever did (Gillis 2015). All greenhouse gases have increased since the Industrial Revolution. In fact, the atmospheric concentration of greenhouse gases is now at its highest level in 400,000 years. It will continue to rise, as will global temperatures, without actions to slow it down (National Academy of Sciences 2008; National Research Council 2011).

Global temperatures have risen about 1.8°F since 1880 (Gillis 2016a). This increase is not due to increased solar radiation. The causes are mainly **anthropogenic**—caused by humans and their activities. Who can reasonably deny that over 7 billion people, along with their animals, crops, machines, and increasing use of fossil fuels, have a greater environmental impact than the 5 million or so pre-Neolithic hunter-gatherers estimated to have lived on our planet 12,000 years ago?

Scientists prefer the term **climate change** to *global warming*. The former term points out that, beyond rising temperatures, there have been changes in storm patterns, ecosystem effects, and especially sea levels. The ocean is extremely sensitive to small fluctuations in the Earth's temperature. During the 19th century, as industrialization proceeded, sea levels began to rise; they have climbed about 8 inches since 1880 (Gillis 2016a). The Intergovernmental Panel on Climate Change, a United Nations body that reviews and summarizes climate research, has estimated that continued high emissions are likely to produce a rise in sea level of 1.7 to 3.2 feet during the 21st century (Gillis 2016a). One consequence of rising sea levels has been a worsening of tidal flooding in coastal communities, including the East coast of the United States. In the decade between 1955 and 1964, a tide gauge at Annapolis, Maryland, measured 32 days of flooding. Fifty years later, in the decade between 2005 and 2014, that figure jumped to 394 days. In Charleston, South Carolina, flood days increased from 34 in the earlier decade to 219 between 2005 and 2014 (Gillis 2016a).

The precise effects of climate change on regional weather patterns have yet to be fully determined (see DiMento and Doughman 2014). Land areas are predicted to warm more than oceans, with the greatest warming in higher latitudes, such as Canada, the northern United States, northern Europe, and Russia. Climate change may benefit these areas, offering milder winters and extended growing seasons. However, many more people worldwide probably will be harmed (see Cribb 2010). Already we know that in the Arctic, temperatures have risen almost twice as much as the global average. Arctic landscapes and ecosystems are changing rapidly and perceptibly, creating hundreds of "climate refugees" in areas of Alaska where the permafrost is melting and indigenous villages are sinking below sea level (see Yardley 2007). Coastal communities worldwide can anticipate increased flooding and more severe storms and surges. At risk are people, animals, plants, freshwater supplies, and such industries as tourism and farming.

Global energy demand is the single greatest obstacle to slowing down climate change. Worldwide, energy consumption continues to grow with economic and population expansion. China and India, in particular, are rapidly increasing their use of energy,

In the global economy, India (shown here) and China in particular have increased their use of fossil fuels and, consequently, their emissions of CO_2. This photo shows school children in New Delhi on November 3, 2016, when a blanket of heavy smog sent air pollution to dangerous levels. Some 16 million people had to breathe this toxic air. Experts warned of severe health problems for children forced to attend school. What's the most polluted place you've ever been to? ©Arvind Yadav/*Hindustan Times* via Getty Images

mainly from fossil fuels, and consequently their emissions. Their cities, most notably Beijing and New Delhi, are now among the most polluted in the world. China currently accounts for about 23 percent of world energy consumption, compared with 9 percent in 2000. The U.S. share has fallen from 25 percent in 2000 to about 16 percent today (see Table 13.1). Among the alternatives to fossil fuels are nuclear power and renewable energy technologies such as solar, wind, and biomass generators.

In 2015 the American Anthropological Association (AAA) issued a "Statement on Humanity and Climate Change."

That statement makes several key points, including the following:

- Human cultures and actions are the most important causes of the dramatic environmental changes that have taken place during the last 100 years. Two key factors influencing climate change are (1) reliance on fossil fuels as the primary energy source, and (2) an ever-expanding culture of consumption.

- Climate change will accelerate migration, destabilize communities, and exacerbate the spread of infectious diseases.

- Most affected will be people living on coasts, in island nations, and in high-latitude (e.g., far north) and high-altitude (e.g., very mountainous) areas.

- The tendency has been to address climate change at the international and national levels. We also need planning at the regional and local levels, because the impacts of climate change vary in specific locales. Affected communities, perhaps working with anthropologists, must be active participants in planning how to adapt to climate change—and in implementing those plans.

Environmental Anthropology

Anthropology always has been concerned with how environmental forces influence humans and how human activities affect the environment. The 1950s–1970s witnessed the emergence of an area of study known as cultural ecology, or **ecological anthropology** (see Haenn, Wilk, and Harnish 2016). That field focused on how cultural beliefs and practices helped human populations adapt to their environments, as well as how people used elements of their culture to maintain their ecosystems. Ecological anthropologists showed that many indigenous groups did a reasonable job of managing their resources and preserving their ecosystems. Such groups had traditional ways of categorizing resources and using them sustainably (see Dagne 2015). The term **ethnoecology** describes a society's set of environmental perceptions and practices (see Vinyeta and Lynn 2013).

Outside forces increasingly challenge indigenous ethnoecologies. Given national and international incentives to exploit and degrade, ethnoecological systems that once preserved local and regional environments increasingly are ineffective or irrelevant (see Dove, Sajise, and Doolittle 2011). Anthropologists routinely witness threats to the people they study and their environments. Among such threats are commercial logging, mining, industrial pollution, and the imposition of external management systems on local ecosystems (see Johnston 2009). Today's ecological anthropology, *environmental anthropology,* attempts not only to understand but also to find solutions to environmental problems. Such problems must be tackled at the national and international levels (e.g., global warming).

Local people and their landscapes, ideas, values, and traditional management systems face attacks from all sides (see Hornborg, Clark, and Hermele 2011). Outsiders attempt to remake native landscapes and cultures in their own image. The aim of many agricultural development projects, for example, seems to be to make the world as much like a midwestern American agricultural state as possible. Often there is an attempt to impose mechanized farming and nuclear family ownership, even though these institutions may be inappropriate in areas far removed from the midwestern United States. Anthropologists know that development projects usually fail when they try to replace indigenous institutions with culturally alien concepts.

Global Assaults on Local Autonomy

A clash of cultures related to environmental change may occur when development threatens indigenous peoples and their environments (see this chapter's "Anthropology Today"). A second clash of cultures related to environmental change may occur when external regulation aimed at conservation confronts indigenous peoples and their ethnoecologies. Like development projects, conservation schemes may ask people to change their ways in order to satisfy planners' goals rather than local goals. In places as different as Madagascar, Brazil, and the Pacific Northwest of the United States, people have been asked, told, or forced to abandon basic economic activities because to do so is good for "nature" or "the globe." "Good for the globe" doesn't play very well in Brazil, whose Amazon region has been a focus of international environmentalist attention. Brazilians complain that outsiders (e.g., Europeans and North Americans) promote "global needs" and "saving the Amazon" after having destroyed their own primary forests for economic growth. Conservation efforts always face local opposition when they promote radical changes without involving local people in planning and carrying out the policies that affect them. When people are asked to give up the basis of their livelihood, they usually resist.

The spread of environmentalism may reveal radically different notions about the "rights" and value of plants and animals versus humans. In Madagascar, many intellectuals and officials complain that foreigners seem more concerned about lemurs and other endangered species than about the people of Madagascar (the Malagasy). As a geographer there remarked to me, "The next time you come to Madagascar, there'll be no more Malagasy. All the people will have starved to death, and a lemur will have to meet you at the airport." Most Malagasy perceive human poverty as a more pressing problem than animal and plant survival.

On the other hand, who can doubt that conservation, including the preservation of biodiversity, is a worthy goal? The challenge for applied ecological anthropology is to devise culturally appropriate strategies for achieving biodiversity conservation in the face of unrelenting population growth and commercial expansion. How does one get people to support conservation measures that may, in the short run at least, diminish their access to resources? Like development plans in general, the most effective conservation strategies pay attention to the needs and wishes of the local people.

Deforestation

Generations of anthropologists have studied how human economic activities (ancient and modern) affect the environment. Anthropologists know that food producers (farmers and herders) typically do more to degrade the environment than foragers do. Population increase and the need to expand farming caused deforestation in many parts of the ancient Middle East and Mesoamerica (see Cairns 2015; Hornborg and Crumley, 2007). Even today, many farmers think of trees as giant weeds to be removed and replaced with productive fields.

Often, deforestation is demographically driven—caused by population pressure. For example, Madagascar's population is growing at a rate of 3 percent annually, doubling every generation. Population pressure leads to migration, including rural–urban migration. Madagascar's capital, Antananarivo, had just 100,000 people in 1967. Its population today is over 2 million. Urban growth promotes deforestation if city dwellers rely on fuelwood from the countryside, as is true in Madagascar. As forested watersheds disappear, crop productivity declines. Madagascar is known as the "great red island," after the color of its soil. On that island, the effects of soil erosion and water runoff are visible to the naked eye. From the look of its rivers, Madagascar appears to be bleeding to death. Increasing runoff of water no longer trapped by trees causes erosion of low-lying rice fields near swollen rivers as well as siltation in irrigation canals (Kottak 2007).

Causes of deforestation include demographic pressure (from births or immigration) on subsistence economies, commercial logging, road building, cash cropping, fuelwood needs associated with urban expansion, and clearing and burning associated with livestock and grazing. The fact that forest loss has several causes has a policy implication: Different deforestation scenarios require different conservation strategies.

What can be done? On this question, applied anthropology weighs in, spurring policy makers to think about new conservation strategies. The traditional approach has been to restrict access to forested areas designated as parks, then employ park guards and punish violators. Modern strategies are more likely to consider the needs, wishes, and abilities of the people (often impoverished) living in and near the forest. Since effective conservation depends on the cooperation of the local people, their concerns must be addressed in devising conservation strategies.

Reasons to change behavior must make sense to local people (see Sillitoe 2007). In Madagascar, the economic value of the forest for agriculture (as an antierosion mechanism and reservoir of potential irrigation water) provides a much more powerful incentive against forest degradation than do such global goals as "preserving biodiversity." Most Malagasy have no idea that lemurs and other endemic species exist only in Madagascar. Nor would such knowledge provide much of an incentive for them to conserve the forests if doing so jeopardized their livelihoods.

To curb the global deforestation threat, we need conservation strategies that work. Laws and enforcement may help reduce commercially driven deforestation caused by burning and clear-cutting. But local people also use and abuse forested lands. A challenge

Applied anthropology uses anthropological perspectives to identify and solve contemporary problems that affect humans. Deforestation is one such problem. Here, women take part in a reforestation project in coastal Tanzania near Dar es Salaam. ©Ed Parker/Alamy Stock Photo

for the environmentally oriented applied anthropologist is to find ways to make forest preservation attractive to local people and ensure their cooperation. Applied anthropologists must work to make "good for the globe" good for the people.

Emerging Diseases

A number of potentially lethal infectious diseases have emerged and spread in the past few decades. These *emerging diseases* include HIV/AIDS, Ebola, West Nile, SARS (severe acute respiratory syndrome), Lyme disease, and Zika. All these diseases have emerged as a result of human activity. Driven by factors including population increase, changing settlement patterns, and commercial expansion, humans have been encroaching on wild lands, particularly forests, and creating conditions that favor the spread of disease pathogens. In the Amazon, for example, one study showed that an increase in deforestation of just 4 percent produced a 50 percent increase in the incidence of malaria. This is because the mosquitoes that transmit malaria thrive in the right mix of sunlight and water in recently deforested areas (Robbins 2012).

Some emerging diseases are *zoonotic*—they spread from animals to humans. The transmission of diseases from wild to domesticated animals and then to humans has been going on since the Neolithic, when animals first were domesticated. Zoonotic diseases pose a huge threat today because of human population increase and forces of globalization. Emerging diseases kill more than 2 million people annually, and 60 percent of those diseases originate in animals (Robbins 2012).

Among the diseases that have jumped from woods and wildlife to humans through their domesticated animals is the Nipah virus, which began its migration from fruit bats to humans in South Asia. Because fruit bats have co-evolved with the Nipah virus for millions of years, it does little damage to their health. When the virus moves from bats into other species, however, it can be lethal. Fruit bats eat the pulp of fruit and spit out the residue. In rural Malaysia in 1999, an infected bat appears to have dropped a piece of chewed fruit into the food supply of a swine herd (a scenario depicted in the movie *Contagion*). The virus then spread from those pigs to humans. Of 276 people infected in Malaysia, 106 died. Eleven more people died in Singapore, when the virus was exported there via live pigs. South Asia has experienced a dozen smaller Nipah outbreaks in recent years.

Spillovers from wildlife to humans have quadrupled in the past half-century, reflecting increasing human encroachment on disease hotspots, especially in the tropics (Robbins 2012). HIV/AIDS originally jumped from chimpanzees to humans through bush-meat hunters in Africa, who kill and butcher chimps. Modern air travel contributes to the potential for a transnational outbreak or even a pandemic. (A *pandemic* is an epidemic with global scope.)

Biologists and doctors are acutely aware of the threat posed by zoonotic diseases. One international project, called PREDICT, funds teams of veterinarians, conservation biologists, medical doctors, and epidemiologists to identify disease-causing organisms in wildlife before they spread to humans (see http://www.vetmed.ucdavis.edu/ohi/predict/index.cfm). PREDICT, which is financed by the United States Agency for International Development (USAID), attempts to "predict," spot, and prevent the spread of zoonotic diseases from world areas with high potential for disease transmission. Some 24 countries in Africa, Latin America, and Asia participate in the program. PREDICT scientists monitor areas where deadly viruses are known to exist and where humans are encroaching. One such locale is a new highway being built to link the Atlantic and Pacific Oceans in South America, traversing Brazil and the Peruvian Andes.

PREDICT scientists also gather blood, saliva, and other samples from wildlife species to create a "library" of viruses, to facilitate identification when a threat is imminent. This library focuses on the animals most likely to carry diseases to people, such as primates, rats, and bats. PREDICT scientists also study ways of preventing disease transmission. Sometimes solutions can be remarkably simple. In Bangladesh, for example, outbreaks of the Nipah virus were contained by placing bamboo screens (which cost 8 cents each) over the containers used to collect date palm sap (Robbins 2012). Because humans, by modifying the environment, create the conditions that allow diseases to emerge and spread, anthropologists can contribute by studying the cultural (including economic) causes of environmental encroachment and by suggesting culturally appropriate and workable solutions.

Interethnic Contact

Since at least the 1920s, anthropologists have been interested in changes that take place where there is sustained contact between industrial and nonindustrial societies. The term *acculturation* refers to the cultural changes that occur when different societies come into continuous firsthand contact (Redfield, Linton, and Herskovits 1936). Most acculturation studies have focused on contact between Western and non-Western cultures. Often, this contact reflects Western domination over a non-Western society. In that case, the cultural patterns of the dominant Western society are more likely to be forced upon or accepted by the non-Western society than vice versa. However, the westerners who take up residence in a non-Western setting will also be affected by the cultural practices of that setting. In postcolonial times, people have been migrating from the former colonies to the former colonial nations. Inevitably, these migrants bring along their own cultural practices. It is not uncommon for their foods, music, art, and clothing styles to influence the cultural practices of the former colonial nation. If contact is sustained long enough, acculturation will be reciprocal—influencing both groups, even if one is influenced more than the other.

Although *acculturation* can be applied to any case of cultural contact and change, the term most often described **Westernization**—the influence of Western expansion on indigenous peoples and their cultures. Thus, local people who wear store-bought clothes, learn Indo-European languages, and otherwise adopt Western customs are called "acculturated." Acculturation may be voluntary or forced, and there may be considerable resistance to the process.

Different degrees of destruction, domination, resistance, survival, adaptation, and modification of native cultures may follow interethnic contact. In the most destructive encounters, native and subordinate cultures face obliteration. When contact with powerful outsiders seriously threatens an indigenous culture, a "shock phase" often follows the initial encounter (Bodley 2012). Outsiders may attack or exploit the native people.

Illustrating both globalization and indigenization, McDonalds's now routinely tries to tailor its offerings to specific cultural appetites. Shown here in downtown Fort-de-France, Martinique (French West Indies), is a billboard advertising a hamburger topped with Italian cheese (Parmigiano-Reggiano). ©Guiziou Franck/hemis.fr/Getty Images

Such exploitation may increase mortality, disrupt subsistence, fragment kin groups, damage social support systems, and inspire new religious movements. During the shock phase, there may be civil repression backed by military force. Such factors may lead to the group's cultural collapse (*ethnocide*) or physical extinction (*genocide*).

Cultural Imperialism and Indigenization

Cultural imperialism refers to the spread or advance of one culture at the expense of others, or its imposition on other cultures, which it modifies, replaces, or destroys—usually because of differential economic or political influence. Thus, children in the French colonial empire learned French history, language, and culture from standard textbooks also used in France. Tahitians, Malagasy, Vietnamese, and Senegalese learned the French language by reciting from books about "our ancestors the Gauls."

Some commentators think that modern technology and the mass media are erasing cultural differences, as a common set of products and brands spread globally. Others, however, see a role for modern technology in allowing social groups (local cultures) to express themselves and to survive (see Lule 2015; Mirrlees 2013). In today's world, radio, TV, film, digital media, and increasingly the Internet (e.g., YouTube) constantly bring local happenings to the attention of a larger public (see Fuchs and Sandoval 2014). For example, Susan Boyle's rendition of "I Dreamed a Dream" on a British TV show soon became an Internet sensation and made her a global star. YouTube similarly fueled

A potter plies his trade for a group of observers (including the author) in Fez, Morocco, in February 2015. Increasingly, local communities perform "traditional" activities, especially ceremonies, celebrations, and arts and crafts for TV and tourists. ©Conrad P. Kottak

the global spread of the hugely popular "Gangnam Style" by the South Korean singer Psy. Without YouTube, appreciation of these performances would be much more limited. Contemporary media play a role in stimulating and organizing local and community activities of many sorts. Think of ways in which this is done by YouTube, Facebook, and Twitter—global networks all.

In Brazil, local practices, celebrations, and performances have changed in the context of outside forces, including the mass media and tourism. In the town of Arembepe (Kottak 2006), TV coverage stimulated increased participation in a traditional annual performance, the Chegança. This is a danceplay that reenacts the Portuguese discovery of Brazil. Arembepeiros have traveled to the state capital to perform the Chegança before television cameras, for a nationally televised program featuring traditional performances from many rural communities, and cameras have gone to Arembepe to record it.

In several towns along the Amazon River, annual folk ceremonies now are staged more lavishly for TV and video cameras. In the Amazon town of Parantíns, for example, boatloads of tourists arriving any time of year are shown a video recording of the town's annual Bumba Meu Boi festival. This is a costumed performance mimicking bullfighting, parts of which have been shown on national TV. This pattern, in which local communities preserve, revive, and intensify the scale of traditional ceremonies to perform for the media and tourists, is expanding. To see whether I could, I just managed to watch snippets of these annual events in Arembepe and Parantíns on YouTube!

In the process of globalization, people continually make and remake culture as they assign their own meanings to the information, images, and products they receive from outside. One example of such a process of **indigenization**—how a globally spreading Evangelical Protestantism adapts to local circumstances—was discussed in Chapter 9. Indigenization occurs in cultural domains as different as fast food, music, housing styles, science, religion, terrorism, celebrations, and political ideas and institutions (Ellen, Lycett, and Johns 2013; Fiske 2011; Wilk 2006).

A Global System of Images

With globalization, more people in many more places imagine "a wider set of 'possible' lives than they ever did before. One important source of this change is the mass media . . ." (Appadurai 1991, p. 197). The United States as a global media center has been joined by Canada, Japan, Western Europe, Brazil, Mexico, Nigeria, Egypt, India, and Hong Kong. Like print, the electronic mass media can diffuse the cultures of different countries within (and often beyond) their own boundaries, thus enhancing national cultural identity. For example, millions of Brazilians who once were cut off (by geographic isolation or illiteracy) from urban, national, and international events and information now participate in a larger "mediascape" (Appadurai 1991) through mass media and the Internet (Kottak 2009).

Brazil's most popular network (Rede Globo) relies heavily on its own productions, especially *telenovelas* (nightly serial programs often compared to American soap operas). Globo plays each night to the world's largest and most devoted audience (perhaps 80 million viewers throughout the nation and beyond—via satellite TV). The programs that attract this horde are made by Brazilians, for Brazilians.

The mass media and the Internet also play a prominent role in maintaining ethnic and national identities among people who lead transnational lives. Arabic-speaking Muslims, including migrants in several countries, follow the TV network Al Jazeera, based in Qatar, which helps reinforce ethnic and religious identities. As groups move, they can stay linked to each other and to their homeland through global media. **Diasporas** (people who have spread out from an original, ancestral homeland) have enlarged the markets for media, communication, brands, and travel services targeted at specific ethnic, national, or religious groups that now live in various parts of the world.

A Global Culture of Consumption

Business and the media have fueled a global culture of consumption, based on a craving for certain lifestyles and the products that go along with them. People also crave and consume knowledge and information, available through the media and the gadgets that allow media access (see Kennedy 2015). The media also provide connectivity and a forum for expressing shared sentiments.

In the Middle East, for example, social media use exploded during the Arab Spring of 2011. In cyberspace Middle Easterners found something missing from their ordinary, offline worlds: platforms permitting social connectivity and the collective airing of grievances. Since then, social media have entered the region commercially, in a big way. Over 40 percent of Middle Easterners have Internet access, and almost 90 percent of them use social media on a daily basis. Facebook is the most popular social network, with 94 percent of Middle Eastern social media users accessing that site. Arabic has become Twitter's fastest-growing language. LinkedIn (a professional social networking and job search site) has almost 6 million Middle Eastern users (Jazra 2014). (This region has one of the world's highest youth unemployment rates.) This rapidly rising Middle Eastern Internet presence is occurring in an area where 40 percent of the population (of 380 million) is younger than 30 years. The smartphone is another key element in the Middle Eastern marketing mediascape. Illustrating the spreading culture of consumption, a global survey by Google found that 93 percent of smartphone users notice mobile ads, and 39 percent of those follow up with an online purchase. Saudi Arabia's mobile phone penetration rate is 190 percent, meaning that everyone has almost two cell phones (Hamdan 2013). Media and marketing are the new "It" couple.

Illustrating the global culture of consumption, few people have never seen a T-shirt advertising a Western product (see Gould 2016). American and English rock stars' recordings blast through the streets of Rio de Janeiro, while taxi drivers from Toronto to Madagascar listen to Brazilian music. The popularity of Korean pop singers spreads internationally via the Internet. Peasants and tribal people participate in the modern world system not only because they have been hooked on cash but also because their products and images are appropriated by world capitalism. They are commercialized by others (like the Quileute nation in the *Twilight* series of books and movies). Furthermore, indigenous peoples also market their own images and products, through outlets like Cultural Survival.

People in Motion

Globalization has both enlarged and erased old boundaries and distinctions. Arjun Appadurai (1990, p. 1) characterizes today's world as a "translocal" "interactive system" that is "strikingly new." Whether as refugees, migrants, tourists, pilgrims, proselytizers, laborers, businesspeople, development workers, politicians, terrorists, soldiers, sports figures, or media-borne images, people travel more than ever.

The scale of human movement has expanded dramatically. Most emigrants maintain their ties with their native land, however—by phoning, Skyping, Facetiming, texting, e-mailing, visiting, sending money, or watching home videos or "ethnic TV." In a sense, they live multilocally—in different places at once. With so many people "in motion," the unit of anthropological study expands from the local community to the diaspora. Anthropologists increasingly follow descendants of the villages they have studied as they move from rural to urban areas and across national boundaries.

Postmodernity describes our time and situation: today's world in flux, these people on the move who have learned to manage multiple identities depending on place and context. In its most general sense, **postmodern** refers to the blurring and breakdown of established canons (rules or standards), categories, distinctions, and boundaries.

With so many people on the move, the unit of anthropological study has expanded from the local community to the diaspora. This refers to the offspring of an area who have spread to many lands, such as the owners of this falafel shop in Paris, France. ©Lionel Derimais/VISUM/The Image Works

The word is taken from **postmodernism**—a style and movement in architecture that succeeded modernism, beginning in the 1970s. Postmodern architecture rejected the rules, geometric order, and austerity of modernism. Modernist buildings were expected to have a clear and functional design. Postmodern design is "messier" and more playful. It draws on a diversity of styles from different times and places—including popular, ethnic, and non-Western cultures. Postmodernism extends "value" globally—well beyond classic, elite, and Western cultural forms. *Postmodern* now is used to describe comparable developments beyond architecture—in music, literature, and visual art. From this origin, postmodernity describes a world in which traditional standards, contrasts, groups, boundaries, and identities are opening up, reaching out, and breaking down.

New kinds of political and ethnic units have emerged along with globalization. In some cases, cultures and ethnic groups have banded together in larger associations. There is a growing pan-Native-American identity as well as an international pantribal movement. Thus, in June 1992, the World Conference of Indigenous Peoples met in Rio de Janeiro concurrently with UNCED (the United Nations Conference on the Environment and Development). Along with diplomats, journalists, and environmentalists came 300 representatives of the tribal diversity that survives under globalization—from Lapland to Mali (Brooke 1992; see also Maybury-Lewis, Macdonald, and Maybury-Lewis 2009).

Indigenous Peoples

All too often, conquest, annexation, and development have been associated with genocide—the deliberate extermination of a specific ethnic group. Examples of genocide include the Holocaust, Rwanda in 1994, and Bosnia in the early 1990s. Bodley (2015) estimates that an average of 250,000 indigenous people perished annually between 1800 and 1950. The causes included warfare, outright murder, introduced diseases, slavery, land grabbing, and other forms of dispossession and impoverishment.

Remaining in the world today are more than 5,000 distinct groups of indigenous peoples, located in some 90 countries. They comprise more than 5 percent of the world's population, numbering about 370 million people. They remain among the world's most disadvantaged and vulnerable populations. Many of them struggle to hold on to their lands and natural resources (see this chapter's "Anthropology Today").

All of the indigenous groups that have survived live today within nation-states. Often, they maintain a distinct ethnic identity, despite having lost their ancestral languages and cultures to varying degrees. Many such groups aspire to autonomy. To describe these original inhabitants of their territories, the term *indigenous people* entered international law in 1982 with the creation of the United Nations Working Group on Indigenous Populations (WGIP). This group meets annually and has members from six continents. The UN General Assembly adopted its Declaration of Indigenous Rights in 2007. Convention 169, a document supporting cultural diversity and indigenous empowerment, had been approved by the International Labor Organization (ILO) in 1989. Such documents, along with the global work of the WGIP, have influenced governments, NGOs, and international agencies to adopt policies favorable to indigenous peoples. In May 2012, the United Nations sponsored a high-level commemoration of the fifth anniversary of the adoption of the UN Declaration on the Rights of Indigenous Peoples (see Doyle 2015; Drahos 2014). In September 2014, the United Nations hosted a World Conference on Indigenous Peoples, to reiterate the U.N.'s ongoing role in promoting and protecting the rights of indigenous peoples (see http://wcip2014.org). Social movements worldwide use *indigenous people* as a self-identifying label in their quests for social, cultural, and political rights (Brower and Johnston 2007; de la Peña 2005).

In Spanish-speaking Latin America, social scientists and politicians favor the term *indígena* (indigenous person) over *indio* (Indian), the colonial term that European conquerors used for Native Americans (de la Peña 2005). Until the mid- to late 1980s, Latin American public policy emphasized assimilation. During the past 30 years, the emphasis has shifted from assimilation—*mestizaje*—to cultural difference. In Ecuador, for example, groups seen previously as Quichua-speaking peasants are classified now as indigenous communities with their own territories. Brazil has recognized 30 new indigenous communities in the northeast, a region previously seen as having lost its native population. Guatemala, Nicaragua, Brazil, Colombia, Mexico, Paraguay, Ecuador, Argentina, Bolivia, Peru, and Venezuela now are officially multicultural (Jackson and Warren 2005). Several national constitutions recognize the rights of indigenous peoples to cultural distinctiveness and political representation (de la Peña 2005).

Ceuppens and Geschiere (2005) comment on a recent upsurge, in multiple world areas, of the notion of *autochthony* (being native to, or formed in, the place where found), with an implicit call for excluding strangers. The terms *autochthony* and *indigenous* go back to classical Greek history, with similar implications. *Autochthony* refers to self and soil. *Indigenous* literally means born inside, with the connotation in classical Greek of being born "inside the house." Both notions stress the rights of first-comers to privileged status and protection versus later immigrants—legal or illegal (Ceuppens and Geschiere 2005; Hornborg, Clark, and Hermele 2011).

During the 1990s, autochthony became an issue in many parts of Africa, inspiring violent efforts to exclude (European and Asian) "strangers." Simultaneously, autochthony became a key notion in debates about immigration and multiculturalism in Europe. European majority groups have claimed the label *autochthon.* This term highlights the prominence that the exclusion of strangers has assumed in day-to-day politics worldwide (Ceuppens and Geschiere 2005). One familiar example is the United States, as represented in ongoing debates over undocumented immigration.

Essentialism describes the process of viewing an identity (e.g., an ethnic label) as established, real, and frozen, thus ignoring the historical processes within which that identity was forged. Identities, however, are not fixed. We saw in Chapter 10 that identities can be fluid and multiple. People draw on particular, sometimes competing, self-labels and identities. Some Peruvian groups, for instance, self-identify as *mestizos* but still see themselves as indigenous. Identity is a fluid, dynamic process, and there are multiple ways of being indigenous. Neither speaking an indigenous language nor wearing "native" clothing is required (Jackson and Warren 2005).

Anthropology's Lessons

Anthropology teaches us that the adaptive responses of humans are more flexible than those of other species because our main adaptive means are sociocultural. However, in the face of globalization, the cultural institutions of the past always influence subsequent adaptation, producing continued diversity in the actions and reactions of different groups as they indigenize global inputs. In our globalizing world, anthropology offers a people-centered vision of social change. The existence of anthropology is itself a tribute to the continuing need to understand similarities and differences among human beings throughout the world.

Anthropology offers relevant, indeed powerful, ways of understanding how the world actually works. Lessons of the past can and should be applied to the present and future, hopefully to benefit humanity. Anthropologists know that civilizations and world powers rise and fall, and that social transformations typically follow major innovations, such as the Neolithic and the Industrial Revolution. There is little chance that the current world system and the power relations within it will last forever. Whatever it may be, our social future will trace its origins to our social present. That is, future developments will need to build on, modify, and perhaps discard preexisting practices and institutions. What trends observable in the world today are most likely to transform society in the long run? Using your new knowledge of anthropology, try to imagine possible futures for humanity.

Anthropology Today *Diversity under Siege: Global Forces and Indigenous Peoples*

Around the globe, diversity is under siege. In Alaska, which has been warming twice as fast as the rest of the United States, displaced villagers have become climate change refugees—forced to move as rising sea levels have eroded and flooded their settlements. In the South Pacific, Marshall Islanders also face rising seas, which render their villages increasingly uninhabitable and their land too salty for productive agriculture (Davenport and Haner 2015). In the Brazilian Amazon, outside settlers, including farmers, cattle herders, gold prospectors, and commercial loggers, are illegally encroaching on areas reserved for indigenous groups. A combination of forces at work globally, including climate change and development, are threatening the lifestyles, livelihoods, and even the lives of indigenous peoples.

We focus now on the Norwegian Arctic, where a Sami (Lapp) population of about 100,000 traditional reindeer herders extends over a vast territory—northern areas of Norway, Sweden, Finland, and Russia's Kola Peninsula. Sami nomads once moved their herds seasonally across this expanse, paying little attention to national borders. Today, a mere one-tenth of the total Sami population, Western Europe's only indigenous Arctic group, continues to herd reindeer for a living (Wallace 2016).

The Sami way of life is being destroyed incrementally rather than by a major project or event. The cumulative effects of a series of smaller constructions, including roads and pipelines, have reduced Norway's undisturbed reindeer habitat by 70 percent in the past century. Like so many other indigenous peoples, the Sami

Sami herder Johann Anders Oskal and his brother tend their reindeer herd in Troms County, Norway (January 27, 2016). ©Scott Wallace/Hulton Archive/Getty Images

continued

Anthropology Today *continued*

must compete with powerful external interests for use of their traditional (grazing) lands. For generations, the Sami have lived under state organization. The state allows the Sami to graze their herds, but the land belongs to the national government. The Sami must deal with decisions made at the national level by planners, legislators, and the courts. What is good for the nation and business interests often takes precedence over what may be best for local people.

External inputs have been both positive and negative. The group benefits from the use of GPS collars and smartphone apps to track their animals, and snowmobiles and all-terrain vehicles to round them up. On the negative side, the steady encroachment of industrial infrastructure has reduced their range and freedom of movement. Current threats include dams, roads, live-fire military drills, high-voltage power lines, wind farms, and a copper mine. Many Sami now have to move their herds by truck and boat between summer and winter pastures—a costly operation. When courts approved large-scale projects that negatively affected the Sami, the herders received only a one-time payment as compensation for their losses (Wallace 2016).

Norway is proceeding with plans to extract more resources and build more industry in the Arctic. The Sami fear that their languages and culture, largely sustained by herding, will ultimately be sacrificed to benefit the larger society. The government has ambitious targets for renewable energy, including more hydroelectric and wind power projects. These projects, although possibly "good for the globe," negatively affect reindeer herding, as well as Arctic biodiversity, wilderness landscapes, and traditional subsistence activities. A proposed wind farm (now under judicial review) and associated power lines would encroach substantially on the summer grazing lands of a group of herders who still speak South Sami, a language listed by UNESCO as endangered (Wallace 2016).

In addition to the threats from development, the Sami have an ongoing conflict with the military. Since the Cold War, Norwegian soldiers have been a regular presence in Sami country, preparing for a possible Russian incursion across northern Scandinavia. These troops stage regular, often daily, war exercises, including live gunfire. Herders must be vigilant to avoid flying bullets as they go about their activities. (The information about contemporary Sami in this feature comes mainly from Wallace 2016.)

Even the most enlightened governments pursue policies that are incompatible with preserving the traditional activities and lifestyles of indigenous peoples. Like certain conservation schemes aimed at preserving biodiversity, efforts that are good for the globe, such as the development of green energy sources, may not be best for local people. Planners must be attentive to the need to seek a delicate balance between what's good for the globe and what's good for the people.

Summary

1. As used in this book, the primary meaning of globalization is *worldwide connectedness,* through contemporary systems of production, distribution, consumption, finance, transportation, and communication (including the Internet and other media). A second meaning of globalization is political, referring to efforts by international financial powers to create a global *free market* for goods and services.

2. Fueling global climate change are human population growth and use of fossil fuels, which produce greenhouse gases. The atmospheric concentration of those gases has increased since the Industrial Revolution, and especially since 1978. Climate change encompasses global warming along with changing sea levels, precipitation, storms, and ecosystem effects.

3. Anthropology always has been concerned with how environmental forces influence humans and how human activities affect the biosphere. Many indigenous groups did a reasonable job of preserving their ecosystems. An ethnoecology is any society's set of environmental practices and perceptions. Indigenous ethnoecologies increasingly are being challenged by global forces that work to exploit and degrade—and that sometimes aim to protect—the environment. The challenge for applied ecological anthropology is to devise culturally appropriate strategies for conservation in the face of unrelenting population growth and commercial expansion.

4. Deforestation is a major factor in the loss of global biodiversity. Causes of deforestation include demographic pressure (from births or immigration) on subsistence economies; commercial logging; road building; cash cropping; fuelwood needs associated with urban expansion; and clearing and burning associated with livestock and grazing. The fact that forest loss has several causes has a policy implication: Different deforestation scenarios require different conservation strategies. Applied anthropologists must work to make "good for the globe" good for the people.

5. The recent emergence and spread of infectious diseases like HIV/AIDS, Ebola, West Nile, SARS, Zika, and Lyme disease are the result of things people have done to their environments. The spread of zoonotic diseases from wild to domesticated animals and then to humans has been going on since the Neolithic. Because human groups create the conditions that allow zoonotic pathogens to jump species and to spread, anthropologists have a key role to play in studying the causes of environmental encroachment and in suggesting culturally appropriate solutions.

6. Cultural imperialism is the spread of one culture and its imposition on other cultures, which it modifies, replaces, or destroys—usually because of differential economic and political power. Some observers worry that modern technology, including the mass media, is destroying traditional cultures. But others see an important role for new technology in allowing local cultures to express themselves. As the forces of globalization spread, they are modified (indigenized) to fit local cultures. The mass media can help diffuse a national culture within and beyond its own boundaries. The media, including the Internet, also play a role in preserving ethnic and national identities among people who lead transnational lives.

7. People travel more than ever. But migrants also maintain ties with home, so they live multilocally. With so many people "in motion," the unit of anthropological study expands from the local community to the diaspora. *Postmodernity* describes this world in flux, with people on the move who manage multiple social identities depending on place and context. With globalization, new kinds of political and ethnic units are emerging as others break down or disappear.

8. Governments, NGOs, and international agencies have adopted policies designed to recognize and benefit indigenous peoples. Social movements worldwide have adopted this term as a self-identifying and political label based on past oppression but now signaling a search for social, cultural, and political rights. In Latin America, several national constitutions now recognize the rights of indigenous peoples. Identity is a fluid, dynamic process, and there are multiple ways of being indigenous.

Think Like an Anthropologist

1. What does it mean to apply an anthropological perspective to contemporary global issues? Can you come up with an anthropological research question that investigates a global issue? Imagine you had a year (and the money!) to carry out this project. How would you spend your time and your resources?

2. The topic of global climate change has been hotly debated during the past few years. Why is there so much debate? Are you concerned about global climate change? Do you think everyone on the planet should be equally concerned and share the responsibility for doing something about it? Why or why not?

3. Consider majority and minority rights in the context of contemporary events involving religion, ethnicity, politics, and law. What kind of rights should be granted based on religious beliefs? What kinds of groups, if any, within a nation should have special rights? How about indigenous peoples?

Key Terms

anthropogenic, *301*
climate change, *301*
cultural
  imperialism, *308*
diaspora, *310*
ecological
  anthropology, *303*

essentialism, *314*
ethnoecology, *303*
greenhouse
  effect, *300*
indigenization, *310*
postmodern, *311*
postmodernism, *312*

postmodernity, *311*
Westernization, *307*

Glossary

A

acculturation   The exchange of cultural features that results when groups come into continuous firsthand contact; the original cultural patterns of either or both groups may be altered, but the groups remain distinct.

achieved status   Social status that comes through talents, actions, efforts, activities, and accomplishments, rather than ascription.

adaptation   The process by which organisms cope with environmental stresses.

African American Vernacular English (AAVE)   A rule-governed dialect of American English spoken by some African Americans in their casual, intimate speech

agriculture   Nonindustrial system of plant cultivation characterized by continuous and intensive use of land and labor.

animism   Belief in souls or doubles.

anthropology   The study of the human species and its immediate ancestors.

anthropology and education   Anthropological research in classrooms, homes, and neighborhoods, viewing students as total cultural creatures whose enculturation and attitudes toward education belong to a larger context that includes family, peers, and society.

applied anthropology   The application of anthropological data, perspectives, theory, and methods to identify, assess, and solve contemporary social problems.

archaeological anthropology   The branch of anthropology that reconstructs, describes, and interprets human behavior and cultural patterns through material remains; best known for the study of prehistory. Also known as *archaeology*.

ascribed status   Social status (e.g., race or gender) that people have little or no choice about occupying.

assimilation   The process of change that a minority group may experience when it moves to a country where another culture dominates; the minority is incorporated into the dominant culture to the point that it no longer exists as a separate cultural unit.

authority   The formal, socially approved use of power, e.g., by government officials.

B

balanced reciprocity   See *generalized reciprocity*.

band   Basic unit of social organization among foragers. A band includes fewer than one hundred people; it often splits up seasonally.

big man   Figure often found among tribal horticulturalists and pastoralists. The big man occupies no office but creates his reputation through entrepreneurship and generosity to others. Neither his wealth nor his position passes to his heirs.

biocultural   Referring to the inclusion and combination (to solve a common problem) of both biological and cultural approaches—one of anthropology's hallmarks.

biological anthropology   The branch of anthropology that studies human biological diversity in time and space—for instance, hominid evolution, human genetics, human biological adaptation; also includes primatology (behavior and evolution of monkeys and apes). Also called *physical anthropology*.

bourgeoisie   One of Karl Marx's opposed classes; owners of the means of production (factories, mines, large farms, and other sources of subsistence).

C

call systems   Systems of communication among nonhuman primates, composed of a limited number of sounds that vary in intensity and duration; tied to environmental stimuli.

capital   Wealth or resources invested in business, with the intent of producing a profit.

capitalist world economy   The single world system, which emerged in the 16th century, committed to production for sale, with the object of maximizing profits rather than supplying domestic needs.

cargo cults   Postcolonial, acculturative, religious movements common in Melanesia that attempt to explain European domination and wealth and to achieve similar success magically by mimicking European behavior.

caste system   Closed, hereditary system of stratification, often dictated by religion; hierarchical social status is ascribed at birth, so that people are locked into their parents' social position.

chiefdom   Form of sociopolitical organization intermediate between the tribe and the state; kin-based with differential access to resources and a permanent political structure. A ranked society in which relations among villages as well as among individuals are unequal, with smaller villages under the authority of leaders in larger villages; has a two-level settlement hierarchy.

clan   Unilineal descent group based on stipulated descent.

climate change   Global warming, plus changing sea levels, precipitation, storms, and ecosystem effects.

cline   Gradual shift in gene (allele) frequencies between neighboring populations.

colonialism   The political, social, economic, and cultural domination of a territory and its people by a foreign power for an extended time.

Communism   Spelled with a capital *C*, a political movement and doctrine seeking to overthrow capitalism and to establish a form of communism such as that which prevailed in the Soviet Union (USSR) from 1917 to 1991.

communism   Spelled with a lowercase *c*, describes a social system in which property is owned by the community and in which people work for the common good.

communitas   Intense community spirit, a feeling of great social solidarity, equality, and togetherness; characteristic of people experiencing liminality together.

conflict resolution   The means by which disputes are socially regulated and settled; found in all societies, but the resolution methods tend to be more formal and effective in states than in nonstates.

core   Dominant structural position in the world system; consists of the strongest and most powerful states with advanced systems of production.

core values   Key, basic, or central values that integrate a culture and help distinguish it from others.

correlation   An association between two or more variables such that when one changes (varies), the other(s) also change(s) (covaries)—for example, temperature and sweating.

cultivation continuum   Continuum of land and labor use, with horticulture at one end and agriculture at the other.

cultural anthropology   The study of human society and culture; describes, analyzes, interprets, and explains social and cultural similarities and differences.

cultural colonialism   Within a nation or an empire, domination by one ethnic group or nationality and its culture/ideology over others—e.g., the dominance of Russian people, language, and culture in the former Soviet Union.

cultural consultant   Someone the ethnographer gets to know in the field, who teaches him or her about the consultant's society and culture; also called an *informant*.

cultural imperialism   The rapid spread or advance of one culture at the expense of others, or its imposition on other cultures, which it modifies, replaces, or destroys—usually because of differential economic or political influence.

cultural relativism   The position that the values and standards of cultures differ and deserve respect. Anthropology is characterized by methodological rather than moral relativism: In order to understand another culture fully, anthropologists try to understand its members' beliefs and motivations. Methodological relativism does not preclude making moral judgments or taking action.

cultural resource management (CRM)   The branch of applied archaeology aimed at preserving sites threatened by dams, highways, and other projects.

cultural rights   Doctrine that certain rights are vested not in individuals but in identifiable groups, such as religious and ethnic minorities and indigenous societies.

cultural transmission   A basic feature of language; transmission through learning.

culture   Traditions and customs that govern behavior and beliefs; distinctly human; transmitted through learning.

curer   Specialized role acquired through a culturally appropriate process of selection, training, certification, and acquisition of a professional image; the curer is consulted by patients, who believe in his or her special powers, and receives some form of special consideration; a cultural universal.

D

daughter languages   Languages developing out of the same parent language; for example, French and Spanish are daughter languages of Latin.

descent   Rule assigning social identity on the basis of some aspect of one's ancestry.

descent group   A permanent social unit whose members claim common ancestry; fundamental to tribal society.

descriptive linguistics   The scientific study of a spoken language, including its phonology, morphology, lexicon, and syntax.

development anthropology   The branch of applied anthropology that focuses on social issues in, and the cultural dimension of, economic development.

diaspora   The offspring of an area who have spread to many lands.

differential access   Unequal access to resources; basic attribute of chiefdoms and states. Superordinates have favored access to such resources, while the access of subordinates is limited by superordinates.

diffusion   Borrowing between cultures either directly or through intermediaries.

diglossia   The existence of "high" (formal) and "low" (familial) dialects of a single language, such as German.

discrimination   Policies and practices that harm a group and its members.

disease   A scientifically identified health threat caused by a bacterium, virus, fungus, parasite, or other pathogen.

displacement   A linguistic capacity that allows humans to speak of things and events that are not present.

domestic   Within or pertaining to the home.

domestic–public dichotomy   Contrast between women's role in the home and men's role in public life, with a corresponding social devaluation of women's work and worth.

dowry   A marital exchange in which the wife's group provides substantial gifts to the husband's family.

E

ecological anthropology   Study of cultural adaptations to environments.

economy   A population's system of production, distribution, and consumption of resources.

emic   The research strategy that focuses on native explanations and criteria of significance.

empire   A mature state that is large, multiethnic, militaristic, and expansive.

enculturation   The social process by which culture is learned and transmitted across the generations.

endogamy   Marriage between people of the same social group.

essentialism   The process of viewing an identity as established, real, and frozen, so as to hide the historical processes and politics within which that identity developed.

estrus   Period of maximum sexual receptivity in female baboons, chimpanzees, and other primates, signaled by vaginal-area swelling and coloration.

ethnic group   Group distinguished by cultural similarities (shared among members of that group) and differences (between that group and others); ethnic group members share beliefs, values, habits, customs, norms, and a common language, religion, history, geography, kinship, and/or race.

ethnicity   Identification with, and feeling part of, an ethnic group and exclusion from certain other groups because of this affiliation.

ethnocentrism   The tendency to view one's own culture as best and to judge the behavior and beliefs of culturally different people by one's own standards.

ethnocide   Destruction by a dominant group of the culture of an ethnic group.

ethnoecology   A culture's set of environmental practices and perceptions.

ethnography   Fieldwork in a particular culture.

ethnology   The theoretical, comparative study of society and culture; compares cultures in time and space.

etic   The research strategy that emphasizes the observer's rather than the natives' explanations, categories, and criteria of significance.

exogamy   Mating or marriage outside one's kin group; a cultural universal.

extended family household   Expanded household including three or more generations.

F

family   A group of people (e.g., parents, children, siblings, grandparents, grandchildren, uncles, aunts, nephews, nieces, cousins, spouses, siblings-in-law, parents-in-law, children-in-law) who are considered to be related in some way, for example, by "blood" (common ancestry or descent) or marriage.

family of orientation   Nuclear family in which one is born and grows up.

family of procreation   Nuclear family established when one marries and has children.

fiscal   Pertaining to finances and taxation.

focal vocabulary   A set of words and distinctions that are particularly important to certain groups (those with particular foci of experience or activity), such as types of snow to Eskimos or skiers.

food production   Cultivation of plants and domestication (stockbreeding) of animals; first developed in the Middle East 10,000 to 12,000 years ago.

foraging   An economy and way of life based on hunting and gathering.

G

gender identity   Identity based on whether a person feels, and is regarded as, male, female, or something else.

gender roles   The tasks and activities that a culture assigns to each sex.

gender stereotypes   Oversimplified but strongly held ideas about the characteristics of males and females.

gender stratification   Unequal distribution of rewards (socially valued resources, power, prestige, and personal freedom) between men and women, reflecting their different positions in a social hierarchy.

genealogical method   Procedures by which ethnographers discover and record connections of kinship, descent, and marriage, using diagrams and symbols.

general anthropology   The field of anthropology as a whole, consisting of cultural, archaeological, biological, and linguistic anthropology.

generality   Culture pattern or trait that exists in some but not all societies.

generalized reciprocity   Principle that characterizes exchanges between closely related individuals: As social distance increases, reciprocity becomes balanced and finally negative.

genocide   Policies aimed at, and/or resulting in, the physical extinction (through mass murder) of a people perceived as a racial group, that is, as sharing defining physical, genetic, or other biological characteristics.

globalization   The accelerating interdependence of nations in a world system linked economically and through mass media and modern transportation systems.

greenhouse effect   Warming from trapped atmospheric gases.

H

health care systems   Beliefs, customs, and specialists concerned with ensuring health and preventing and curing illness; a cultural universal.

hegemony   The internalization of a dominant ideology.

historical linguistics   Subdivision of linguistics that studies languages over time.

holistic   Interested in the whole of the human condition: past, present, and future; biology, society, language, and culture.

hominid   A member of the taxonomic family that includes humans and the African apes and their immediate ancestors.

hominin   A member of the human lineage after its split from ancestral chimps; used to describe all the human species that ever have existed, including the extinct ones, but excluding chimps and gorillas.

horticulture   Nonindustrial system of plant cultivation in which plots lie fallow for varying lengths of time.

human rights   Doctrine that invokes a realm of justice and morality beyond and superior to particular countries, cultures, and religions. Human rights, usually seen as vested in individuals, include the right to speak freely, to hold religious beliefs without persecution, and not to be enslaved.

hypodescent   Rule that automatically places the children of a union or mating between members of different socioeconomic groups in the less privileged group.

I

illness   A condition of poor health perceived or felt by an individual.

imperialism   A policy of extending the rule of a nation or an empire over foreign nations and of taking and holding foreign colonies.

incest   Sexual relations with a close relative.

increased equity   A reduction in absolute poverty, with a more even distribution of wealth.

independent invention   Development of the same culture trait or pattern in separate cultures as a result of comparable needs and circumstances.

indigenization   Process by which cultural items introduced from outside are modified to fit the local culture.

Industrial Revolution   The historical transformation (in Europe, after 1750) of "traditional" into "modern" societies through industrialization of the economy.

informed consent   Agreement to take part in research, after the people being studied have been told about that research's purpose, nature, procedures, and potential impact on them.

intellectual property rights (IPR)   Each society's cultural base—its core beliefs and principles. IPR is claimed as a group right—a cultural right, allowing indigenous groups to control who may know and use their collective knowledge and its applications.

international culture   Cultural traditions that extend beyond national boundaries.

intersex   Pertaining to a group of conditions reflecting a discrepancy between the external genitals (penis, vagina, etc.) and the internal genitals (testes, ovaries, etc.).

intervention philosophy   Guiding principle of colonialism, conquest, missionization, or development; an ideological justification for outsiders to guide native peoples in specific directions.

interview schedule   Ethnographic tool for structuring a formal interview. A prepared form (usually printed) that guides interviews with households or individuals being compared systematically. Contrasts with a questionnaire because the researcher has personal contact and records people's answers.

K

key cultural consultant   An expert on a particular aspect of local life who helps the ethnographer understand that aspect. Also called *key informant*.

kinesics   The study of communication through body movements, stances, gestures, and facial expressions.

L

law   A legal code, including trial and enforcement; characteristic of state-organized societies.

levirate   Custom by which a widow marries the brother of her deceased husband.

lexicon   Vocabulary; a dictionary containing all the morphemes in a language and their meaning.

life history   Of a cultural consultant; provides a personal cultural portrait of existence or change in a culture.

liminality   The critically important marginal or in-between phase of a rite of passage.

lineage   Unilineal descent group based on demonstrated descent.

linguistic anthropology   The branch of anthropology that studies linguistic variation in time and space, including interrelations between language and culture; includes *historical linguistics* and *sociolinguistics*.

lobola   A customary gift before, at, or after marriage from the husband and his kin to the wife and her kin.

longitudinal research   Long-term study of a community, society, culture, or other unit, usually based on repeated visits.

M

magic   Use of supernatural techniques to accomplish specific aims.

mana   Sacred impersonal force in Melanesian and Polynesian religions.

market principle   Profit-oriented principle of exchange that dominates in states, particularly industrial states. Goods and services are bought and sold, and values are determined by supply and demand.

matrilineal descent   Unilineal descent rule in which people join the mother's group automatically at birth and stay members throughout life.

matrilocality   Customary residence with the wife's relatives after marriage, so that children grow up in their mother's community.

means (or factors) of production   Land, labor, technology, and capital—major productive resources.

medical anthropology   Unites biological and cultural anthropologists in the study of disease, health problems, health care systems, and theories about illness in different cultures and ethnic groups.

mode of production   Way of organizing production—a set of social relations through which labor is deployed to wrest energy from nature by means of tools, skills, and knowledge.

monotheism   Worship of an eternal, omniscient, omnipotent, and omnipresent supreme being.

morphology   The study of form; used in linguistics (the study of morphemes and word construction) and for form in general—for example, biomorphology relates to physical form.

multiculturalism   The view of cultural diversity in a country as something good and desirable; a multicultural society socializes individuals not only into the dominant (national) culture but also into an ethnic culture.

N

nation   Once a synonym for *ethnic group*, designating a single culture sharing a language, religion, history, territory, ancestry, and kinship; now usually a synonym for *state* or *nation-state*.

nation-state   An autonomous political entity; a country like the United States or Canada.

national culture   Cultural experiences, beliefs, learned behavior patterns, and values shared by citizens of the same nation.

nationalities   Ethnic groups that once had, or wish to have or regain, autonomous political status (their own country).

natural selection   Originally formulated by Charles Darwin and Alfred Russel Wallace; the process by which nature selects the forms most fit to survive and reproduce in a given environment, such as the tropics.

negative reciprocity   See *generalized reciprocity*.

neoliberalism   Revival of Adam Smith's classic economic liberalism, the idea that governments should not regulate private enterprise and that free market forces should rule; a currently dominant intervention philosophy.

neolocality   Postmarital residence pattern in which a couple establishes a new place of residence rather than living with or near either set of parents.

norms   Cultural standards or guidelines that enable individuals to distinguish between appropriate and inappropriate behavior in a given society.

O

office   Permanent political position.

overinnovation   Characteristic of development projects that require major changes in people's daily lives, especially ones that interfere with customary subsistence pursuits.

P

pantribal sodality   A non-kin-based group that exists throughout a tribe, spanning several villages.

participant observation   A characteristic ethnographic technique; taking part in the events one is observing, describing, and analyzing.

particularity   Distinctive or unique culture trait, pattern, or integration.

pastoral nomadism   Movement throughout the year by the whole pastoral group (men, women, and children) with their animals; more generally, such constant movement in pursuit of strategic resources.

pastoralists   People who use a food-producing strategy of adaptation based on care of herds of domesticated animals.

patriarchy   Political system ruled by men in which women have inferior social and political status, including basic human rights.

patrilineal descent   Unilineal descent rule in which people join the father's group automatically at birth and stay members throughout life.

patrilineal–patrilocal complex   An interrelated constellation of patrilineality, patrilocality, warfare, and male supremacy.

patrilocality   Customary residence with the husband's relatives after marriage, so that children grow up in their father's community.

peasant   Small-scale agriculturist living in a state, with rent fund obligations.

periphery   Weakest structural position in the world system.

phenotype   An organism's evident traits; its "manifest biology"—anatomy and physiology.

phoneme   Significant sound contrast in a language that serves to distinguish meaning, as in minimal pairs.

phonemics   The study of the sound contrasts (phonemes) of a particular language.

phonetics   The study of speech sounds in general; what people actually say in various languages.

phonology   The study of sounds used in speech.

plural marriage   Marriage of a man to two or more women (polygyny) or marriage of a woman to two or more men (polyandry) at the same time; see also *polygamy*.

plural society   A society that combines ethnic contrasts, ecological specialization (i.e., use of different environmental resources by each ethnic group), and the economic interdependence of those groups.

polyandry   Variety of plural marriage in which a woman has more than one husband.

polygamy   Marriage with three or more spouses, at the same time; see also *plural marriage*.

polygyny   Variety of plural marriage in which a man has more than one wife.

polities   Political entities or systems.

polytheism   Belief in several deities who control aspects of nature.

popular culture: Aspects of culture that have meaning for many or most people within the same national culture, including media, fast-food restaurant chains, sports, and games.

postcolonial   Referring to interactions between European nations and the societies they colonized (mainly after 1800); more generally, *postcolonial* may be used to signify a position against imperialism and Eurocentrism.

postmodern   In its most general sense, describes the blurring and breakdown of established canons (rules, standards), categories, distinctions, and boundaries.

postmodernism   A style and movement in architecture that succeeded modernism. Compared with modernism, postmodernism is less geometric, less functional, less austere, more playful, and more willing to include elements from diverse times and cultures; *postmodern* now describes comparable developments in music, literature, and visual art.

postmodernity   Condition of a world in flux, with people on-the-move, in which established groups, boundaries, identities, contrasts, and standards are reaching out and breaking down.

potlatch   Competitive feast among Indians on the North Pacific Coast of North America.

power   The ability to exercise one's will over others—to do what one wants; the basis of political status.

prejudice   Devaluing (looking down on) a group because of its assumed behavior, values, capabilities, or attributes.

prestige   Esteem, respect, or approval for acts, deeds, or qualities considered exemplary.

productivity   The ability to use the rules of one's language to create new expressions comprehensible to other speakers; a basic feature of language.

protolanguage   Language ancestral to several daughter languages.

public anthropology   Efforts to extend anthropology's visibility beyond academia and to demonstrate its public policy relevance.

R

race   An ethnic group assumed to have a biological basis.

racial classification   The attempt to assign humans to discrete categories (purportedly) based on common ancestry.

racism   Discrimination against an ethnic group assumed to have a biological basis.

reciprocity   One of the three principles of exchange; governs exchange between social equals; major exchange mode in band and tribal societies.

reciprocity continuum   Regarding exchanges, a range running from generalized reciprocity (closely related/deferred return) through balanced reciprocity to negative reciprocity (strangers/immediate return).

redistribution   Major exchange mode of chiefdoms, many archaic states, and some states with managed economies.

refugees   People who have been forced (involuntary refugees) or who have chosen (voluntary refugees) to flee a country, to escape persecution or war.

religion   Beliefs and rituals concerned with supernatural beings, powers, and forces.

revitalization movements   Movements that occur in times of change, in which religious leaders emerge and undertake to alter or revitalize a society.

rites of passage   Culturally defined activities associated with the transition from one place or stage of life to another.

ritual   Behavior that is formal, stylized, repetitive, and stereotyped, performed earnestly as a social act; rituals are held at set times and places and have liturgical orders.

S

sample   A smaller study group chosen to represent a larger population.

Sapir-Whorf hypothesis   Theory that different languages produce different ways of thinking.

science   A systematic field of study or body of knowledge that aims, through experiment, observation, and deduction, to produce reliable explanations of phenomena, with reference to the material and physical world.

scientific medicine   As distinguished from Western medicine, a health care system based on scientific knowledge and procedures, encompassing such fields as pathology, microbiology, biochemistry, surgery, diagnostic technology, and applications.

semantics   A language's meaning system.

semiperiphery   Structural position in the world system intermediate between core and periphery.

sexual dimorphism   Marked differences in male and female biology, besides the contrasts in breasts and genitals, and temperament.

sexual orientation   A person's habitual sexual attraction to and activities with persons of the opposite sex (*heterosexuality*), the same sex (*homosexuality*), or both sexes (*bisexuality*).

shaman   A part-time religious practitioner who mediates between ordinary people and supernatural beings and forces.

social control   Those fields of the social system (beliefs, practices, and institutions) that are most actively involved in the maintenance of any norms and the regulation of any conflict.

society   Organized life in groups; typical of humans and other animals.

sociolinguistics   Study of relationships between social and linguistic variation; study of language in its social context.

sociopolitical typology   Classification scheme based on the scale and complexity of social organization and the effectiveness of political regulation; includes band, tribe, chiefdom, and state.

sororate   Custom by which a widower marries the sister of the deceased wife.

state   Complex sociopolitical system that administers a territory and populace with substantial contrasts in occupation, wealth, prestige, and power. An independent, centrally organized political unit; a government. A form of social and political organization with a formal, central government and a division of society into classes.

status   Any position that determines where someone fits in society; may be ascribed or achieved.

stereotypes   Fixed ideas—often unfavorable—about what members of a group are like.

style shifts   Variations in speech in different contexts.

subcultures   Different cultural symbol-based traditions associated with subgroups in the same complex society.

subgroups   Languages within a taxonomy of related languages that are most closely related.

subordinate   The lower, or underprivileged, group in a stratified system.

superordinate   The upper, or privileged, group in a stratified system.

survey research   Characteristic research procedure among social scientists other than anthropologists. Studies society through sampling, statistical analysis, and impersonal data collection.

symbol   Something, verbal or nonverbal, that arbitrarily and by convention stands for something else, with which it has no necessary or natural connection.

syntax   The arrangement and order of words in phrases and sentences.

T

taboo   Prohibition backed by supernatural sanctions.

totem   An animal, plant, or geographic feature associated with a specific social group, to which that totem is sacred or symbolically important.

transgender   A category of varied individuals whose gender identity contradicts their biological sex at birth and the gender identity that society assigned to them in infancy.

transhumance One of two variants of pastoralism; part of the population moves seasonally with the herds while the other part remains in home villages.

tribe Form of sociopolitical organization usually based on horticulture or pastoralism. Socioeconomic stratification and centralized rule are absent in tribes, and there is no means of enforcing political decisions.

U

underdifferentiation Planning fallacy of viewing less-developed countries as an undifferentiated group; ignoring cultural diversity and adopting a uniform approach (often ethnocentric) for very different types of project beneficiaries.

unilineal descent Matrilineal or patrilineal descent.

universal Something that exists in every culture.

urban anthropology The anthropological study of life in and around world cities, including urban social problems, differences between urban and other environments, and adaptation to city life.

V

variables Attributes (e.g., age, occupation, income) that differ from one person or case to the next.

village head Leadership position in a village (as among the Yanomami, where the head is always a man); has limited authority; and leads by example and persuasion.

W

wealth All a person's material assets, including income, land, and other types of property; the basis of economic status.

Westernization The acculturative influence of Western expansion on other cultures.

working class (or proletariat) Those who must sell their labor to survive; the antithesis of the bourgeoisie in Marx's class analysis.

world-system theory Argument for the historic and contemporary social, political, and economic significance of an identifiable global system, based on wealth and power differentials, that extends beyond individual countries.

Bibliography

Adams, S. 2012. The World's Next Genocide. *New York Times,* November 15.

Ahearn, L. M. 2012. *Living Language: An Introduction to Linguistic Anthropology.* Malden, MA: Wiley-Blackwell.

Amadiume, I. 1987. *Male Daughters, Female Husbands.* Atlantic Highlands, NJ: Zed.

Amos, T. D. 2011. *Embodying Difference: The Making of the Burakumin in Modern Japan.* Honolulu: University of Hawaii Press.

Anderson, B. 2006 (orig. 1991). *Imagined Communities: Reflections on the Origin and Spread of Nationalism,* rev. ed. New York: Verso.

Anderson-Levitt, K. M. 2012. *Anthropologies of Education: A Global Guide to Ethnographic Studies of Learning and Schooling.* New York: Berghahn Books.

Andersson, R., 2014. *Inequality Inc.: Clandestine Migration and the Business of Bordering Europe.* Berkeley: University of California Press.

Anemone, R. L. 2011. *Race and Human Diversity: A Biocultural Approach.* Upper Saddle River, NJ: Prentice Hall/Pearson.

Antoun, R. T. 2008. *Understanding Fundamentalism: Christian, Islamic, and Jewish Movements,* 2nd ed. Lanham, MD: AltaMira.

Ansell, A. E. 2013. *Race and Ethnicity: The Key Concepts.* New York: Routledge.

Appadurai, A. 1990. Disjuncture and Difference in the Global Cultural Economy. *Public Culture* 2(2):1–24.

———. 1991. Global Ethnoscapes: Notes and Queries for a Transnational Anthropology. In *Recapturing Anthropology: Working in the Present,* R. G. Fox, ed., pp. 191–210. Santa Fe, NM: School of American Research Advanced Seminar Series.

Appiah, K. A. 1990. Racisms. In *Anatomy of Racism,* David Theo Goldberg, ed., pp. 3–17. Minneapolis: University of Minnesota Press.

Arrighi, G. 2010. *The Long Twentieth Century: Money, Power, and the Origins of Our Times,* new and updated ed. New York: Verso.

Ashcroft, B., G. Griffiths, and H. Tiffin. 2013. *Postcolonial Studies: The Key Concepts,* 3rd ed. New York: Routledge, Taylor and Francis.

Atran, S. 2016. The Devoted Actor: Unconditional Commitment and Intractable Conflict across Cultures. *Current Anthropology* 57 (Supplement 13): S192–S203.

Atran, S., et al. 2014. The Devoted Actor, Sacred Values, and Willingness to Fight: Preliminary Studies with ISIL Volunteers and Kurdish Frontline Fighters. University of Oxford, United Kingdom: ARTIS Research. http://johnjayresearch.org/ct/files/2015/05/The-Devoted-Actor-Sacred-Values-and-Willingness-to-Fight.pdf.

Baer, H. A., M. Singer, and I. Susser. 2013. *Medical Anthropology and the World System,* 3rd ed. Santa Barbara, CA: Praeger.

Banton, M. 2015. *What We Now Know about Race and Ethnicity.* New York: Berghahn Books.

Barfield, T. J. 2010. *Afghanistan: A Cultural and Political History.* Princeton, NJ: Princeton University Press.

Baron, D. E. 2009. *A Better Pencil: Readers, Writers, and the Digital Revolution.* New York: Oxford University Press.

———. 2015. Singular They Is Word of the Year. The Web of Language, November 19. University of Illinois. https://illinois.edu/blog/view/25/280996.

Barth, F. 1968. (orig. 1958). Ecologic Relations of Ethnic Groups in Swat, North Pakistan. In *Man in Adaptation: The Cultural Present,* Yehudi Cohen, ed., pp. 324–331. Chicago: Aldine.

———. 1969. *Ethnic Groups and Boundaries: The Social Organization of Cultural Difference.* London: Allen and Unwin.

Bartlett, B. 2010. America's Foreign Owned National Debt. *Forbes,* March 12. http://www.forbes.com/2010/03/11/treasury-securities-national-debt-chinatrade-opinions-columnists-bruce-Bartlett_print.html.

Beck, S., and C. A. Maida, eds. 2013. *Toward Engaged Anthropology*. New York: Berghahn Books.

————. 2015. *Public Anthropology in a Borderless World*. New York: Berghahn Books.

Bellah, R. N. 2011. *Religion in Human Evolution: From the Paleolithic to the Axial Age*. Cambridge, MA: Belknap Press of Harvard University Press.

Benedict, R. F. 1946. *The Chrysanthemum and the Sword*. Boston: Houghton Mifflin.

Bennett, J. W. 1969. *Northern Plainsmen: Adaptive Strategy and Agrarian Life*. Chicago: Aldine.

Berger, P. 2010. Pentecostalism—Protestant Ethic or Cargo Cult? *Peter Berger's blog,* July 29. http://blogs.the-american-interest.com/berger/2010/07/29/pentecostalism-%E2%80%93-protestant-ethic-or-cargo-cult/.

Berlin, B., and P. Kay. 1992 (orig. 1969). *Basic Color Terms: Their Universality and Evolution,* 2nd ed. Berkeley: University of California Press.

Bernard, H. R. 2011. *Research Methods in Anthropology: Qualitative and Quantitative Approaches*. 5th ed. Lanham, MD: AltaMira.

————. 2013. *Social Science Research Methods: Qualitative and Quantitative Approaches,* 2nd ed. Los Angeles: Sage.

Bernard, H. R., and C. C. Gravlee, eds. 2014. *Handbook of Methods in Cultural Anthropology,* 2nd ed. Lanham: Rowman & Littlefield.

Besnier, N., and S. Brownell. 2016. The Untold Story behind Fiji's Astonishing Gold Medal. *SAPIENS*, August 19. http://www.sapiens.org/culture/fiji-rugby-racial-sexual-politics/.

Bielo, J. S. 2015. *Anthropology of Religion: The Basics*. New York: Routledge.

Bjuremalm, H. 1997. Rattvisa kan skiruppas i Rwanda: Folkmordet 1994 gar attt forklara och analyseras pa samma satt som forintelsen av judarna. *Dagens Nyheter* [06-03-1977, p. B3].

Black, J. 2015. *The British Empire: A History and a Debate*. Burlington, VT: Ashgate.

Blackwood, E. 2010. *Falling into the Lesbi World: Desire and Difference in Indonesia*. Honolulu: University of Hawaii Press.

Blommaert, J. 2010. *Sociolinguistics of Globalization*. New York: Cambridge University Press.

Blurton-Jones N.G., et al. 2000. Paternal Investment and Hunter-Gatherer Divorce Rates. In *Adaptation and Human Behavior: An Anthropological Perspective*. L. Cronk, N. Chagnon, and W. Irons, eds., pp. 69-90. New York: Aldine.

Boas, F. 1966 (orig. 1940). *Race, Language, and Culture*. New York: Free Press.

Bodley, J. H. 2012. *Anthropology and Contemporary Human Problems,* 6th ed. Lanham, MD: AltaMira.

————. 2015. *Victims of Progress*, 6th ed. Lanham, MD: Rowman & Littlefield.

Bonvillain, N. 2012. *Language, Culture, and Communication: The Meaning of Messages,* 7th ed. Boston: Pearson Prentice Hall.

————. 2016. *The Routledge Handbook of Linguistic Anthropology*. New York: Routledge.

Borneman, J., and L. K. Hart. 2015. The Institution of Marriage Our Society Needs: Anthropological Investigations over the Last Century Have Shown That Marriage Is an Elastic Institution. *Aljazeera America*, July 12. http://america.aljazeera.com/opinions/2015/7/the-institution-of-marriage-our-society-needs.html.

Borofsky, R. 2000. Public Anthropology: Where To? What Next? *Anthropology Newsletter* 41(5): 9–10.

Bouckaert, R., et al. 2012. Mapping the Origins and Expansion of the Indo-European Language Family. *Science* 337: 957–960.

Bourdieu, P. 1977. *Outline of a Theory of Practice*. R. Nice (trans.). Cambridge: Cambridge University Press.

————. 1982. *Ce Que Parler Veut Dire*. Paris: Fayard.

————. 1984. *Distinction: A Social Critique of the Judgment of Taste*. R. Nice (trans.). Cambridge, MA: Harvard University Press.

Bourque, S. C., and K. B. Warren. 1987. Technology, Gender and Development. *Daedalus* 116(4):173–197.

Bowen, J. R. 2014. *Religions in Practice: An Approach to the Anthropology of Religion,* 6th ed. Boston: Pearson.

Braudel, F. 1981. *Civilization and Capitalism, 15th–18th Century,* Volume I, *The Structure of Everyday Life: The Limits.* S. Reynolds (trans.). New York: Harper and Row.

———. 1982. *Civilization and Capitalism, 15th–18th Century,* Volume II, *The Wheels of Commerce.* New York: Harper and Row.

———. 1992. *Civilization and Capitalism, 15th–18th Century,* Volume III, *The Perspective of the World.* Berkeley: University of California Press.

Briggs, C. L. 2005. Communicability, Racial Discourse, and Disease. *Annual Review of Anthropology* 34:269–291.

Briody, E. K., and R. T. Trotter II. 2008. *Partnering for Organizational Performance; Collaboration and Culture in the Global Workplace.* Lanham, MD: Rowman & Littlefield.

Brooke, J. 1992. Rio's New Day in Sun Leaves Laplander Limp. *New York Times,* June 1, p. A7.

Brookings Institution. 2010. *State of Metropolitan America: On the Front Lines of Demographic Transition.* The Brookings Institution Metropolitan Policy Program. http://www.brookings.edu/~/media/Files/Programs/Metro/state_of_metro_america/metro_america_report1.pdf.

Brown, A. 2001. Communism. *International Encyclopedia of the Social & Behavioral Sciences,* pp. 2323–2326. New York: Elsevier.

Brown, M. F. 2003. *Who Owns Native Culture?* Cambridge, MA: Harvard University Press.

Brown, P. J., and R. L. Barrett. 2010. *Understanding and Applying Medical Anthropology,* 2nd ed. New York: McGraw-Hill.

Brownstein, R. 2010. The Gray and the Brown: The Generational Mismatch. *National Journal,* July 24. http://www.nationaljournal.com/njmagazines/cs_20100724_3946php.

Buettner, E. 2016. *Europe after Empire: Decolonization, Society, and Culture.* Cambridge, UK: Cambridge University Press.

Burbank, J., and F. Cooper. 2010. *Empires in World History: Power and the Politics of Difference.* Princeton, NJ: Princeton University Press.

Burdick, J. 1993. *Looking for God in Brazil: The Progressive Catholic Church in Urban Brazil's Religious Arena.* Berkeley: University of California Press.

Burn, S. M. 2011. *Women Across Cultures,* 3rd ed. New York: McGraw-Hill.

Butler, J. 1988. Performative Acts and Gender Constitution: An Essay in Phenomenology and Feminist Theory. *Theatre Journal* 40(4):519–531.

———. 1990. *Gender Trouble: Feminism and the Subversion of Identity.* New York: Routledge.

———. 2015. *Notes toward a Performative Theory of Assembly.* Cambridge, MA: Harvard University Press.

Buvinic, M. 1995. The Feminization of Poverty? Research and Policy Needs. In *Reducing Poverty through Labour Market Policies.* Geneva: International Institute for Labour Studies.

Cairns, M. F. 2015. *Shifting Cultivation and Environmental Change: Indigenous People, Agriculture and Forest Conservation.* New York: Routledge.

Caldararo, N. L. 2014. *The Anthropology of Complex Economic Systems: Inequality, Stability, and Cycles of Crisis.* Lanham, MD: Lexington Books.

Carballo, D. M. 2016. *Urbanization and Religion in Ancient Central Mexico.* New York: Oxford University Press.

Carneiro, R. L. 1956. Slash-and-Burn Agriculture: A Closer Look at Its Implications for Settlement Patterns. In *Men and Cultures.* Selected Papers of the Fifth International Congress of Anthropological and Ethnological Sciences, pp. 229–234. Philadelphia: University of Pennsylvania Press.

————. 1968 (orig. 1961). Slash-and-Burn Cultivation among the Kuikuru and Its Implications for Cultural Development in the Amazon Basin. In *Man in Adaptation: The Cultural Present,* Y. A. Cohen, ed., pp. 131–145. Chicago: Aldine.

————. 1970. A Theory of the Origin of the State. *Science* 69:733–738.

————. 1990. Chiefdom-Level Warfare as Exemplified in Fiji and the Cauca Valley. In *The Anthropology of War,* J. Haas, ed., pp. 190–211. Cambridge: Cambridge University Press.

————. 1991. The Nature of the Chiefdom as Revealed by Evidence from the Cauca Valley of Colombia. In *Profiles in Cultural Evolution,* A. T. Rambo and K. Gillogly, eds. Anthropological Papers 85, pp. 167–190. Ann Arbor: University of Michigan Museum of Anthropology.

Carrier, J. G. 2012. *A Handbook of Economic Anthropology.* Cheltenham, UK: Edward Edgar.

Carsten, J. 2004. *After Kinship.* New York: Cambridge University Press.

Casanova, J. 2001. Religion, the New Millennium, and Globalization. *Sociology of Religion* 62:415–441.

Cefkin, M., ed. 2009. *Ethnography and the Corporate Encounter: Reflections on Research in and of Corporations.* New York: Berghahn Books.

Cernea, M., ed. 1991. *Putting People First: Sociological Variables in Rural Development,* 2nd ed. New York: Oxford University Press (published for the World Bank).

Ceuppens, B., and P. Geschiere. 2005. Autochthony: Local or Global? New Modes in the Struggle over Citizenship and Belonging in Africa and Europe. *Annual Review of Anthropology* 34:385–407.

Chagnon, N. A. 1992 (orig. 1983). *Yanomamo: The Fierce People,* 4th ed. New York: Harcourt Brace.

————. 1997. *Yanomamo,* 5th ed. Fort Worth, TX: Harcourt Brace.

————. 2013. *Noble Savages: My Life among Two Dangerous Tribes—the Yanomamo and the Anthropologists.* New York: Simon and Schuster.

Chambers, E. 1987. Applied Anthropology in the Post-Vietnam Era: Anticipations and Ironies. *Annual Review of Anthropology* 16:309–337.

Chapais, B. 2008. *Primeval Kinship: How Pair Bonding Gave Birth to Human Society.* Cambridge, MA: Harvard University Press.

Chatterjee, P. 2004. *The Politics of the Governed: Reflections on Popular Politics in Most of the World.* New York: Columbia University Press.

Chibnik, M. 2011. *Anthropology, Economics, and Choice.* Austin: University of Texas Press.

Chomsky, N. 1957. *Syntactic Structures.* The Hague: Mouton.

————. 2014. *Aspects of the Theory of Syntax,* 50th Anniversary ed. Cambridge, MA: MIT Press.

Clark, G. 2010. *African Market Women: Seven Life Stories from Ghana.* Indianapolis: Indiana University Press.

Coburn, N. 2011. *Bazaar Politics: Power and Pottery in an Afghan Market Town.* Stanford, CA: Stanford University Press.

Cody, D. 1998. British Empire. The Victorian Web. http://www.victorianweb.org/history/empire/Empire.html

Cohen, P. 2008. The Pentagon Enlists Social Scientists to Study Security Issues. *New York Times,* June 18.

Cohen, R. 1967. *The Kanuri of Bornu.* New York: Holt, Rinehart & Winston.

Cohen, Y. 1974. Culture as Adaptation. In *Man in Adaptation: The Cultural Present,* 2nd ed., Y. A. Cohen, ed., pp. 45–68. Chicago: Aldine.

Colson, E., and T. Scudder. 1988. *For Prayer and Profit: The Ritual, Economic, and Social Importance of Beer in Gwembe District, Zambia, 1950–1982.* Stanford, CA: Stanford University Press.

Conklin, A. L., S. Fishman, and R. Zaretsky. 2015. *France and Its Empire since 1870*. New York: Oxford University Press.

Cooper, F. 2014. *Africa in the World: Capitalism, Empire, Nation-State*. Cambridge, MA: Harvard University Press.

Council of Economic Advisers. 2014. *Nine Facts about American Families and Work*. Executive Office of the President of the United States. https://www.whitehouse.gov/sites/default/files/docs/nine_facts_about_family_and_work_real_final.pdf.

Coy, P. 2014. The Richest Rich Are in a Class by Themselves. *Bloomberg News,* April 14. http://www.bloomberg.com/news/articles/2014-04-03/top-tenth-of-1-percenters-reaps-all-the-riches.

Crewe, E., and R. Axelby. 2013. *Anthropology and Development: Culture, Morality, and Politics in a Globalised World*. Cambridge, UK: Cambridge University Press.

Cribb, J. 2010. *The Coming Famine: The Global Food Crisis and What We Can Do to Avoid It*. Berkeley: University of California Press.

Cultural Survival Quarterly. Quarterly journal. Cambridge, MA: Cultural Survival, Inc.

Dagne, T. W. 2015. *Intellectual Property and Traditional Knowledge in the Global Economy: Translating Geographical Indications for Development*. New York: Routledge.

DaMatta, R. 1991. *Carnivals, Rogues, and Heroes: An Interpretation of the Brazilian Dilemma*. Translated from the Portuguese by John Drury. Notre Dame, IN: University of Notre Dame Press.

D'Andrade, R. 1984. Cultural Meaning Systems. In *Culture Theory: Essays on Mind, Self, and Emotion,* R. A. Shweder and R. A. Levine, eds., pp. 88–119. Cambridge: Cambridge University Press.

Darwin, J. 2013. *Unfinished Empire: The Global Expansion of Britain*. New York: Bloomsbury Press.

Das, V., and D. Poole, eds. 2004. *Anthropology in the Margins of the State*. Santa Fe, NM: School of American Research Press.

Davenport, C., and J. Haner. 2015. The Marshall Islands Are Disappearing. *New York Times,* December 1. http://www.nytimes.com/interactive/2015/12/02/world/The-Marshall-Islands-Are-Disappearing.html.

Day, E. 2015. #BlackLivesMatter: The Birth of a New Civil Rights Movement. *The Guardian,* July 19. http://www.theguardian.com/world/2015/jul/19/blacklivesmatter-birth-civil-rights-movement.

Degler, C. 1970. *Neither Black nor White: Slavery and Race Relations in Brazil and the United States*. New York: Macmillan.

de la Peña, G. 2005. Social and Cultural Policies toward Indigenous Peoples: Perspectives from Latin America. *Annual Review of Anthropology* 34:717–739.

DeNavas-Walt, C., and B. D. Proctor. 2015. *Income and Poverty in the United States: 2014*. U.S. Census Bureau, Current Population Reports, P60-252. Washington, DC: U.S. Government Printing Office. https://www.census.gov/content/dam/Census/library/publications/2015/demo/p60-252.pdf.

————. 2008. *Overwhelming Terror: Love, Fear, Peace and Violence among the Semai of Malaysia*. Lanham, MD: Rowman & Littlefield.

De Vos, G. A., and H. Wagatsuma. 1966. *Japan's Invisible Race: Caste in Culture and Personality*. Berkeley: University of California Press.

DiMento, J. F. C., and P. Doughman. 2014. *Climate Change: What It Means for Us, Our Children, and Our Grandchildren*. Cambridge, MA: MIT Press.

Donham, D. L. 2011. *Violence in a Time of Liberation: Murder and Ethnicity at a South African Gold Mine, 1994*. Durham, NC: Duke University Press.

Donnelly, J. 2013. *Universal Human Rights in Theory and Practice*, 3rd ed. Ithaca, NY: Cornell University Press.

Donovan, J. M. 2007. *Legal Anthropology*. Lanham, MD: Altamira.

Dorward, D. C., ed. 1983. *The Igbo "Women's War" of 1929: Documents Relating to the Aba Riots in Eastern Nigeria*. Wakefield, England: East Ardsley.

Dove, M. R., and C. Carpenter, eds. 2008. *Environmental Anthropology: A Historical Reader*. Malden, MA: Blackwell.

Dove, M. R., P. E. Sajise, and A. A. Doolittle, eds. 2011. *Beyond the Sacred Forest: Complicating Conservation in Southeast Asia*. Durham, NC: Duke University Press.

Doyle, C. M. 2015. *Indigenous Peoples, Title to Territory, Rights, and Resources: The Transformative Role of Free Prior and Informed Consent*. New York: Routledge.

Drahos, P. 2014. *Intellectual Property, Indigenous People, and Their Knowledge*. Cambridge, UK: Cambridge University Press.

Dresch, P., and H. Skoda, eds. 2012. *Legalism: Anthropology and History*. New York: Oxford University Press.

Dressler, W. W., K. S. Oths, and C. C. Gravlee. 2005. Race and Ethnicity in Public Health Research. *Annual Review of Anthropology* 34:231–252.

Duffield, M., and V. Hewitt, eds. 2009. *Empire, Development, and Colonialism: The Past in the Present*. Rochester, NY: James Currey.

Duranti, A., ed. 2009. *Linguistic Anthropology: A Reader*. Malden, MA: Wiley Blackwell.

Durkheim, E. 1951 (orig. 1897). *Suicide: A Study in Sociology*. Glencoe, IL: Free Press.

———. 2001 (orig. 1912). *The Elementary Forms of the Religious Life*. Translated by Carol Cosman. Abridged with an introduction and notes by Mark S. Cladis. New York: Oxford University Press.

Dürr, E., and R. Jaffe, eds. 2010. *Urban Pollution: Cultural Meanings, Social Practices*. New York: Berghahn Books.

Eckert, P. 1989. *Jocks and Burnouts: Social Categories and Identity in the High School*. New York: Teachers College Press, Columbia University.

———. 2000. *Linguistic Variation as Social Practice: The Linguistic Construction of Identity in Belten High*. Malden, MA: Blackwell.

Eckert, P., and S. McConnell-Ginet. 2013. *Language and Gender*, 2nd ed. Cambridge, UK: Cambridge University Press.

Eckert, P., and N. Mendoza-Denton. 2002. Getting Real in the Golden State. *Language*, March 29.

Edelman, M., and A. Haugerud. 2005. *The Anthropology of Development and Globalization: From Classical Political Economy to Contemporary Neoliberalism*. Malden, MA: Blackwell.

Edwards, J. 2013. *Sociolinguistics: A Very Short Introduction*. New York: Oxford Universiry Press.

Ellen, R., S. J. Lycett, and S. E. Johns, eds. 2013. *Understanding Cultural Transmission in Anthropology: A Critical Synthesis*. New York: Berghahn.

Ellick, C. J., and J. E. Watkins. 2011. *The Anthropology Graduate's Guide: From Student to a Career*. Walnut Creek, CA: Left Coast Press.

Entmacher, J., et al. 2013. *Insecure and Unequal: Poverty and Income among Women and Families 2000–2012*. Washington, DC: National Women's Law Center. http://www.nwlc.org/resource/insecure-unequal-poverty-among-women-and-families-2000-2012.

Erickson, J. 2016. Minority, Low-Income Neighborhoods Targeted for Hazardous Waste. University of Michigan, *The University Record*, January 20.

Eriksen, T. H. 2014. *Globalization: The Key Concepts*, 2nd ed. New York: Bloomsbury Academic.

Errington, F., and D. Gewertz. 1987. *Cultural Alternatives and a Feminist Anthropology: An Analysis of Culturally Constructed Gender Interests in Papua New Guinea*. New York: Cambridge University Press.

Ervin, A. M. 2005. *Applied Anthropology: Tools and Perspectives for Contemporary Practice*, 2nd ed. Boston: Pearson/Allyn & Bacon.

———. 2014. *Cultural Transformation and Globalization: Theory, Development and Social Change*. Boulder, CO: Paradigm.

Escobar, A. 2012. *Encountering Development: The Making and Unmaking of the Third World*. Princeton, NJ: Princeton University Press.

Evans-Pritchard, E. E. 1970. Sexual Inversion among the Azande. *American Anthropologist* 72:1428–1433.

Fairbanks, D. J. 2015. *Everyone Is African: How Science Explodes the Myth of Race.* New York: Prometheus Books.

Fairclough, N. 2015. *Language and Power.* New York: Routledge.

Fearon, J. D. 2003. Ethnic and Cultural Diversity by Country. *Journal of Economic Growth* 8:195–222.

Ferguson, D. 2015. First Black Player on PGA Tour Dies. *Associated Press, Post and Courier.* Charleston, SC, February 5.

Ferguson, R. B. 1995. *Yanomami Warfare: A Political History.* Santa Fe, NM: School of American Research Press.

Ferraro, G., and E. Briody. 2013. *The Cultural Dimension of Global Business,* 7th ed. Boston: Pearson.

Field, L. W., and R. G. Fox. 2007. *Anthropology Put to Work.* New York: Berg.

Finnan, C. 2016. Residential Schooling Brings Opportunity to India's Poorest Indigenous Children. *Sapiens,* October 12. http://www.sapiens.org/culture/india-indigenous-education/.

Finnstrom, S. 1997. Postcoloniality and the Postcolony: Theories of the Global and the Local. http://www.postcolonialweb.org/poldiscourse/finnstrom/finnstrom2.html.

Fiske, J. 2011. *Reading the Popular,* 2nd ed. New York: Routledge.

Fleisher, M. L. 2000. *Kuria Cattle Raiders: Violence and Vigilantism on the Tanzania/Kenya Frontier.* Ann Arbor: University of Michigan Press.

Ford, C. S., and F. A. Beach. 1951. *Patterns of Sexual Behavior.* New York: Harper Torchbooks.

Fortes, M. 1950. Kinship and Marriage among the Ashanti. In *African Systems of Kinship and Marriage,* A. R. Radcliffe-Brown and D. Forde, eds., pp. 252–284. London: Oxford University Press.

Fortier, J. 2009. The Ethnography of South Asian Foragers. *Annual Review of Anthropology* 39:99–114.

Foster, G. M. 1965. Peasant Society and the Image of Limited Good. *American Anthropologist* 67:293–315.

Foster, G. M., and B. G. Anderson. 1978. *Medical Anthropology.* New York: McGraw-Hill.

Foucault, M. 1979. *Discipline and Punish: The Birth of the Prison.* A. Sheridan (trans.). New York: Vintage Books.

———. 1990. *The History of Sexuality,* Volume 2, *The Use of Pleasure.* R. Hurley (trans.). New York: Vintage.

Freeman, M., and D. Napier, eds. 2009. *Law and Anthropology.* New York: Oxford University Press.

Freilich, M., D. Raybeck, and J. Savishinsky. 1991. *Deviance: Anthropological Perspectives.* Westport, CT: Bergin and Garvey.

Freston, P., ed. 2008. *Evangelical Christianity and Democracy in Latin America.* New York: Oxford University Press.

Fricke, T. 1994. *Himalayan Households: Tamang Demography and Domestic Processes,* 2nd ed. New York: Columbia University Press.

Fried, M. H. 1960. On the Evolution of Social Stratification and the State. In *Culture in History,* S. Diamond, ed., pp. 713–731. New York: Columbia University Press.

———. 1967. *The Evolution of Political Society: An Essay in Political Anthropology.* New York: McGraw-Hill.

Friedl, E. 1962. *Vasilika: A Village in Modern Greece.* New York: Holt, Rinehart, and Winston.

———. 1975. *Women and Men: An Anthropologist's View.* New York: Holt, Rinehart & Winston.

Friedman, J., ed. 2003. *Globalization, the State, and Violence.* Walnut Creek, CA: AltaMira.

Friedman, K. E., and J. Friedman. 2008. *The Anthropology of Global Systems.* Lanham, MD: AltaMira.

Fuchs, C., and M. Sandoval, eds. 2014. *Critique, Social Media, and the Information Society.* New York: Routledge/Taylor and Francis.

Garcia-Navarro, L. 2013. Brazilian Believers of Hidden Religion Step Out of Shadows, September 16. National Public Radio. http://www.npr.org/blogs/parallels/2013/09/16/216890587/brazilian-believers-of-hidden-religion-step-out-of-shadows.

Geertz, C. 1973. *The Interpretation of Cultures.* New York: Basic Books.

Gell-Mann, M., and M. Ruhlen. 2011. The Origin and Evolution of Word Order. *Proceedings of the National Academy of Sciences* 108(42):17290–17295. http://www.pnas.org/content/early/2011/10/04/1113716108.

Giddens, A. 1973. *The Class Structure of the Advanced Societies.* New York: Cambridge University Press.

Gillis, J. 2015. Short Answers to Hard Questions about Climate Change. *New York Times,* November 28. http://www.nytimes.com/interactive/2015/11/28/science/what-is-climate-change.html.

———. 2016a. 2015 Was Hottest Year in Historical Record, Scientists Say. *New York Times,* January 20. http://www.nytimes.com/2016/01/21/science/earth/2015-hottest-year-global-warming.html.

———. 2016b. Seas Are Rising at Fastest Rate in Last 28 Centuries. *New York Times,* February 22. http://www.nytimes.com/2016/02/23/science/sea-level-rise-global-warming-climate-change.html.

Gilmore, D. D. 1987. *Aggression and Community: Paradoxes of Andalusian Culture.* New Haven, CT: Yale University Press.

Gimpel, J. 1988. *The Medieval Machine: The Industrial Revolution of the Middle Ages,* 2nd ed. Aldershot, Hants, UK: Wildwood House.

Gluckman, M. 2012. *Politics, Law, and Ritual in Tribal Society.* New Brunswick, NJ: Transaction.

Gmelch, G. 1978. Baseball Magic. *Human Nature* 1(8):32–40.

———. 2006. *Inside Pitch: Life in Professional Baseball.* Lincoln: University of Nebraska Press.

Goleman, D. 1992. Anthropology Goes Looking for Love in All the Old Places. *New York Times,* November 24, p. B1.

Gonzalez-Barrera, A. 2015. More Mexicans Leaving Than Coming to U.S.: Net Loss of 140,000 from 2009 to 2014; Family Reunification Top Reason for Return. Pew Research Center-Hispanic Trends. November 19. http://www.pewhispanic.org/2015/11/19/more-mexicans-leaving-than-coming-to-the-u-s/.

Gotkowitz, L., ed. 2011. *Histories of Race and Racism: The Andes and Mesoamerica from Colonial Times to the Present.* Durham, NC: Duke University Press.

Gough, E. K. 1959. The Nayars and the Definition of Marriage. *Journal of the Royal Anthropological Institute* 89:23–34.

Gould, T. H. P. 2016. *Global Advertising in a Global Culture.* Lanham, MD: Rowman & Littlefield.

Graber, M., and J. Atkinson. 2012. Business Anthropology Unlocks Opportunities. *Memphis Daily News* 127(185), September 21. https://www.memphisdailynews.com/news/2012/sep/21/business-anthropology-unlocks-opportunities/.

Graburn, N. H. H., et al., eds. 2008. *Multiculturalism in the New Japan: Crossing the Boundaries Within.* New York: Berghahn Books.

Gramsci, A. 1971. *Selections from the Prison Notebooks.* Q. Hoare and G. N. Smith, ed. and trans. London: Wishart.

Green, G. M., and R. W. Sussman. 1990. Deforestation History of the Eastern Rain Forests of Madagascar from Satellite Images. *Science* 248 (April 13):212–215.

Green, P. 1999. Mirror, Mirror; The Anthropologist of Dressing Rooms. *New York Times,* May 2. http://www.nytimes.com/1999/05/02/style/mirror-mirror-the-anthropologist-of-dressing-rooms.html.

Gremaux, R. 1993. Woman Becomes Man in the Balkans. In *Third Sex, Third Gender: Beyond Sexual Dimorphism in Culture and History,* G. Herdt, ed. Cambridge, MA: MIT Press.

Griffin, P. B., and A. Estioko-Griffin, eds. 1985. *The Agta of Northern Luzon: Recent Studies.* Cebu City, Philippines: University of San Carlos.

Gu, S. 2012. *Language and Culture in the Growth of Imperialism.* Jefferson, NC: McFarland.

Gudeman, S. F. 2016. *Anthropology and Economy.* New York: Cambridge University Press.

Gunewardena, N., and A. Kingsolver, eds. 2007. *The Gender of Globalization: Women Navigating Cultural and Economic Marginalities.* Santa Fe, NM: School for Advanced Research Press.

Gupta, A., and J. Ferguson. 1997a. Culture, Power, Place: Ethnography at the End of an Era. In *Culture, Power, Place: Explorations in Critical Anthropology,* A. Gupta and J. Ferguson, eds., pp. 1–29. Durham, NC: Duke University Press.

———. 1997b. Beyond "Culture": Space, Identity, and the Politics of Difference. In *Culture, Power, Place,* A. Gupta and J. Ferguson, eds., pp. 33–51. Durham, NC: Duke University Press.

Ha, K. O. n. d. Anthropologists Dig into Business: Researchers Observe Consumer Habits to Design New Products. *Mercury News.* http://www.antropologi.info/antromag/corporate/kopi/business.html.

Haenn, N., R. R. Wilk, and A. Harnish, eds. 2016. *The Environment in Anthropology: A Reader in Ecology, Culture, and Sustainable Living.* New York: New York University Press.

Hallowell, A. I. 1955. *Culture and Experience.* Philadelphia: University of Pennsylvania Press.

Hamdan, S. 2013. Social Media Firms Move to Capitalize on Popularity in Middle East. *New York Times,* February 6. http://www.nytimes.com/2013/02/07/world/middleeast/social-media-firms-move-to-capitalize-on-popularity-in-middle-east.html.

Handwerk, B. 2008. Half of Humanity Will Live in Cities by Year's End. *National Geographic News,* March 13. www.nationalgeographic.com/news/pf30472163.html.

Handwerker, W. P. 2009. *The Origins of Cultures: How Individual Choices Make Cultures Change.* Walnut Creek, CA: Left Coast Press.

Hann, C., and K. Hart. 2011. *Economic Anthropology: History, Ethnography, Critique.* Malden, MA: Polity Press.

Hann, C., and K. Hart, eds. 2009. *Market and Society: The Great Transformation Today.* New York: Cambridge University Press.

Hansen, K. V. 2005. *Not-So-Nuclear Families: Class, Gender, and Networks of Care.* New Brunswick, NJ: Rutgers University Press.

Harris, M. 1964. *Patterns of Race in the Americas.* New York: Walker.

———. 1970. Referential Ambiguity in the Calculus of Brazilian Racial Identity. *Southwestern Journal of Anthropology* 26(1):1–14.

———. 1974. *Cows, Pigs, Wars, and Witches: The Riddles of Culture.* New York: Random House.

———. 1978. *Cannibals and Kings.* New York: Vintage Books.

Harris, M., and C. P. Kottak. 1963. The Structural Significance of Brazilian Racial Categories. *Sociologia* 25:203–209.

Harrison, G. G., W. L. Rathje, and W. W. Hughes. 1994. Food Waste Behavior in an Urban Population. In *Applying Anthropology: An Introductory Reader,* 3rd ed., A. Podolefsky and P. J. Brown, eds., pp. 107–112. Mountain View, CA: Mayfield.

Harrison, K. D. 2007. *When Languages Die: The Extinction of the World's Languages and the Erosion of Human Knowledge.* New York: Oxford University Press.

———. 2010. *The Last Speakers: The Quest to Save the World's Most Endangered Languages.* Washington, DC: National Geographic.

Hart, C. W. M., A. R. Pilling, and J. C. Goodale. 1988. *The Tiwi of North Australia,* 3rd ed. Fort Worth, TX: Harcourt Brace.

Harvey, D. J. 1980. French Empire. *Academic American Encyclopedia,* Volume 8, pp. 309–310. Princeton, NJ: Arete.

Haugerud, A., M. P. Stone, and P. D. Little, eds. 2011. *Commodities and Globalization: Anthropological Perspectives.* Lanham, MD: Rowman & Littlefield.

Helliwell, J., R. Layard, and J. Sachs. 2016. *Word Happiness Report 2016.* http://world-happiness.report/wp-content/uploads/sites/2/2016/03/HR-V1_web.pdf.

Herdt, G. H. 2006. *The Sambia: Ritual, Sexuality, and Change in Papua New Guinea.* Belmont, CA: Thomson/Wadsworth.

Herdt, G. H., ed. 1984. *Ritualized Homosexuality in Melanesia.* Berkeley: University of California Press.

Herdt, G. H., and N. Polen. 2013. *Sexual Literacy: Sexuality in Human Nature, Culture and Society.* New York: McGraw-Hill.

Herzog, T. 2015. *Frontiers of Possession: Spain and Portugal in Europe and the Americas.* Cambridge, MA: Harvard University Press.

Hicks, D., ed. 2010. *Ritual and Belief: Readings in the Anthropology of Religion*, 3rd ed. Lanham, MD: AltaMira.

Hill, K. R., et al. 2011. Co-residence Patterns in Hunter-Gatherer Societies Show Unique Human Social Structure. *Science* (March 11):1286–1289.

Hill-Burnett, J. 1978. Developing Anthropological Knowledge through Application. In *Applied Anthropology in America,* E. M. Eddy and W. L. Partridge, eds., pp. 112–128. New York: Columbia University Press.

Hinton, A. L., and K. L. O'Neill, eds. 2011. *Genocide: Truth, Memory, and Representation.* Durham, NC: Duke University Press.

Hirai, T., ed. 2015. *Capitalism and the World Economy: The Light and Shadow of Globalization.* New York: Routledge.

Hobhouse, L. T. 1915. *Morals in Evolution,* rev. ed. New York: Holt.

Hoebel, E. A. 1954. *The Law of Primitive Man.* Cambridge, MA: Harvard University Press.

———. 1968 (orig. 1954). The Eskimo: Rudimentary Law in a Primitive Anarchy. In *Studies in Social and Cultural Anthropology,* J. Middleton, ed., pp. 93–127. New York: Crowell.

———. 2006. *The Law of Primitive Man: A Study in Comparative Legal Dynamics.* Cambridge, MA: Harvard University Press.

Hogan, B., N. Li, and W. H. Dutton. 2011. *A Global Shift in the Social Relationships of Networked Individuals: Meeting and Dating Online Comes of Age* (February 14). Oxford Internet Institute, University of Oxford. http://ssrn.com/abstract=1763884 or http://dx.doi.org/10.2139/ssrn.1763884.

Hoge, W. 2001. Kautokeino Journal; Reindeer Herders, at Home on a (Very Cold) Range. *New York Times,* March 26, late ed.—final, sec. A, p. 4.

Hornborg, A., B. Clark, and K. Hermele, eds. 2011. *Ecology and Power: Struggles over Land and Material Resources in the Past, Present and Future.* New York: Routledge.

Hornborg, A., and C. L. Crumley, eds. 2007. *The World System and the Earth System: Global Socioenvironmental Change and Sustainability since the Neolithic.* Walnut Creek, CA: Left Coast Press.

Hornborg, A., J. R. McNeill, and J. Martinez-Alier, eds. 2007. *Rethinking Environmental History: World-System History and Global Environmental Change.* Lanham, MD: AltaMira.

Horton, R. 1993. *Patterns of Thought in Africa and the West: Essays on Magic, Religion, and Science.* Cambridge, UK: Cambridge University Press.

Hunt, R. C. 2007. *Beyond Relativism: Comparability in Cultural Anthropology.* Lanham, MD: AltaMira.

Hunter, M. L. 2005. *Race, Gender, and the Politics of Skin Tone.* New York: Routledge.

Hyde, J. S., and J. D. DeLamater. 2016. *Understanding Human Sexuality*, 13th ed. New York: McGraw-Hill Education.

Ingraham, C. 2008. *White Weddings: Romancing Heterosexuality in Popular Culture,* 2nd ed. New York: Routledge.

Inhorn, M. C., and P. J. Brown. 1990. The Anthropology of Infectious Disease. *Annual Review of Anthropology* 19:89–117.

Inhorn, M. C., and E. A. Wentzell, eds. 2012. *Medical Anthropology at the Intersections: Histories, Activisms, and Futures*. Durham, NC: Duke University Press.

Iqbal, S. 2002. A New Light on Skin Color. *National Geographic Online Extra*. http://magma.nationalgeographic.com/ngm/0211/feature2/online_extra.html.

Jablonski, N. G. 2006. *Skin: A Natural History*. Berkeley: University of California Press.

―――. 2012. *Living Color: The Biological and Social Meaning of Skin Color*. Berkeley: University of California Press.

Jablonski, N. G., and G. Chaplin. 2000. The Evolution of Human Skin Coloration. *Journal of Human Evolution* (39):57–106.

Jackson, J., and K. B. Warren. 2005. Indigenous Movements in Latin America, 1992–2004: Controversies, Ironies, New Directions. *Annual Review of Anthropology* 34:549–573.

Jazra, K. 2014. 15 Stats about Social Media in the Middle East That You Need to Know. Social4ce/Blog, July 1. http://social4ce.com/blog/2014/07/01/15-stats-you-need-to-know-about-social-media-in-the-middle-east/.

Johnson, A. W., and T. K. Earle. 2000. *The Evolution of Human Societies: From Foraging Group to Agrarian State,* 2nd ed. Stanford, CA: Stanford University Press.

Johnston, B. R. 2009. *Life and Death Matters: Human Rights, Environment, and Social Justice,* 2nd ed. Walnut Creek, CA: Left Coast Press.

Joralemon, D. 2010. *Exploring Medical Anthropology,* 3rd ed. Boston: Pearson.

Jordan, A. 2003. *Business Anthropology*. Prospect Heights, IL: Waveland.

Jordan, B., ed. 2013. *Advancing Ethnography in Corporate Environments: Challenges and Emerging Opportunities*. Walnut Creek, CA: Left Coast Press.

Joyce, R. 2015. Aztec Marriage: A Lesson for Chief Justice Roberts. *Psychology Today,* June 26. https://www.psychologytoday.com/blog/what-makes-us-human/201506/aztec-marriage-lesson-chief-justice-roberts.

Jurafsky, D. 2014. *The Language of Food: A Linguist Reads the Menu*. New York: Norton.

Kamrava, M. 2011. *The Modern Middle East: A Political History since the First World War,* 2nd ed. Berkeley: University of California Press.

Kan, S. 1986. The 19th-Century Tlingit Potlatch: A New Perspective. *American Ethnologist* 13:191–212.

―――. 1989. *Symbolic Immortality: The Tlingit Potlatch of the Nineteenth Century*. Washington, DC: Smithsonian Institution Press.

Kaneshiro, N. K. 2009. Intersex. Medline Plus. National Institutes of Health, U.S. National Library of Medicine. http://www.nlm.nih.gov/medlineplus/ency/article/001669.htm.

Kaplan, H. R. 2014. *Understanding Conflict and Change in a Multicultural World*. Lanham, MD: Rowman & Littlefield.

Kaufman, S. R., and L. M. Morgan. 2005. The Anthropology of the Beginnings and Ends of Life. *Annual Review of Anthropology* 34:317–341.

Kellenberger, J. 2008. *Moral Relativism: A Dialogue*. Lanham, MA: Rowman & Littlefield.

Kelly, R. C. 1976. Witchcraft and Sexual Relations: An Exploration in the Social and Semantic Implications of the Structure of Belief. In *Man and Woman in the New Guinea Highlands,* P. Brown and G. Buchbinder, eds., pp. 36–53. Special Publication No. 8. Washington, DC: American Anthropological Association.

Kelly, R. L. 1995. *The Foraging Spectrum: Diversity in Hunter-Gatherer Lifeways*. Washington, DC: Smithsonian Institution Press.

Kennedy, P. 2010. *Local Lives and Global Transformations: Towards a World Society*. New York: Palgrave Macmillan.

Kent, S., ed. 2002. *Ethnicity, Hunter-Gatherers, and the "Other": Association or Assimilation in Africa*. Washington, DC: Smithsonian Institution Press.

Kent, S., and H. Vierich. 1989. The Myth of Ecological Determinism: Anticipated Mobility and Site Organization of Space. In *Farmers as Hunters: The Implications of Sedentism,* S. Kent, ed., pp. 96–130. New York: Cambridge University Press.

Kerbo, H. R. 2012. *Social Stratification and Inequality: Class Conflict in Historical, Comparative, and Global Perspective*, 8th ed. New York: McGraw-Hill.

Kershaw, S. 2009. For Teenagers, Hello Means "How about a Hug?" *New York Times*, May 28.

Keynes, J. M. 1927. *The End of Laissez-Faire*. London: L. and Virginia Woolf.

_____. 1936. *General Theory of Employment, Interest, and Money*. New York: Harcourt Brace.

Kimmel, M. S. 2013. *The Gendered Society*, 5th ed. New York: Oxford University Press.

King, E. 2012. Stanford Linguists Seek to Identify the Elusive California Accent. *Stanford Report*, August 6. http://news.stanford.edu/news/2012/august/california-dialect-linguistics-080612.html.

King, T. F., ed. 2011. *A Companion to Cultural Resource Management*. Malden, MA: Wiley-Blackwell.

Kinsey, A. C., W. B. Pomeroy, and C. E. Martin. 1948. *Sexual Behavior in the Human Male*. Philadelphia: W. B. Saunders.

Kjaerulff, J. 2010. *Internet and Change: An Ethnography of Knowledge and Flexible Work*. Walnut Creek, CA: Left Coast Press.

Kluckhohn, C. 1944. *Mirror for Man: A Survey of Human Behavior and Social Attitudes*. Greenwich, CT: Fawcett.

Kochhar, R., and W. Fry. 2014. Wealth Inequality Has Widened along Racial, Ethnic Lines since End of Great Recession. *Facttank, News in the Numbers,* December 12. Pew Research Center. http://www.pewresearch.org/fact-tank/2014/12/12/racial-wealth-gaps-great-recession/

Konopinski, N., ed. 2014. *Doing Anthropological Research: A Practical Guide*. New York: Routledge.

Kontopodis, M., C. Wulf, and B. Fichtner, eds. 2011. *Children, Development, and Education: Cultural, Historical, and Anthropological Perspectives*. New York: Springer.

Kottak, C. P. 1980. *The Past in the Present: History, Ecology, and Social Organization in Highland Madagascar*. Ann Arbor: University of Michigan Press.

_____. 1990. *Prime-Time Society: An Anthropological Analysis of Television and Culture*. Belmont, CA: Wadsworth.

_____. 1999. The New Ecological Anthropology. *American Anthropologist* 101(1):23–35.

_____. 2006. *Assault on Paradise: The Globalization of a Little Community in Brazil*, 4th ed. New York: McGraw-Hill.P

_____. 2007. Return to Madagascar: A Forty Year Retrospective. *General Anthropology: Bulletin of the General Anthropology Division of the American Anthropological Association* 14(2):1–10.

_____. 2009. *Prime-Time Society: An Anthropological Analysis of Television and Culture,* updated ed. Walnut Creek, CA: Left Coast Press.

Kottak, C. P., and K. A. Kozaitis. 2012. *On Being Different: Diversity and Multiculturalism in the North American Mainstream*, 4th ed. New York: McGraw-Hill.

Kottak, N. C. 2002. *Stealing the Neighbor's Chicken: Social Control in Northern Mozambique*. PhD dissertation. Department of Anthropology, Emory University, Atlanta, GA.

Kotz, D. M. 2015. *The Rise and Fall of Neoliberal Capitalism*. Cambridge, MA: Harvard University Press.

Kozlowski, K. 2016. Virginia Tech Expert Helped Expose Flint Water Crisis. *Detroit News*, January 24. http://www.detroitnews.com/story/news/politics/2016/01/23/virginia-tech-expert-helped-expose-flint-water-crisis/79251004/

Krogstad, J. M. 2014. 11 Facts for National Hispanic Heritage Month. Pew Research Center, September 16. http://www.pewresearch.org/fact-tank/2014/09/16/11-facts-for-national-hispanic-heritage-month/.

Kulick, D. 1998. *Travesti: Sex, Gender, and Culture among Brazilian Transgendered Prostitutes*. Chicago: University of Chicago Press.

Labov, W. 1972a. *Language in the Inner City: Studies in the Black English Vernacular.* Philadelphia: University of Pennsylvania Press.

_____. 1972b. *Sociolinguistic Patterns.* Philadelphia: University of Pennsylvania Press.

_____. 2006. *The Social Stratification of English in New York City.* New York: Cambridge University Press.

_____. 2012. *Dialect Diversity in America: The Politics of Language Change.* Charlottesville: University of Virginia Press.

Lakoff, G. 2008. *The Political Mind: Why You Can't Understand 21st-Century Politics with an 18th-Century Brain.* New York: Viking.

Lakoff, G., and E. Wehling. 2012. *The Little Blue Book: The Essential Guide to Thinking and Talking Democratic.* New York: Free Press.

Lakoff, R. T. 2004. *Language and Women's Place: Text and Commentaries,* rev. ed., M. Bucholtz, ed. New York: Oxford University Press.

Lambek, M., ed. 2008. *A Reader in the Anthropology of Religion.* Malden, MA: Blackwell.

Lange, M. 2009. *Lineages of Despotism and Development: British Colonialism and State Power.* Chicago: University of Chicago Press.

Lassiter, L. E. 1998. *The Power of Kiowa Song: A Collaborative Ethnography.* Tucson: University of Arizona Press.

Leach, E. R. 1955. Polyandry, Inheritance and the Definition of Marriage. *Man* 55:182–186.

_____. 1961. *Rethinking Anthropology.* London: Athlone Press.

Lee, R. B. 1984. *The Dobe !Kung.* New York: Harcourt Brace.

_____. 2003. *The Dobe Ju/'hoansi,* 3rd ed. Belmont, CA: Wadsworth.

_____. 2012. The !Kung and I: Reflections on My Life and Times with the Ju/Hoansi People. *General Anthropology* 19(1):1–4.

Lee, R. B., and R. H. Daly. 1999. *The Cambridge Encyclopedia of Hunters and Gatherers.* New York: Cambridge University Press.

Leman, J. 2001. *The Dynamics of Emerging Ethnicities: Immigrant and Indigenous Ethnogenesis in Confrontation.* New York: Peter Lang.

Lenski, G. 1966. *Power and Privilege: A Theory of Social Stratification.* New York: McGraw-Hill.

Levinson, B. A. U., and M. Pollock, eds. 2011. *A Companion to the Anthropology of Education.* Malden, MA: Blackwell.

Lévi-Strauss, C. 1963. *Totemism.* R. Needham (trans.). Boston: Beacon Press.

_____. 1967. *Structural Anthropology.* New York: Doubleday.

Levy, J. E., with B. Pepper. 1992. *Orayvi Revisited: Social Stratification in an "Egalitarian" Society.* Santa Fe, NM: School of American Research Press, and Seattle: University of Washington Press.

Lewin, E., and L. M. Silverstein, eds. 2016. *Mapping Feminist Anthropology in the Twenty-First Century.* New Brunswick, NJ: Rutgers University Press.

Lie, J. 2001. *Multiethnic Japan.* Cambridge, MA: Harvard University Press.

Lim, L., and U. Ansaldo. 2016. *Languages in Contact.* New York: Cambridge University Press.

Lindenbaum, S. 1972. Sorcerers, Ghosts, and Polluting Women: An Analysis of Religious Belief and Population Control. *Ethnology* 11:241–253.

Lindquist, G., and D. Handelman, eds. 2013. *Religion, Politics, and Globalization: Anthropological Approaches.* New York: Berghahn Books.

Little, K. 1971. Some Aspects of African Urbanization South of the Sahara. Reading, MA: Addison-Wesley, McCaleb Modules in Anthropology.

Lockwood, W. G. 1975. *European Moslems: Economy and Ethnicity in Western Bosnia.* New York: Academic Press.

Loomis, W. F. 1967. Skin-Pigmented Regulation of Vitamin-D Biosynthesis in Man. *Science* 157:501–506.

López, A. A. 2011. New Questions in the Immigration Debate. *Anthropology Now* 3(1):47–53.

Lowie, R. H. 1961 (orig. 1920). *Primitive Society*. New York: Harper & Brothers.

Lowrey, A. 2013. The Rich Get Richer through the Recovery. *New York Times,* September 13. http://economix.blogs.nytimes.com/2013/09/10/the-rich-get-richer-through-the-recovery/.

Lugo, A. 1997. Reflections on Border Theory, Culture, and the Nation. *Border Theory: The Limits of Cultural Politics,* Scott Michaelsen and David Johnson, eds., pp. 43–67. Minneapolis: University of Minnesota Press.

Lugo, A., and B. Maurer. 2000. *Gender Matters: Rereading Michelle Z. Rosaldo.* Ann Arbor, University of Michigan Press.

Lule, J. 2015. *Globalization and Media: Global Village of Babel.* Lanham, MA: Rowman & Littlefield.

Lupton, D. 2012. *Medicine as Culture: Illness, Disease, and the Body.* Los Angeles: Sage.

Lyons, A. P., and H. D. Lyons. 2011. *Sexualities in Anthropology: A Reader.* Walden, MA: Wiley Blackwell.

Madra, Y. M. 2004. Karl Polanyi: Freedom in a Complex Society. *Econ-Atrocity Bulletin: In the History of Thought.*

Madsbjerg, C., and M. B. Rasmussen. 2014. An Anthropologist Walks into a Bar. *Harvard Business Review,* March. https://hbr.org/2014/03/an-anthropologist-walks-into-a-bar.

Maguire, M., C. Frois, and N. Zurawski, eds. 2014. *The Anthropology of Security: Perspectives from the Frontline of Policing, Counterterrorism, and Border Control.* Sterling, VA: Pluto Press.

Malinowski, B. 1927. *Sex and Repression in Savage Society.* London and New York: International Library of Psychology, Philosophy and Scientific Method.

———. 1929. Practical Anthropology. *Africa* 2:23–38.

———. 1961 (orig. 1922). *Argonauts of the Western Pacific.* New York: Dutton.

———. 1978 (orig. 1931). The Role of Magic and Religion. In *Reader in Comparative Religion: An Anthropological Approach,* 4th ed., W. A. Lessa and E. Z. Vogt, eds., pp. 37–46. New York: Harper and Row.

———. 2013. *Crime and Custom in Savage Society.* New Brunswick, NJ: Transaction.

Malkki, L. H. 1995. *Purity and Exile: Violence, Memory, and National Cosmology among Hutu Refugees in Tanzania.* Chicago: University of Chicago Press.

Mann, C. C. 2011. *1493: Uncovering the New World Columbus Created.* New York: Knopf.

Marcus, G. E., and M. M. J. Fischer. 1986. *Anthropology as Cultural Critique: An Experimental Moment in the Human Sciences.* Chicago: University of Chicago Press.

Marger, M. 2015. *Race and Ethnic Relations: American and Global Perspectives*, 10th ed. Stamford, CT: Cengage.

Margolis, M. L. 2000. *True to Her Nature: Changing Advice to American Women.* Prospect Heights, IL: Waveland.

Marks, R. 2015. *The Origins of the Modern World: A Global and Environmental Narrative from the Fifteenth to the Twenty-First Century*, 3rd ed. Lanham, MD: Rowman & Littlefield.

Marshall, R. C., ed. 2011. *Cooperation in Economy and Society.* Lanham, MD: Rowman & Littlefield.

Martin, D. 1990. *Tongues of Fire: The Explosion of Protestantism in Latin America.* Cambridge, MA: Blackwell.

Martin, K., and B. Voorhies. 1975. *Female of the Species.* New York: Columbia University Press.

Martin, S. M. 1988. *Palm Oil and Protest: An Economic History of the Ngwa Region, South-Eastern Nigeria, 1800–1980.* New York: Cambridge University Press.

Marx, K., and F. Engels. 1976 (orig. 1848). *Communist Manifesto.* New York: Pantheon.

Mascia-Lees, F. 2010. *Gender & Difference in a Globalizing World: Twenty-First Century Anthropology.* Long Grove, IL: Waveland.

Maugh, T. H., III. 2007. One Language Disappears Every 14 Days; About Half of the World's Distinct Tongues Could Vanish This Century, Researchers Say. *Los Angeles Times,* September 19.

Maybury-Lewis, D., T. Macdonald, and B. Maybury-Lewis, eds. 2009. *Manifest Destinies and Indigenous Peoples*. Cambridge, MA: David Rockefeller Center for Latin American Studies and Harvard University Press.

Mazzeo, J., A. Rödlach, and B. P. Brenton. 2011. Introduction: Anthropologists Confront HIV/AIDS and Food Insecurity in Sub-Saharan Africa. American Anthropological Association, *Annals of Anthropological Practice* 35(1–7).

Mba, N. E. 1982. *Nigerian Women Mobilized: Women's Political Activity in Southern Nigeria, 1900–1965*. Berkeley: University of California Press.

McConnell-Ginet, S. 2010. *Gender, Sexuality, and Meaning: Linguistic Practice and Politics*. New York: Oxford University Press.

McElroy, A., and P. K. Townsend. 2009. *Medical Anthropology in Ecological Perspective*, 5th ed. Boulder, CO: Westview Press.

McGregor, W. 2015. *Linguistics: An Introduction*. New York: Bloomsbury Academic.

McLaughlin, E. C. 2016. 5 Things to Know about Flint's Water Crisis. CNN, January 21. http://www.cnn.com/2016/01/18/us/flint-michigan-water-crisis-five-things/.

Mead, M. 1937. *Cooperation and Competition among Primitive Peoples*. New York: McGraw-Hill.

————. 1950 (orig. 1935). *Sex and Temperament in Three Primitive Societies*. New York: New American Library.

————. 1977. Applied Anthropology: The State of the Art. In *Perspectives on Anthropology, 1976*. Washington, DC: American Anthropological Association.

Meigs, A., and K. Barlow. 2002. Beyond the Taboo: Imagining Incest. *American Anthropologist* 104(1):38–49.

Menzies, C. R., ed. 2006. *Traditional Ecological Knowledge and Natural Resource Management*. Lincoln: University of Nebraska Press.

Mesthrie, R., ed. 2011. *The Cambridge Handbook of Sociolinguistics*. Cambridge, UK: Cambridge University Press.

Meyer, B. 1999. *Translating the Devil: Religion and Modernity among the Ewe in Ghana*. Trenton, NJ: Africa World Press.

Miller, C. C. 2015. The Search for the Best Estimate of the Transgender Population. *New York Times,* June 8. http://www.nytimes.com/2015/06/09/upshot/the-search-for-the-best-estimate-of-the-transgender-population.html.

Mintz, S. 1985. *Sweetness and Power: The Place of Sugar in Modern History*. New York: Viking Penguin.

Mirrlees, T. 2013. *Global Entertainment Media: Between Cultural Imperialism and Cultural Globalization*. New York: Routledge.

Mohai, P., and R. Saha. 2015. Which Came First, People or Pollution? Assessing the Disparate Siting and Post-Siting Demographic Change Hypotheses of Environmental Injustice. *Environmental Research Letters* 10:1–17. http://iopscience.iop.org/article/10.1088/1748-9326/10/11/115008/pdf.

Mooney, A. 2011. *Language, Society, and Power*. New York: Routledge.

Mooney, A., and B. Evans, eds. 2015. *Language Society and Power: An Introduction*. New York: Routledge.

Moore, J. D. 2012. *Visions of Culture: An Introduction to Anthropological Theories and Theorists,* 4th ed. Lanham, MD: AltaMira.

Moro, P. A., and J. E. Myers. 2012. *Magic, Witchcraft, and Religion: A Reader in the Anthropology of Religion*, 9th ed. New York: McGraw-Hill.

Motseta, S. 2006. Botswana Gives Bushmen Tough Conditions. *Washington Post,* December 14. http://www.washingtonpost.com/wp-dyn/content/article/2006/12/14/.

Mukhopadhyay, C. C., R. Henzie, and Y. T. Moses. 2014. *How Real Is Race?: A Sourcebook on Race, Culture, and Biology*, 2nd ed. Lanham, MD: Altamira.

Murchison, J. M. 2010. *Ethnography Essentials: Designing, Conducting, and Presenting Your Research.* San Francisco: Jossey Bass.

Murdock, G. P. 1957. World Ethnographic Sample. *American Anthropologist* 59:664–687.

Murdock, G. P., and C. Provost. 1973. Factors in the Division of Labor by Sex: A Cross-Cultural Analysis. *Ethnology* 12(2):203–225.

Murray, S. O., and W. Roscoe, eds. 1998. *Boy-wives and Female Husbands: Studies in African Homosexualities.* New York: St. Martin's Press.

Nadeem, S. 2011. *Dead Ringers: How Outsourcing Is Changing the Way Indians Understand Themselves.* Princeton, NJ: Princeton University Press.

Nanda, S. 1996. Hijras: An Alternative Sex and Gender Role in India. *Third Sex Third Gender: Beyond Sexual Dimorphism in Culture and History,* G. Herdt, ed., pp. 373–418. New York: Zone Books.

————. 1998. *Neither Man nor Woman: The Hijras of India.* Belmont, CA: Thomson/Wadsworth.

————. 2014. *Gender Diversity: Crosscultural Variations,* 2nd ed. Long Grove, IL: Waveland.

National Academy of Sciences. 2008. *Understanding and Responding to Climate Change: Highlights of National Academies Reports.* http://dels.nas.edu/dels/rpt_briefs/climate_change_2008_final.pdf.

National Research Council. 2011. *America's Climate Choices.* http://nas-sites.org/americasclimatechoices/sample-page/panel-reports/americas-climate-choices-final-report/.

Nayar, P. K., ed. 2016. *Postcolonial Studies: An Anthology.* Malden, MA: Wiley.

Nolan, R., ed. 2013. *The Handbook of Practicing Anthropology.* Malden, MA: Wiley-Blackwell.

Nolan, R. W. 2002. *Development Anthropology: Encounters in the Real World.* Boulder, CO: Westview Press.

Nononi, D. M, ed. 2014. *A Companion to Urban Anthropology.* Malden, MA: Wiley-Blackwell.

Nordstrom, C. 2004. *Shadows of War: Violence, Power, and International Profiteering in the Twenty-First Century.* Berkeley: University of California Press.

Northover, A. 2016. Words of 2015 Round-Up. Oxford Dictionaries, January 16. Oxford University Press. http://blog.oup.com/2016/01/words-2015-round-up/.

O'Donnell, J., 2016. The Big Business of Europe's Migration Crisis. *SAPIENS,* June 21. http://www.sapiens.org/culture/migration-crisis-illegality-industry/.

Okely, J. 2012. *Anthropological Practice: Fieldwork and the Ethnographic Method.* New York: Berg.

Omohundro, J. T. 2001. *Careers in Anthropology,* 2nd ed. New York: McGraw-Hill.

Ong, A. 1987. *Spirits of Resistance and Capitalist Discipline: Factory Women in Malaysia.* Albany: State University of New York Press.

————. 1989. Center, Periphery, and Hierarchy: Gender in Southeast Asia. In *Gender and Anthropology: Critical Reviews for Research and Teaching,* S. Morgen, ed., pp. 294–312. Washington, DC: American Anthropological Association.

Ong, A., and S. J. Collier, eds. 2005. *Global Assemblages: Technology, Politics, and Ethics as Anthropological Problems.* Malden, MA: Blackwell.

————. 2010. *Spirits of Resistance and Capitalist Discipline: Factory Women in Malaysia,* 2nd ed. Albany: State University of New York Press.

Ontario Consultants on Religious Tolerance. 2007. Santeria: A Syncretistic Caribbean Religion. http://www.religioustolerance.org/santeri2.htm.

————. 2011. Religions of the World: Number of Adherents of Major Religions, Their Geographical Distribution, Date Founded, and Sacred Texts. http://www.religioustolerance.org/worldrel.htm.

Oriji, J. N. 2000. Igbo Women from 1929–1960. *West Africa Review* 2:1.

Ortner, S. B. 1984. Theory in Anthropology since the Sixties. *Comparative Studies in Society and History* 126(1):126–166.

Ottenheimer, H. J. 2013. *The Anthropology of Language: An Introduction to Linguistic Anthropology*, 3rd ed. Belmont, CA: Wadsworth Cengage Learning.

Oxford, University of. 2013. Social Media: The Perils and Pleasures. http://www.ox.ac.uk/media/news_stories/2013/130411_1.html.

Oxford University Press. 2015. Oxford Dictionaries Word of the Year 2015 Is…. http://blog.oxforddictionaries.com/2015/11/word-of-the-year-2015-emoji.

Pace, R., and B. P. Hinote. 2013. *Amazon Town TV: An Audience Ethnography in Gurupá, Brazil.* Austin: University of Texas Press.

Paine, R. 2009. *Camps of the Tundra: Politics through Reindeer among Saami Pastoralists.* Oslo: Instituttet for sammenlignende kulturforskning.

Pardo, I., and G. B. Prato, eds. 2012. *Anthropology in the City: Methodology and Theory.* Burlington, VT: Ashgate.

Parrillo, V. N. 2016. *Understanding Race and Ethnic Relations*, 5th ed. Boston: Pearson.

Pasquali, V. 2016. The World's Richest and Poorest Countries, *Global Finance,* December 2. https://www.gfmag.com/global-data/economic-data/worlds-richest-and-poorest-countries.

Patel, J. K. 2017. How 2016 Became Earth's Hottest Year on Record. *New York Times,* January 18. https://www.nytimes.com/interactive/2017/01/18/science/earth/2016-hottest-year-on-record.html.

Peletz, M. 1988. *A Share of the Harvest: Kinship, Property, and Social History among the Malays of Rembau.* Berkeley: University of California Press.

———— 2009. *Gender Pluralism; Southeast Asia since Early Modern Times.* New York: Routledge.

Petraglia-Bahri, D. 1996. *Introduction to Postcolonial Studies.* http://www.emory.edu/ENGLISH/Bahri/.

Pew Research Center. 2011. *The Pew Forum on Religion and Public Life.* Global Christianity – A Report on the Size and Distribution of the World's Christian Population. http://www.pewforum.org/2011/12/19/global-christianity-exec/.

————. 2012a. *The Global Religious Landscape: A Report on the Size and Distribution of the World's Major Religious Groups as of 2010, Analysis,* December 18. http://www.pewforum.org/global-religious-landscape-exec.aspx#src=global-footer.

————. 2012b. *"Nones" on the Rise, One-in-Five Adults Have No Religious Affiliation,* October 9. http://www.pewforum.org/unaffiliated/nones-on-the-rise.aspx.

————. 2015a. *America's Changing Religious Landscape,* May 12. http://www.pewforum.org/2015/05/12/americas-changing-religious-landscape/.

————. 2015b. *The Future of World Religions: Population Growth Projections, 2010–2050,* April 2. http://www.pewforum.org/files/2015/03/PF_15.04.02_ProjectionsFullReport.pdf.

Piddocke, S. 1969. The Potlatch System of the Southern Kwakiutl: A New Perspective. In *Environment and Cultural Behavior,* A. P. Vayda, ed., pp. 130–156. Garden City, NY: Natural History Press.

Pirie, F. 2013. *The Anthropology of Law.* New York: Oxford University Press.

Polanyi, K. 1968. *Primitive, Archaic and Modern Economies: Essays of Karl Polanyi,* G. Dalton, ed. Garden City, NY: Anchor Books.

Pospisil, L. 1963. *The Kapauku Papuans of West New Guinea.* New York: Holt, Rinehart & Winston.

Price, R., ed. 1973. *Maroon Societies.* New York: Anchor Press/Doubleday.

Proctor, B. D., J. L. Semega, and M. A. Kollar. 2016. *Income and Poverty in the United States: 2015.* U.S. Census Bureau, Current Population Reports, P60-256. Washington, DC: U.S. Government Printing Office. https://www.census.gov/content/dam/Census/library/publications/2016/demo/p60-256.pdf.

Radcliffe-Brown, A. R. 1965 (orig. 1952). *Structure and Function in Primitive Society.* New York: Free Press.

Radcliffe-Brown, A. R. 1952 (orig. 1924). The Mother's Brother in South Africa. In A. R. Radcliffe-Brown, *Structure and Function in Primitive Society,* pp. 15–31. London: Routledge & Kegan Paul.

Ramos, A. R. 1995. *Sanumá Memories: Yanomami Ethnography in Times of Crisis.* Madison: University of Wisconsin Press.

Ranger, T. O. 1996. Postscript. In *Postcolonial Identities,* R. Werbner and T. O. Ranger, eds. London: Zed.

Rapoza, K. 2012. Disturbing Trend for Putin, Russian Poverty Rising. *Forbes.* April 12. http://www.forbes.com/sites/kenrapoza/2012/04/12/disturbing-trend-for-putin-russian-poverty-rising/.

Rappaport, R. A. 1974. Obvious Aspects of Ritual. *Cambridge Anthropology* 2:2–60.

———. 1999. *Holiness and Humanity: Ritual in the Making of Religious Life.* New York: Cambridge University Press.

Rathje, W. L., and C. Murphy. 2001. *Rubbish! The Archaeology of Garbage.* Tucson: University of Arizona Press.

Rathus, S. A., J. S. Nevid, and J. Fichner-Rathus. 2014. *Human Sexuality in a World of Diversity,* 9th ed. Boston: Allyn & Bacon.

Reardon, S. 2015. Psychologists Seek Roots of Terror: Studies Raise Prospect of Intervention in the Radicalization Process. *Nature* 517 (421). http://www.nature.com/polopoly_fs/1.16756!/menu/main/topColumns/topLeftColumn/pdf/517420a.pdf.

Redfield, R. 1941. *The Folk Culture of Yucatan.* Chicago: University of Chicago Press.

Redfield, R., R. Linton, and M. Herskovits. 1936. Memorandum on the Study of Acculturation. *American Anthropologist* 38:149–152.

Renfrew, C. 1987. *Archaeology and Language: The Puzzle of Indo-European Origin.* London: Pimlico.

Reyhner, J., et al. eds. 2013. *Honoring Our Children: Culturally Appropriate Approaches for Teaching Indigenous Students.* Flagstaff: Northern Arizona University.

Rhodes, R. A. W., and P. 't Hart. 2014. *The Oxford Handbook of Political Leadership.* Oxford, UK: Oxford University Press.

Riach, J. 2013. Golf's Failure to Embrace Demographics across Society Is Hard to Stomach. *The Guardian,* May 22. http://www.theguardian.com/sport/blog/2013/may/22/uk-golf-clubs-race-issues.

Robbins, Jim. 2012. The Ecology of Disease, *New York Times,* July 14. http://www.nytimes.com/2012/07/15/sunday-review/the-ecology-of-disease.html.

Robbins, Joel. 2004. The Globalization of Pentecostal and Charismatic Christianity. *Annual Review of Anthropology* 33:17–143.

Robertson, J. 1992. Koreans in Japan. Paper presented at the University of Michigan Department of Anthropology, Martin Luther King Jr. Day Panel, January. Ann Arbor: University of Michigan Department of Anthropology (unpublished).

Robson, D. 2013. There Really Are 50 Eskimo Words for Snow. *Washington Post,* January 14. http://articles.washingtonpost.com/2013-01-14/national/36344037_1_eskimo-words-snow-inuit.

Romero, S. 2008. Rain Forest Tribe's Charge of Neglect Is Shrouded by Religion and Politics. *New York Times,* October 7, 2008.

Rosaldo, M. Z. 1980a. *Knowledge and Passion: Notions of Self and Social Life.* Stanford, CA: Stanford University Press.

———. 1980b. The Use and Abuse of Anthropology: Reflections on Feminism and Cross-Cultural Understanding. *Signs* 5(3):389–417.

Roscoe, W. 1991. *Zuni Man-Woman.* Albuquerque: University of New Mexico Press.

———. 1998. *Changing Ones: Third and Fourth Genders in Native North America.* New York: St. Martin's Press.

Rothstein, E. 2006. Protection for Indian Patrimony That Leads to a Paradox. *New York Times,* March 29.

Ryang, S., and J. Lie. 2009. *Diaspora without Homeland: Being Korean in Japan.* Berkeley: University of California Press.

Rylko-Bauer, B., M. Singer, and J. Van Willigen. 2006. Reclaiming Applied Anthropology: Its Past, Present, and Future. *American Anthropologist* 108(1):178–190.

Sack, K. 2011. In Tough Times, a Boom in Cremations as a Way to Save Money. *New York Times,* December 8. http://www.nytimes.com/2011/12/09/us/in-economic-downturn-survivors-turning-to-cremations-over-burials.html.

Saez, E., and G. Zucman. 2014. Wealth Inequality in the United States since 1913: Evidence from Capitalized Income Tax Data. Working Paper 20625, National Bureau of Economic Research, Cambridge, MA. http://gabriel-zucman.eu/files/SaezZucman2014.pdf.

Sahlins, M. D. 1968. *Tribesmen.* Englewood Cliffs, NJ: Prentice Hall.

———. 2011 *Stone Age Economics.* New Brunswick, NJ: Transaction Books.

Salazar, C., and J. Bestard, eds. 2015. *Religion and Science as Forms of Life: Anthropological Insights into Reason and Unreason.* New York: Berghahn Books.

Saleh, A. 2013. *Ethnic Identity and the State in Iran.* New York: Palgrave Macmillan.

Salzman, P. C. 1974. Political Organization among Nomadic Peoples. In *Man in Adaptation: The Cultural Present,* 2nd ed., Y. A. Cohen, ed., pp. 267–284. Chicago: Aldine.

———. 2008. *Culture and Conflict in the Middle East.* Amherst, NY: Humanity Books.

Salzmann, Z., J. M. Stanlaw, and N. Adachi. 2015. *Language, Culture, and Society: An Introduction to Linguistic Anthropology,* 6th ed. Boulder, CO: Westview Press.

Sanday, P. R. 1974. Female Status in the Public Domain. In *Woman, Culture, and Society,* M. Z. Rosaldo and L. Lamphere, eds., pp. 189–206. Stanford, CA: Stanford University Press.

———. 2002. *Women at the Center: Life in a Modern Matriarchy.* Ithaca, NY: Cornell University Press.

———. 2003. Public Interest Anthropology: A Model for Engaged Social Science. http://www.sas.upenn.edu/anthro/CPIA/PAPERS/SARdiscussion%20paper.65.html.

Sanjek, R. 2004. Going Public: Responsibilities and Strategies in the Aftermath of Ethnography. *Human Organization* 63(4): 444–456.

———. 2014. *Ethnography in Today's World: Color Full before Color Blind.* Philadelphia: University of Pennsylvania Press.

Sapir, E. 1931. Conceptual Categories in Primitive Languages. *Science* 74:578–584.

———. 1956 (orig. 1928). The Meaning of Religion. In *Culture, Language and Personality: Selected Essays,* E. Sapir. Berkeley: University of California Press.

Scheidel, W. 1997. Brother-Sister Marriage in Roman Egypt. *Journal of Biosocial Science* 29(3):361–371.

Schwartz, M. J., V. W. Turner, and A. Tuden, eds. 2011. *Political Anthropology.* New Brunswick, NJ: Aldine Transaction.

Scott, James C. 1985. *Weapons of the Weak.* New Haven, CT: Yale University Press.

———. 1990. *Domination and the Arts of Resistance.* New Haven, CT: Yale University Press.

Scott, S., and C. Duncan. 2004. *Return of the Black Death: The World's Greatest Serial Killer.* Hoboken, NJ: Wiley.

Scudder, T., and E. Colson. 1980. *Secondary Education and the Formation of an Elite: The Impact of Education on Gwembe District, Zambia.* London: Academic Press.

Scupin, R. 2012. *Race and Ethnicity: An Anthropological Focus on the United States and the World,* 2nd ed. Upper Saddle River, NJ: Prentice Hall.

Service, E. R. 1962. *Primitive Social Organization: An Evolutionary Perspective.* New York: McGraw-Hill.

———. 1966. *The Hunters.* Englewood Cliffs, NJ: Prentice Hall.

Sharma, A., and A. Gupta, eds. 2006. *The Anthropology of the State: A Reader.* Malden, MA: Blackwell.

Shivaram, C. 1996. Where Women Wore the Crown: Kerala's Dissolving Matriarchies Leave a Rich Legacy of Compassionate Family Culture. *Hinduism Today.* http://www.spirit-web.org/HinduismToday/96_02_Women_Wore_Crown.html.

Shore, C., S. Wright, and D. Però, eds. 2011. *Policy Worlds: Anthropology and the Analysis of Contemporary Power.* New York: Berghahn Books.

Shryock, A. 1988. Autonomy, Entanglement, and the Feud: Prestige Structures and Gender Values in Highland Albania. *Anthropological Quarterly* 61(3):113–118.

Sillitoe, P., ed. 2007. *Local Science versus Global Science: Approaches to Indigenous Knowledge in International Development.* New York: Berghahn Books.

Singer, M. 2012. *Introducing Medical Anthropology: A Discipline in Action,* 2nd ed. Lanham, MD: AltaMira.

_____. 2015. *Anthropology of Infectious Disease.* Walnut Creek, CA: Left Coast Press.

Slaughter, A.-M. 2013. Women Are Sexist, Too: If Women Are Equal at the Office, Why Can't Men Be Equal at Home? *Time.* http://time.com/women-are-sexist-too/.

_____. 2015. *Unfinished Business: Men, Women, Work, Family.* New York: Random House.

Solway, J., and R. Lee. 1990. Foragers, Genuine and Spurious: Situating the Kalahari San in History (with CA Treatment). *Current Anthropology* 31(2):109–146.

Sotomayor, S. 2009. (orig. 2001). A Latina Judge's Voice. Judge Mario G. Olmos Memorial Lecture, University of California, Berkeley School of Law. Reprinted by the *New York Times,* http://www.nytimes.com/2009/05/15/us/politics/15judge.text.html.

Spencer, E. T. 2010. *Sociolinguistics.* Hauppauge, NY: Nova Science.

Spickard, P., ed. 2004. *Race and Nation: Ethnic Systems in the Modern World.* New York: Routledge.

_____. 2012. *Race and Immigration in the United States: New Histories.* New York: Routledge.

_____. 2013 *Multiple Identities: Migrants, Ethnicity, and Membership.* Bloomington: Indiana University Press.

Spindler, G. D., and L. Hammond, eds. 2006. *Innovations in Educational Ethnography: Theory, Methods, and Results.* Mahwah, NJ: Erlbaum.

Stack, C. B. 1975. *All Our Kin: Strategies for Survival in a Black Community.* New York: Harper Torchbooks.

Starn, O. 2011. *The Passion of Tiger Woods: An Anthropologist Reports on Golf, Race, and Celebrity Scandal.* Durham, NC: Duke University Press.

Statistics Canada. 2001. *Census.* Nation Tables. http://www.statcan.ca/english/census96/nation.htm.

_____. 2010. *Study: Projections of the Diversity of the Canadian Population.* http://www.statcan.gc.ca/daily-quotidien/100309/dq100309a-eng.htm.

Stearns, P. N. 2016. *Globalization in World History,* 2nd ed. New York: Routledge.

Stein, R. L., and P. L. Stein, eds. 2011. *The Anthropology of Religion, Magic, and Witchcraft,* 3rd ed. Upper Saddle River, NJ: Pearson Prentice Hall.

Stoler, A. L.., ed. 2013. *Imperial Debris: On Ruins and Ruination*: Durham, NC: Duke University Press.

Stoler, A. L., C. McGranahan, and P. C. Perdue, eds. 2007. *Imperial Formations.* Santa Fe, NM: School for Advanced Research Press.

Strathern, A., and P. J. Stewart. 2010. *Kinship in Action: Self and Group.* Boston: Prentice Hall.

Strathern, M. 1988. *Dealing with Inequality: Analysing Gender Relations in Melanesia and Beyond: Essays by Members of the 1983/1984 Anthropological Research Group at the Research School of Pacific Studies, the Australian National University.* New York: Cambridge University Press.

Streets-Salter, H., and T. Getz. 2016. *Empires and Colonies in the Modern World: A Global Perspective.* New York: Oxford University Press.

Stryker, R., and R. J. Gonzalez, eds. 2014. *Up, Down, and Sideways: Anthropologists Trace the Pathways of Power.* New York: Berghahn Books.

Sunstein, B. S., and E. Chiseri-Strater. 2012. *Fieldworking: Reading and Writing Research,* 4th ed. Upper Saddle River, NJ: Prentice Hall.

Suttles, W. 1960. Affinal Ties, Subsistence, and Prestige among the Coast Salish. *American Anthropologist* 62:296–305.

Tannen, D. 1990. *You Just Don't Understand: Women and Men in Conversation.* New York: Ballantine Books.

———. ed. 1993. *Gender and Conversational Interaction.* New York: Oxford University Press.

Tannen, D., and A. M. Trester, eds. 2012. *Discourse 2.0: Language and New Media.* Washington, DC: Georgetown University Press.

Tattersall, I., and R. De Salle. 2011. *Race? Debunking a Scientific Myth.* College Station: Texas A&M University Press.

Tavernise, S. 2012. Whites Account for Under Half of Births in U.S. *New York Times,* May 17. http://www.nytimes.com/2012/05/17/us/whites-account-for-under-half-of-births-in-us.html.

Taylor, P., M. H. Lopez, J. H. Martínez, and G. Velasco. 2012. *When Labels Don't Fit: Hispanics and Their Views of Identity.* Pew Research Hispanic Center, April 4. http://www.pewhispanic.org/2012/04/04/when-labels-dont-fit-hispanics-and-their-views-of-identity/.

Telegraph. 2005. Third Sex Finds a Place on Indian Passport Forms. March 10. http://infochangeindia.org/human-rights/news/third-sex-finds-a-place-on-indian-passport-forms.html.

Tishkov, V. A. 2004. *Chechnya: Life in a War-Torn Society.* Berkeley: University of California Press.

Titiev, M. 1992. *Old Oraibi: A Study of the Hopi Indians of Third Mesa.* Albuquerque: University of New Mexico Press.

Totten, S., and R. Ubaldo, eds. 2011. *We Cannot Forget: Interviews with Survivors of the 1994 Genocide in Rwanda.* New Brunswick, NJ: Rutgers University Press.

Tougher, S. 2008. *The Eunuch in Byzantine History and Society.* New York: Routledge.

Trudgill, P. 2010. *Investigations in Sociohistorical Linguistics: Stories of Colonisation and Contact.* New York: Cambridge University Press.

Turner, V. W. 1974 (orig. 1967). *The Ritual Process.* Harmondsworth, England: Penguin Press.

Tylor, E. B. 1958 (orig. 1871). *Primitive Culture.* New York: Harper Torchbooks.

Underhill, P. 2009. *Why We Buy? The Science of Shopping.* New York: Random House.

U.S. Bureau of Labor Statistics. 2014. *Women in the Labor Force: A Databook.* BLS Reports 1052. http://www.bls.gov/opub/reports/cps/women-in-the-labor-force-a-databook-2014.pdf.

———. 2017. Union Members Summary. January 26. https://www.bls.gov/news.release/union2.nr0.htm.

U.S. Census Bureau. 2014. Marital Status. Families and Living Arrangements. http://www.census.gov/hhes/families/data/marital.html.

Vallegia, C. R., and J. J. Snodgrass. 2015. Health of Indigenous Peoples. *Annual Review of Anthropology* 44:117–135.

Van Allen, J. 1971. *"Aba Riots" or "Women's War"? British Ideology and Eastern Nigerian Women's Political Activism.* Waltham, MA: African Studies Association.

Vayda, A. P. 1968 (orig. 1961). Economic Systems in Ecological Perspective: The Case of the Northwest Coast. In *Readings in Anthropology,* 2nd ed., Volume 2, M. H. Fried, ed., pp. 172–178. New York: Crowell.

Veblen, T. 1934. *The Theory of the Leisure Class: An Economic Study of Institutions.* New York: The Modern Library.

Ventkatesan, S., and T. Yarrow, eds. 2014. *Differentiating Development: Beyond an Anthropology of Critique.* New York: Berghahn Books.

Vigil, J. D. 2010. *Gang Redux: A Balanced Anti-Gang Strategy.* Long Grove, IL: Waveland.

———. 2012. *From Indians to Chicanos; The Dynamics of Mexican-American Culture,* 3rd ed. Boulder, CO: Westview Press.

Vinyeta, K., and K. Lynn. 2013. *Exploring the Role of Traditional Ecological Knowledge in Climate Change Initiatives.* Portland, OR: U. S. Department of Agriculture, Forest Service, Pacific Northwest Research Station.

Wade, P. 2010. *Race and Ethnicity in Latin America,* 2nd ed. New York: Pluto Press.

Wallace, A. F. C. 1966. *Religion: An Anthropological View.* New York: McGraw-Hill.

Wallace, S. 2016. Dodging Wind Farms and Bullets in the Arctic. *National Geographic,* March 1. http://news.nationalgeographic.com/2016/03/160301-arctic-sami-norway-reindeer/.

Wallerstein, I. M. 1982. The Rise and Future Demise of the World Capitalist System: Concepts for Comparative Analysis. In *Introduction to the Sociology of "Developing Societies,"* H. Alavi and T. Shanin, eds., pp. 29–53. New York: Monthly Review Press.

———. 2004. *World-Systems Analysis: An Introduction.* Durham, NC: Duke University Press.

Walton, D., and J. A. Suarez, eds. 2016. *Culture, Space, and Power: Blurred Lines.* Lanham, MD: Lexington Books.

Ward, M. C., and M. Edelstein. 2013. *A World Full of Women,* 6th ed. Upper Saddle River, NJ: Pearson.

Wardhaugh, R., and J. Fuller. 2015. *An Introduction to Sociolinguistics,* 7th ed. Malden, MA: Wiley-Blackwell.

Warms, R., J. Garber, and R. J. McGee, eds. 2009. *Sacred Realms: Readings in the Anthropology of Religion,* 2nd ed. New York: Oxford University Press.

Warne, A. D., ed. 2015. *Ethnic and Cultural Identity: Perceptions, Discrimination, and Social Challenges.* Hauppauge, NY: Nova Science.

Wasson, C., M. O. Butler, and J. Copeland-Carson, eds. 2012. *Applying Anthropology in the Global Village.* Walnut Creek, CA: Left Coast Press.

Weber, M. 1958 (orig. 1904). *The Protestant Ethic and the Spirit of Capitalism.* New York: Scribner.

———. 1968 (orig. 1922). *Economy and Society.* E. Fischoff et al. (trans.). New York: Bedminster Press.

Webster's New World Encyclopedia. 1993. College Edition. Englewood Cliffs, NJ: Prentice Hall.

Weiner, M. 2009. *Japan's Minorities: The Illusion of Homogeneity,* 2nd ed. New York: Routledge.

White, L. A. 2009. *Modern Capitalist Culture,* abridged ed. Walnut Creek, CA: Left Coast Press.

Whorf, B. L. 1956. A Linguistic Consideration of Thinking in Primitive Communities. In *Language, Thought, and Reality: Selected Writings of Benjamin Lee Whorf,* J. B. Carroll, ed., pp. 65–86. Cambridge, MA: MIT Press.

Whyte, M. F. 1978. Cross-Cultural Codes Dealing with the Relative Status of Women. *Ethnology* 12(2):203–225.

Wiley, A. S., and J. S. Allen. 2012. *Medical Anthropology: A Biocultural Approach,* 2nd ed. New York: Oxford University Press.

Wilk, R. R. 2006. *Fast Food/Slow Food: The Cultural Economy of the Global Food System.* Lanham, MD: AltaMira.

Williams, L. M., and D. Finkelhor. 1995. Paternal Caregiving and Incest: Test of a Biosocial Model. *American Journal of Orthopsychiatry* 65(1):101–113.

Wilmsen, E. N. 1989. *Land Filled with Flies: A Political Economy of the Kalahari.* Chicago: University of Chicago Press.

Winzeler, R. L. 2012. *Anthropology and Religion,* 2nd ed. Lanham, MD: Rowman & Littlefield.

Wittfogel, K. A. 1957. *Oriental Despotism: A Comparative Study of Total Power.* New Haven, CT: Yale University Press.

Wolcott, H. F. 2008. *Ethnography: A Way of Seeing,* 2nd ed. Lanham, MD: AltaMira.

Wolf, E. R. 1966. *Peasants.* Englewood Cliffs, NJ: Prentice Hall.

———. 1982. *Europe and the People without History.* Berkeley: University of California Press.

Womack, M. 2010. *The Anthropology of Health and Healing.* Lanham, MD: AltaMira.

Worsley, P. 1985 (orig. 1959). Cargo Cults. In *Readings in Anthropology* 85/86. Guilford, CT: Dushkin.

Yardley, W. 2007. Victim of Climate Change, a Town Seeks a Lifeline. *New York Times,* May 27. http://www.nytimes.com/2007/05/27/us/27newtok.html.

Young, A. 2000. *Women Who Become Men: Albanian Sworn Virgins.* New York: Berg.

Zhang, Y. 2016. *Trust and Economics: The Co-evolution of Trust and Exchange Systems.* New York: Routledge.

Zimmer-Tamakoshi, L. 1997. The Last Big Man: Development and Men's Discontents in the Papua New Guinea Highlands. *Oceania* 68(2):107–122.

Zimring, C. A., ed. 2012. *Encyclopedia of Consumption and Waste: The Social Science of Garbage.* Thousand Oaks, CA: Sage.

Zukin, S., P. Kasinitz, and X. Chen, eds. 2015. *Global Cities, Local Streets: Everyday Diversity from New York to Shanghai.* New York: Routledge.

Index

Note: Tables, figures, and illustrations are indicated by t, f, and i.